The experience of urban poverty, 1723–82

Manchester University Press

The experience of urban poverty, 1723–82

Parish, charity and credit

ALANNAH TOMKINS

Manchester University Press
Manchester and New York

distributed exclusively in the USA by Palgrave

Published by Manchester University Press
Oxford Road, Manchester M13 9NR, UK
and Room 400, 175 Fifth Avenue, New York, NY 10010, USA
www.manchesteruniversitypress.co.uk

Distributed exclusively in the USA by
Palgrave, 175 Fifth Avenue, New York,
NY 10010, USA

Distributed exclusively in Canada by
UBC Press, University of British Columbia, 2029 West Mall,
Vancouver, BC, Canada V6T 1Z2

British Library Cataloguing-in-Publication Data
A catalogue record for this book is available from the British Library

Library of Congress Cataloging-in-Publication Data applied for

ISBN 0 7190 7504 1 *hardback*
EAN 978 0 7190 7504 9

First published 2006

15 14 13 12 11 10 09 08 07 06   10 9 8 7 6 5 4 3 2 1

Typeset in Sabon by
Koinonia, Manchester
Printed in Great Britain
by Bell & Bain Ltd, Glasgow

For Mum and Dad

Contents

Tables, figures and appendices

Tables

Figures

Appendices

Acknowledgements

I owe thanks to many people for their advice and assistance during the production of this book. My greatest debts are to Joanna Innes who supervised the original research, Richard Smith whose support and good humour have been unfailing, and Steve King whose encouragement and guidance have been invaluable. More broadly my academic debts extend to many friends and tutors at Oxford, along with colleagues and students at Keele, who have listened to research papers and asked searching questions. Similarly the anonymous reviewers for this manuscript tested my analysis and offered constructive criticism, while the staff at Manchester University Press proved kind and efficient guides through the publishing process.

I should also like to thank the staff of the Bodleian Library, Borthwick Institute, British Library, Cheshire Record Office, Chester Archives, Leeds District Archives, Greater London Record Office, Lichfield Record Office, National Archives, Northamptonshire Record Office, Oxfordshire Local Studies Library, Oxfordshire Record Office, Oxford University Archives, Shropshire Archives, and the York City Archives for their help and patience.

In addition I owe particular gratitude to Richard Adair, Ian Atherton, Amanda Berry, Bob Cromarty, Alun Davies, Rita Freedman, Steve Hindle, Tim Hitchcock, Linda Homfray, Katherine Keats-Rohan, Peter King, Mr J. B. Lawson, Alysa Levine, Angus MacInnes, Mary Prior, Paul Slack, Hugh Walton, and Samantha Williams, variously for their friendship, advice and cups of tea.

Finally I would like to thank my extended family for their unfeigned interest in the byways of my research and for their technical assistance at crucial points over the last fourteen years.

Abbreviations

Alk	St Alkmund
Bod. Lib.	Bodleian Library
CRO	Cheshire Record Office
GLRO	Greater London Record Office
HC	Holy Cross
HT Gdgt	Holy Trinity Goodramgate
MBp sr	St Mary Bishophill senior
MC	St Michael
MleB	St Michael le Belfrey
MM	St Mary Magdalen
ORO	Oxford Record Office
Ox	Oxford
PinE	St Peter in East
PleB	St Peter le Bailey
PP	Parliamentary Papers
PRO	National Archive
SA	Shropshire Archives
Sh	Shrewsbury
Yk	York

1

Introduction

Francis 'Nack' Wheeler was an able-bodied, adult pauper, a sometime criminal, and in 1739 he felt aggrieved. In May of that year he was in the Oxford town bridewell, probably for his trademark offences of violence or threats; by September he had progressed to the town prison for threatening the life of Sir John Boyce.[1] While in the bridewell he used threatening words against parish officials. On the testimony of Mary Buddard who had visited to give him a clean shirt he apparently swore, 'God D'mn my Liver if I would not run this knife through some of them if I was sure I should be hanged at Green Ditch for it',[2] while simultaneously stabbing his knife into the table for emphasis. Later in the same month, one of his children was baptised at the parish expense and some veal and ale were conveyed to him at the house of correction so that he might share the christening feast. This roused his anger once more; he swore again, 'God D--n them that bought it, them that bought it and them that sent it, that the longer he was kept in it should be the worse for 'em for were it forty years hence he would be revenged of them'.

These quotes drawn from jotted memoranda in a volume of overseers' accounts suggest that Francis Wheeler's experience of life and of poverty were characterised by instability, brutality, criminality and, in something of a contrast, the dogged presence of parish poor-relief mechanisms. All of these experiences were repeated over the following decade. In 1740 first Francis and then his wife ran away from Oxford, leaving their children to the overseers' care. It is not surprising that when Wheeler returned with the proposal that he go to Chester, the parish readily contributed 7s 6d towards his journey. By 1741 though, Francis was back in Oxford, on relief, and was carried to gaol on 30 October; a warrant for his arrest had been issued at his parish's expense on 25 August (although his misdemeanour on this occasion is unknown). Three years later on 26 November 1744 the parish paid again to take him up and in the following February Wheeler was indicted at the town quarter sessions for the theft of a brass kettle from James Sadler. It is fairly clear he was a violent man but it would be wrong to brand him a thief as a consequence; he was found not guilty. The later 1740s saw a lull in this activity but by 1749 the Wheelers were in town as the parish paid for the birth of Francis's son James and by February 1750 Francis was back in bridewell, for offences unknown. The parish paid both to have him committed and to provide him with meat and bread during his four weeks inside. In May 1751 the parish had to pay a constable a shilling to bring Francis's wife home after he beat her. This violence continued as on 11 September 1752 he was bound over for wounding William Winfield by the county quarter sessions.

Francis Wheeler's defiance of the system brought him before the town and county quarter sessions and probably before a magistrate for summary punishment. He saw the inside of both the town bridewell and prison. These experiences were intimately connected with the parish, which paid for his arrest on more than one occasion while continuing to relieve him. Francis (or Nack), his wife and children are named on relief in their parish in 1739, 1770 and most of the years in between, establishing them as a long-term pauper family.

How unusual was Wheeler's experience, as someone charged with a comprehensive catalogue of deviancy but whose outstretched hand repeatedly found relief? Wheeler is different in part because he is visible, his words and behaviour being so outrageous as to warrant a special entry in the parish ledgers with an apparently verbatim account of his threatening words in 1739. His experience of life in Oxford was seemingly marked by frustration at his dependency, since an obvious interpretation of his second outburst is that he viewed the gift of veal and ale as a painful reminder of what he was missing, and of the authorities that had committed him, rather than as an opportunity to share a celebration. His repeated incarcerations had no discernible impact on his impulse to lash out. It also did nothing to bar his access to parish relief. Furthermore Francis Wheeler's experience was not unique in that similar cases of repeated offenders who bounced between prison and pauperdom can be found in mid-eighteenth-century Oxford.[3]

It is possible to get closer to Wheeler and his family than is usually the case with people blandly listed as parish paupers because the extremity of his case generated additional written source material but there are still problems of interpretation and incompleteness. It is quite possible that he was a tragically misunderstood man, taken up for crimes not of his commission, but even if his reported words and actions are accepted at their most obvious interpretation there is always the matter of experiences unreported. There is a paucity of accounts of poverty by the poor and where these survive their interpretation is problematic. Individuals' passage into or through poverty, their changing perceptions of their own experiences and the probably conflicting opinions of their contemporaries all make the subject difficult to grasp. The experience of poverty, when broadened from a relatively high-profile high-maintenance individual to a group, will always be acutely difficult to define. Beyond the identification of a generalised list of causes which either precipitated or lulled individuals or families into poverty, such as the life-cycle dip, the instability of employment or the uncertainties of health, the specifics of what it was like to be poor are rarely glimpsed. This book tries to secure a few new sightings of poverty.

In the process it inevitably addresses the issue of the character of the old poor law and the balance of alternative welfare or survival resources. The vignette of eighteenth-century life offered by Francis Wheeler has been couched in terms of criminal transgression and parish relief (largely because his story is derived from legal and parochial records) but just how persistent was the parish relief system in the lives of working people en masse? Did it provide a comprehensive safety net for the vulnerable or improvident poor, or was it typically a distant source of authority, a constant part of the backdrop to life but an unreliable source of succour? Historians have constructed different, often competing characterisations of the poor law and the practices of parish authorities, and close attention to the experiences of numerous individual paupers can shed new light on these problems.

Why eighteenth-century urban poverty?

In 1990, Sir Tony Wrigley argued that 'urban history may be said to be in the very bloom of youth', despite the presence of urban history as a discrete discipline for some years. He stressed the specificity of the urban experience and recommended the study of urban systems, since they possessed regularities that throw light on pre-industrial society generally.[4] At that time there seemed little in the way of detailed work on the eighteenth-century urban (and non-metropolitan) poor, since earlier local studies had often chosen the rural parish or the county as a focus.[5] Acknowledgement of the impact of towns had probably outrun the state of research on life within them. This situation has changed somewhat in the intervening sixteen years, particularly with the completion of the authoritative Cambridge Urban Histories.[6] Yet the need to consider the subtleties of urban life is increasingly imperative given new perceptions of the exposure of the English population to town-dwelling. The role of towns in driving migration (traditionally in pulling people from rural areas, but also now perceived as pushing people towards other towns or smaller settlements) generated a much wider experience of urban life at some point during the life-cycle across all English regions than is evident from urban population statistics.[7] Aspects of urban social history remain quite remote; both gender and poverty require attention.[8] Furthermore, distinctively urban poverty may also lose out if the emphasis of social and economic history moves from the traditional rural/urban dichotomy to concentrate instead on regional variation.[9]

This research employs a new methodology to tackle the perennial problem of the elusive urban poor. The mobility of town populations will always make them harder to pin down than the inhabitants of small, more static communities; it is no surprise most parish reconstruction work, for example, which relies on a consistent report of vital events for the vast majority of residents, has concentrated on villages. Reconstitution of mobile urban populations proves highly taxing if not impossible. Very large or rapidly growing towns are also at a disadvantage for historical research on poor individuals as a consequence of the often patchy state of their written records. Rapid change apparently militated against the creation, retention and ultimate survival of records relating to the labouring and poor populations of towns. The Liverpool vestry stopped recording the minutiae of poor relief decisions in the early eighteenth century, for example.[10] Thus it may have been justified for one writer to assert in 1752 that 'the excellent Oeconomy observed among the numerous poor of *Liverpool*, seems to plead in favour of large Districts' but the minutiae of such systems cannot now be appreciated.[11] Conversely some of the best runs of parochial, charity and other records have survived for towns that did not undergo rapid change but housed slow-growing populations. The experiences of the poor were by no means homogenous in these 'traditional' towns but the survival of sources makes possible a consideration and comparison of the experience of poverty in such towns. Of course, it is likely that the terrors of poverty were also substantially different between the categories of 'traditional' and 'industrial' or other rapidly growing towns, if only because in the former there was less acute overcrowding or consequential need to utilise all available living space including cellars and garrets. Therefore this is emphatically not an attempt to tackle 'urban' poverty on aggregate but instead a treatment of poverty in those quieter county towns where at least some measures of comparability are possible and plausible.

This book takes the towns of Oxford, Shrewsbury and York for its main focus, drawing on additional evidence from other traditional towns, particularly Northampton and Chester. The rationale for this derives from both an empirical, source-driven perspective and also from an apprehension of appropriate similarities and differences. In the first instance, all of these towns aside from Northampton enjoy a conjunction of good collections of overseers of the poor accounts (covering at least a substantial portion of the eighteenth century) along with caches of rich, alternative sources for reaching the poor. Oxford possesses detailed lists of the beneficiaries of parish and town charities, while Shrewsbury and Northampton have some excellent (if chronologically patchy) infirmary records. Finally York holds the distinction of a unique source, an eighteenth-century pawnbroker's pledge book. The towns also experienced some interesting coalescences around their populations and economies. All were essentially market towns, all with fairly large populations in the early eighteenth century and all with industrial sectors in relative decline but with leisure sectors of increasing buoyancy. Therefore while no comparative historical study will be capable of strictly comparing like with like, these towns seemed to offer broadly similar canvases upon which the practices of welfare and experiences of poverty were drawn (and therefore any differences in these practices and experiences could not simply be attributable to widely differing contexts). In this sense the issue of region will not be ignored, since the argument here occasionally reverts to what Steve King has characterised 'a southern culture of dependency' versus 'a northern culture of making do', but it puts the urban experience decisively to the fore.[12]

If the geographical focus has been somewhat dictated by the availability of sources for towns undergoing gradual demographic and economic change, the chronological range of this book was determined by another measure of calm namely the absence of legislative change. The eighteenth century saw a significant, if periodic, pamphlet debate about the characteristics and treatment of the poor. There was overwhelming support for the contention that the poor posed an enormous problem; beyond this central agreement, however, views were fragmented. The amorphous labouring poor were subdivided into the idle, industrious, ignorant or honest poor depending on the preconceptions and interests of each writer. The characteristics which defined these groups were either presumed to be self-evident, or were left vague because writers did not know how or whether to attempt a literal, coherent definition, or because further specification was deemed unnecessary. Some pamphleteers were primarily concerned with the economic and organisational aspects of the poor law. Their various suggestions for amendments and refinements of the existing poor laws tended to focus on making the dependent poor less expensive, less idle or less visible, often suggesting a new administrative unit for relief other than the parish. Yet these did not inspire any changes to the legislation which governed the relief of the resident poor between Knatchbull's act of 1723, permitting the establishment of workhouses, and Gilbert's act of 1782 which substantially altered the nature of any workhouse founded under its aegis. Numerous local acts were passed during these sixty years, including those to authorise incorporations of parishes in Norfolk and Suffolk, but laws that would have been nationally applicable were not forthcoming. Moves to overhaul the poor laws in the 1750s foundered. Modern historians have blamed this on localism and the inability to agree on the practical steps required to achieve goals, despite consensus on the nature of those goals.[13] Consequently, the period 1723 to 1782 was one of the most prolonged periods of governance under the old poor law when the terms whereby relief was offered to the settled poor did not undergo structural change.[14]

This is not to say, however, that the experience of poverty had stopped changing in this period; rather change was dependent on broad national trends and local economies instead of direct legislative intervention in the affairs of the poor. There was perhaps a measure of stability in such trends in the years up to 1760.[15] Demographic pressure had eased and the price of corn was generally deemed reasonable in the years 1723–60, with a couple of notable exceptions. There was no dramatic boost to the fortunes of the poorest, nor was there any reversal or decline as has been identified for the later sixteenth century.[16] But there were new challenges including the occasional requirement to conform to life in a workhouse, opposition to the education of the poor, and the need to withstand increasing scrutiny given concerns about fluctuating or rising poor rates and the persistently popular perception of the link between poverty and crime. From around 1760 a different national picture inevitably made an impact on the experience of poverty. Rising prices and population both placed renewed pressure on the poorest in a period that began to see the emergence of horizontal social groupings, the beginnings of the much debated class system.[17] Still the focus of this book is decidedly on the period before 1789, when continental events raised the stakes for governors and governed alike.

One relevant European trend is the alleged 'great confinement' of the insane poor and marginal, said to date from the seventeenth century. If an argument were to be made for the same process taking place in England the origins of the movement would probably be located between 1723 and 1782, and given the emphasis of this book on welfare and institutional settings it would have comprised a central element of the experience of poverty examined here; however, I do not think that it did. The empirical evidence for a 'great confinement' in England, particularly one beginning in the mid-seventeenth century, is slim and there is some agreement that the concept does not express the experience of the age before 1800.[18] Therefore the potentially punitive or incarcerating functions of the institutions treated here are played down or in some cases contradicted.

Sentiments towards the poor were undoubtedly changing in the period 1723–82 but the timing of change is contestable. It is widely accepted that there was a hardening of attitude towards the poor in the early nineteenth century, giving rise first to a poor-law abolition movement in the 1810s and eventually to the New Poor Law of 1834. There is less agreement on how far back into the eighteenth century this brusque attitude emerged. Lynn Hollen Lees emphasises that the legal right to poor relief was persistently asserted by the eighteenth-century poor (if with reluctance on the part of some) and that the right was accepted with more or less good grace by local authorities and taxpayers. Consensus is identified as the crucial issue, rather than the perceived generosity or meanness of disbursements.[19] Furthermore she points up the extent to which the poor took charge of their own access to welfare, stressing the initial decision to apply for relief and the negotiation of varied forms of support by individual paupers (with magistrates' help if necessary).[20] She positions a significant change or hardening of attitude around 1800, but not earlier than 1780, suggesting at least a grudging mutual agreement which was recognisable throughout England before that date.[21] Other research gestures towards an earlier sea change in public opinion. Anne Borsay implies a slightly earlier chronology, pointing up the significance of declining paternalist obligation and the rise of voluntary, polite civility and aligning it with the contemporary economic shift from mercantilism to laissez-faire. The combined effects of these sentiments left 'the poor wide open to moral disapprobation at a time when traditional paternalism was retreating'.[22] Similarly, Donna Andrew concludes from the reduced flow of begging letters published in the London press in the 1770s that there was a hardening of attitude among the intended audience.[23] Deborah Valenze finds that 'charitable sentiment was notably in eclipse' in the second half of the eighteenth century, and characterises a shift in sentiment from the 1750s based on a new apprehension of the dangers of wealth in that decade and an allied negativity about the poor.[24] This negative view began with a renewed perception of the poor as a social threat (exemplified by Fielding's *Enquiry into the Causes of the late Increase of robbers*) and inspired a heightened anxiety about the ways in which labourers might be motivated to work (and about the ways they might be tempted to spend their wages, classically a concern about tea-drinking).[25] In related work she identifies an increasingly negative image of working women in this period, in terms of their perceived disregard for both morality and property law. Consequently she endorses the idea that a variety of underclass was emerging by the 1750s, which

exercised the imaginations of the rich (even if it were not readily identifiable in the behaviour of the poor) and resulted in the withdrawal of
sympathies from poor labouring women.[26]

Pushing back the start of significant change to 1750 fits with Richard
Smith's research on the provision of parish pensions. His survey of
45,000 pension payments during 1750–80 revealed that there was no
appreciable increase in the face value of pensions at a time when the cost
of living was rising sharply. Notwithstanding the role of workhouses
in this period, and the demographic shifts in the pauper body which
saw an increasing proportion of able-bodied men taking pensions, he
concluded that the well-being of paupers heavily dependent upon their
parish relief (specifically elderly women) went into decline.[27] A failure
or strong resistance by parishes to match increased hardship with extra
funds is indicative of a growing reluctance to supply the needs of the
poor (including those poor who might earlier have been regarded as
uncontroversially deserving).

These shifting sentiments form part of a cyclical process of redefining the 'deserving' and 'undeserving' poor. The appropriate balance of
responsibility between individual, family and community is never static
but is in constant renegotiation.[28] The elderly and incapable, and very
young orphans, typically form the core of those held virtually blame-
less for their plight at all periods, but all other categories of poor are
regarded as more suspect (or loom large in the public consciousness,
even where they do not register as a numerically significant problem).
It is ironic that at the end of the eighteenth century an apparently more
expansive attitude to desert on the part of some parish authorities (that
employed the bread scale for example, and so drew numbers of young
families within the remit of the poor law) should so quickly give rise to
a more stringent stance towards all the poor by ratepayers. Stringency
is always latent but can be notably slow to emerge (if the example of
Wheeler at the start of this chapter is any guide), creating in this period
'extraordinary differentials in the generosity of relief even between adja-
cent parishes'.[29]

Given that there is also a revisionist emphasis on the continuities
between the old poor law and the new, there is clearly a range of views
about the timing and nature of changes in attitudes to and treatment of
the poor in the period between 1750 and 1850. By treating the earlier
decades of this period, this research contributes eighteenth-century
urban sentiments and practices to the picture, revealing the first stirrings
of change in communities that clearly had to deal with their share of the
problems of poverty but were not seriously challenged by them.[30]

Sources and methods

Almost all research into the experience of poverty in England before the nineteenth century must rely on the records left by welfare agencies of one sort or another, and this is a standard 'caveat' for historians of the topic.[31] The sorts of poverty excluded from overt welfare mechanisms are very shadowy, but relief was not always distributed solely on the basis of observable material need. It has been shown that vestries in the north-east of England, for example, routinely brought into play considerations of the moral desert of applicants and their plausible alternatives to parish money when determining levels of relief.[32] Furthermore, the process of impoverishment, via sharply fluctuating or gradually declining material resources, presented individuals and families with choices (albeit unpalatable ones). The poor had publicly to assert their level of need before assistance could be given, and people were not always willing to admit to themselves or others that they had reached that level of need, or asserted their needs in different ways. Those poor enough to register in the welfare process still fell through the net, no matter how tightly or loosely the net was strung; consequently the poor cannot be defined solely in relation to receipt of material assistance.[33] Tom Arkell and Steve King have outlined some innovative ways to calculate the extent of the community of poor, while Steve Hindle's comprehensive treatment of the rural 'penumbral' poor has shown something of their plight.[34]

England held an unusual position in Europe with regard to the poor in the early modern period as one of the few countries to provide relief financed from a local tax.[35] The administration of this levy and consequent disbursements generated multiple volumes of overseers' accounts, supported by vestry minutes, sheaves of settlement certificates, bastardy bonds, and even pauper correspondence; such sources have fuelled many local studies recounting, and in some cases analysing, the practices of individual parishes. Parish relief may have been organisationally distinctive but it was not necessarily systematic (in other words predictable) in its manifestations, and it is unlikely that it was comprehensive. Parishes supplied a wide variety of props on different occasions but there was still room for shortfall between the perception of need on the part of the poor applicants and the perception of adequate or appropriate provision on the part of vestries and parish officers. Also there was demonstrably a range of alternative expedients for making ends meet comprising an 'economy of makeshifts'.

One alternative to the parish was to tap into the funds of formal charity, in other words monies or other benefits supplied from funds given voluntarily and not extracted as revenue. English towns and villages possessed their own share of charitable foundations that were usually administered independently from the poor-law authorities. The experience of poverty must have consisted (in some part) in having to negotiate and deal with a variety of such agencies. If these had their own agenda to serve, and did not consult financial needs of recipients solely or firstly, the study of charity will necessitate the consideration of more diverse aspects of the experiences of poverty. Where sources for statutory and non-statutory forms of relief (or other avenues of support, although these are more rare) can be consulted together, a unique series of insights into the nature of poverty and the experiences of the poor can be gained via the compilation of partial pauper biographies. These are not the rich biographies discernible from narrative sources such as pauper letters or trial proceedings, but instead the piecemeal, fragmentary biographies of people who ran up against two or more institutions; 'biography is primarily concerned with the lives of individuals, while prosopography deals with the connections between individuals in a group'.[36] Therefore the prosopography featured here chiefly involves identification of overlapping groups, not unpicking pre-existing narratives.

Parish records and particularly overseers' accounts lie at the heart of this study. Overseers' accounts provide a list of people who were considered by their home community to be so poor as to require and in some measure deserve to be given relief and occasionally reveal details of their marital status and family ties. In addition the distribution of extraordinary relief for specific purposes provides glimpses of people's experiences of some key life-cycle events, such as birth, burial or apprenticeship, and experiences of common short-term problems, such as illness. Name lists of paupers (whether in need of long-term or temporary relief), and in individual cases information about the relief they took, can be used to compile information about people and groups who crop up in other contexts. These parish-relief lists cannot be used as a proxy for a census of the poor, and there are a number of problems with using them at all, but they are often the best route we can now adopt to identify people in the lowliest, most impoverished strata of early modern society; the only people in a worse situation would have been those who were similarly poor but who would not assert a claim for relief or whose claims were considered ineligible (by criteria such as settlement, or readily apparent alternative means of support). Provision of parish relief provides a convenient threshold for a person's inclusion among 'the poor', even if the failure to take such relief does not categorically exclude someone from that group. Historians are developing increasingly sophisticated ways for dealing with stark lists of relief recipients.[37]

The records of non-statutory relief or charitable bodies can be used in a similar way. Trustees' minute books, printed annual reports and charity account books can all be used to find the identities of beneficiaries, the extent to which they were eligible for assistance and some specific details about their experiences of that foundation. It is more doubtful whether receipt of charity always qualified a person for inclusion among the very poor. Charities could sometimes confer status on their beneficiaries, with the result that benefits might be sought by people who possessed the means to supply their own minimum requirements of food, shelter and fuel. There is no guarantee that any particular person given charity was all that poor; however, charity disbursements were usually supposed to be directed at people thought to be poor on some level (ranging from the absolutely destitute, to the relatively deprived) so disbursement lists provide another way in to the community of 'the poor'. This book uses lists of paupers in overseers' accounts in conjunction with other sources to build up a more rounded picture of the experiences of the poor. Chapter two looks in detail at the treatment which paupers received in urban workhouses particularly in relation to their material environment and diet (and so concentrates exclusively on the experience of poverty via the parish) but thereafter parish material is interleaved with evidence from charities and other agencies. In this way the functions fulfilled by different charities, principally their accessibility for paupers and the facilities they offered, can be compared with parish initiatives and responses in the same spheres of accommodation, health and education. Chapter three investigates the older formal charities such as almshouses that may have been founded much earlier than the eighteenth century but which continued to dispense a variety of welfare. The roles of these in the lives of the poor have been neglected in the aftermath of Jordan's overambitious claims for charity.[38] In contrast, this research goes some way to extend our understanding of the place of more traditional charities in the lives of urban poor. Chapters four and five deal with provincial hospitals and charity schools respectively, both specifically eighteenth-century expressions of the charitable impulse. Confusion about the groups likely to benefit from these charities, particularly about the tendency of pauper children to occupy places at charity schools, can be tentatively resolved via a comparison of paupers and beneficiaries. Finally, chapter six looks at the relationship between the poor, the use of credit by pawning, and the intervention of parish relief.

When this research was initially conceived, this sort of prosopographical approach to the history of poverty had rarely been undertaken before despite the logic of such a practice, and the specific mechanics of my research varied from existing attempts in English history in that it did not rely on the parish reconstruction as a starting point.[39] It remains methodologically innovative, since in existing published work it is the preserve of a few chapters and articles rather than a widespread tactic for accessing pauper lives, and it is used here because the primary concern is with poor populations of multiple parishes rather than with total populations of single parishes.[40] Therefore I have used overseers' accounts to identify one subset of urban poor, charity accounts and a pawnshop register for other cohorts of the poor, and sought vital events only for selected individuals who occurred in multiple lists. The result is a 'limited prosopography'.[41] Yet a comparison of names cited in these varied contexts is problematic; the main methodological difficulty with this procedure related to proving conclusively that a person named on one list was the same individual on another list whenever an identical first and surname overlapped (appendix 1.1: 'Prosopographical methodology'). It has been heartening to discover that the procedure that developed as this research progressed has subsequently found effective endorsement in the systematic methodological treatment advocated by Williams and Ottaway.[42] The result, I hope, is an echo of Kevin Siena's work on venereal patients, comprising a history based on institutional records but revealing the outward experience of dependent poverty.

The historiography of eighteenth-century poverty

Early twentieth-century histories of poverty tended to be administrative in focus and negative in tone.[43] The Webbs' research (particularly for the post-1834 period) can be challenged and criticised for the extent to which their political bias and their sense of timing prompted them to draw questionable inferences from their material and cut corners in its presentation.[44] Readers have regretted their anachronistic criticisms of the law as 'irredeemably punitive',[45] being harsh and controlling, managed with ignorance or indifference, neglect or malicious manipulation.[46] Their damning depiction of parish welfare as the cause of early, improvident family formation was effectively overturned in the 1960s. Blaug acquitted the wage subsidy policy in particular of responsibility for population growth by presenting evidence that the old poor law was responding to changing family needs and not inspiring those changes (in work which has found critics but no decisive contradictions).[47] Most unfortunate of all has been their stylistic legacy. For many years the main product of welfare research was the unambitious vignette of relief within a single parish, which developed in miniature the same sort of institutional history for one place that the Webbs had attempted nationally. The result was that the records of poor relief were treated fairly uncritically, and that very little attention was paid to the life experiences of paupers, the central actors on the poor-relief stage. The challenge to see poverty from the viewpoint of the poor was only taken up forty years later, with the injunction to study 'history from below'.[48] Latterly though, issues of parish government have been given a much more positive, updated treatment in terms of authority, the balance of power within local communities, and 'micro-politics'.[49]

Recent work on welfare may be characterised under a number of broad headings such as the 'demographic' (broadly defined) causes and consequences of poverty, the multiple strands of the English 'economy of makeshifts', the experiences of the poor (particularly their scope for autonomous action), and increasingly sophisticated variants on the study of place (as parish, town or region). None of these artificial categories is self-contained, of course, but each approach has a recognisable trajectory and has opened up different opportunities.

Demographic issues have been more accurately labelled the 'life-cycle' causes of poverty. Tim Wales drew out the explicit connections between stress points in people's personal or family life-cycle and the experience of poverty, specifically the need for parish relief, in one of the first books to grapple explicitly with the influence of life-cycle.[50] Barry Stapleton took up the challenge to elucidate life-cycle poverty for an entire community over more than one generation, and formulated the alternative phrase 'life-time poverty' to describe families subjected to unrelenting hardship from the birth of a first child through to old age.[51] Few studies have attempted to replicate, test, extend or refine this work. Latterly the poles of childhood and old age have attracted interest from welfare historians as discrete phases requiring discernible and relatively uncontroversial welfare activity but without coverage of the whole life-cycle.[52] Thus the concept of life-cycle poverty has been absorbed and turned to account by historians of welfare, but there seems to be some doubt about how to take this sort of research forward. Can we develop some analytical subtleties to differentiate between different strains of widowhood, different experiences of being orphaned, and the rigidity or otherwise with which people were constrained by their birth or family circumstances to a lifetime of dependent poverty? Steve King has recently demonstrated the potential of parish reconstitutions, when analysed alongside poverty indicators, to reveal the percentages of populations who were never poor, always poor or intermittently poor over the course of their life-cycle.[53] Similarly imaginative use of labour-intensive researches may be required to advance our conception of life-cycle poverty.

The demographic consequences of poverty have inspired debate about both the minutiae of pauper experiences and the big questions facing an industrialising society. Under the first heading, Laslett's controversial theory about the size and simplicity of pauper households has proved persistent despite Thomas Sokoll's work on Essex, which shows that pauper households could be larger and more complex than their neighbours'.[54] On the broader question of the utility of a poor law for industrialising England, historians have become entangled with the question of whether the old poor law constituted a 'welfare state in miniature' or was a fragmentary, only notionally systematic phenomenon that was wholly unpredictable. Both interpretations have great significance for ideas about employment. Snell was primarily concerned with the question of the quality of life experienced by ordinary agricultural labourers in counties south of Staffordshire. In the process of illuminating the rhythms of seasonal employment and unemployment in eighteenth- and nineteenth-century England he characterised parish relief under the old poor law as a relatively generous and flexible safety net (particularly before 1780), which was able to support the mobility of labourers between different geographical places and between jobs.[55] Peter Solar writing in 1995 argued that the flexibility of the old poor law allowed it to be applied by officials in such a way as to regulate the local supply of labour. The aggregate (national) consequence of these multiple independent decisions, he alleges, promoted a mobile, responsive workforce.[56] But this level of optimism has not yet proved entirely convincing. At its broadest, the role of the poor law has been considered in a demographic macroeconomic sense. Blaug, Williams and Boyer have attempted to summarise the nature of cause and effect in the spheres of social policy and population growth in the late eighteenth and early nineteenth centuries.[57]

Most recently research has swung round to the experiences of poverty, both via the regional variations in the range and quantity of relief offered to the local poor and by looking beyond the parish to the alternative sources of income or benefits which could be gleaned, exploited or even stolen. Steve King has emphasised the significant variations between parish practices in the north and south, demonstrating that the safety net provided by the poor law was much less comprehensive in the north. Penny Lane has illustrated how crime was viewed as a 'legitimate' income-generating activity among certain groups particularly rural industrial workers.[58] Detailed work on the range of alternatives to poor relief, often summarised using the oft-quoted heading of 'the economy of makeshifts', was effectively begun some time ago by Roger Smith in relation to Nottingham and has been taken up again by John Broad who makes a convincing appeal for a holistic approach to the history of local welfare opportunities.[59] The state of play on English makeshifts is surveyed in *The Poor in England 1700–1850: An Economy of Makeshifts*.[60] A recent innovation has been the use of narrative sources generated by parish procedures (like pauper letters and settlement examinations) to gain access to the range of alternative survival strategies employed by the poor.[61] The most ambitious attempts to tackle poverty via a compilation of evidence about poor relief, charity and work or kinship lie outside the period of this book (or employ sources not available for the eighteenth century).[62]

One consequence of attempts to write genuine history from below has been to instate some acknowledgement of the autonomy of the poor, albeit limited. Thompson's brilliant depiction of a culture of resistance is unusually emphatic; most writers are more cautious.[63] Ostensibly intimate perspectives on the lives of the poor are currently being wrested from pauper letters,[64] whereby the people who approached their parishes for relief are depicted as negotiators rather than passive recipients. The dialogue between poor and parish officers, vestry men, magistrates and aldermen may frequently have been unequal, but the balance of power could shift in some surprising ways. Poor applicants for relief could couch their requests in such a way as to maximise their immediate takings, by threatening greater subsequent expense if demands were not met, promising independence from the parish for the future or in numerous other ways. The most stereotypical was perhaps the oft-repeated warning of pauper letter writers, that their demands on the parish would be greater if they returned home to their parish of settlement than if they were given the cash they requested in their location of choice.[65] Cleverly this strategy both emphasised economy for the parish and secured their homes according to their own geographical preference. Having said this, it is possible to go too far in according autonomy to the very poor. The fact that outright workhouse riots were rare in the eighteenth century is possibly evidence of moderation within workhouses but it may also point to a measure of acquiescence on the part of the poor, and choices might be exercised in the context of limited room for manoeuvre.[66]

Given these broadly defined preoccupations, what are the resulting limitations of the current historiographical picture? These approaches to the history of welfare have generated some heated debates and supplied limited information about poverty but there are still many areas of life for the poor, which should be at least partly recoverable from the known source base, but which have been tackled in only a partial, desultory or unsustained way. Themed research, into one aspect of relief in many different places, remains rather rare. Richard Smith's co-ordination of work on pensions is one of the few good examples of this (and as he says, poor-relief topics often suffer from the absence of good doctoral work from the published canon).[67] I do not know of any equivalent to Tim Hitchcock's large-scale survey for workhouse life, for example, and the deficiencies of workhouse literature for the period before 1834 are discussed at the start of chapter two as a preface to the comparative study offered here of life in urban workhouses.[68] There has also been recognisable reticence about exploring the function of extraordinary (or short-term) relief. Tim Wales implied in 1984 that extraordinary relief essentially augmented parish pensions, generating a variety of total support for some individuals in seventeenth-century Norfolk, but little work has been undertaken to confirm this idea, or extend it in time.[69] Therefore one of the main aims of this research has been to trace patterns of extraordinary relief distributions under key headings such as medical-related payments.

Welfare histories that consider poor relief and charity together, not just as theoretically accessible benefits but as quantifiable distributions to specific people or families, are fairly thin on the ground. Mary Fissell's research on the Bristol infirmary used local parish records to try to map the use of either the infirmary or the parish but depended on a rough and ready comparison of surnames rather than a painstaking hooking-up of individual case studies. Fiddly work like this has been undertaken but the empirical base for conclusions remains very small.[70] Therefore the research offered in this book explicitly attempts to reach the experience of poverty as revealed by interactions between paupers and formally run charities, particularly long-term institutions or establishments, the majority of which were found much more frequently in urban settings than in rural locations.

Population and economy in three 'traditional' towns: Oxford, Shrewsbury and York

In 1700, county towns like Oxford, Shrewsbury and York, in company with numerous others such as Chester and Northampton, had reached or passed their peak of national significance and were in relative decline in comparison with expanding industrial centres. York had sustained a blow to its status with the loss of the Council of the North in 1641 and Oxford, once the Royalist headquarters, was fast becoming a provincial backwater. As regional centres they provided the venue for markets and fairs crucial to the economy of their regions and housed influential institutions like cathedrals, schools and universities. They played host to gatherings of wider relevance than those required to administer the town itself, including county quarter sessions, assize courts and parliamentary elections. These events along with other social occasions such as races and assemblies generated business, drew visitors and occasionally inhabitants but could not provide the same impetus to growth and

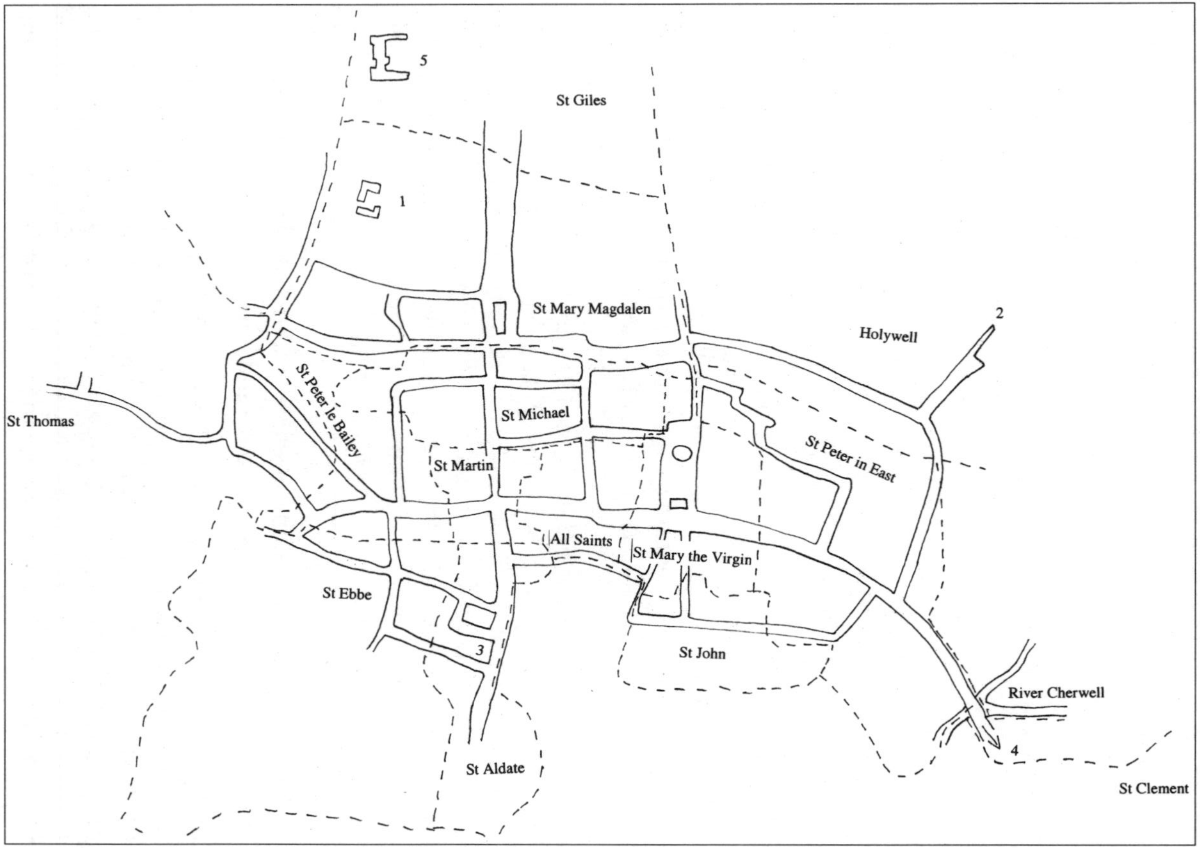

Figure 1.1
Map of Oxford

1 Woodroffes Folly
  (workhouse)
2 Holywell work-
  house
3 Christ Church
  Almshouse
4 Towards St Bartho-
  lomew's Almshouse
5 House of Industry
  (opened 1771)

Figure 1.2
Map of Shrewsbury

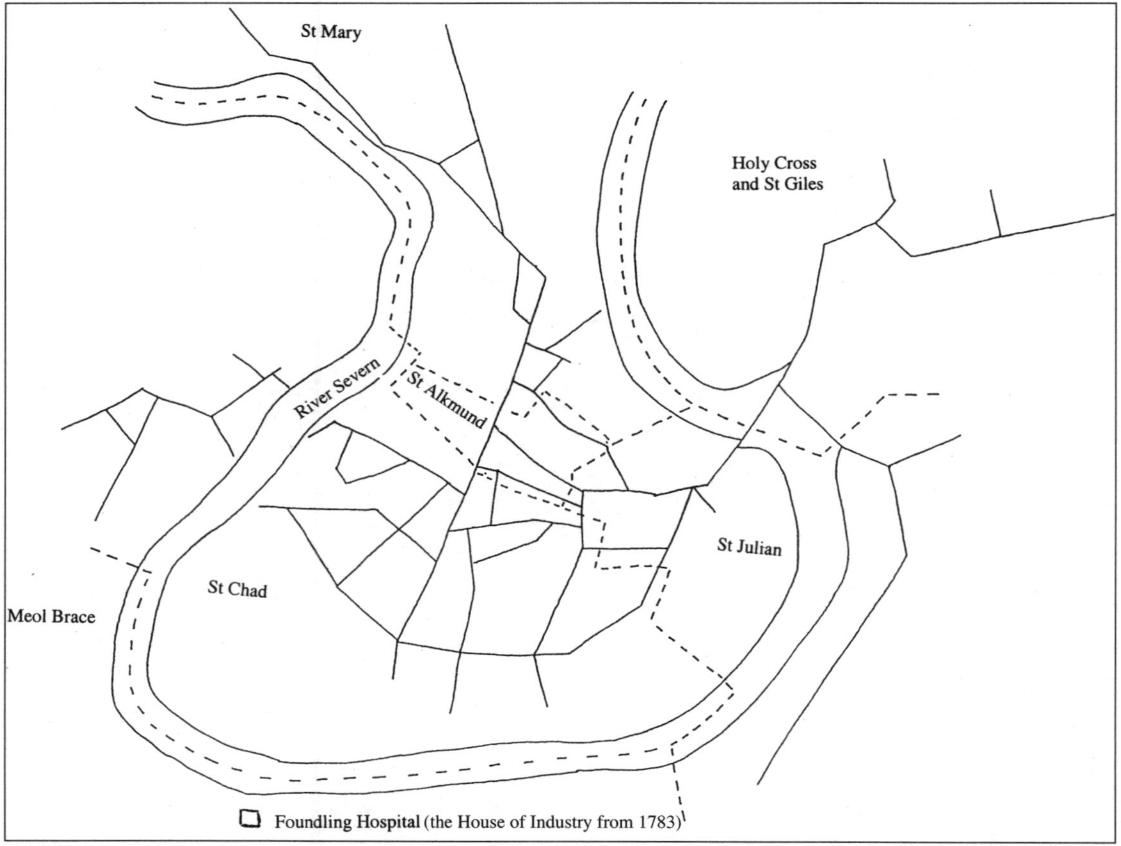

St Mary

Holy Cross
and St Giles

River Severn

St Alkmund

St Julian

St Chad

Meol Brace

☐ Foundling Hospital (the House of Industry from 1783)[1]

prosperity in eighteenth-century England as a thriving staple industry or a vibrant port. The attitude of these towns' ruling bodies (in the face of expansion of industry elsewhere) varied but tended to be conservative, emphasising protectionism and insularity. Without industry or another source of employment, there was a limit to how much these towns could expand, since marketing services were also supplied by other, smaller market towns.[71] In Cheshire, for example, the vast majority of goods produced in the region passed through Chester for redistribution or for export out of the region but smaller towns forged some interconnections, enabling goods to bypass Chester.[72]

The three towns studied most closely here, Oxford, Shrewsbury and York, had populations of between 8,000 and 14,000 people in the period 1723–82. Oxford (figure 1.1) was relatively immune from any dramatic change to either population or economy. The size and rate of change of Oxford's population can be assessed from numerous counts of houses and inhabitants 1737–74; a pre-census count put inhabitants at 8,292 in 1751, spread across fourteen parishes.[73] The housing stock of many parishes was static if not in decline. Two of only three parishes exhibiting observable growth, St Mary Magdalen and St Thomas, were located on the outskirts of the town and were each on one of the main approach roads. Such newcomers as there were to the town may have been more likely to settle in these parishes. In 1738 St Mary Magdalen in particular was noted to contain many single people or lodgers.[74]

Shrewsbury (figure 1.2) was clearly very similar in size to Oxford around 1750; the only population estimate taken for Shrewsbury in the eighteenth century counted 8,141 inhabitants across just five parishes.[75] Holy Cross was the smallest parish with fewer than 1,000 people, while St Chad was the largest with 3,771. Unlike Oxford, however, Shrewsbury experienced a spurt of population growth in the later part of the century which pre-dated 'vigorous' manufacturing expansion 1790–1820 but the general increase did not affect all parishes equally.[76] St Mary's experienced the most rapid growth-rate with the population more than doubling from 1,399 in 1750 to 3,324 in 1801. Population density also increased as the available housing tended not to keep pace with the increase of people, so in St Mary's the number of people per house increased from 4.4 to 5.8.[77] In contrast the calculations by William Gorsuch, the vicar of Holy Cross, show that between 1755 and 1780 the population of his parish remained remarkably steady, at between 1,050 and 1,100 people.[78] He was able to account minutely for fluctuations in the total by reference to numerous families moving into houses previously vacant, or demolition of dwellings to make way for a new bridge over the Severn, constructed in 1769.[79]

Figure 1.3 *Map of York*

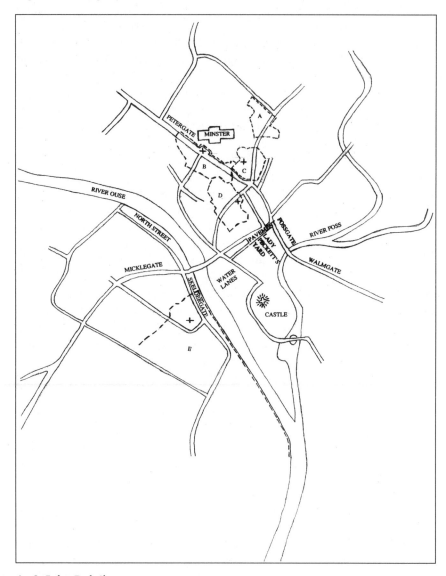

A St John Delpike
B St Michael le Belfrey
C Holy Trinity Goodramgate
D St Sampson
E St Mary Bishophill senior

York (figure 1.3), like Oxford, seems to have experienced virtually no population growth up to 1760 but probably underwent persistent growth at the end of the century (without any industrial underpinning). Mid-century stagnation was ascribed at the time to the restrictive policy of the corporation, which tended to discourage outside manufacturers from settling in York.[80] The inhabitants were spread over twenty-eight tiny parishes. Contemporary research used city baptisms to estimate that the population in 1735 had stood at approximately 10,800 but that it had risen very slightly to 12,750 or 12,800 in 1781.[81] If accurate these figures suggest that the city experienced relatively rapid growth in the twenty years 1781–1801, as the total had reached 16,145 in 1801.[82]

The three towns' economies exhibited broad similarities. Oxford, Shrewsbury and York were all primarily market towns which supplied consumers in their immediate hinterlands but each enjoying local variants on their spheres of influence; Shrewsbury had a privileged access to the Welsh cloth trade and was home to an increasingly prestigious public school, Oxford was in the unusual position of supplying the university, while York and Oxford contained cathedrals.

In Oxford the prosperity of several sectors relied heavily on the university itself or the students and this dependence had some negative aspects. The town had a distinctive seasonal unemployment pattern that hinged on the academic terms. Vacations meant less work for those who made a living from the university and many artisans and labourers could expect regular periods of unemployment.[83] Student numbers declined from the late seventeenth century onwards which may have forced the town's economy to contract, although this blow may have been softened by students' increasing conspicuous consumption.[84] Also, a dilemma for tradesmen surrounded the extension of credit. If students were refused credit they might boycott a particular establishment, but if too much was advanced businesses could be ruined.[85] The presence of the university also affected the numbers of freemen in the town. Those employed in businesses associated closely with supplying the needs of the university were designated 'matriculated' or privileged tradesmen and did not have to take up the freedom. Those privileged included booksellers, printers, and less immediately obvious groups like barbers.[86]

Marketing was central to both York and Shrewsbury. York's chief economic importance throughout the eighteenth century remained its role in the regional economy, as a centre of wheat and dairy distribution. It was home to one of the most important grain markets in northern England and a wholesale butter market thrived in Micklegate until the 1750s.[87] Similarly the extent of the goods that Shrewsbury offered to the local population made it 'the greatest market … in all the western part of England'.[88] One of the most distinctive and visible aspects of Shrewsbury's economy in the eyes of contemporaries was the trade in Welsh textiles. Cloth would be brought to Shrewsbury to be 'finished' and sold on to clothiers. Defoe commented on the high visibility of this association in the 1720s, as 'on market day you would think you were in Wales'.[89] At some time in the eighteenth century this trade began to wane as new markets were established at Oswestry and other places nearer to the sites of production and in the 1790s it collapsed entirely. This was a double loss as the Welsh traders had sold cloth for cash and then spent it in town on groceries and shop goods.[90]

Industry was waning or barely significant in these towns. Both Oxford and Shrewsbury had traditional connections with leather-work that were more or less in decline. From the late seventeenth century onwards one branch of the Oxford trade, gloving, shifted focus to Woodstock. Also, Oxford's shoemakers may have suffered from regional competitors.[91] Shrewsbury's leather-working industry apparently suffered a more substantial decline.[92] Manufacturing of all descriptions remained a relatively minor component of York's economy throughout the century; leather and textiles combined were responsible for only around ten percent of admissions to the freedom in the eighteenth century, and small-scale handcrafts accounted for less than ten percent more.[93]

The spirit of industrial enterprise was not encouraged; Oxford has been described as having carried on 'the psychology of the walled town' in the eighteenth century.[94] Conditions inside Shrewsbury may have been even more restrictive. For many years prior to 1774 admission to the freedom was by descent or grant of the corporation only, which generated considerable resentment in the town.[95] A mandamus had to be issued from King's Bench directing the corporation to admit on the grounds of servitude.[96] Also the power of the companies and guilds in the town amounted to a stranglehold. It was complained that a retailer might have to compound for membership of three or more companies in order to trade. There was apparently evidence that some branches of trade had been abandoned altogether as a result of this control. The municipal corporations commissioners cited it as a failing on the part of the town corporation that the excesses of the guilds had not been curbed. Similarly in York the corporation actively deterred incoming investors and attempted to enforce the freedom regulations strictly throughout the eighteenth century.[97] In 1781 it was assumed that few people moved to the town 'as there is no settled manufactory here' and the urban authorities were still being urged to 'open the gates to all tradesmen and manufacturers inclinable to settle among us' in 1790.[98] The two confectionery businesses which were later to prove important to York, Rowntree's and

Terry's sweet manufactories, were both established between 1750 and 1770 but for the duration of the eighteenth century these were small concerns.[99]

In contrast, all three towns functioned as regional social centres. Shrewsbury also developed a luxury sector to attract and amuse gentry custom. McInnes suggests that this increased to fill the gap left by leather and textiles.[100] Shrewsbury may have had more resident gentry (as opposed to visitors, or students in Oxford). By the end of the seventeenth century the town had an 'abundance of people of quality' and thirty years later was still 'full of gentry'.[101] Oxford and York also developed some features of the leisure town.[102] In the early eighteenth century Defoe referred to York as a place of 'good company and cheap living; a man converses here with all the world as effectually as at London' but enjoying 'no trade indeed, except such as depends upon the confluence of the gentry'.[103] In 1745 he was echoed by another commentator: 'the chief support of the city, at present, is the resort to and residence of several country gentlemen with their families in it'. It has been described as the social and intellectual capital of the north between the seventeenth and the nineteenth centuries.[104] Nevertheless, by the 1770s not all of its visitors thought it a particularly vibrant social centre. One of Horace Walpole's correspondents described it in 1771 as 'this dullest of all provincial towns'.[105]

In common with many urban centres these towns benefited from turnpiking, and also from the eighteenth-century enthusiasm for urban improvement, but it was access to water that lay at the heart of their external communications and flavoured their economies. Staithes or wharfs on the River Ouse were vital to the economic life of York, and this was reflected in a high percentage of admissions to the freedom for sailors or mariners. Corn and coal were typically transported into the city via the river, along with other commodities such as salt and lime. The corporation remained eager to improve the river in the immediate vicinity of York and to promote the maintenance of the harbour at Hull (the city's ultimate connection with the sea).[106] Shrewsbury was connected by water via the Severn. The river is an integral part of Shrewsbury, and in the eighteenth century its horse-shoe curve must have encompassed the greater part of the town. Its depth meant the Severn was navigable through and beyond Shrewsbury. River craft did not necessarily ply the entire length of the river from Bristol to Welshpool but mostly travelled particular stretches of the upper or lower waterway. One or two vessels sailed directly between Shrewsbury and Bristol.[107] The proximity of the Severn was not always beneficial to the town as it was (and remains) prone to flooding. In 1767, St Julian's parish overseers paid to have people transported by boat from the workhouse and mentioned floods specifically again in 1768 and 1770.[108] The reliability of the Severn declined in the late eighteenth century as it became more liable to flood.[109] Oxford's relationship with the Thames was more quiescent but the prosperity of trade varied.[110] In mid-century Oxford fuel was described as 'scarce'.[111] Coal had to travel by sea from Newcastle to London and then on barges up the Thames to Oxford.

Poverty and parish relief in Oxford, Shrewsbury and York

These towns were not unduly marked out by the poverty of their inhabitants. Some perspective on the scale of poverty towards the end of the period treated here, in a format that is at least ostensibly comparable from place to place, is available via an examination of the returns made to parliament in 1777 and 1787 regarding poor-relief expenditure.

In relation to the three towns principally considered here, it is clear that significantly less money was being raised in York than in either Oxford or Shrewsbury. This finding does not arise from some peculiarity associated with York as such, but reflects regional differences which saw *per capita* spending in the northern midlands and north-east as substantially less than spending in the south midlands and south-east.[112] By the 1780s the amount of money raised in York had exceeded the equivalent amount for Oxford, but the different populations in the towns mean that *per capita* spending in York was still rather distant from the totals for the more southerly towns. The rate of increase over time was generally upwards in all locations, but was not uniformly so; the *per capita* cost of parish welfare in Oxford apparently went down over the decade, while the increase was much less marked in York than in Shrewsbury. Oxford and Shrewsbury were clearly within the same orbit of experience and broadly in the same geographical region, although they may have been diverging by the 1780s.

Comparison with a variety of other urban centres is striking. Regional coalescence becomes obvious given the similarity between the experiences of, for example, York and Leeds. However, there are also parallels to be drawn between the same types of town even where their regional location was rather different, such that Liverpool and Newcastle-upon-Tyne had similar though not identical trajectories. Finally, none of these towns was in the same league as Colchester where the cost of poor relief gave rise to an inordinate *per capita* expenditure.

The relative distribution of wealth and poverty in these three towns during 1723–82 can be gauged impressionistically from an analysis of levies for poor rates and the estimates of property rental values on which rates were based.[113] In the majority of parishes that have surviving

Table 1.1 *Spending on poor relief in selected towns, 1776 and 1783–85*

	Poor rates 1776	Estimated population 1770s	Per capita cost of poor relief 1776	Poor rates, average 1783–85	Estimated population 1780s	Per capita cost of poor relief 1783–58
Chester	£1,249 5s	11,940	2.1s	£2,018 12s	11,670	3.5s
Northampton	£1,207 6s	5,633	4.1s	£2,000 15s	5,433	7.3s
Oxford	£2,203 13s	7,965	5.5s	£2,287 19s	8,700	5.3s
Shrewsbury	£2,674 4s	10,290	5.2s	£3,891 7s	10,810	7.2s
York	£1,749 3s	12,960	2.8s	£2,657 16s	14,260	3.7s
Birmingham	£5,894 17s	40,920	2.9s	£11,385 6s	55,210	4.1s
Colchester	£3,587 9s	6,975	10.3s	£4,334 0s	6,480	13.4s
Leeds	£3,692 15s	28,530	2.6s	£4,397 10s	33,980	2.6s
Liverpool	£3,043 18s	45,030	1.4s	£6,117 15s	55,630	2.2s
Newcastle-Upon-Tyne	£1,738 13s	17,925	1.9s	£3,561 8s	18,950	3.8s

Source: House of Commons Sessional Papers of the Eighteenth Century ed. S. Lambert (Wilmington Delaware, 1975) 31, 'Abstracts of the returns made by the overseers of the poor' 1777; 60, 'Abstracts of the returns made by overseers of the poor' 1787.
Note: Population estimates are based on decadal baptism rates reported at the time of the 1801 census.

poor-rate lists, the parish officer levying the tax either noted the approximate rent that occupiers were paying or the rate that was being raised on the basis of that rent.[114] Rents may not necessarily be a good guide to individuals' wealth in the mid-eighteenth century, but they do provide a rough impression of the economic composition of a parish. Attempts to tax wealth not represented in the rental values of properties were notoriously fraught. The only clear attempt to raise money on the value of stock-in-trade can be seen in Oxford in St Peter le Bailey, which raised an annual levy on the butchers' shops in the parish. In York parishes made a concerted effort to tax personal wealth in addition to real estate and made separate assessments for properties and people (demanding in St Michael le Belfrey, for example, payment of 2s for every £120 of personal estate). This survey of parochial wealth is based on rental values only.

Figure 1.4 *Rental values from poor-rate levies, 1740–80*

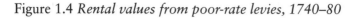

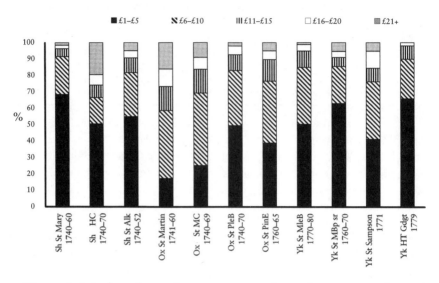

Figure 1.4 is based on the average number of ratepayers in each rent-band during selected years in the period 1740 to 1780.[115] Of the Oxford parishes, St Martin was clearly the wealthiest. This parish had both the smallest proportion of inhabitants paying rent of between one and five pounds and one of the largest proportions paying over twenty-one pounds. St Michael and St Peter in East were both less wealthy, as their groups of low-rent-payers was larger and their high-rent-payers smaller. St Peter le Bailey was certainly the poorest as the vast majority of inhabitants paid ten pounds or less in rent. These graphs are based on ratepayers only and therefore exclude all households that were exempt. As a result, many more homes may have existed within each parish in the poorer rent-bands. Only one rate in Oxford, for St Peter le Bailey in 1739, numbered both houses rated and houses exempt. In that year, parish officers noted 149 houses and 46 exempt, implying that in this parish around thirty-one percent of houses were untaxed. Furthermore St Peter le Bailey combined lack of wealth in the rate base with numerous poor in need of relief. As a result it received rates in aid from other town parishes. Around £17 per year was collected via this system but the legal expenses of applying for them each year, coupled with the money spent when overseers received these funds, may have accounted for the expenditure of up to ten percent of the income.

The larger size of Shrewsbury parishes meant that the groups of rent-payers would be more likely to reflect the profile of rent-payers in the town as a whole rather than highlight differences between parishes.

Nevertheless, all of the Shrewsbury parishes contained the same proportion as or a greater proportion of the poorest rent-payers than St Peter le Bailey in Oxford. This probably reflects the fact that rents were pitched lower in Shrewsbury; alternatively, it might be evidence that Shrewsbury parishes had poorer rate-bases than Oxford parishes. There are also one or two differences that can be discerned between the Shrewsbury parishes. Holy Cross contained a much larger percentage of the highest ratepayers among town residents than St Mary. It is likely though that St Chad's parish (lacking poor rates for this period) was both the largest parish and the poorest. The approach roads from Wales arrived at the town in St Chad and Welsh migrant workers tended to settle there in the sixteenth and seventeenth centuries when looking for work in the textile industry. For the seventeenth century, the parish has been described as 'ghetto-like'.[116] Of course, the size of the Shrewsbury parishes could conceal considerable variations in the wealth of their populations; in the 1690s poverty was particularly marked on some streets including Frankwell, Castle Foregate, Coleham and Abbey Foregate, which were distributed between most of the town parishes.[117]

Rate-bases in York (in the admittedly few places where these were available) had more in common with Shrewsbury than Oxford, which is interesting given the vast difference in sizes of parish between the two towns. Ratepayers in the lowest band dominate the picture for York, with only St Sampson containing over half of its rated properties in bands above the lowest. The graph for St Mary Bishophill senior, a relatively large and mixed parish by York standards, looks very similar to that of St Mary in Shrewsbury.

This book will focus mainly on around twelve of the forty eight town parishes that comprised Oxford, Shrewsbury and York. In Oxford, the parishes of St Martin, St Mary Magdalen, St Michael, St Peter in East and St Peter le Bailey are examined most intensively. These parishes possessed overseers' accounts for some or all of the period from 1723 until 1771 (when the town incorporated for poor-relief purposes and parish accounts were no longer kept). They also possessed a variety of other records useful to this study of poverty such as overseers' vouchers and charity records. Furthermore they represented a selection of the types of parish found in Oxford; for example, St Martin's was a small and wealthy parish that was located at the centre of the town's trading area, while St Mary Magdalen was a large, poor parish sited around the northern approach roads to Oxford. The Shrewsbury parishes of St Julian, St Mary and Holy Cross also possessed overseers' accounts. Holy Cross was the smallest central parish while St Mary was one of the largest and most densely populated parishes in Shrewsbury in the second half of the eighteenth century. Holy Cross and St Julian lay chiefly on the east of the town while St Mary contained the castle and approach roads from the north. The York parishes of St Mary Bishophill senior, St Sampson and particularly St Michael le Belfrey, provide the main focus. The overseers' accounts for York were dated later in the eighteenth century than those found for Oxford or Shrewsbury and were less detailed but the retention of St Michael le Belfrey workhouse accounts for the 1740s and 1750s provided some points for direct comparison. Also the accounts had the advantage of overlapping chronologically with the unique pawnbroker's pledge book that is central to chapter six.

One of the core roles of parish relief was the provision of long-term assistance for people who fell into dependency. The forms of long-term relief, which typically comprised a regular cash payment or pension, or later a place in a workhouse, went a long way to define the material experiences of people who were fully maintained by their parish of settlement. The lot of parish pensioners in the mid-eighteenth century has been given considerable attention by other historians and the sources surviving for Oxford, Shrewsbury and York are not well suited to a study of pensioners. In contrast, conditions of life inside mid-century workhouses have been relatively under-explored. In consequence the next chapter will address key questions relating to workhouse life.

Notes

1 Oxford Record Office (hereafter ORO), Oxford City Archives, O.1.1. Gaol indenture September 1739. Boyce was a city alderman.
2 Green Ditch was the site of the Oxford gallows. ORO, Mss dd par Oxford St Peter le Bailey b.15 inside volume cover. Men who frequently acted as churchwardens and overseers were the targets of Wheeler's animosity on this occasion.
3 See the conclusion of this book for the case of the Wildgoose family.
4 E. A. Wrigley, *Poverty, Progress and Population* (Cambridge, 2004), p. 267. This chapter was first given as a paper at the Anglo-American conference at the Institute of Historical Research in July 1990.
5 E. M. Hampson, *The Treatment of Poverty in Cambridgeshire, 1597–1834* (Cambridge, 1934) provides a good example of a county study; parochial studies are numerous. The work on deprivation in towns was, in 1990, limited but the leading work was undoubtedly P. Slack, *Poverty and Policy in Tudor and Stuart England* (London, 1988).
6 P. Clark (ed.), *The Cambridge Urban History of Britain. Volume 2, 1540–1840* (Cambridge, 2001).
7 C. G. Pooley and J. Turnbull, *Migration and Mobility in Britain since the Eighteenth Century* (London, 1998), chapter 4.

8 R. Sweet, 'Introduction', in R. Sweet and P. Lane (eds), *Women and Urban Life in Eighteenth-Century England* (Aldershot, 2003), p. 1.

9 P. Hudson, *The Industrial Revolution* (London, 1992), for example, stresses the importance of regional economic history; S. King, *Poverty and Welfare in England 1700–1850: A Regional Perspective* (Manchester, 2000) takes the regional issue into poverty.

10 H. Peet, *Liverpool Vestry Minutes 1681–1834* (Liverpool, 1912).

11 *A Letter to the Author of Considerations on Several Proposals for the Better Maintenance of the Poor* (London, 1752), p. 20.

12 King, *Poverty and Welfare*, p. 221.

13 See the assessment in S. Lloyd, 'Perceptions of Poverty in England 1660–1770' (DPhil thesis, Oxford University, 1991), p. 330; N. Rogers, 'Confronting the crime wave: the debate over social reform and regulation 1749–1753', in L. Davison *et al* (eds), *Stilling the Grumbling Hive: The Response To Social And Economic Problems in England, 1689–1750* (Stroud, 1992); J. Innes, 'The "mixed economy of welfare" in early modern England: assessments of the options from Hale to Malthus (c.1683–1803)', in M. Daunton (ed.), *Charity, Self-interest and Welfare in the English Past* (London, 1996).

14 The situation was different for the vagrant and begging poor; laws relating to them changed repeatedly, see T. Hitchcock, 'Begging on the streets of eighteenth-century London', *Journal of British Studies* 44 (2005), 479.

15 P. Langford, *A Polite and Commercial People* (Oxford, 1992), p. 442 and *passim*.

16 K. Wrightson and D. Levine, *Poverty and Piety in an English Village: Terling, 1525–1700* (New York, 1979), p. 182.

17 P. J. Corfield, 'Class by name and number in eighteenth-century Britain', *History* 72 (1987); it is no coincidence that E. P. Thompson, *The Making of the English Working Class* (London, 1980) essentially deals with the period after 1780.

18 H. C. E. Midelfort, 'Madness and civilisation in early modern Europe: a reappraisal of Michel Foucault', in B. C. Malament (ed.), *After the Reformation: Essays in Honor of J. H. Hexter* (Manchester, 1980).

19 L. Hollen Lees, *The Solidarities of Strangers: The English Poor Laws and the People, 1700–1948* (Cambridge, 1998), pp. 19, 77–9.

20 Ibid., pp. 37–9.

21 Ibid., chapter 3.

22 A. Borsay, *Medicine and Charity in Georgian Bath: A Social History of the General Infirmary c.1739–1830* (Aldershot, 1999), p. 211.

23 D. Andrew, '"To the Charitable and Humane": appeals for assistance in the eighteenth-century London press', in H. Cunningham and J. Innes (eds), *Charity, Philanthropy and Reform* (Basingstoke, 1998), pp. 102–4.

24 D. Valenze, 'Charity, custom and humanity: changing attitudes towards the poor in eighteenth-century England', in J. Garnett and C. Matthew (eds), *Revival and Religion Since 1700* (London, 1993), pp. 61–2.

25 Ibid., pp. 66–71.

26 D. Valenze, *The First Industrial Woman* (Oxford, 1995), pp. 25–7.

27 R. M. Smith, 'Reflections from demographic and family history', in M. Daunton (ed.), *Charity, Self Interest and Welfare in the English Past* (London, 1996), pp. 39–40.
28 D. Thomson, 'The welfare of the elderly in the past', in M. Pelling and R. M. Smith (eds), *Life, Death and the Elderly: Historical Perspectives* (London, 1991), pp. 213–17.
29 S. Hindle, *On the Parish? The Micro-Politics Of Poor Relief In Rural England c. 1550–1750* (Oxford, 2004), p. 287.
30 These trends are probably tackled most directly in relation to workhouse food and pauper burial (in chapters two and four respectively).
31 J. Boulton, '"It is extreme necessity that makes me do this": some "survival strategies" of pauper households in London's West End during the early 18th century', *International Review of Social History* 45 (2000), 49–50; K. Siena, *Venereal Disease, Hospitals and the Urban Poor: London's 'Foul Wards', 1600–1800* (Rochester, 2004), p. 4.
32 M. Hanly, 'The economy of makeshifts and the role of the poor law: a game of chance?', in S. King and A. Tomkins (eds), *The Poor in England 1700–1850: An Economy of Makeshifts* (Manchester, 2003).
33 The same conclusion has been reached by historians of poverty on the continent; S. Cavallo, 'Conceptions of poverty and poor relief in Turin in the second half of the eighteenth century', in S. J. Woolf, (ed.) *Domestic Strategies: Work and Family in France and Italy 1600–1800* (Cambridge, 1991), p. 168. Identification of 'the poor' in the past has been addressed via criteria including sex, age, the type and level of occupational label and community status labels. It has been suggested that poverty is also (or primarily) a state of mind; see B. Geremek, *Poverty: A History* (Oxford, 1994), p. 237.
34 T. Arkell, 'The incidence of poverty in England in the later seventeenth century', *Social History* 12 (1987); King, *Poverty and Welfare*, p. 114–16; Hindle, *On the Parish?*, p. 4.
35 See J. Innes, 'The state and the poor: eighteenth-century England in European perspective', in J. Brewer and E. Hellmuth (eds), *Rethinking Leviathan: The Eighteenth Century State in Britain and Germany* (Oxford, 1999) for an explanation of the distinctive English experience. Switzerland exhibited some similarities with relief on the English model; see R. Jütte, *Poverty and Deviance in Early Modern Europe* (Cambridge, 1994), p. 110.
36 P. Magdalino, 'Prosopography and the Byzantine identity', in A. Cameron (ed.), *Fifty Years of Prosopography* (Oxford, 2003), p. 43.
37 For examples of this procedure with different aims see T. Sokoll, 'Negotiating a living: Essex pauper letters from London, 1800–34', *International Review of Social History* 45 (2000), and Boulton, 'Survival strategies'.
38 W. K. Jordan, *Philanthropy in England, 1480–1660* (London, 1959).
39 Parish reconstruction naturally offers important opportunities for studying the rural poor; see for example S. Williams, 'Poor relief, labourers' households and living standards in rural England c. 1770–1834: a Bedfordshire case study', *Economic History Review* 58: 3 (2005).
40 For example J. Robin, 'The relief of poverty in mid nineteenth-century Coly-

ton', *Rural History* 1: 2 (1990) makes use of surviving sources in the context of the censuses 1851–81. Eighteenth-century instances are even more rare but see S. Barratt, 'Kinship, poor relief and the welfare process in early modern England', in King and Tomkins (eds), *The Poor in England*. The methodology of compiling pauper biographies from poor-law records without employing total parish reconstruction has found endorsement in the ESRC-funded project on the Westminster poor headed by Jeremy Boulton and Leonard Schwarz; see www.staff.ncl.ac.uk/j.p.boulton/esrcframeset.htm, accessed 10 October 2003.

41 A similar technique has been used in an American context to study independent labourers as opposed to the dependent poor (giving rise to bulkier biographies); see B. G. Smith, *The 'Lower Sort': Philadelphia's Laboring People, 1750–1800* (Ithaca, 1990), pp. 201–3.

42 S. Ottaway and S. Williams, 'Reconstructing the life-cycle-experience of poverty in the time of the Old Poor Law', *Archives* 23 (1998), 26–7.

43 S. Webb and B. Webb, *English Poor Law History part one: The Old Poor Law* (London [1927] 1963); D. Marshall, *The English Poor in the Eighteenth Century* (London, 1926).

44 A. Kidd, 'Historians or polemicists? How the Webbs wrote their history of the English poor laws', *Economic History Review* 40: 3 (1987).

45 P. Thane, 'Histories of the welfare state', in W. Lamont (ed.), *Historical Controversies and Historians* (London, 1998), p. 55.

46 S. King, 'Poor relief and English economic development reappraised', *Economic History Review* 50: 2 (1997), 360.

47 M. Blaug, 'The myth of the old poor law and the making of the new', *Journal of Economic History* 23: 2 (1963); K. Williams, *From Pauperism to Poverty* (London, 1981).

48 Thompson, *English Working Class*, first published in 1963.

49 Hindle, *On the Parish?*; K. Wrightson, 'The politics of the parish in early modern England', in P. Griffiths *et al* (eds), *The Experience of Authority in Early Modern England* (Basingstoke, 1996).

50 T. Wales, 'Poverty, poor relief and life-cycle: some evidence from seventeenth-century Norfolk', in R. M. Smith (ed.), *Land, Kinship and Life-Cycle* (Cambridge, 1984).

51 B. Stapleton, 'Inherited poverty and life-cycle poverty: Odiham, Hampshire, 1650–1850', *Social History* 18 (1993).

52 P. Thane, *Old Age in English History: Past Experiences, Present Issues* (Oxford, 2000); S. Ottaway, *The Decline of Life: Old Age in Eighteenth-Century England* (Cambridge, 2004); J. Henderson and R. Wall (eds), *Poor Women And Children in the European Past* (London, 1994); Pam Sharpe is unusual in having tackled more than one aspect of lifecycle poverty, see P. Sharpe, 'Poor children as apprentices in Colyton, 1598–1830', *Continuity and Change* 6: 2 (1991) and P. Sharpe, 'Survival strategies and stories: poor widows and widowers in early industrial England', in S. Cavallo and L. Warner (eds), *Widowhood in Medieval and Early Modern Europe* (Harlow, 1999).

53 King, *Poverty and Welfare*, p. 132.
54 P. Laslett (ed.), *Household and Family in Past Time: Comparative Studies in the Size and Structure of the Domestic Group over the Last Three Centuries in England, France, Serbia, Japan, and Colonial North America, With Further Materials from Western Europe* (Cambridge, 1972), particularly chapter 4; T. Sokoll, 'The pauper household small and simple', *Ethnologia Europaea* 17: 1 (1987); T. Sokoll, 'Household and Family Among the Poor: The Case of Two Essex Communities in the Late Eighteenth and Early Nineteenth Centuries' (PhD thesis, Cambridge University, 1988).
55 K. D. M. Snell, *Annals of the Labouring Poor: Social Change and Agrarian England 1660–1900* (Cambridge, 1985), pp. 104–8.
56 P. Solar, 'Poor relief and English economic development before the Industrial Revolution', *Economic History Review* 48 (1995).
57 Blaug, 'Myth'; Williams, *From Pauperism*; G. Boyer, *An Economic History of the English Poor Law 1750–1850* (Cambridge, 1990).
58 King, *Poverty and Welfare*; P. Lane, 'Work on the margins: poor women and the informal economy of eighteenth and early nineteenth century Leicestershire', *Midland History* 22 (1997).
59 R. Smith, 'Relief of urban poverty outside the poor law, 1800–1850: a study of Nottingham', *Midland History* 2: 4 (1974); J. Broad, 'Parish Economies of Welfare, 1650–1834', *Historical Journal* 42: 4 (1999).
60 King and Tomkins (eds), *The poor in England*.
61 Boulton, 'Survival strategies'; A. Tomkins, 'Poverty, kinship support and the case of Ellen Parker, 1818–1827', in S. King (ed.), *The British Experience of Welfare* [forthcoming].
62 For example see J. Long, *Conversations in Cold Rooms: Women, Work and Poverty in 19th-Century Northumberland* (Woodbridge, 1999); M. McIntosh, 'Networks of care in Elizabethan English towns: the example of Hadleigh, Suffolk', in P. Horden and R. M. Smith (eds), *The Locus of Care: Families, Communities, Institutions and the Provision of Welfare Since Antiquity* (London, 1998); B. Reay, *Microhistories: Demography, Society and Culture in Rural England, 1800–1930* (Cambridge, 1996) – chapter 4 draws extensively on oral history sources, although it depicts an 'economy of makeshifts' highly reminiscent of earlier periods.
63 E. P. Thompson, *Customs in Common* (London, 1993).
64 T. Sokoll, *Essex Pauper Letters 1731–1837* (Oxford, 2001) and elsewhere; P. Sharpe, '"The bowels of compation": a labouring family and the law, c.1790–1834', in T. Hitchcock *et al* (eds*)*, *Chronicling Poverty: The Voices and Strategies of the English Poor, 1640–1840* (Basingstoke, 1997).
65 Parishes usually concurred with this financial analysis; Sokoll, *Essex Pauper Letters*, p. 14.
66 For one workhouse riot see P. Muskett, 'A picturesque little rebellion? The Suffolk workhouses in 1765', *Bulletin of the Society for the Study of Labour History* 41 (1980).
67 Smith, 'Reflections', p. 35.
68 T. Hitchcock, 'The English Workhouse: A Study in Institutional Poor Relief

in Selected Counties 1696–1750' (DPhil thesis, Oxford University, 1985).

69 Wales, 'Poverty', p. 357.

70 M. Fissell, *Patients, Power and the Poor in Eighteenth Century Bristol* (Cambridge, 1991); R. Adair, 'Age composition of pensioners in early modern England', paper given at the Wellcome Unit for the History of Medicine, Oxford seminar (1993), and see note 39 above.

71 C. W. Chalklin, *The Provincial Towns of Georgian England: A Study of the Building Process 1740–1820* (London, 1974), pp. 19, 30.

72 J. Stobart, 'Regional Structure and the Urban System: North-West England, 1700–1760', *Transactions of the Historic Society of Lancashire and Cheshire* (Liverpool, 1996), 67–9.

73 Derived from *Articles of Enquiry Addressed to the Clergy of the Diocese of Oxford at the primary Visitation of Dr Thomas Secker 1738* ed. Rev. H. A. Lloyd Jukes (Oxford Record Society 38, 1957); ORO, Mss Oxf. dioc. Papers d.556, d.559, d.562, and d.565 for visitation returns 1759,1768, 1771 and 1774; British Library, Add Mss 5832 fo.189 for an account of houses in Oxford, 1737; *Map of the University and City of Oxford 1750* surveyed by I. Taylor 1750 (Oxford, 1751); A. Wood, *The Antient and Present State of the City of Oxford* with additions by Rev. Sir John Peshall (London, 1773).

74 *Articles 1738*.

75 T. Phillips, *History and Antiquities of Shrewsbury* (Shrewsbury, 1779); unfortunately the estimate excluded Meol Brace, a peripheral parish that was regarded as part of the town by 1801.

76 B. S. Trinder, 'The Textile Industry in Shrewsbury in the Late Eighteenth Century' paper given at the ESRC Colloquium on urban industry in the long eighteenth century (1993). This industrial activity was short-lived however; see A. McInnes, '1638–1780', *Victoria County History of Shropshire* [Shrewsbury volume, forthcoming].

77 PP *Abstract of the Answers and Returns made pursuant to 'An act for taking an account of the population of Great Britain 1801'* (London, 1802).

78 W. Gorsuch, 'An extract of the register of the parish of Holy Cross in Salop, from Michaelmas 1750 to Michaelmas 1760', *Philosophical Transactions of the Royal Society of London* 52 (1761–62), 140–1; W. Gorsuch, 'An extract from the register of the parish of Holy Cross in Salop, being a second decade of years from Michaelmas 1760 to Michaelmas 1770', *Philosophical Transactions of the Royal Society of London* 61 (1771), 57–8; W. Gorsuch, 'An extract of the register of the parish of Holy Cross Salop being a third decade of years from Michaelmas 1770 to Michaelmas 1780', *Philosophical Transactions of the Royal Society of London* 72 (1782), 53–7.

79 H. Owen, *Some Account of the Ancient and Present State of Shrewsbury* (Shrewsbury, 1808), p. 86.

80 P. M. Tillott (ed.), *The Victoria History of Yorkshire: The City of York* (Oxford, 1961), p. 212.

81 W. White, 'Observations on the Bills of Mortality in York', *Philosophical Transactions of the Royal Society of London* 72 (1782), 40.

82 Ibid., p. 40; PP *Abstract of the Answers and Returns made pursuant to 'An act for taking an account of the population of Great Britain 1801'* (London, 1802).

83 A. Crossley (ed.), *Victoria County History of Oxfordshire* 4 (Oxford, 1979), p. 211.

84 L. Stone (ed.), *University in Society* 1 (Princeton, 1975), pp. 37–57.

85 Crossley, *Oxfordshire* 4, p. 211.

86 M. Graham (ed.), *Oxford City Apprentices 1697–1800* (Oxford Historical Society 31, 1987), p. ix.

87 Tillott, *City of York*, pp. 220–1.

88 D. Defoe, *A Tour Through England and Wales* 2 ([1727] 1959), p. 76.

89 Ibid., p. 75.

90 J. B. Blakeway and H. Owen, *A History of Shrewsbury* 1 (London, 1825), pp. 511–12.

91 Crossley, *Oxfordshire* 4, p. 120.

92 A. McInnes, 'The emergence of a leisure town: Shrewsbury 1660–1760', *Past and Present* 120 (1988), 56–7.

93 Tillott, *City of York*, pp. 218–19; relies on a survey of admissions to the freedom for decades 1720–29, 1750–58, 1780–89 and 1790–99.

94 R. Fasnacht, *A History of the City of Oxford* (Oxford, 1954), p. 139.

95 McInnes, 'Leisure town', 59.

96 PP *Reports of the Municipal Corporations Commissioners* (1835) 25, pp. 2,014, 2,021.

97 Tillott, *City of York*, pp. 215, 219–21.

98 White, 'Observations', 41; Tillott, *City of York*, pp. 215–16; *York Chronicle* 27 August 1790 quoted in A. Armstrong, *Stability and Change in an English County Town: A Social Study of York 1801–1851* (Cambridge, 1974), p. 20.

99 Tillott, *City of York*, p. 225.

100 McInnes, 'Leisure town', 58.

101 *The Journeys of Celia Fiennes* ed. C. Morris (London, 1947), p. 227 and Defoe, *A Tour* 1, p. 75.

102 Crossley, *Oxfordshire* 4, p. 119.

103 Defoe, *A Tour* 2, pp. 230, 234.

104 Tillott, *City of York*, p. 215; D. M. Palliser, *Tudor York* (Oxford, 1980), p. 1.

105 W. S. Lewis (ed.), *Correspondence of Horace Walpole* 28 (New Haven, 1955), p. 23.

106 Tillott, *City of York*, pp. 223–5.

107 McInnes, 'Leisure town', 79.

108 Shropshire Archives, 2711/P/2 Shrewsbury St Julian overseers' accounts 1766–74.

109 B. S. Trinder, *The Industrial Revolution in Shropshire* (London, 1981), p. 67–8.

110 Crossley, *Oxfordshire* 4, pp. 208, 292.

111 J. Savary des Brulons and M. Postlethwayt, *Universal Directory of Trade and Commerce* (London, 1757), p. 392.

112 King, *Poverty and Welfare*, p. 84.

113 This technique has been used to good effect elsewhere, particularly where additional listings help to fill out the picture; see J. Boulton, *Neighbourhood and Society: A London Suburb in the Seventeenth Century* (Cambridge, 1987), pp. 105–19.

114 Rates were levied per pound of rent paid. Only St Peter le Bailey quoted neither rates nor rents. As a result, it was assumed that this parish was levying a rate of 2d in the pound, a figure found in several other Oxford parishes.

115 Figures were taken for 1740, 45, 50, 55, 60, 65, 70, 75 and 1780 where overseers' records survive.

116 J. Hill, 'A Study of Poverty and Poor Relief in Shropshire 1550–1685' (MA dissertation, Liverpool University, 1973), p. 197.

117 J. Hindson, 'The Marriage Duty Acts and the social topography of the early modern town: Shrewsbury 1695–8', *Local Population Studies* 31 (1983), 21–8.

2

Life in urban workhouses[1]

The organisation of poor relief in the towns of Oxford, Shrewsbury and York did not change dramatically between 1723 and 1782 because, like urban and rural parishes elsewhere, they drew on a fairly limited range of options for relieving their poor. In particular, the two main choices for the relief of the dependent poor, the workhouse and the parish pension, were used with different emphases in different years with the result that spending usually remained within certain bounds. Yet parish policy could fluctuate in the weighting given to the various components of relief. Changes in policy in this period saw parishes oscillating between the major alternatives rather than progressing in a purposeful or linear fashion. The most eloquent example of this was the repeated return to the workhouse as a means to relieve all the needy poor. This idea remained beguiling even in those parishes which had already tried to set the poor to work or where one workhouse experiment had been seen to fail. Alternatively, workhouses could be reserved for the few paupers who through age or incapacity could not maintain a household, or scrapped altogether.

The widespread adoption of workhouses as an important component of parish relief was essentially an early to mid-eighteenth-century phenomenon, as a result of the changing emphasis of public (published) opinion and the law on providing work for paupers generally and workhouses specifically. The idea that able-bodied paupers should be set to work had been present in the Elizabethan legislation, and a number of metropolitan and provincial examples sprang up (particularly in the 1630s), yet the workhouse 'movement' did not begin in earnest until a century later.[2] Workhouses as places for the joint maintenance and employment of the poor were opened and built by the Corporations of the Poor launched in Bristol in 1696.[3] These were initially unions of urban parishes, established by acts of parliament, formed with several ambitious objectives. Corporations hoped that the systematic and institutional provision of work would enable communities of paupers to become partially or wholly self-supporting. Other aims included the reduction of legal costs, as parishes in the same town would no longer need to engage in settlement disputes with each other, and possibly the deterrence of idle paupers who would not have to be relieved if they refused to work. It was anticipated that all of these measures would tend to reduce the poor rates. Individual parishes soon followed the lead of the Corporations and established their own workhouses. These experiments culminated in, and were further encouraged by, the Knatchbull workhouse act of 1723 that permitted parishes (alone or in concert) to rent houses and contract with workhouse managers to maintain the poor. Contractors (or 'farmers') were remunerated either per head of the inmates from each parish or by an agreed lump sum. Such contractors made a profit either by charging *per capita* rates and admitting as many poor residents as possible or by charging a fixed amount and operating a reluctant admissions policy. In both cases profits might be boosted by the income from inmates' work. With this thought in mind many of the men who applied for work-house management were weavers or competent in some other area of production, not highly skilled, which they could hope to practice in the house (using paupers as more or less coerced employees). The alternative was for a parish to run the workhouse directly, using a housekeeper for daily domestic oversight and relying upon overseers to manage the supply of food and other necessaries. Paupers refusing to enter the house could be denied access to other forms of relief, a manoeuvre known as the workhouse test. The most intense period of workhouse foundation throughout England occurred in the ten years after 1723 and by 1777 there was apparently the capacity to accommodate over 90,000 people in workhouses.[4]

Naturally, urban parishes accounted for a significant proportion of these workhouse places, but capacity and occupancy were two different matters. Workhouses clearly had a notional maximum capacity but it was not necessarily the aim to keep numbers up to the maximum. A comparison of alleged capacities with later recorded occupancy reveals some telling discrepancies. Some places changed the premises of their workhouse between the two assessment dates (as was the case with Shrewsbury, giving rise to a ratio that was lower for occupancy in 1803 than it was for capacity in 1777) but in Chester and Bristol, for example, the house apparently had a much larger capacity than its regular rate of occupancy. Therefore in many urban communities, a much higher proportion of the population could technically have been accommodated than was the case in practice. This was probably not true wherever the difference between capacity and occupancy was dramatic; there it was likely that rapid population growth had outstripped the original capacities of

Table 2.1 *Workhouse capacity, 1777 versus occupancy, 1803*

	Capacity in 1777 and population (date)	Ratio	Occupancy in 1803 and population 1801	Ratio
Birmingham	340/30,804 (1770)	1:91	360/60,822	1:169
Bristol	450/c. 60,000 (1777)	1:133	308/63,645	1:207
Cambridge	140/c. 8,500 (1777)	1:61	108/10,087	1:93
Chester	250/14,713 (1774)	1:59	89/15,052	1:169
Exeter	Not given		233/17,398	1:75
Gloucester	200/c. 6,000	1:30	216/7,579	1:35
Hull	200/22,286 (1792)	1:111	199/27,609	1:139
Leeds	342/16,380 (1771)	1:48	245/53,162	1:217
Leicester	358/12,784 (1785)	1:36	183/16,953	1:93
Liverpool	600/34,407 (1773)	1:57	852/77,653	1:91
Manchester	180/27,246 (1773/4)	1:151	264/70,409	1:267
North-ampton	126/c.6,000 (1777)	1:48	68/7,020	1:103
Norwich	1560/c. 36,000 (1777)	1:23	702/36,832	1:52
Nottingham	270/17,584 (1779)	1:65	595/28,861	1:49
Oxford	200/c. 10,000 (1777)	1:50	233/11,694	1:50
Salisbury	220/c. 7,300 (1777)	1:33	184/7,668	1:42
Sheffield	160/26,538 (1788)	1:166	76/31,314	1:412
Shrewsbury	191/c. 11,000 (1777)	1:58	262/14,739	1:56
Winchester	82/c. 4,500 (1777)	1:55	45/5,826	1:129
Worcester	90/13,104 (1779)	1:146	174/11,352	1:65
York	Not given		122/16,145	1:132

Source: Workhouse capacity and occupancy are taken from Parliamentary papers; population estimates prior to 1801 are derived from sundry urban histories.[5]

workhouses (such as in Sheffield, Manchester and Leeds).

The ideal and the actual place of the workhouse in eighteenth-century poor relief was much debated. Pamphlets which trumpeted national poor-law reform jostled with local printed ephemera advertising the advantages or shortcomings of particular houses. It soon became clear that work schemes could not generate enough income to contribute substantially to the running-costs of workhouses, and in practice the workhouse test was rarely enforced with rigour for any length of time. Contemporary local attitudes to the foundation of workhouses followed a fairly typical cycle of initial enthusiasm that waned as the impossibility of employing the poor at a profit became evident. Disillusion and apathy among the organisers were inevitable, although the tendency of the workhouse to recur as a new project in parishes country-wide throughout the century is testament to the intrinsic attraction of the idea of setting the poor to work. Yet local practice was often inconsistent with widespread apprehensions about the potential of workhouses. When the parishes of Chester and Shrewsbury incorporated for the purposes of poor relief in 1762 and 1783 respectively, naïve clauses in the relevant acts still urged that when the earnings of the poor were sufficient to maintain them, poor rates would cease.[6] The accumulating evidence contradicting these ambitious hopes gradually encouraged a more realistic understanding of what a parish workhouse could achieve. Eventually work was demanded from the poor for their moral improvement and as a disincentive for dependence rather than for their outright economic maintenance.[7]

The Shrewsbury House of Industry that opened in 1784 demonstrated this familiar cycle of attitudes. The house was an immediate success in that it reduced the poor rates and appeared to run a more rigorous, systematic and sanitary regime than most houses. Indeed, it acquired a small measure of fame as a result when its chief promoter, Isaac Wood, published a pamphlet to advertise its achievements. Unfortunately, on Wood's death in 1801 (and lacking his personal energy and oversight) the house suffered a decline in fortunes and local popularity. Owen wrote as an amendment to his history of Shrewsbury that 'public opinion in this town has experienced a great revolution on the subject of Houses of Industry ... the system detailed in the pages referred to is now in a great measure abandoned'.[8] The comments of another Shrewsbury historian, J. B. Blakeway, demonstrate some of the contradictions which swayed opinion on workhouses first one way and then another. In his manuscript additions to a copy of Phillips' history of Shrewsbury, Blakeway listed three 'invincible'[9] objections to the use of workhouses; they deprived people of their liberty, severed the natural links of reliance between children and parents, and brought the innocent into close contact with the wicked. These criticisms suggest that the writer had given some thought to the sensibilities of the poor yet in the same passage Blakeway reverts to type, judging the two advantages of workhouses to be a reduction in the rates and their discouragement of applications for relief.

Susannah Ottaway has unpicked a further strand of opinion that promoted or denigrated workhouses on their credentials as asylums for the elderly. Expressions in favour of workhouses as caring institutions seem to have clustered in the first half of the eighteenth century (although Ottaway cites examples running up to 1800) and opponents of this view became more vocal towards the end of the century (with high-profile support from Malthus).[10] Slack has identified 'a gradual swing of opinion against workhouses' from the mid-eighteenth century onwards.[11] The philanthropic endeavours of Hanway and others drew attention and sympathy towards the poor, particularly poor children. Gilbert's act of 1782 was another relief statute that both reflected and encouraged a trend away from setting the poor on work and towards providing residential care only. By 1800 Thomas Bernard was writing that if workhouses 'are made the common receptacle of all who apply for relief, they will, in their general effect, be the cause of injustice and unkindness to many individuals'.[12]

Previous studies of workhouses have tended to concentrate on the workhouse movement, the administrative options and difficulties which houses posed for individual parishes, and the key personalities influential to the movement such as John Cary and Matthew Marryott.[13] Yet workhouses continued to house habitual paupers long after pioneering spirits had faded away. What was it like to live in a parish workhouse? Our (modern) view has been strongly influenced by the work of early historians of welfare, who condemned the houses as poorly managed, insanitary 'promiscuous' institutions (mingling the young and old, strong and weak, innocent and reprehensible). Dorothy Marshall relied on the evidence of contemporary pamphleteers, and despite qualifying statements about the living conditions of the poor generally she still judged that, in relation to contractors' workhouses, 'it is perhaps impossible to colour the canvas too darkly'; she painted a picture of unmitigated overcrowding, dirt, hunger and neglect.[14] James Taylor raised doubts about the acceptance of this line in 1972 but practical attempts to reassess pre-1834 workhouses have been sparse.[15] Multiple vignettes of parish workhouses supplied by local studies present standard genres of information in the form of aspirational rules and dietaries with little attempt to analyse the lived experience of the poor inhabitants or to compare these experiences between places.[16] Tim Hitchcock's review of workhouses throws some light on the age and sex of the average workhouse inmate and assesses what life should have been like via lists of rules and diets. Yet as Hitchcock himself points out, there were factors that militated against rule enforcement and his more recent work tries to access the experiences of individual pauper occupants.[17]

Attitudes of the poor to the experience of workhouse life at any point in the eighteenth century remain elusive, but the available evidence seems negative. Literate contemporaries of a sensitive bent opined 'the poor themselves, being intimidated by the prospect of a poor house prison, will almost perish before they apply for parochial relief' while more utilitarian writers (particularly among the parish officer class) were relieved to think that the poor might shrink from entry to a workhouse.[18] The words of the poor are notable by their virtual absence from the written record before 1800 and even Essex pauper letter writers from the early nineteenth century remain tight-lipped about workhouses, although one man was keen 'to try every honest means wee posably could to Keep out of the workhouse'.[19] Therefore the recorded actions of inmates are currently the best guide to their stance on workhouse living. Ottaway pointed to a workhouse fire, runaways and in-house protests to characterise attitudes as ranging from unwilling to fractious.[20]

This chapter will try to get beyond the surface of workhouse life, and underneath the public profile of these institutions, to look at the day-to-day pulse of workhouse-dwelling and in particular at the material existence of inmates. In doing so it is necessary to look briefly at the administrative aspects of workhouse usage but for the most part discussion will analyse the experiences of inmates in Oxford, Shrewsbury and York. Who was accommodated in these houses? What were their diets and was nutrition adequate, both in terms of calorific value and in the context of inmates' expectations? Consideration of workhouse food-ways will occupy the largest section of this chapter; however it will also address the comfort or deprivation of workhouse material surroundings. Did parishes consign paupers to workhouses and shut the door, or did they remain aware of individuals' ongoing needs for clothing, medicines or other necessaries?

Expenditure on workhouses

Parishes in Oxford, Shrewsbury and York made their first attempts to run (but not build) a workhouse in the decade after Knatchbull's act. In Oxford the first workhouse was opened in the later 1720s, when it was suggested that the poor of the city already had an antipathy to residential relief; the poor were said in 1727 to 'work to keep themselves out of these (as they call them) confinements'.[21] A large house run by a contractor became the main workhouse experiment in the town from the 1730s to the 1760s. Individual parishes did try to run their own smaller workhouses in the charge of a salaried manager but most overseers or vestries preferred to pay the contractor a fixed sum per pauper per week.

This large workhouse was located in St Mary Magdalen parish, opposite the entrance to Worcester College.[22] The building had inauspicious origins. It had been built by a Dr Woodroffe of Gloucester Hall at the beginning of the eighteenth century to form part of Worcester College, but the failure of a scheme to attract Greek students to Oxford meant that the new building was not needed. In 1714, Hearne claimed disparagingly that this structure had been built 'with such slight materials' that it would not last very long; no-one 'hath presumed to lodge in it'.[23] 'Woodroffe's Folly' was used as a workhouse by numerous parishes under two main contractors, James and Esther Piggot in the 1730s and Solomon and Ann Cross in the 1750s and 1760s. Despite its dubious construction the folly was still standing in 1767 when St Michael's parish bought it to act as their own parish workhouse. It was not demolished until 1806. Nonetheless, it was superseded when eleven of Oxford's parishes united for the purposes of poor relief in 1771 and a joint workhouse with capacity for 200 paupers was built in 1772 at 'Rats and Mice Hill'.[24]

Shrewsbury parishes were also keen to try the efficacy of workhouses but did not co-operate to achieve this end, perhaps because the larger parishes in Shrewsbury made individual parish workhouse experiments more viable. Each of the five main urban parishes came to acquire their own house via either purchase or lease.[25] Parishes seem to have fluctuated between running houses which were directly under the control of overseers and paying contractors to take over the individual houses. Like Oxford, Shrewsbury eventually decided to incorporate for poor-relief purposes, and opened a joint, purpose-built workhouse for all town parishes in 1784.

In York the poor were managed by individual parishes, but overseers of the poor were supervised by the corporation (perhaps in an attempt to secure some order across a fragmented administration). It is one of the intricacies of urban welfare that town and parish authorities were often in some measure in competition for control of poor relief. In York the town corporation agreed regulations to be enforced by overseers across the city, defended some overseers at law and compiled statistics relating to poor rates and expenses.[26] Therefore proposals to found a workhouse were initially considered by the town rather than by separate parishes, but a committee established in 1729 to consider a workhouse scheme quickly folded in the face of local opposition. In 1736 Francis Drake urged the necessity of a workhouse, but the town remained largely uninspired by the need for change and schemes to cover the whole city failed.[27] In 1768, several parishes chose to unite for the purpose of running a joint workhouse that was established in Marygate but individual parishes continued to administer their own funds and to payout-relief.[28] The Marygate house apparently had a maximum capacity of ninety paupers.[29]

The distribution of out-relief in the three towns was never decisively ended by the use of the workhouse test in the mid-eighteenth century. As elsewhere, attempts to compel all of the poor to enter the house lasted only for short periods after which pension and other payments began again. Fluctuations in total overseers' spending, and the proportions of the total spent on either pensions or workhouses, illustrate the emphasis placed on the different components of poor relief in each parish.[30] In Shrewsbury Holy Cross, this can be seen to good effect in the 1740s. The workhouse was the key element of relief in the parish until early 1742. Then in 1743 the parish house was damaged by fire, ensuring that any revival of its use would entail some expense. As a result, parish pensions became the main source of long-term relief in the period 1742–48. These were the only years up to 1770 when pensions cost more per year in this parish than the workhouse, accounting for forty percent or more of annual expenditure. This was doubtless the result of paying pensions to former workhouse inmates but may also have been a consequence of the absence of the workhouse test. In June 1748 the parish decided to revert to the workhouse despite the immediate expenses involved. After the reintroduction of the house, spending on pensions commonly fell to between ten and twenty percent of all money paid. The amounts paid per year suggest that between ten and twenty people were paid as pensioners when the workhouse was not open, compared with five to ten pensioners when the workhouse was operational.

Figure 2.1 *Spending on the workhouse in Shrewsbury Holy Cross*

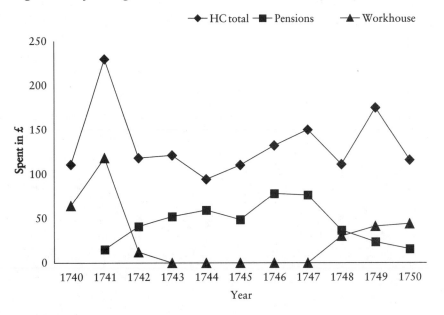

Figure 2.2 *Spending on the workhouse in Oxford St Peter le Bailey*

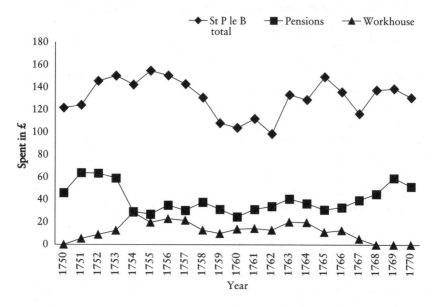

By contrast, Oxford St Peter le Bailey eschewed the workhouse as a method for relieving the bulk of the dependent poor in the 1750s and 1760s; instead it chose to rely heavily on pensions and used a workhouse

Figure 2.3 *Spending on the workhouse in York St Michael le Belfrey*

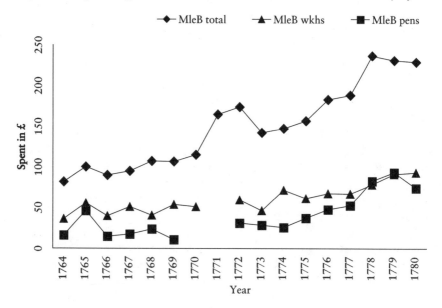

only for keeping a few elderly widows, pregnant women and children. As a result the percentage of all expenditure allocated to pensions was higher than in Holy Cross. There is good evidence to suggest, however, that the workhouse test was used quite consciously over the 1750s to keep the pensioner list as short as possible. The introduction of a workhouse option from 1751 onwards made an impression on spending on long-term paupers out of proportion to its direct use. York's St Michael le Belfrey parish supplies a third model, in that it prioritised use of the workhouse in the period 1764–75. Both workhouses and pensions were used concurrently, but the workhouse was the most important element of regular relief in most years, and around forty percent of spending was devoted to its maintenance. Pensions were used fairly minimally, comprising between ten and twenty percent of annual spending, until the mid-1770s when there was an upswing in pensions expenditure.

Workhouse inmates

The persistent use of workhouses in urban parishes (albeit with fluctuating insistence on *work*) raises questions about the material lives of inmates and the deprivations or consolations of institutional life. The remainder of this chapter will address some of these questions in relation to three workhouses with good inmate records, one each from Shrewsbury, Oxford and York.

Shrewsbury St Mary's parish had decided to open a workhouse at a vestry of June 1731. The parish resolved to contract 'with persons for the lodging, maintaining and employing all such poor as shall desire to receive relief';[31] however, when the workhouse became established, it was neither run by a contractor nor catered for all who required relief. A salaried master ran the house on a daily basis and the workhouse test was probably never enforced to the point of abolishing outdoor relief. This chapter concentrates on the use of this workhouse in 1742 and 1745, by which time a mistress (probably the original master's widow) was running the house.

The Oxford house was quite different, being a large workhouse run by a contractor to which various town parishes subscribed. In 1747, St Mary Magdalen parish was the first to contract with Solomon Cross (a weaver from St Ebbe's parish) to accommodate all of the parish poor for a fixed annual sum at Woodroffe's Folly. From around 1750, other parishes bought Cross's services until the contractor ceased in 1767. This chapter will concentrate on three: St Peter le Bailey 1751–57, St Michael 1754–58 and St Martin 1753–54.[32] The contract which Cross signed with St Mary Magdalen did not provide a prototype that was universally adopted. All three of these parishes paid Cross per head of the parishioners they chose to send, at 2s or 2s 6d per person, so even the level of the *per capita* payments was not uniform. The contract with Cross made the most dramatic (if temporary) impact on the poor of St Michael because the parish wholeheartedly embraced the opportunity to farm out their poor, scrapped the pension list and in 1753 sent all the poor in need of regular relief to the house. The honeymoon period was soon over, however, and in March 1756 a list of pensioners was re-established. St Martin, by contrast, began paying Cross in 1749 but did not abolish the pension list until 1752 or 1753, which suggests that this parish may have waited to see whether Cross's establishment would stand the test of time before committing itself more fully.

In York no contractors like Cross emerged to service the city's paupers and parishes were fairly tentative about taking up the challenge to run houses directly. St Michael le Belfrey parish decided in 1744 to establish a workhouse on its own and rented a small house in Monk Bar for the purpose (featuring at least five rooms and a cellar). Initially there was not enough money to stock the house, so twelve inhabitants each advanced 1 guinea to the parish to defray immediate costs, to be repaid when the opportunity arose. The parish took the investment in the new house seriously, supplying all the necessary furniture and household goods. Thomas and Rachel Plaxton were appointed as the master and mistress and in May 1744 Rachel Plaxton was sent to Knaresborough to learn the art of workhouse management. A representative of Knaresborough made a return visit to York for a week in June. Yet all this energetic activity in one of York's most populous parishes was devoted to a surprisingly small establishment. The lists of inmates found for 1747 onwards sometimes contain just two paupers (the 'family' comprising four including the master and mistress) and never more than twelve, a testament to the attractions of the workhouse ideal even where its continuance must have been highly inefficient.[33]

What was the age and gender profile of workhouse inmates? Were parishes using the house and its associated test to target certain groups? In one of the largest comparative exercises conducted to date, Tim Hitchcock assembled a substantial sample of paupers drawn from three large houses.[34] By contrast, far fewer paupers were involved as workhouse residents in the towns studied here, but the data has the advantage of relating to the varied use of smaller workhouses by six parishes, and after all smaller parish workhouses were the norm; the most frequent numbers of inmates cited in the returns to parliament 1776-1803 were between twenty and thirty per house.[35] Cross's workhouse begins to look like a sizeable establishment, but the 111 inmates identified were sent over an eight-year period so not all were present at the same time. A comparison can also be drawn with a small Chester workhouse.[36]

The most striking aspect of the information in table 2.2. is the large proportion of children found in the Shrewsbury and Chester work-houses, more than twenty percent above Hitchcock's figures. In Shrews-bury the workhouse was being directed at families overburdened with children, both from having large numbers of children and from family requirements outstripping resources. In 1742, four of the nineteen chil-dren listed came from homes where their mother was also provided with a parish pension specifically for two or three more children. While this is not very many in percentage terms, it must be borne in mind that only the poorest families would have had both a child removed to the

Table 2.2 *Men, women and children in provincial urban workhouses*

	Adult women (%)	Adult men (%)	Children / adolescents (%)	Not known (%)	Total (no.)
Oxford St Peter le Bailey 1751–57	47.6	9.5	33.3	9.5	21
Oxford St Michael 1754–58	35.7	8.9	39.3	16.1	56
Oxford St Martin 1753–54	41.2	20.6	29.4	8.8	34
Total in Cross's house	39.6	12.6	35.1	12.6	111
Shrewsbury St Mary 1742, 1745	28.8	11.5	59.6	Nil	52
York St Michael le Belfrey 1747–51	35.7	14.3	42.9	7.1	14
Chester St John 1731–33	30.8	10.3	56.4	2.6	39
Hitchcock's three workhouses[a]	50.2	15.2	34.0	Nil	1,742

Note: [a] Hitchcock, 'The English Workhouse'.

workhouse and a pension to maintain the rest. Of the nineteen children in the house in the earlier year, only three shared the workhouse with either parent, indicating that children rather than whole families were being targeted for the workhouse. Yet one-third of children in 1742 were accompanied by a sibling suggesting some link between specific families and the workhouse. Perhaps taking two or more children into the house was an alternative to providing a pension for the rest of the family. Motives for overseers' actions (in deciding which families to manage in this way) regrettably remain elusive, but ideas about children's futures are more clear. In 1742, six children went directly from the workhouse to an arranged apprenticeship place. This progression for children from the family home to the workhouse and finally to an apprenticeship had two advantages. It removed from home one of the older children who was most likely to consume and be a burden on scarce family resources, and also prevented their being on the parish for very long. In addition it gave the parish a chance to ensure that the child's settlement was transferred to another parish. Wolverhampton was cited as the destination of three of these apprentices.

This policy of bringing children into the house did not indicate a single or unified approach to the problem of pauper children. Marshall has claimed that one of the advantages supposed to stem from the use of a workhouse was that children would not need to be boarded out.[37] The domestic care of infants and children could be undertaken in the house (by the housekeeper, contractor or possibly by other paupers) and presumably the youngest children would be fed on dairy milk rather than breast-fed. Yet throughout 1742, St Mary's continued to pay for placing certain children out to nurse; Sarah Cooper and Sarah Blower looked after two parish infants each. The decision to bring a child to the house was probably connected to its age, given the specialised feeding requirements of babies. The only child aged less than two in the house in 1742 was probably there with its mother. This implies that the Shrewsbury parish officers considered the workhouse an inappropriate environment for maintaining babies, particularly when mothers were not also present. Parishes may have appreciated the health risks to very young children in these institutions because workhouses attracted the attention of contemporaries for their role in child mortality. One parliamentary committee found that the survival rate of infants in their first year of life in London workhouses 1763–65 was only seven percent. Yet Hanway judged that 'an overall survival rate in a parish of fifty per cent for its infant parish poor under the age of four was a good one, and he noted that the survival rate for all infants to age three within the Bills of Mortality in 1765 was only twenty-two per cent'.[38] Information from the provinces is also equivocal. Of the eight children born in the Oxford and Shrewsbury workhouses, four are known to have died within a year, but the degree of responsibility that should be placed on the two workhouses for this outcome is disputable. Two of the mothers were brought into the house only to lie in, and their infants died less than one month after birth. The short time-span involved means that their deaths were endogenous, probably related to genetics, birth trauma or weight at birth (and therefore to maternal nutrition). It is doubtful whether their mothers' immediate surroundings would have had time to make an impact on their chances of survival.

An underlying trend may manifest itself in different ways in different years. The decision to have a large proportion of children in the Shrewsbury house (in both years more than fifty-five percent of inhabitants were children) does not necessarily indicate a static policy. In 1745, twelve of the fifteen children in the house had one or both of their parents with them implying a switch to relieving whole families in the house. Also, in the later year, only one child was apprenticed from the house. However, the basic use of workhouses primarily as establishments for children was familiar in other towns, as confirmed by Chester's St John and elsewhere.[39] Susannah Ottaway found that the house in Terling was targeting the young in the mid-eighteenth century (but had shifted to cater increasingly for the elderly by the 1790s).[40]

The proportions of men, women and children which Oxford parishes sent to Cross's workhouse match more closely with Hitchcock's average picture of workhouse inmates, particularly in the case of St Peter le Bailey. Adult women were the largest group in the Oxford workhouse. This is predictable given the typical predominance of women over men as paupers receiving outdoor relief at this time, and has been ascribed to the greater difficulties faced by women aiming for economic independence (whether they were elderly, widows or women with children but no spouse).[41] Certainly, these figures do not challenge the stereotypical picture of the low representation of adult men in the house. Even if all the males of uncertain age in the house from St Michael are assumed to have been adults, their possible occupancy only rises to 16.1 percent. There is also (slender) evidence that the men admitted were in a much poorer state of health than their fellow female inmates. In York, neither of the two men were thought to be capable of work.

These findings receive additional support from MacKay's work, which is based on St Martin in the Fields workhouse 1817–18. She was able to employ more scrupulous divisions between her classifications of inmate. Adult men were somewhat better represented there (totalling 261 or twenty-six percent of the intake November 1817 to November 1818);

they were resident for a shorter period than women and were more likely than women to be elderly, or experience illness or death in the house. Children or adolescents of both sexes (up to age fifteen) comprised a predictable thirty-two percent of incoming paupers. The data also shows up an interesting refinement on the situation for children, since young-sters admitted aged seven to fifteen were much more likely to be boys than girls.[42] Anderson's evidence for Leeds provides a further model. In that expanding industrial setting men were much more likely to occupy a workhouse place but were still in the minority of around twenty-five percent.[43]

In Oxford, settlement papers show another way in which the parishes differed; at least twelve of the fifty-six people from St Michael's in the workhouse, and ten of the thirty-four people from St Martin's, had been removed from another parish at some time compared with only one possible connection between the law of settlement and a family in the workhouse from St Peter le Bailey. The former parishes were sending their mobile poor to the house, while the latter sent parishioners who were long-term residents. Five of the people and families from St Michael and eight from St Martin were placed in the workhouse immediately on their arrival in the parish having been removed from elsewhere. Others used the workhouse as a stopgap measure between an enforced removal and a voluntary one. Edward Herring deposited his family in the house and then left them to look for work. His travels took him to North-ampton and finally to Deptford where he gained a post in the merchant navy. He wrote to his wife 'I am fixed at Mr Westes yard & have an Admiralty Protection to keep me from the Press'.[44] He was therefore able to withdraw his family from workhouse residence. He informed his wife 'my Master & I was looking this morning at a Pleasant little house near my work which he proposes to take for us at £3 10s P Ann'; however, his sanguine hopes that the parish would provide his wife with five or six guineas to carry her and their three children to Deptford (and to 'prevent taking ready furnished lodgings' in the meantime) were to be disappointed. St Michael's overseers gave her only 2 guineas when she left Oxford.

Food provision in a parish workhouse

An appreciation of the quantity, quality and palatability of workhouse food is central to an understanding of experiences of institutional life, yet close research on workhouse diets under the old poor law seems effectively to have stalled.[45] Valerie Johnston collated evidence about workhouse food after 1834 but, given that diet was one of the central elements in the drive for less eligibility in the immediate aftermath of 1834, it would be perverse to assume that her findings could be applicable earlier.[46] The best recent work undertakes an assessment of nutritional sufficiency. In 1990 Carole Shammas examined the nutritional value of pre-1834 institutional diets and estimated the nutritional value of sundry institutional diets in London and provincial towns. She found that eighteenth-century institutions typically supplied between 2,000 and 2,500 calories per person, and that where it was possible to calculate the distribution of calories according to the age and sex of inmates the totals rose by about 500 calories per institution. In other words, the diets could be adequate assuming no special reasons for higher calorie requirements by inmates (such as the need to undertake hard labour or struggle against illness).[47] Indeed when set in a national context, their calorific value was potentially rather impressive; the *per capita* calorie supply in Britain over the eighteenth century ranged from 2,095 to 2,237.[48] The quality of institutional diets was much more suspect with very few houses or hospitals providing sufficient calcium, for example, and the scale of insufficiency becoming more pronounced over the 1700s.

My central aim here is to test the quantity and quality of food offered in workhouses, but also to point up the role of food and other consumables as consolations (desirable aside from considerations of their nutritional worth). In particular, eighteenth-century workhouse food must be seen in the light of dietary developments in the 1790s and later, to appreciate the evolution of inmates' sentiments prior to the institutional stringency of the 1830s. Most work to date (Shammas excepted) has been based on menu-style dietaries but selected institutions have also left purchasing accounts that itemise the nature and (at their best) the quantity and quality of ingredients. Given the variable state of accounts compiled by parish overseers of the poor, these can be difficult to use. Nonetheless, in order to secure new insights into workhouse food it is necessary to all but jettison the use of dietaries (or retain them only as corroborating evidence) and concentrate instead on shopping-list accounts. Dietaries were essentially statements of intended policy, often drawn up at the time a workhouse was opened along with a set of rules for the inmates. There is no guarantee that they were followed meticulously or even loosely in the following months and years, particularly in smaller houses where even the rules may only ever have been aspirational. Only shopping-list accounts used in conjunction with well-kept lists of inmates can reliably speak to the ongoing nutritional experiences of the indoor pauper; this combination of sources has the potential to reveal the accuracy or otherwise of dietaries, and leave open to view the gap between policy and practice (or between the unspoken assumptions informing the compilation of dietaries and the ways in which historians read them). The gap may not be large, but the interstices between stated policy and practice may have made all the difference to our understanding of these institutions, and for inmates provided just enough leeway to render the mid-eighteenth century workhouse a place characterised by nutritional comforts and props.

Furthermore, the cultural value of the foodstuffs on offer but not written into dietaries can be appreciated only via a sense of the relationship between institutional and domestic foods. Historians of food have tended to regard workhouses and the like either as discrete microcosms without much of a place in the appreciation of changing foodways or, ironically, as the basis of comments about the diets of the labouring poor wherever no domestic evidence is available.[49] Neither of these approaches is strictly appropriate; the overlaps and divergences between food at home and food in workhouses are crucial for understanding the changing status of the latter.

First, though, what generalisations have been made on the basis of dietaries? Workhouse and other institutional dietaries of the eighteenth and nineteenth centuries assumed the provision of three meals per day for inmates: breakfast, dinner and supper.[50] Breakfast and supper would often consist of similar dishes. Gruel, porridge, broth or simply bread were often served at either meal. Another common dish, frumenty or furmety, was a milk pottage comprising milk, wheat and sometimes sugar.[51] Dinner could be more varied, and could reflect local foods (such as the availability of fresh fish at the coast), but usually comprised one of four basic types of meal: meat with potatoes, soup or stew, pudding, or bread and cheese. Meat was most frequently boiled, although some dietaries did specify that it should be roasted. Puddings were made with suet or rice and were also boiled or steamed. Where the type of meat was not specified, diets used the general term 'butcher's meat' which meant that animal muscle tissue was to be served rather than offal. Four known eighteenth-century dietaries which survive from institutions in Oxford, Shrewsbury and York conform exactly to this broad outline of workhouse meals.[52]

Diets sometimes specified the different amounts of food to be given to men and women, or adults and children. The bill of fare drawn up for the Society of Friends workhouse in Clerkenwell in 1713 distinguished between 'ancient' friends, 'big' children and 'small' children when allocating amounts of food.[53] Alternatively, some institutions allowed themselves to be guided somewhat by the desires of inmates; at Wisbech in the 1720s, the supply of food at dinner was determined 'according to everyone's stomach' whereas the quantities of food available at breakfast and supper were more restricted. Similarly, in the 1790s inhabitants of the workhouse in All Saints parish Northampton were allegedly given as much bread and meat as they could eat.[54] Yet institutional attitudes towards food could be punitive, as at Leeds where inmates were required to sit decently at meals, avoid talking, and not leave the room without giving thanks; infractions of other rules resulted in the loss of meals.[55]

The calorie intake of all inmates was dominated by carbohydrate as 'Bread was the basis of most workhouse diets'.[56] Protein was technically available in the form of meat and cheese. Calcium could be obtained from cheese or the milky meals and puddings which workhouses favoured. Salt was most likely to have been derived from salted meat or from salt added to dishes during or after cooking. Some energy was also obtained from the alcohol present in small beer. The most likely deficiencies in institutional diets were vitamins A, C and D, although as many diets mentioned vegetables only as unquantified 'greens' or 'garden stuff' which was often grown in a workhouse garden, the provision of vitamin C may have been higher than can now be measured.

The style of workhouse diets can be explained by the need to feed fairly large numbers of people with ease and economy. Meals had to be cheap and the cheaper cuts of meat were often more suited to use in stews, soups or puddings than they were as boiled or roast joints. Boiling needed less equipment and less skill than some other styles of cooking and could be made to supply large quantities at one time. Liquid foods like soup, stew, gruel or porridge could be doled out to inmates fairly equally if bowls or containers of the same size were used. There may also be an explanation in dental health, as the mid-century population suffered both tooth decay and scurvy.

The quality of food served in workhouses was probably variable and not so high in nutritional value as equivalent foodstuffs today. Some cheeses could be particularly poor.[57] Yet there is little reason to suppose that food in the eighteenth century was subjected to widespread, organised adulteration (as it was to be in the nineteenth century).[58] Aside from very large cities, the producer or retailer and consumer would have lived near to one another and fraud would have been detected and acted upon. Yet paupers confined to workhouses would have had less opportunity to seek redress of this sort on their own behalf. Perhaps the fact that, in a parish-run workhouse, the mistress had to eat the same diet would have encouraged her to ensure that foodstuffs served had not been tampered with.

It is tempting to assume that 'The rich man considers what might please his palate, the poor householder is simply concerned to fill his stomach'.[59] Nonetheless, I disagree; nutritional status is partly dependent on disposable income but this does not mean that the poor were unswayed by considerations of taste. Furthermore, the sense of entitlement to food is shaped by more than mere availability (or the rationale for buying cheap, bulky, filling foods over the impractical purchase of small amounts of expensive, tasty foods).[60] Therefore the points of overlap between the workhouse diet and the habitual foodways of the local poor could be important for the acceptability of the former. It seems likely that in smaller workhouses, diets were effectively much more informal than they were in large institutions, regimented by virtue of a large, paid staff. In smaller houses, it has been argued, 'the supply and preparation of food [was] very similar to that of any ordinary household' wherein the 'diet compared very favourably with that of the local working community'.[61] Ideally, therefore, the workhouse diet should be seen in the context of the diet of inmates before their admission, or at the least the likely range of local labouring diets. Unfortunately, local dietary habits are difficult to unearth. The diets gathered and published by David Davies and Frederick Morton Eden in the 1780s and 1790s have tended to provide the most confident starting point for any close study of labourers' diets. The issue has been picked up more robustly by Burnett and others for the period 1815 onwards.[62]

So far as we can tell, workhouse diets generally differed from labourers' diets in several key points. Labourers' families relied on bread or (to a lesser extent but noticeably in the north) potatoes as the main source of nourishment but preferred to eat white bread than any other variety. This trend towards white bread occurred in southern and midland England between 1715 and 1755. Once people had been converted they were reluctant to eat other breads.[63] It is not always clear which bread overseers or contractors bought for consumption in workhouses but it seems unlikely that white or the most expensive bread would have been the usual fare. Other differences related to the conditions of urban life; town labourers placed greater reliance on food retailers than their rural equivalents, and long working hours meant that the ideal foods were hot, tasty and quickly prepared.[64] This led to greater consumption of butter, tea, sugar and eggs in households then in workhouses. A favourite food was bacon as it was both salty and fatty, making it palatable, and was quick to cook. Bacon was not supplied very often in workhouses as it was less easy to prepare in large quantities. Furthermore, labourers did not often make the stews or puddings prepared in workhouses as these required time and fuel which labourers did not always have.

It is a standard feature of the existing literature that, nutritionally, some groups were better off in workhouses than in their own homes and this was acknowledged at the time as well as being pointed up by historians.

For example, all workhouse inmates received more meat than labourers outside, and the absence of meat from the labouring diet from week to week (and exclusive reliance on bread or potatoes) was often the occasion of distress and comment.[65] If very poor families could afford only a little meat, the male family members may have received it all. What was more, men were more likely to buy ready-made foods for consumption outside the home.[66] This means that women and children received a substantially more protein-filled diet in workhouses than outside (always assuming that they received the foods notionally allocated to them, hung on to it in the face of depredations by other inmates, and consented to eat the pappy dishes in which this food was presented). Similarly, the amount of calcium available in the diets of ordinary labouring families was dangerously low. Carole Shammas calculated that even if all sources of calcium (primarily milk, cheese and cereals) were accounted for and converted to equivalent intake in pints of milk, fewer than ten percent of families in both the north and south of England enjoyed sufficient milk for the needs of its women and children.[67] This percentage is again based on the assumption of equal division of resources in a society where men took a greater share of milk and cheese leaving less for their dependants.

Nutritional advantage is one thing, but contentment is another. As Thompson put it, 'People may consume more goods and become less happy ... at the same time.'[68] There is no first-person testimony to speak to the joys or deprivations of the diet in an eighteenth-century workhouse; however, this pattern of both meals and foodstuffs was repeated across institutions and across the country in infirmaries, other residential charities and boarding schools. The trials of institutional food could attract pungent criticism from participants other than workhouse inmates. Food in the Middlesex hospital arguably left much to be desired by following the pattern of institutional dietaries but apparently leaving patients desperately hungry. One wrote in 1813 'wee have no tee no suger no buter no chis and onley meet 3 days and Broth and Gruel and that is all that wee ar all most starved for wont'.[69]

The references to broth and gruel are telling. Perhaps the most important difference between individuals and institutions arose from their propensity to make the gruels or broths so favoured by workhouse founders. These required time and fuel to prepare that working people often found hard to supply. Wilson argues that cereal pottages were consumed by all classes in late seventeenth-century England, but that they underwent a decline in popularity, characterised by regional variation; broadly, they remained acceptable in the north much longer than in the south. She also alleges that dislike of pottages may have intensified due to their extensive use in workhouses.[70] But plausibly the blame for hatred of pottages must be levelled at wider discourses of poverty (rather than simply at what became standard workhouse practice). Sandra Sherman has argued that commentators in the 1790s endeavoured to render the poor as abstract masses rather than individuals via a welter of statistical material, in an attempt to 'manage the poor into inconsequence'. In her view, working people were reduced in contemporary publications to ciphers, a group to be fuelled efficiently and kept working productively, so 'teaching them how to behave industrially'.[71] In this way, the self-satisfied view of Benjamin Rumford on the supply of food to the poor for example, and the promotion of his famous soup, was just one instance among many concerned with engineering a change in the tastes of the poor in favour of a scientifically adequate diet (wherein a full stomach should induce both personal and political contentment). Sherman's work concentrates mainly on the published voices, but what of the ciphers themselves? Arguably it was this calculating approach to food, and the trumpeted role of soups and gruels as efficient, that hardened the attitudes of the poor. Pottages that had been regarded as a regrettable, occasional necessity (including on the 'occasion' of workhouse residency) before the 1790s were now being promoted as 'normal' in ways that 'affront traditional foodways'.[72] It was this scientific normalising that aroused such resentment and prompted the workhouse poor to view these pappy dishes as despicable. In this context, the comments of the hospital patient in 1813 post-date the shifts in both regional and chronological trends. Aside from calorific insufficiency, this southerner feels starved partly *because* the hospital diet is dominated by broth and gruel.

If the evidence of formal dietaries is set aside, what can be achieved via a study of shopping-list accounts used in conjunction with inmate lists? In Shrewsbury St Mary, the 1742 and 1745 overseers' records contain accounts of food bought for workhouse inmates, as do the records for York St Michael le Belfrey in 1751. These contain some information about the weight and price per pound of meat, cheese, and other consumables, which in some cases makes it possible to calculate the average amounts of foodstuffs available per person per day (appendix 2.1, 'Food per person per day in two workhouses 1742, 1745 and 1751'). Notably both of these houses were run by overseers and housekeepers rather than contractors, and so were possibly quite different to the contractor Cross's house in Oxford in their dietary regime. In both cases, the housekeepers were assumed to share the workhouse diet; their salaries (at around £2 per annum only) suggest that this was a necessary part of their remuneration.

In both Shrewsbury during 1742 and York in 1751, the average amount of raw beef available per person per day was identical at 4.8 ounces. At

York this was intended to supply two dinners plus three other meals of broth per week; if the average quantity of beef per day is converted to represent the average amount per person per day on the two days when it was served there was over a pound of uncooked beef per person in the house. Beef and other meats would have been presented in a variety of cooked forms, but cooking alters the weight and calorific value of food-stuffs. If stewed, then the food energy transferred to the cooking medium (water) in the form of fats and juices may not have been lost to the pauper consumers. Gravies and broths were often an integral part of workhouse dishes. Alternatively, if food was boiled and the water thrown away, a substantial proportion of the calorific value of the raw food would have been lost. It will be assumed here that, on average, twenty-five percent of the weight of meat purchased was lost during cooking.[73] The calories yielded by cooked meats can then be estimated more accurately. Modern assessments of calories for different meats depend on the cut of meat and the style of cooking. Here, it has been assumed that on average cooked beef supplies 70 calories per ounce. This would mean that, if the same value applied, the daily *per capita* allowance for cooked beef in 1742 and 1751 provided paupers with 252 calories. The fact that these two houses in different towns and accommodating differing numbers and types of population supplied, on average, the same amount of meat to each inmate is suggestive; there may have been widespread, tacit agreement on the acceptable scale of provision or even size of portions for paupers.

The picture of meat consumption in 1745 was apparently quite different, because the total amount of raw meat available rested near the lowest levels extrapolated in 1742 and 1751. The advantage for 1745 inmates was a greater variety of meat with an alternative to beef being offered almost every week. If meat other than beef constituted one main meal per week, this explains the apparently tiny amount per day. A daily intake of one-tenth of an ounce of raw pork (for example) amounts to a more satisfying three and a half ounces once every fifth week. In the matter of meat purchases, however, the experience in Shrewsbury was probably dictated by the national, economic context. In 1745, a cattle disease was raging which prompted Horace Walpole to comment in November 'we dare not eat milk, butter, beef, nor anything from that species'.[74] The subsequent shortage of animal foods lasted into the 1750s. This could well explain both the increased variety of meat in 1745 and the lower price of beef per pound. Modern assessments suggest that an average portion of raw meat of 3.6 ounces would (when cooked) provide 190 calories.

In these calculations, the inmates were assumed to have required and received an equal amount of food. No allowance was made for discrimination between the amounts needed by men and women or between adults and children, nor was the age of inmates taken into account. This may substantially affect the results of average food availability in 1745 when three infants were in the Shrewsbury house for a total of 92 weeks between them, almost the equivalent of two people for a full year each. If these are excluded on the grounds that they were either breast-fed or consumed only small quantities of bought foodstuffs, the average availability of raw meat in 1745 increases to 4 ounces per day. This accords much more favourably with the aggregate year averages for 1742 and 1751.

The two houses operated completely different purchasing policies in relation to cheese. In Shrewsbury it was a vital component of the diet, where as in York it was never offered to inmates. The amount of cheese available per day was around 1.5 ounces in 1742. If cheese yielded 117 calories per ounce (as it would today), the nutritional value of an average portion would have been 175 calories. In 1745 the average availability of cheese was more generous at around 2 ounces per day, possibly yielding 257 calories. According to Shammas, 2.6 ounces of cheese was the nutritional equivalent (in containing calcium and protein) of one pint of milk.[75] The Shrewsbury house was supplying a minority proportion of the calcium requirements of inmates in the form of cheese, whereas York would have needed to supply this requirement in the form of significant provision of milk. Calcium could also be derived from meat, but as the two houses supplied meat equally the inmates at York would not have gained any more calcium from this source than their Shrewsbury counterparts would.

These types of working make it relatively easy to visualise the quantities and types of food probably set before the poor. Unfortunately, there can be no easy comprehension of the amount of bread available per day. Corn was purchased in bulk by the strike, bushell or peck then ground and baked privately. It is difficult to assess how a farthing or a halfpence of corn per person per day translated into bread in ounces, which is unfortunate since bread was the staple foodstuff. By way of comparison, prisoners in the Shrewsbury town bridewell in the late 1750s and early 1760s cost the town ten and a half pence for a week's bread or one and a half pence per day.[76]

The amounts of foodstuffs available per head of inmates in St Mary can be compared with the recommended portions in the Shrewsbury House of Industry, which opened in 1784, and with early nineteenth-century workhouse diets in Lancashire. The Shrewsbury House of Industry allocated between 6 and 12 ounces of bread per adult per meal (according to the rest of the dish), or between 3 and 5 ounces for children. Adults were given 10 ounces of meat when it was served boiled or roasted but only 5 ounces when it had been stewed. Children were given 5 and 2 ounces from each dish respectively. Yet meat was served on only four days in the week. As a result, adults could expect an average daily portion of just over 4 ounces of meat. Cheese was doled out to adults in portions of 6 ounces, but this was served only once per week giving a daily average of under 1 ounce.[77] Alan Crosby has found that in the crisis years of 1826–27, the workhouse inmates at Tottington near Bury saw a decline in their diet, particularly its protein component; inmates could look forward to over a pound of meat per week each in November 1825 but this fell to approximately 4 ounces per week by mid-1827.[78] The St Mary's diet also compares favourably with labourers' diets later in the late eighteenth century. Davies and Eden projected a meat intake among labourers of under 1 ounce per person per day in the 1780s and 1790s, while Burnett found that the diet of a compositor's family in 1810 included 4 ounces of meat per person per day and 1.75 ounces of cheese or butter.[79] That workhouse paupers may have enjoyed substantial nutritional superiority over the labourers surveyed by Davies and Eden is not surprising, given the inflation and other economic difficulties associated with the 1780s and 1790s, but the fact that they apparently enjoyed a measure of equity with a well-paid worker's family seventy years later adds weight to the argument that, by some nutritional yardsticks, workhouse diets compared favourably with labouring diets outside.

Given that the sources comprise inmate lists supplying the sex and age of workhouse paupers, it is plausible to look at the total nutritional requirement represented by the inmates over the course of a year. The combined calorie needs of inmates can be compared with the maximum calories that could have been obtained from meat and cheese. The difficulties inherent with this research are daunting. Dietary requirements depend on sex, age, activity, health and other factors specific to individuals, when nationally the population of Britain has been found to be shorter and lighter than today, being judged 'severely stunted by modern standards'.[80] Calorific needs also depend on environments; in cold weather or poorly heated buildings, there will be a greater need for dietary energy than in summer or adequately heated surroundings.[81] Here it is assumed rather pessimistically that dietary requirements today do match those of eighteenth-century paupers. On this basis, workhouse inmates' daily calorie requirements ranged from 800 calories per day (for those under one year old) to 2,800 calories (for some adult males).[82] As most inmates were women or children, the calories needed per day by most people fell within the range 1,800 to 2,200.[83]

Table 2.3 *Calories needed and received by workhouse inmates*

	Total calories needed	Maximum calories received from meat and cheese		Shortfall	
		No.	% of requirement	No.	% of requirement
1742	11,404,050	2,585,593	22.7	8,818,457	77.3
1745	13,338,500	3,264,034	24.5	10,074,466	75.5
1751	5,915,700	753,541	12.7	5,162,159	87.3

In Shrewsbury, there was a striking similarity between the proportion of energy in the workhouse diet derived from meat and cheese in both years. This suggests there may have been some sort of dietary in operation, which specified how much of each foodstuff adults and children were to receive per day. The table also shows that, in Shrewsbury, the proportion of energy in the workhouse diet derived from meat and cheese fell in the range twenty-two to twenty-five percent. Even allowing for wastage and inedible material it is likely that around a fifth of the required calories were derived from protein, particularly given that individuals' nutritional requirements have been assumed to be modern. In contrast, the absence of cheese from the diet in York made a dramatic difference to the intake of protein from these sources. Protein is a vital component of the human diet (for tissue construction and repair) and should comprise a minimum of ten percent of total intake, and the York diet ran perilously close to this minimum; the only good news for York paupers here is that (according to some modern commentators) some protein can also be extracted from bread.[84]

If the shortfall in calories were to be made up in these years from bread alone, how much bread (in weight) would have had to be served on average per person per day? If it is assumed that the nutritional values of food were the same in the past as they are today, and if the workhouse inmates were usually provided with wheaten (brown) bread, then the average daily portion would have been around one pound six ounces of bread. The weight of wheaten loaves in Shrewsbury for these years is not known but in Oxford it would have cost between one penny and one and a half pence to buy this quantity of wheaten bread.[85] St Mary spent between only a farthing and one half pence on corn per inmate per day, which may mean that they made a considerable saving by making their own dough, that they did not provide their paupers with sufficient food, or that inmates obtained some more calories from other sources.

One qualitative way to look at shopping-list accounts is to compare the variety of consumables other than cheese, meat and corn bought during the year.

In Shrewsbury the overall picture of greater generosity but less variety in 1742 is maintained by this qualitative test. Inmates of 1745 had the opportunity to eat eggs and butter where neither had been offered in 1742.

Table 2.4 *Purchases for workhouse consumption*

	Shrewsbury St Mary 1742		Shrewsbury St Mary 1745		York St Michael le Belfrey 1751	
	No. of purchases	Maximum spent	No. of purchases	Minimum spent	No. of purchases	Spent
Ale	0		12	£0 3s 9.5d	16	£0 7s 4.5d
Butter	0		24	£1s 10d	0	
Currents/ Raisins	0		0		3	£0 0s 8d
Eggs	0		18	£0 2s 8d	0	
Malt/ hops	27	£4 13s 3d	30	£6 5s 1d	0	
Milk	46	£4 7s 3d	45	£1 18s 5d	12	£3 2s 10d
Oatmeal	57	£2 1s 6d	47	£0 17s 4.5d	11	£0 10s 6d
Oil/hogs lard	0		0		3	£0 0s 4d
Pease	8	£0 9s 8d	9	£0 6s 9d	0	
Potatoes	4	£0 6s 1d	15	£0 5s	0	
Rice	0		0		11	£0 19s 3d
Salt	46	£1 5s 2d	37	£0 10s 0.5d	11	£0 4s 8d
Sugar	4	£0 0s 7d	20	£0 3s 6.5d	3	£0 0s 2.5d
Tobacco	0		14	£0 1s 10.5d	12	£0 3s 9d
Treacle	1	£0 0s 2d	14	£0 1s 6d	15	£0 7s 4.5d
Turnips	8	£0 6s	5	£0 0s 7.5d	1	£0 0s 4d
White bread	0		17	£0 3s 1.5d	8	£0 3s 3.5d
Average occupancy	17		21		8	

Conversely, if prices did relate fairly consistently to quantity purchased, there was probably much less porridge being made in 1745. The reduced quantity of milk purchased may also relate to the cattle disease but if all dairy products were suspect, to the point that the overseers chose to buy less milk, why did provision of cheese and butter go up? It may be more likely that milk became cheaper as the cattle disease reduced overall demand for dairy products and as a consequence overseers could afford to buy more of these for their paupers. Fresh produce looks poorly represented, but this is deceptive. Small amounts of vegetables purchased in both years were supplemented by greens grown in the workhouse garden. Each year St Mary paid for four or five hundred 'plants' for the garden, and on one occasion onion seed.

One of the most noticeable qualitative differences between the two years in Shrewsbury is the provision of more luxury goods in 1745; however, increased purchases of sugar and white bread may have been linked to need rather than dietary sophistication, as these were commonly supplied by overseers to those pregnant, ill or dying; in 1745 four people died in the house and two gave birth, whereas neither event had occurred in 1742.[86] One facet of life in the house not brought out by this table was the provision of treats at Christmas. In 1745, treats included a currant pudding, gingerbread and gin.

In York, the dominance of flour, corn, rice, oatmeal and milk give testimony to the many dishes of wheat gruels and puddings served. The complete absence of other dairy products or eggs, however, raises further doubts about the diet's sufficiency of calcium (given the proportion of small children and ageing women in the house). Shammas found that only a fifth of eighteenth-century institutions supplied even a pint of milk per person (when children and lactating mothers would have needed at least one and a half to two pints) and that all of these houses were in the north and west of England.[87] Ironically, the York house with its multiple servings of milk porridge did not necessarily manage to meet the minimum (although in the absence of information about the amounts of milk purchased it is difficult to be sure). If milk cost 1d per quart then inmates received a pint of milk per person per day before calcium in bread and meat is considered. The absence of vegetables from both the dietary and the shopping is also ominous, since only one purchase of turnips (probably to augment the Christmas meal) had to suffice for the whole year and this impression is not mitigated by knowledge about plants grown in a workhouse garden, since there is no evidence that any fresh produce was home-grown.[88]

Crucially the evidence from York provides a rare instance where a planned institutional dietary may be compared with subsequent spending on food in order to judge whether the parish officers adhered to the diet. The weekly distribution of food across the standard three meals of breakfast, dinner and supper set out for paupers in St Michael le Belfrey in 1745 was designedly very bland and repetitive, demonstrating all the features of the typical dietary outlined at the start of this section. Breakfast and supper were given over entirely to milk porridge or broth. Dinner featured boiled beef twice per week (timed to supply the ingredients for broth later in the day) and a limited variety of alternative dishes, chiefly in the form of wheat-based puddings (rice pudding, hasty pudding, creed wheat, furmety and dumplings).

The shopping-list accounts of 1751 unpicked in this section confirm that this diet was being implemented, but with some important additions.[89] The diet though says nothing of the small beer (which may have been implied or assumed by contemporaries) or the treacle and salt, the former consumed in some quantity, which gave savour to the many puddings and made them more palatable. Treacle was plainly a key component of the York diet; a conservative estimate of treacle purchases finds that three stone of treacle was consumed over the year (by a workhouse population of eight people or fewer). It is likely that the use of treacle elsewhere was implicit in a label like 'hasty pudding' rather than it being a later addition to the grocery bill.[90] Treacle at this time was dark molasses (rather than golden syrup) and notably it was a prominent feature of labouring diets in the north of England over the lengthy period 1780–1900, where a spoonful of treacle was added to oatmeal porridge.[91] On the evidence of these purchasing accounts almost every dinner comprising a pudding was given savour from treacle. This is particularly significant given the role of treacle (and later jam) in workhouses under the New Poor Law. Johnston reported that salt was the only flavouring allowed in puddings up to the 1870s but that treacle and jam increasingly featured in workhouse diets after this date. She concluded that without these additions puddings might often be wasted. In other words she implied that treacle could make all the difference to the acceptability of these dishes, that it was usually denied under the strictures of 1834, but was effectively reintroduced as the conditions of workhouse life eased over the final quarter of the nineteenth century.[92] These later developments put a different cast on the implicit presence of treacle in the 1745 dietary, when hasty pudding was uncontroversially made with this ingredient. Paupers and overseers alike probably expected its presence and the former at least were in future destined to resent its omission.

There was also the important addition of tobacco in both houses. Tobacco was the first of the new, non-European products to gain a mass market in England and its diffusion was so extensive that by the period 1748–52, legal and illegal imports of tobacco permitted the consumption of nearly two pounds of tobacco for every man, woman and child in England per year.[93] Tim Hitchcock suggested that workhouse smoking might be strictly forbidden in sets of rules (based on London workhouses in the first half of the eighteenth century), but that tobacco was characteristic of houses where more latitude was allowed to inmates than a straight diet implied, and Shammas also assumed that tobacco was technically forbidden, but occasionally purchased and excused as medicinal.[94] On the evidence from Shrewsbury and York, 'latitude' over tobacco consumption was routinely extended in the mid-eighteenth century in smaller workhouses and this sort of leeway was integral to the way in which smaller houses were run. It is telling that purchases in York continued constantly throughout the year, irrespective of the composition of workhouse inmates (and some at a time when there were no adult male inmates at all), so tobacco was plainly being enjoyed by adult women. Two people were consuming a pipe of tobacco (or equivalent) per day throughout the year.

This research offers concrete evidence that some workhouse inmates not only subsisted throughout the year but were occasionally treated generously. In line with Shammas, diets were largely sufficient in quantity. They were almost certainly lacking in quality, being in some cases demonstrably deficient in calcium and vitamins, if fairly sufficient in protein. In assessing workhouse diets, though, context is everything. The pattern of local food consumption, and the concurrent discourses of poverty, had a profound impact on the reception of workhouse food by inmates. The York dietary of 1745 would have proved a severe punishment to a Berkshire labourer in 1795, but in York in the 1740s and 1750s it probably proved acceptable. Furthermore extra dietary benefits, or other consumables that did not feature on dietaries, routinely made a difference to the character of workhouse life. The milky porridges, wheat puddings, or rice paps that featured so heavily in dietaries were rendered more varied, tasty and acceptable by the routine addition of savour, particularly here via treacle (which was almost certainly an integral part of the local labouring diet). Therefore the image of the pre-1800 workhouse diet should be updated; it was not merely generous in quantity and deficient in quality, nor was the monotony broken only by occasional but unsustainable additions (such as a Christmas treat, details which catch the eye of poor-law historians but were relatively rare in the ongoing experiences of inmates). Instead workhouse diets contained regular weekly or daily comforts which may have done little to restore their nutritional sufficiency but made life in the mid-century house much more acceptable. Eighteenth-century houses must also be seen in the light of later developments. The New Poor Law insisted that tobacco and treacle, for example, be excluded from workhouse provision. The point here is that appetising additions or extras were not a result of alleged poor-law abuses arising in the early nineteenth century; they were part of a long tradition of extending the dietary and making workhouse existence more acceptable before 1800.

Material standards of living in workhouses

Another factor conditioning the experience of life in the workhouse will have been material surroundings; but much less has been written on this topic than on diet. Surviving examples of pre-1800 workhouse buildings have been catalogued by the Royal Commission for Historical Monuments. In that study Morrison distinguished between large, purpose-built workhouses and smaller domestic institutions (commonly of brick, with two storeys and an attic) and also regretted the extent to which surviving institutions have been remodelled.[95] None of the smaller houses studied here have survived. The virtual absence of artefacts known to have comprised workhouse contents is even more striking. This has effectively forestalled discussion of workhouse interiors. Therefore it is not possible to become so combatively engaged in this issue as was the case above with food. Nonetheless, an appreciation of paupers' surroundings is possible from a close reading of workhouse inventories (see appendix 2.2, Inventories of workhouses 1730–67).[96]

Workhouse inventories must be read with the intentions of compilers in mind. Three from Oxford and the one from York were drawn up when parishes were establishing a new workhouse or switching to a new manager. None of the lists used here attempted to place a value on the goods, although some parishes did take itemised inventories to assess their fixed capital.[97] The Shrewsbury example had no evident or specific purpose, but it was completed two years after the workhouse had been refitted in 1748. It is possible to check off a number of the items in the inventory against the shopping-list accounts kept for the new furniture and contents in 1748, and perhaps this was exactly the point; the parish wanted to see what it still had, and what had been lost, broken or purloined.[98] Holy Cross along with St Peter le Bailey in Oxford made a separate note of contents brought into the house by paupers. This may have been to prevent them from removing parish goods if and when they left the house again, although it is more likely that a pauper brought into the house with their goods also died there. It may have been a variety of shorthand, used to distinguish between two similar pieces of furniture.

Some urban workhouses compelled paupers to bring their household goods with them when they were admitted. In Leeds, paupers were periodically forced to surrender their goods when entering the workhouse, a strategy on the part of the parish that apparently increased the severity of the 'workhouse test' and reduced the number of relief claimants. In Mansfield the workhouse rules required every inmate to bring their goods and chattels with them, although this may not have been consistently enforced. There was a similar condition attached to workhouse entry in Lincoln, but there paupers could take their goods away with them again if and when they left.[99] This control of pauper possessions by parish authorities is reminiscent of the spasmodic requisition of pauper goods after a person's death. Entries in overseers' accounts demonstrating that a portion of parish income derived from the sale of paupers' goods, or the speculative taking of pauper inventories, is often the only evidence for the practice.[100] Parish authority to act in this way was customary rather than statutory. Burn tacitly acknowledged that parishes enjoyed no technical right to requisition pauper possessions, but judged 'In case of removing poor persons to the workhouse, a power (as it seemeth) should be given to the overseers, to take with them their cloaths, bedding, tools of their trade, or other effects.'[101] Yet acts concerning the poor cited different circumstances under which goods might be taken and parishes may have inferred such a right at other times; 5 Geo I c.8. 1718–19 gave churchwardens and overseers permission to seize the goods of paupers who had run away and left their wives and children chargeable to the parish. Historians have customarily viewed this in a negative light, taking the view that poor people lost their liberty and control of their possessions simultaneously, but it is just possible that paupers preferred to enter the workhouse with 'at least some of their own more cherished belongings'.[102] Either way, the entanglement of pauper possessions with workhouse stock raises the possibility that some inventories omitted items which were not the property of the parish but which were nonetheless in use in the workhouse. The same problem applies to household stock supplied by workhouse masters and mistresses.

Even so, some facets of paupers' material lives are clear, helping to place institutions on a spectrum from comfortable to institutional.[103] The most well-represented category of contents is bedding. There were 482 separate items in this section (appendix 2.2). This fits with Cornford's findings for pauper possessions, where a bed and bedding were judged 'the most essential and valuable item of furniture'.[104] All of the workhouses contained multiple beds and bedsteads, with blankets and usually with a lesser number of sheets. Rugs were also used. St Michael's house in Oxford made the most comprehensive provision for its inmates as regards bedding, with at least two blankets and a pair of sheets to every mattress; as the house contents were brand new at this point, this may not have remained the case. Chester's St John's workhouse inventory specified bed materials, giving five feather, three flock and seven chaff beds (leaving one unidentified).

It was a common contemporary complaint that workhouse beds were habitually shared. None of the workhouses with inventories used here have inmate lists for the same dates, but the number in the house in Chester St John fell between twenty-six and forty-eight (where there were twenty bedsteads) and an inventory and inmate list from North-leigh in Oxfordshire taken around 1800 revealed that twelve beds were shared by twenty-five inhabitants.[105] Paupers were accommodated with a bed each in Terling, but were forced to share in Ovenden.[106] In some establishments accommodation became very cramped indeed; in the Birmingham workhouse, there were four adults or six children in each bed in 1783.[107] Yet bed-sharing was a feature of a number of institutions including infirmaries and schools.[108] Also the experience of bed-sharing may have been substantially different depending on whether one had to share with a member of one's family or a stranger. In Northleigh, at least nineteen of the people in the house shared a surname with other inmates, so beds might have been shared by spouses, siblings or parents with children. Bed-sharing might also have been viewed by inmates as another way of keeping warm in winter when bedding, clothing and heating became insufficient. In his recommendations relating to the education of girls in boarding schools, Erasmus Darwin actively advised bed-sharing.[109] For workhouse paupers, bed-sharing was possibly prefer-able to no bed at all.[110]

Workhouses could contain a considerable amount of furniture. Most houses contained a table and chairs, but the only item to feature in all was a bench or form. It makes sense that furniture designed to cater for numbers of people would be popular with institutions like workhouses. Still, some of the furniture listed by Oxford's St Michael and Chester's St John was placed in a 'committee' room, so although the chairs and tables were included in the workhouse inventory it is unlikely that paupers had access to them. On the other hand, there was an apparent scarcity of fire and light equipment. Each house would technically need only one of each item like a shovel and tongs to start fires in any number of hearths; however, it seems more likely that heating was skimped. If the lists are accurate, then the absence of many candlesticks is interesting. Corn-ford found at least one in most pauper houses.[111] Perhaps the absence of candlesticks from workhouses reflects an element of parish policy, to compel people to go to bed when it got dark and also save on candles.

When it came to feeding the poor, trenchers and spoons seem to have proved the most popular option or combination. These two types of item account for over half of all crockery and cutlery. Knives and forks are hardly found outside of Oxford St Michael.

There is evidence of some workhouse work in all these houses except St Martin's. As this house was run by a mistress alone, it may have been more like a poorhouse than a workhouse. St Michael's was relatively well equipped, but again as this was a new house, the parish was probably experiencing the type of optimism characteristic of the early stages of a workhouse experiment. Yet in one respect the houses were alike, in the lack of variety of work done there. The carding and spinning of fibre into thread was the only occupation except in St Michael le Belfrey, where workhouse accounts show that oakum picking was also conducted. The York workhouse also paid 'encouragement money', small occasional sums to the paupers who worked to give them an incentive to continue, disbursing a total of just 1s 2d in 1751 for example. This was a sop, being a tiny fraction of the £2 1s 6.5d that paupers earned for the parish over the course of the same year.

Inventories are not always broken down into a room-by-room study but they sometimes give an indication of the living space available. In St Peter le Bailey the writers of the inventory noted that the workhouse had three floors, denoted as 'below stairs', 'up one pair of stairs' and 'up 2 pair of stairs'. Beds were found on all three floors but it was clear that the ground floor was primarily used for cooking and eating. The more detailed room-by-room account of St Michael's workhouse in 1767 is valuable, as the parish was using the building which had been occupied by Cross as a contractor's house. The rooms comprised a kitchen, cellar, dining hall, master and mistress's room, working room, wool room, committee room, working mistress's room and three bedrooms. It seems probable that these eleven rooms were the main apartments that had been used for the preceding thirty years as in November 1741, St Mary Magdalen overseers had paid 3s 6d to have eleven chimneys swept at the workhouse.

St John's workhouse in Chester was the best equipped house in terms of bedrooms with five bedrooms on the first and second storeys of the house; there were a further five bedsteads in 'the old house' but the absence of additional beds and bedding suggests that it was a storage room rather than a place to sleep. It seems that if overseers ever tried to segregate workhouse inmates, the limited number of bedrooms in workhouses meant that at the most inmates could be divided between men, women and children. Pressure on spaces in beds might have meant that rigid rules would have had to be relaxed if paupers were not to sleep on the floor. In all of these houses paupers must have had to sleep in dormitories rather than individual rooms.

Finally, the inventory for St Michael le Belfrey, which lists rooms but not storeys, is intriguing on the subject of the separation of the sexes. The house was equipped with a women's ward, containing all the bedding in the house, but no other rooms allocated for sleeping. This suggests that at the outset the house was designed to hold the adult female poor. Presumably, children joined the women in this ward as they were admitted. But this arrangement begs the question, where were the occasional adult male inmates lodged? In a room furnished later in the 1740s or in the same room as the women and children? One of the men present in the later 1740s was the husband of one of the female inmates; she would presumably have been content to share a room and bed with him, but what would the other women have made of his presence? They may have been as disgruntled as some contemporary commentators were shocked by the prospect of men and women sharing the same rooms.

Extraordinary relief for workhouse inmates

Once paupers had been fed and accommodated in workhouses, what other costs might be met by the parish on their behalf? In Oxford parishes had surrendered part of their responsibility to a contractor. Did this mean that any further needs of paupers would be ignored, as overseers no longer had daily or weekly contact with them? Patterns of parish behaviour were probably influenced by the type of contract signed. It would be surprising indeed to find a parish supplying clothes, shoes and other necessaries when their contractor was legally supposed to meet such costs from his lump sum or *per capita* payments. The terms of the contract between Solomon Cross and St Michael's parish which were agreed 2 April 1751 specified that Cross was to provide food, drink, washing and lodging while the parish remained responsible for paupers 'in Sickness, so far as Advice or Medicine is wanting, in Apparel and Bedding'.[112] Yet when it was left to parishes to provide clothes, it does not follow that they would necessarily have remained alert to their paupers' needs in these respects. Given contemporary rhetoric, paupers might have feared they would be abandoned in contractors' houses.

Therefore it is slightly surprising but valuable to learn that Oxford parishes did not totally ignore the needs of their paupers once they had been transferred to the contractor's workhouse.

Table 2.5 shows the number of inmates receiving extraordinary relief, the proportion of money spent on each type of benefit and the proportion of inmates receiving that benefit. Between forty and eighty percent

The experience of urban poverty, 1723–82

of inmates received extraordinary relief payments in Oxford, which was similar to the interest that the Shrewsbury and York parishes maintained in their paupers where the workhouse was run by the overseers and a housekeeper. Also, this table is more likely to underestimate relief to workhouse paupers than overstate it. Extraordinary relief to children was particularly difficult to isolate. Furthermore, the tendency of overseers to maintain contact with workhouse paupers may have fluctuated from year to year. This may have been a reflection of prevailing policy as well as (or instead of) a reflection of paupers' needs in any year. For instance, St Michael's parish spent £2 7s 2d and £1 6s 9d on named paupers in 1754 and 1755 respectively, when the average number of poor from St Michael's in Cross's house was twenty-six. This average number fell to thirteen in 1756–58, yet spending on extraordinary relief for workhouse inmates rose to over three pounds in 1756 and 1758. The impetus which resulted in St Michael's sending all of their long-term poor to the house in 1753 probably also had a restraining influence on overseers' spending on the workhouse poor. This restraint was partially or wholly lifted in 1756 when the pension list returned, which resulted

Table 2.5 *Extraordinary relief directed to workhouse inmates*

	Oxford St Peter le Bailey 1751–57		Oxford St Michael 1754–58		Oxford St Martin 1733–34		Shrewsbury St Mary 1742, 45		York St Michael le Belfrey 1747–51	
Inmates receiving relief	15	71%	32	57%	14	41%	29	56%	7+	50+%
Total spent	£4 18s 7d		£18 5s 8.5d		£12 7s 7d		£11 7s 1d		£2 1s 5d	

	% of £ spent	% inmates	% of £ spent	% inmates	% of £ spent	% inmates	% of £ spent	% inmates	% of £ spent	% inmates
Cash doles	5.2	23.8	3.8	19.6	Nil	Nil	23.2	23.0	2.1	21.4
Shoes	5.1	19.0	29.1	32.1	23.4	32.4	49.5	32.7	8.6	21.4
Clothes	57.1	42.9	36.2	25.0	1.8	8.8	19.6	21.2	89.2	42.8
Food/ale	2.6	Not known	9.8	Not known	5.0	Not known	Nil	Nil	Nil	Nil
Birth Costs	13.2	9.5	3.8	3.6	Nil	Nil	7.7	5.8	Nil	Not known
Illness	16.7	23.8	17.2	26.8	69.7	14.7	Nil	Nil	Nil	Not known

in more attention and relief for workhouse inmates. The relatively poor parish of St Peter le Bailey had a more long-term incentive to limit costs, but still paid for some extraordinary relief for inmates. Inmates from St Peter le Bailey may have developed more acute needs before the parish relieved them.

Money was spent most often on clothes or shoes. These items commonly accounted for sixty to seventy percent of spending on extraordinary relief for workhouse inmates. St Michael's had contractually agreed to meet these needs and it is possible that St Martin's and St Peter le Bailey had made similar arrangements. Yet it is interesting that Shrewsbury St Mary, which ran its own workhouse via a salaried manageress, spent a similar proportion of relief money on the same commodities. York appears to have spent almost all its money on these items but this is partly because payments for extras in illness have been excluded from the reckoning (because these were not identified in the accounts as being for individual paupers). Workhouse inmates were less likely to need extraordinary relief in the form of food or fuel as these items were (at least theoretically) supplied in the house. As a result, clothing and illness would predictably be the two most significant or legitimate needs which remained to be satisfied. This finding accords with Steve King's judgement, that the poor in this period were relatively well clothed and that clothing the poor well became a basic task of parish relief 1750–1840.[113] Medical relief is another matter. A sixth to a quarter of inmates in Oxford received payments in illness; the use of workhouses as repositories for the sick poor is discussed further in chapter four.

Conclusion

Experience of workhouse life was conditioned in part by parish policy (to impose a workhouse test, or build up a list of outdoor pensioners) but also by responses to the needs of the poor. Parishes developed their workhouse policy in respect to different groups of poor, such that many establishments housed a substantial group of adult women but some locations preferred to target other vulnerable groups such as children (or, in effect, families overburdened with children). Policy choices like this did not constitute an inviolable template, and the emphasis of workhouse use could shift quite quickly, but the finer grades of parish motivation are difficult to discern.

Workhouse life was not decisively comfortable in any of the foundations in Oxford, Shrewsbury or York, but they were not the repositories of squalor and neglect depicted by the most pessimistic contemporaries. Once inside the workhouse paupers received bed and board. The bed

was in all probability shared with someone else, but this was not necessarily a surprise or the occasion of distress. It may even be possible to
wax lyrical about the cosy potentialities of bed-sharing. Consideration of
'board' has occupied a good deal of the discussion in this chapter, in an
attempt to set the mid-eighteenth century workhouse diet in its proper
context. Dietaries were bland and of doubtful nutritional sufficiency, but
the evidence of shopping-list accounts permits an alternative view. Diets
were routinely augmented with goods not specified in dietaries (although
their presence there may have been implicit for contemporaries who
enjoyed a confident knowledge of appropriate recipes), and consequently
it seems likely that workhouse food in the 1750s did not attract the
extreme distaste expressed in the 1830s. Nor were paupers incarcerated
in workhouses and forgotten, at least not in the smaller urban examples
examined here. Overseers continued to monitor people's needs and to
some extent met them with goods and services (sometimes occasioning a
good deal of expenditure over and above workhouse maintenance). This
chapter has been concerned only with the material aspects of workhouse
life, but it has provided support for Hitchcock's recent characterisation
of workhouses as 'porous institutions', casual and consensual, fashioned
as much by the poor as by parish officers or even contractors, where
lived experiences were often far removed from rules and aspirational
regimes.[114] Workhouse inmates may not have been actively pleased with
their lot, but neither were they entirely dispossessd.

Notes

1 Small sections of this chapter were first published in my article 'Almshouse
  versus workhouse: residential welfare in eighteenth-century Oxford', *Family
  and Community History* 7: 1 (2004). I am grateful to the editor for permission to reproduce them here.
2 K. Morrison, *The Workhouse: A Study of Poor Law Buildings in England*
  (Swindon, 1999), pp. 67–8.
3 P. Slack, *Poverty and Policy in Tudor and Stuart England* (London, 1988),
  pp. 195–200; earlier experiments may not have been residential and stood
  in a complicated relationship with houses of correction, see J. Innes, 'Prisons
  for the poor: English bridewells 1555–1800', in F. Snyder and D. Hay (eds),
  Labour, Law and Crime: An Historical Perspective (London, 1987).
4 T. Hitchcock, 'The English Workhouse: A Study of Institutional Poor Relief
  in Selected Counties 1696-1750' (DPhil thesis, Oxford University, 1985),
  p. 221; T. Hitchcock (ed.), *Richard Hutton's Complaints Book: The Notebook of the Steward of the Quaker Workhouse at Clerkenwell, 1711–1737*
  (London Record Society, 1987), p. xxi; J. S. Taylor, 'The unreformed workhouse 1776–1834', in E. W. Martin (ed.), *Comparative Development in
  Social Welfare* (London, 1972), pp. 61–2.

5 PP *House of Commons Sessional Papers of the Eighteenth Century* ed. S. Lambert (Wilmington Delaware, 1975) 31, 'Abstracts of the returns made by the overseers of the poor' 1777, pp. 107–350; PP *Abstract of the Answers and Returns made pursuant to … An act for taking an account of the population of Great Britain, 1801'* (London, 1802); *Abstract of the answers and returns made pursuant to … An act for procuring returns relative to the expense and maintenance of the poor in England* (London, 1804). Population counts are found in C. W. Chalklin, *The Provincial Towns of Georgian England: A Study of the Building Process 1740–1820* (London, 1974), pp. 36, 338–9; P. J. Corfield, *The Impact of English Towns 1700–1800* (Oxford, 1982), pp. 129, 183. Population estimates dated 1777 are guesstimates based on earlier enumerations and 1801 census totals.

6 Cheshire Record Office (hereafter CRO), CLA/6 *An Act for better regulating the poor* (1762) p. 240; Shropshire Archives (hereafter SA), 681/56 *An Act for the better relief and employment of the poor belonging to several parishes within the town of Shrewsbury and the liberties thereof* (1783).

7 Hitchcock, *Quaker Workhouse*, p. xx.

8 H. Owen, *Some Account of the Ancient and Present State of Shrewsbury* (Shrewsbury, 1808), p. 555.

9 Bodleian Library (hereafter Bod. Lib.), MS Blakeway 16 T. Phillips' *History and Antiquities of Shrewsbury* (Shrewsbury, 1779) with mss notes by J. B. Blakeway.

10 S. Ottaway, *The Decline of Life: Old Age in Eighteenth-Century England* (Cambridge, 2004), pp. 267–9.

11 P. Slack, *The English Poor Law 1531–1782* (London, 1990), p. 44.

12 Sir T. Bernard (ed.), *Reports of the Society for Bettering the Condition and Increasing the Comforts of the Poor* 2 (London, 1800), p. 23.

13 T. Hitchcock, 'Paupers and preachers: the S.P.C.K. and the parochial workhouse movement', in L. Davison *et al* (eds), *Stilling the Grumbling Hive: The Response to Social and Economic Problems in England, 1689–1750* (Stroud, 1992).

14 D. Marshall, *The English Poor in the Eighteenth Century* (London, 1926), p. 137.

15 Taylor, 'The unreformed workhouse'.

16 For an honourable exception (looking at diets only) see A. G. Crosby, 'A poor diet for poor people?: workhouse food in Lancashire, 1750–1834', *Lancashire Local History* 9 (1995).

17 Hitchcock, 'English Workhouse', p. 167; T. Hitchcock, '"Unlawfully begotten on her body": illegitimacy and the parish poor in St Luke's, Chelsea', in T. Hitchcock *et al* (eds), *Chronicling Poverty: The Voices and Strategies of the English Poor 1640–1840* (Basingstoke, 1997).

18 Bod. Lib., MS Blakeway 16; *The Present Situation of the Town of Birmingham Respecting its Poor* (Birmingham, 1782), p. 4.

19 T. Sokoll, *Essex Pauper Letters 1731–1837* (Oxford, 2001) p. 469.

20 Ottaway, *Decline of Life*, pp. 258, 273–4.

21 *An Account of Several Workhouses* (London, 1732), pp. 157–8.

22 See figure 1.1, map of Oxford.
23 D. W. Rannie (ed.), *Remarks and Collections of Thomas Hearne* 4 (Oxford Historical Society 34 old series, 1897), p. 349.
24 A. Crossley (ed.), *Victoria County History of Oxfordshire* 4 (Oxford, 1979), p. 347; Morrison, *Workhouse*, p. 29.
25 PP *House of Commons Sessional Papers of the Eighteenth Century* 31, 'Abstracts of the returns made by the overseers of the poor' 1777.
26 P. M. Tillott (ed.), *The Victoria History of Yorkshire: The City of York* (Oxford, 1961), p. 237.
27 P. Wallis, 'Charity, politics and the establishment of York county hospital: a "party job"?', *Northern History* 38 (2001), 246; Tillott, *City of York*, p. 227.
28 Tillott, *City of York*, pp. 226–9.
29 Ibid., pp. 279–80.
30 Information from the various overseers' accounts listed in the bibliography.
31 SA, P257/L/3/2 Shrewsbury St Mary overseers' accounts 1695–1732.
32 Inmates from St Peter le Bailey were listed among the overseers' annual accounts; people from St Martin and St Michael were identified from overseers' vouchers (the receipted bills which Cross or his wife presented to overseers).
33 Borthwick Institute, Y/MB 53 St Michael le Belfrey accounts of the workhouse master 1744–56; Y/MB 54 St Michael le Belfrey overseers' book of workhouse admissions 1744–62; Y/MB 55 St Michael le Belfrey accounts of poorhouse 1744.
34 Hitchcock, 'English Workhouse.
35 Taylor, 'The unreformed workhouse', p. 77.
36 CRO, P51/22, St John poorhouse book 1731–56.
37 Marshall, *English Poor*, p. 128.
38 J. S. Taylor, *Jonas Hanway Founder of the Marine Society* (London, 1985), p. 115.
39 CRO, P51/22 St John poorhouse book 1731–56.
40 Ottaway, *Decline of Life*, pp. 249–50.
41 L. Mackay, 'A culture of poverty? the St Martin in the Fields workhouse in 1817', *Journal of Interdisciplinary History* 26 (1995), 220–1.
42 Ibid., 219, 224.
43 P. Anderson, 'The Leeds workhouse under the old poor law: 1726–1834', *Publications of the Thoresby Society* 56: 2 (1980), 94–5; MacKay, 'Culture of poverty', 219–20.
44 Oxford Record Office (hereafter ORO), Mss dd par Oxford St Michael c. 31, miscellaneous papers including pauper inventories and correspondence.
45 B. Harvey, *Living and Dying in England 1100–1540* (Oxford, 1993), p. 46; J. Reinarz, *The Birth of a Provincial Hospital: The Early Years of the General Hospital, Birmingham, 1765–1790* (Dugdale Society Occasional Papers, 2003), p. 29.
46 V. J. Johnston, *Diets in Workhouses and Prisons 1835–1895* (New York, 1985).
47 C. Shammas, *The Pre-Industrial Consumer in England and America* (Oxford,

1990), pp. 140–3.

48 R. W. Fogel, *The Escape from Hunger and Premature Death, 1700–2100* (Cambridge, 2004), p. 9.

49 Sir J. Drummond and A. Wilbraham, *The Englishman's Food: A History of Five Centuries of English Diet* revised with additions by D. Hollingsworth (London, 1958); C. A. Wilson, *Food and Drink in Britain* (London, 1976).

50 Johnston, *Diets in Workhouses*, chapter five.

51 Hitchcock, *Quaker Workhouse*, p. 1.

52 Greater London Record Office, Foundling Country Hospital at Shrewsbury, committee minutes 27 February 1759; SA, 83/1/309 Shrewsbury House of Industry directors' order book 1784–1808; F. M. Eden *The State of the Poor* (London [1797] 1928) pp. 284–88; Borthwick Institute, Y/MB 53 St Michael le Belfrey accounts of the workhouse master 1744–56.

53 Hitchcock, *Quaker Workhouse*, pp. 96–7.

54 E. M. Hampson, *The Treatment of Poverty in Cambridgeshire, 1597–1834* (Cambridge, 1934), p. 74; Eden, *State of the Poor*, pp. 262–4.

55 *Rules and Orders for Relieving and Employing the Poor of the Township of Leeds* (Leeds, 1771), pp. 8, 11.

56 Johnson, *Diets in Workhouses*, p. 110.

57 Wilson, *Food and Drink*, p. 159.

58 J. Burnett, *Plenty and Want* (London, 1979), pp. 100–1.

59 R. Jütte. 'Diets in welfare institutions and in outdoor poor relief in early modern Western Europe', *Ethnologia Europaea* 16: 2 (1988), 119.

60 S. Pennell, ' "Great quantities of gooseberry pye and baked clod of beef": victualling and eating out in early modern London', in P. Griffiths and M. Jenner (eds), *Londinopolis: Essays in the Cultural and Social History of Early Modern London* (Manchester, 2000), p. 242.

61 P. Brears, 'Bastille soup and skilly: workhouse food in Yorkshire', in C. A. Wilson (ed.), *Food for the Community: Special Diets for Special Groups* (Edinburgh, 1993), p. 125.

62 Shammas, *Pre-Industrial Consumer*, chapter five surveys the scanty material relating to diet in England before 1800; Eden, *State of the Poor*, and D. Davies, *The Case of Labourers in Husbandry Stated and Considered* (London, 1795); Burnett, *Plenty and Want*.

63 Wilson, *Food and Drink*, pp. 235–6; Shammas, *Pre-Industrial Consumer*, p. 136.

64 Burnett, *Plenty and Want*, p. 54.

65 Shammas, *Pre-Industrial Consumer*, p. 137; M. Barker-Read, 'The Treatment of the Aged Poor in Five Selected West Kent Parishes from Settlement to Speenhamland 1662–1797' (PhD thesis, Open University, 1988), p. 256; Sokoll, *Essex Pauper Letters*, pp. 409, 468, 472, 477, 545.

66 This is usually confirmed, however, by reference to the nineteenth-century picture; Johnston, *Diets in Workhouses*, p. 245; Burnett, *Plenty and Want*, p. 55; B. Reay, *Microhistories: Demography, Society and Culture in Rural England, 1800–1930* (Cambridge, 1996), p. 123.

67 Shammas, *Pre-Industrial Consumer*, pp. 138–9.

68 E. P. Thompson, *The Making of the English Working Class* (London, 1980), p. 231.
69 Sokoll, *Esssex Pauper Letters*, p. 622.
70 Wilson, *Food and Drink*, p. 191.
71 S. Sherman, *Imagining Poverty: Quantification and the Decline of Paternalism* (Columbus Ohio, 2001), pp. 4, 6.
72 Ibid., p. 49.
73 Various cooking methods reduce the weight of meat by twenty to forty percent but the fact that workhouses favoured serving stews and broths may have meant that less weight and fewer nutrients were effectively lost; see R. A. McCance *et al.* (eds), *The Composition of Foods* (Royal Society of Chemists and Ministry of Agriculture Fisheries and Foods, 1991), n.p.
74 T. S. Ashton, *Economic Fluctuations in England 1700–1800* (Oxford, 1959), p. 20.
75 Shammas, *Pre-Industrial Consumer*, p. 139.
76 SA, Shrewsbury Borough Records 3365/683, Town public stock vouchers 1715–63.
77 SA, 83/1/309 Shrewsbury House of Industry directors' order book 1784–1808 (inside front cover).
78 Crosby, 'A poor diet', 24–5.
79 Burnett, *Plenty and Want*, p. 62; Shammas, *Pre-Industrial Consumer*, p. 138.
80 Fogel, *Escape from Hunger*, p. 13.
81 Harvey, *Living and Dying*, p. 71.
82 Department of Health, *Dietary Reference Values for Food Energy and Nutrients for the United Kingdom* (Report on Health and Social Subjects 41, HMSO 1991), n.p.
83 Barker-Read, 'Aged Poor', p. 252 estimated that the elderly would have required 2,000–2,500 calories per day; Shammas, *Pre-Industrial Consumer*, p. 135.
84 J. Yudkin, 'Some basic principles of nutrition', in D. Oddy and D. Miller (eds), *The Making of the Modern British Diet* (London, 1976), p. 209.
85 The average weight of the 1d wheaten loaf in Oxford 1742 and 1745 was 17.5 oz and 15 oz respectively, see Bod. Lib., Oxford University Archives MR/3/5/1 Clerk of the market corn book 1733–53
86 See chapter four for a discussion of the workhouse in medical relief.
87 Shammas, *Pre-Industrial Consumer*, pp. 138–41.
88 J. H. Treble, *Urban Poverty in Britain 1830–1914* (London, 1979) p. 150, on reported antipathy to vegetables in York in 1900.
89 Ottaway, *Decline of Life*, p. 264 also found Ovenden purchasing extras that were not on the dietary.
90 Treacle remained demonstrably in use in Yorkshire workhouse diets in the 1790s; Eden, *State of the Poor*, p. 358. Workhouse recipes rarely survive, but some for St James Westminster feature sugar and salt; I am indebted to Tim Hitchcock for this information.
91 Wilson, *Food and Drink*, p. 306; Drummond and Wilbraham, *English-*

man's *Food*, p. 332; Johnston, *Diets in Workhouses*, p. 242; Shammas, *Pre-Industrial Consumer*, pp. 136–7; R. Scola, *Feeding the Victorian City: The Food Supply of Manchester, 1770–1870* (Manchester, 1992), p. 277.

92 Johnston, *Diets in Workhouses*, pp. 112, 151.

93 C. Shammas, 'Changes in English and Anglo-American consumption from 1550 to 1800', in J. Brewer and R. Porter (eds), *Consumption and the World of Goods* (London, 1993), p. 180.

94 Hitchcock, 'English Workhouse', pp. 186, 188; Shammas, *Pre-Industrial Consumer*, p. 144.

95 Morrison, *Workhouse*, p. 17.

96 B. Cornford, 'Inventories of the poor', *Norfolk Archaeology* 35 (1970), 118–25.

97 CRO, P51/22 St John poorhouse book 1731–56. An Oxfordshire workhouse inventory c. 1800 contained an estimate value of the clothes on paupers' backs; see ORO, NP lX/17 Inventory of goods at Northleigh workhouse 1800.

98 SA, Shrewsbury Borough Records 3365/727 Holy Cross Overseers' Accounts 1638–1754.

99 J. W. F. Hill, *Georgian Lincoln* (Cambridge, 1966), p. 161; Anderson, 'Leeds workhouse', pp. 91, 98; J. D. Chambers, *Nottinghamshire in the Eighteenth Century* (London, 1966), p. 240.

100 For example, see Borthwick Institute, Y/MB 53 St Michael le Belfrey accounts of the workhouse master 1744–56, removal of Ann Weatherill's goods to the workhouse 12 November 1745; ORO, Mss dd par Oxford St Peter le Bailey b.18 redistribution of Elizabeth Cooling's goods after her death 1765; requisitioning of goods was practised extensively in seventeenth-century London, see J. Boulton, 'Going on the parish: the parish pension and its meaning in the London suburbs, 1640–1724', in T. Hitchcock *et al* (eds), *Chronicling Poverty*, pp. 35–6.

101 R. Burn, *History of the Poor Laws: With Observations* (London, 1764), p. 287.

102 P. King, 'Pauper inventories and the material lives of the poor in the eighteenth and early nineteenth centuries', in Hitchcock *et al* (eds), *Chronicling Poverty*, pp. 158–60; A. McInnes, '1638–1780', *Victoria County History of Shropshire* [Shrewsbury volume, forthcoming].

103 Ottaway, *Decline of Life*, pp. 256, 262, uses this helpful dichotomy.

104 Cornford, 'Inventories', 119.

105 R. V. H. Burne, 'The treatment of the poor in the eighteenth century in Chester', *Journal of the Chester and North Wales Architectural, Archaeological and Historic Society* 52 (1965), 47; ORO, NP lX/17 Inventory of goods at Northleigh workhouse 1800.

106 Ottaway, *Decline of Life*, pp. 256, 262.

107 M. McNaulty, 'Some Aspects of the History of the Administration of the Poor Laws in Birmingham between 1730 and 1834' (MA dissertation, Birmingham University, 1942), p. 26.

108 SA, 3909/1/1 Royal Salop Infirmary trustees' minute book 8 December

1750; S. Grubb, *Some Account of Life and Religious Labours of Sarah Grubb* (Dublin, 1792), p. 250; *An Account of the Charity School at York* (York, 1705), p. 4; J. H. Cardwell, *The Story of a Charity School* (London, 1899), p. 58; R. Canning, *An Account of the Gifts and Legacies that have been Given and Bequeathed to Charitable Uses in the Town of Ipswich* (Ipswich, 1747), pp. 8–9 for bed-sharing in almshouses.

109 E. Darwin, *A Plan for the Conduct of Female Education in Boarding Schools* (Wakefield, [1797] 1968), p. 105.

110 S. Lloyd, 'Cottage conversations: poverty and manly independence in eighteenth-century England', *Past and Present* 184 (2004), 80 for a portrait of squalid destitution comprising in part the absence of a bed.

111 Cornford, 'Inventories', 120.

112 ORO, Mss dd par Oxford St Michael b.30 fo. 35.

113 S. King, 'Reclothing the English poor, 1750–1840', *Textile History* 33 (2002).

114 T. Hitchcock, *Down and Out in Eighteenth-Century London* (London, 2004), pp. 134–7.

3

Traditional forms of voluntary charity[1]

The role of voluntary charity as both a religious virtue and an element in national welfare ensured that many general discussions of life in eighteenth-century England included some consideration of it. Particularly there is a long history of discussions relating to the spiritual and social benefits accruing to donors. English contemporaries generally wished to eschew the Catholic notion that good works were one route to salvation but at the same time commentators lauded and encouraged charity as 'pleasing to God in a way that the mere payment of taxes to support welfare activity was not'.[2] Furthermore, there were social and political implications to giving that went beyond the basic use of charity as a symbol of the donor's power and although these considerations were not necessarily made explicit by charity promoters at the time, some were quite obvious to contemporary observers.[3] Even a royal charity like Greenwich Hospital, which was founded by William and Mary in 1694, was not exempt from this taint since 'from the first there were complaints that the needs of the pensioners were subjugated to the aspirations of the architects'.[4] The self-interest of charity donors has been given some concentrated attention by historians of both England and Europe in the eighteenth century.[5]

Considerable attention was also directed by contemporaries to the impact of giving on the recipients of charities for the poor. Advocates of indiscriminate giving were rare, because it was increasingly argued that such casual alms encouraged fecklessness by failing to discriminate between 'genuine' objects of charity and the idle, but many endorsed the view that the voluntary (and, for recipients, unreliable) nature of charity meant that it was altogether superior in effect to rate-funded relief. Beneficiaries of charity were not able, or less frequently able, to become dependent on it than on relief, and consequently would be inspired by gratitude and deference. One contributor to the *Gentleman's Magazine* in 1739 therefore represented the views of many when they wrote 'What is given to the Poor now, they look on as a *legal Due*, and give no Thanks

to any one for; whereas if the Poore were supported by voluntary Charities, This would be the means of producing a mutual Harmony between
their *Superiors* and them.'[6] This sentiment was bolstered by a change in
the perception of the relationship between charity and property. Donna
Andrew has identified a rethinking on the part of some clergy who moved
from stressing the obligations of wealth to give charitably (in order to
do justice to the poor) to a rather different position, which emphasised
the sanctity of private property and enshrined only the poor's right to
ask for charity, not the duty of the rich to give.[7] Support for voluntary
over statutory provision for the deserving poor was particularly vocal
in the early 1750s[8] but the judgement, that continuous charity which
could be relied on by the poor was ultimately detrimental to welfare,
proved highly persistent. Thomas Bernard, writing about soup kitchens
in 1818, thought the argument self-evident: 'I need not now observe that
such establishments should never be permanent', and this philosophy
remained very influential throughout the nineteenth century.[9]

There was very little in the way of a legislative framework to regulate
'the chaotic world of private charity'[10] in the eighteenth century and
there was some limited agitation for reform of this oversight. Yet aside
from the Statute of Mortmain (passed in 1735 to restrict devises of land
to charitable trusts, a law that was widely ignored or evaded) there was
no statutory change to the picture of charity management and account-
ability in the eighteenth century because there was no consensus on
how to organise charity, or reform relief along charitable lines. Schemes
designed to integrate voluntary charities and parish relief foundered,
except where incorporations of parishes were authorised to assume
responsibility for local charities.[11] For the most part, charities were left
in the hands of a range of people depending on the provisions made
by testators and the subsequent evolution of local administrative practice; parish officers, trustees, members of testators' families, city councils
and others were either given responsibility for the disposal of charity,
or assumed responsibility in the face of neglect or corruption by other
authorities. The failure of projected schemes and bills to become law
may be a testament to the success of voluntary charity in serving a variety
of purposes (not necessarily or chiefly the relief of the poor), but the legal
picture for eighteenth-century charity has been characterised as sliding
from autonomy to anarchy.[12]

Voluntary charity as opposed to rate-based relief could take various
forms. First, a traditional, common form of charity was the bequest by
individual testators of money, investments or land to produce income
for specific charitable purposes such as building almshouses, providing
cash disbursements, or for regular distributions of other material benefits

such as free clothing, loaves or fuel. This form was becoming less popular during the eighteenth century, both in England and elsewhere, but testamentary charity was never in danger of dying out altogether. Second, the reigning monarch or government might issue or establish a charity. The impressive and ancient foundations of St Bartholomew's and St Thomas's hospitals in London, for example, were merely central and highly visible examples of state munificence; countless free grammar schools and cathedral bedesmen's charities effectively touched life in the provinces. A third option was primarily open to urban populations. Town dwellers might have been members of craft or trade organisations that, although in decline in the eighteenth century, continued to dispense a brand of corporate charity to members and their widows; 'Guilds did not originate to provide welfare, but by the 18th century this had become one of their *raisons d'être*.'[13] Fourth, individuals or groups like town councils traditionally made voluntary collections for specific purposes, for example following severe weather such as flooding. Losers by fire could acquire a charity brief, permitting begging within counties and collections in churches nationwide;[14] only the rise of the modern insurance industry has superseded some of the need for these briefs and voluntary collections. Also, despite opposition, informal giving continued as the fifth familiar type of private charity. For the impoverished this might have derived from kin, friendship or neighbourhood networks, whereby small gifts or loans continually propped up failing household economies, or from begging and receipt of alms from strangers.[15] Alternatively, a begging letter inserted in a newspaper or sent to a prominent wealthy family might solicit funds and enable a poor 'gentle' family to maintain appearances; however, the use of the relatively new medium of the printed press is a reminder of the changing forms of casual charity and the disappearance of some sources of alms. Slack has judged that door-to-door requests for money were rare by 1700; on the testimony of Anthony Wood, the practice was gone from Oxford by 1670.[16] Philanthropic effort was noticeably concentrated in large urban centres, particularly London, Norwich and Bristol, with an observable shift after 1660 towards Warwickshire and the West Riding. Wilson stressed that this suggested 'a direct connection between the stage of economic development and the sources of charity'.[17] Nonetheless, a sixth important source of charity, particularly for the rural poor, survived in the form of gentry largesse. The well-documented decline of ancient, expansive 'hospitality' has masked the persistence of informal giving by prosperous if not elite families to their poor neighbours. Eighteenth-century scions of gentry families based in such disparate counties as Cumberland and Northamptonshire may be found giving up to one-fifth of their annual income for informal charitable purposes in some years.[18]

After the foundation of the poor laws, the limits of poor relief shaped some aspects of charitable activity, as subsequent philanthropy aimed to cater for groups of needy who were not overtly included in the remit of relief. Furthermore, the forms of charity were not immutable. The eighteenth century saw the rise of the subscription charity whereby people made regular contributions during their lifetimes to support specific causes. Charity schools and infirmaries funded by subscription were joined in the last quarter of the eighteenth century by a proliferation of subscriptions and voluntary associations to alleviate specific ills.[19] The popularity of subscription charity can partly be attributed to a growing suspicion that any fund with a reliable income would become subject to abuse (just as any poor who could rely on assistance would become recalcitrant and idle).[20]

In considerations of 'the mixed economy of welfare', voluntary charity has endured a long period in the doldrums as the poor relation of parish relief. Jordan's work claimed a prominent place for private charity in the relief of the poor in his study of benefactions and resulting investments made 1480–1660, yet his findings were attacked and undermined.[21] He failed to deflate the value of charity given in the seventeenth century to make it directly comparable to charity given in the late fifteenth century, and did not allow for the fact that charity might be lost or diverted from its intended objects.[22] The flurry of opposition which overruled Jordan's thesis tended to leave charity sidelined as an insignificant source of income. Charities were characterised as 'seemingly flimsy'[23] from the fact that they were voluntary and sometimes annual rather than compulsory or permanent. They were denigrated (often by champions of the poor law) as 'usually small scale and of relatively slight importance';[24] their impact was allegedly 'marginal'.[25] Charles Wilson attempted to adjust these judgements, asserting that there was a 'vigorous continuation' of the tradition of individual philanthropic giving, as did Slack who argues that to see Jordan's work as fruitless is too dismissive.[26]

There is a gap in the available statistics that give an impression of the national picture; there is nothing between the close of Jordan's research in 1660 and the parliamentary inquiry undertaken in the 1780s. But the latter provides evidence that £259,000 per annum was produced by charitable endowments, a total that excluded both regular giving to subscription charity and those endowments managed by corporations. Set against the two million pounds spent on parish poor relief, endowed charity was clearly a substantial if apparently minority source of support, since even the limited brief of the 1780s inquiry revealed spending equal to thirteen percent of poor relief. In 1798, Sir Thomas Bernard guessed that more money was raised annually by charity than by poor relief.[27] A little later in 1806 Patrick Colquhoun estimated that private charity (testamentary and subscription combined) nearly matched the total disbursed by parishes.[28] It is not at all certain that this estimate is reliable nor that it was universally accepted at the time as a credible guess but even if the true figure was nearer half or quarter Colquhoun's sum, it would still challenge the notion of the dominance of parish relief in the scholarship of early modern English welfare. Prochaska highlighted that even in the early years of the twentieth century, when the state had already begun to assume a more comprehensive role in welfare provision, 'the sums contributed each year, not including church and chapel collections and unremembered alms, far exceeded government expenditure on poor relief'.[29] This volume of charity may be attributable to nineteenth-century developments in charity organisation but it serves to reinforce the possibility that unquantifiable voluntary charity may have been at least as significant as poor relief in other, much earlier decades.

A reassessment of the role of charity is now well underway. Donna Andrew's work on London has provided an updated model of how to approach institutional charity, and how to treat the contemporary discourses informing the foundation and operation of charity.[30] Essays edited by Martin Daunton have broadened the scope of enquiry into welfare strategies.[31] The proceedings of the Anstey conference of 1997, edited by Jo Innes and Hugh Cunningham, have refocused attention on voluntary measures, and have properly drawn the philanthropic trends and experiments of the seventeenth and eighteenth centuries into current debates about the weighting of the roles of the state and voluntary sectors.[32] Nevertheless, just as the poor-relief system was based on the parish, specific to locality and 'shaped by local communities',[33] so charities carefully defined their sphere of influence in terms of place, time, or the qualifications of recipients. Our picture of the poor laws has been compiled painstakingly from numerous studies of individual parishes, towns and regions, and a comprehensive understanding of the role of charity will require similar, detailed examinations of individual charities (such as the work undertaken by Martin Gorsky for Bristol relating to a later period).[34] Perhaps the most surprising omission to date is the neglect of charity as an element of the 'economy of makeshifts'; the latter concept has provided a new direction for welfare historians in the last quarter of the twentieth century, but has not spurred many investigations into the close workings of charity.[35]

What were the experiences of poverty when refracted through the lens of charity? It has been estimated that around twenty to thirty percent of urban populations both in England and on the Continent were reliant on some form of charity, as opposed to four to eight percent who were wholly dependent on relief.[36] Only a relatively small elite could be confident that they would never need to consider an application to charity. Yet within the potential pool of charity applicants there was room for substantial variation between the groups likely to benefit from individual charities. Testators limited possible applicants by sex, age and behaviour, or specified necessary qualifications such as lengthy residence in a parish, membership of a particular trade, or having taken up the freedom. Royal, ecclesiastical or governmental charity was usually directed at definite groups such as orphans and ex-servicemen. Crucially, the extremity of some people's poverty put them beyond the reach of certain charities; some funds explicitly excluded parish paupers as beneficiaries of the charity, or tacitly directed charity to groups not typically found among the parish poor. This may have been 'so as the wealthy inhabitants are not eased'[37] (by a reduction of the burden on the poor rates). Alternatively, it may have been an attempt to discriminate between the deserving and undeserving poor. Poor labouring people not on relief would be rewarded for continuing self-reliance while parishioners who had declined into dependence would not gain (a second time) from the generosity of others. A third possibility is that benefactors wished to spread the benefits of relief as widely as possible and so excluded the people who already received some relief; some benefactions achieved this by specifying that money should be distributed in many small sums with an upper and lower limit on the size of doles. Whatever the motive, the result was that paupers who desired to receive charity simultaneously with relief were technically denied access to some funds and faced stiff competition for others. People may have encountered the problem that, once receiving either charity or relief, they would appear to have been catered for; one contemporary confirmed of an Ipswich charity 'when a Person is in the Foundation, their Friends are apt to think them provided for, and they find more Difficulty in getting Relief elsewhere'.[38] This sort of limitation might have appeared peculiarly ironic to some of the recipients of charity, but then charity was never designed to be responsive to the changing needs of poverty. It was much more self-regarding than that, partly of necessity. Charity benefits were commonly fixed in value, sometimes by the charity's rules but frequently by the finite nature of its income from investments, whereas the amounts spent on relief each year could fluctuate since additional rates could be raised; therefore an inadequate charity might have effectively compelled recipients to find other incomes and done nothing to reduce the number of people seeking poor relief.

The breadth and depth of traditional charity was geographically patchy leading to wide variations in coverage. Formal endowed charities clustered in towns. Where the collective impact of charity appeared munificent, the poor went to some lengths to become eligible. In the nineteenth century, the ready availability of charity in some towns was condemned. York, for example, always enjoyed a large number of charities in relation to its population but this became a matter of criticism in the 1830s when the quantity and quality of charity in some parishes encouraged poor people to establish their settlement in such a parish. A report in the *York Herald* in 1833 alleged that parents prevented the apprenticeship or employment of their children if it altered their legal settlement.[39]

Is it possible to characterise the groups of people who received urban charities? To what extent could the total pool of available charity benefit the people who were parish poor? Is it possible that where paupers were not rigorously excluded they had a good opportunity for collecting charity money? Were there some types of charity that were more likely to be dominated by paupers than others? Were these all necessarily the low-grade, small-income charities? This chapter will consider these questions in the context of traditional types of charity including residential or institutional charities (such as almshouses), and endowments which supplied disbursements of cash doles or clothing; subscription charities represented by infirmaries and charity schools will be dealt with in chapters four and five. Endowed charity may have been less important to the incomes of the poor than informal giving or other benefits, but it does have the advantage that it left more evidence of distribution than other, ephemeral forms of income. The extent of casual or irregular giving in response to verbal or written appeals can be gauged for individual donors but not for the recipients in a particular town or parish,[40] and general treatments of the subject have been achieved elsewhere.[41] Also, the sources used in this chapter could not be adapted to comment decisively on the attitudes of the poor towards receiving charity. Instead, it will focus on the material advantages for beneficiaries (rather than the range of responses and meanings that they might attach to charity), particularly on the minute relationships between individual beneficiaries, the patterns of their charity receipts in the context of eligibility for poor relief, and key life-cycle events (especially burial). This will show the essential fluidity of the eighteenth-century urban population as people moved between welfare agencies. There were no identifiable 'charity-prone' groups but there were individuals both personally inclined and well placed to construct incomes from formal relief and charity sources.

This analysis is confined exclusively to Oxford. Comparative work on this topic is effectively barred by the paucity of full overseers' accounts that survive concurrently with charity disbursements. Evidence of charity foundation is plentiful, but accompanying evidence of distribution or application is vital (as it cannot be assumed that a charity was always set up and run along intended lines). In Oxford a fairly rich supply of charity accounts survive for the mid-eighteenth century, for almshouses, municipal charities and parish charities, disbursing sums from a few shillings to over five pounds per year, to named individuals. Unfortunately, the same is not true for Shrewsbury or York. In the former, five municipal charities were the subject of a case in Chancery in the 1750s, 1760s and 1770s. The corporation retained the capital sums and made virtually no disbursements for the period under study.[42] Details of recipients of other town and parish charities in Shrewsbury could not be found in any numbers, probably because the house of industry collected all such records and apparently did not keep them.[43] York enjoyed an extraordinarily rich collection of charities but barely any of them leave detailed distribution records. The Chamberlain's account books prove that selected town charities were disbursed but do not usually reveal the beneficiaries, while parish charity accounts are very spotty in terms of both survival and quality.[44]

Almshouses

In the first age of the workhouse, from 1723–82, almshouses comprised an alternative, older model of institutional welfare. Founded by testators and others from the medieval period into the twentieth century, they clearly held an enduring appeal for the philanthropic; however, almshouses endured fluctuations in their popularity, and the mid-eighteenth century saw relatively few new charities of this type. There was a resurgence of interest in the early nineteenth century.[45] Often located at the heart of a village or urban community, seventeenth-century almshouses typically comprised a simple row of houses along a road close to the parish church.[46] Individual houses consisted of one or two rooms, on one or two storeys, with one or two hearths and occasionally a piece of garden. Almshouses were often purpose-built but the materials and resilience of houses could vary considerably. Sturdy stone or brick houses sporting a tablet that advertised the terms of the foundation provided a stereotype, but there were also examples in west Kent where a shortage of local brick-making meant that almshouses were timber-framed and not very resistant to the elements (making them little or no better than labourers' cottages).[47] In addition to accommodation it was usual for almshouses to supply a cash pension, but the value of pensions varied widely. Stone's almshouse in Oxford paid inhabitants £20 per year each but in Chester three of the almshouses gave only about £1 a year to inhabitants.[48] Wealthy foundations might also supply extras like fuel; Robert Veel's almshouse in Ilchester supplied clothing, medical aid and funeral costs.[49] Most almshouse pensions reacted very slowly to changes in cost of living (if they reacted at all); it is not impossible to find that pensions were raised in response to rising costs of provisions, as was the case with the Shrewsbury Hospital in Sheffield by 1770 where pensions were increased from 2s 6d to 3s 6d over the mid-century period, but it was more common for pensions to have lagged far behind price rises.[50]

Almshouse foundations often tried to define quite closely what sort of person was eligible for admittance, based on people's age, gender, capacities and demeanor. Almspeople were typically required to be elderly (although not necessarily of a specific age), ill or incapacitated, honest, relatively poor, locally resident, perhaps with a designated marital status. Some had extensive lists of people to be excluded (on the basis of specific faults like gambling, drinking, fighting or scolding, or attributes like Catholicism). Control of almshouse inhabitants once they had been admitted was apparently fairly light; the provisions of the charity might include the employment of a nurse or chaplain to minister to the poor, but rarely gave anyone a directive or disciplinary role. Eccentricities were generally tolerated; for example Richard Hart, inmate of St Cross, built his own coffin and kept it in his rooms for twenty years before his death in 1790, raised to the ceiling on pulleys.[51] Curfews might be employed but it is not clear how these would have been enforced.[52] Yet the relative autonomy of inmates, and the reliability of almshouse charity (in that election to the charity was usually for life), was perceived by founders to be a problem. It was feared that almspeople might become complacent, ungrateful, or worst of all disorderly and 'undeserving'. Therefore founders attempted to forestall these outcomes via behavioural clauses for inmates, to ensure that almspeople would continue to conform to accepted patterns for the 'deserving' poor. Nevertheless, the day-to-day running of almshouses required more pragmatism and less proscription than founders typically tried to enforce; 'this tightening of the screws of social discipline was easier to inscribe on paper than in ... practice'.[53] The only practical sanctions for breaches of behavioural clauses were material admonishments or expulsion, but these were rarely applied for inappropriate behaviour and expulsion was 'very much a last resort'.[54] In Shrewsbury, an almsman in the Drapers' almshouses called Henry Graty was guilty of 'insolence' in 1740, but his punishment stopped short of expulsion. The Drapers' Company simply ordered that 'the money due to him [for a limited period] is to be given to the other poor of the Almshouses'.[55] An inmate of the Lady Margaret Hungerford almshouse in Corsham, Wiltshire, was expelled only after allowing her granddaughter (who was a convicted thief) to stay with her against the express injunction of the trustees, and then permitting the girl to use her almshouse as a brothel.[56]

Research on almshouses to date has concentrated on the provisions of individual institutions, architectural matters and finance, preferences that initially arose from physical survivals of buildings and founding documents.[57] The emphasis is shifting, however, and the launch in 2006 of the Family and Community History Historical Research Society's project on the English almshouse should ultimately yield answers to a range of alternative questions about the experience of almshouse life.

The occasionally comprehensive nature of this type of charity, where a beneficiary might have had most or all of their basic living expenses supplied, makes almshouses of particular interest since well-funded charities had the potential to remove people entirely and permanently from the purview of the parish relief system. This was tacitly acknowledged in the eighteenth century, when almshouses were differentiated from other charities by poor-law legislators. In the local acts of parliament obtained to establish houses of industry in towns like Shrewsbury and Chester, parochial charity money was allocated to the use of the new house unless it had already been directed to a particular use such as the maintenance of an almshouse and its inhabitants. Presumably the new Corporations [Corporations of the Poor not town corporations] wanted to leave well alone those charities that evidently reduced the net burden falling on ratepayers. But not all almshouses insulated residents from the need for additional income. Poorly funded houses, such as the Hospital of St Anthony and St Eloy in Cambridge, compelled beneficiaries to seek further help or income; the charity provided only brick cottages and inmates relied on the master of the hospital who sent out a basket to beg for relief for them and himself.[58]

It is worthwhile considering the relationship between these residential charities and parish poor relief because both were ostensibly directed at representatives of the deserving poor. Almshouses were typically reserved for the elderly and infirm who could no longer work and support themselves. Where the charity was directed at widows or spinsters, there should have been a considerable overlap in terms of life-cycle or circumstances between the people who benefited and those who qualified for relief under the poor law (although the two might still form two distinct subgroups of the elderly). The same was not true when almshouse foundations specified male inhabitants. Before the late eighteenth century, men were much less likely than women to be in receipt of regular parish relief and if they entered a workhouse, for example, it was often for just a short period before their death. Men who made a successful claim for regular parish help had often endured particularly difficult circumstances, perhaps caused by disability. Therefore although places in women's almshouses might all be taken by women who had never required any other form of charity or assistance, and although almswomen probably enjoyed higher status than parish widows, the two forms of welfare were catering to the same sort of need. In contrast, men's almshouses met a need not often recognised by parishes and potentially enabled beneficiaries to wind down gradually rather than dip in and out of destitution as their earning capacity fell away. Some charities specifically eased the transition from work to retirement. The twelve male inmates of the Holy Trinity hospital in Salisbury were permitted to continue their occupations so long as they did not cause annoyance to the other men.[59] In Bristol, residents of the Merchant's Hospital for poor, old or decayed sailors were not prevented from continuing as ship-keepers, or even from going abroad.[60] These charities were not necessarily picking up an intrinsically higher-status group than the people who eventually became paupers, but rather they might have picked people up at an earlier point in their life-cycle. This does not mean, though, that almshouses enjoyed a simple relationship with the poor law, or that the two resources were entirely separate. Helen Caffrey found in nineteenth-century Yorkshire that those receiving poor relief were technically ineligible for admission, but that a scanty pension might necessitate recourse to the parish after successful election to a charity. Some charities even preferred applicants to have access to a private income before admission, raising serious doubts about the depth of inmates' poverty.[61] Furthermore, in supporting independence almshouses may have offered a dignified way to enter a form of retirement, but they did not meet the profile of a modern nursing home. Residents are generally judged to have been 'favourably circumstanced compared with their peers in the workhouse' but they might potentially be compelled to transfer to a hospital or workhouse if their physical needs became extensive (and if charity trustees, or fellow almspeople, would not or could not attend to them).[62]

The distribution of almshouses across the country was inevitably patchy given the ad hoc nature of their establishment but, like other large-scale institutions, tended to cluster in towns. This was particularly noticeable in towns of ancient foundation, and towns that held relatively large populations in the sixteenth and seventeenth centuries (when founding almshouses was a favourite form of philanthropy with wealthy testators).

Almshouse provision could vary wildly between communities but, more importantly, table 3.1 illustrates two key points. First, the ratio of almshouse places to population could be 1:200 or higher; nine of the eighteen towns listed fall into this category, all of them among the

Table 3.1 *Almshouse places in eighteenth-century towns*

	No. of places/year	Pop./Year	Almshouse places: population
Traditional and county towns			
Cambridge	47+/post 1729	7,728/1728	1:164
Chester	12/post 1720	14,713/1774	1:1,226
Exeter	89/1700	c. 14,000/1700	1:157
Gloucester	82/1750	5,291/1743	1:64
Hull	185/1765	22,286/1792	1:120
Northampton	14/1736	5,136/1746	1:367
Nottingham	71/1720	26,861/1801	1:378
Oxford	22/1750	c. 9,000/1750	1:409
Salisbury	66/1700	6,976/1695	1:106
Shrewsbury	45/1755	8,141/1750	1:181
Winchester	42/1675	3,600/1676	1:86
Worcester	60+/post 1703	c. 10,300/1750	1:172
York	147/1740	10,800/1730	1:73
Rapidly expanding industrial and port towns			
Birmingham	42/1750	23,688/1750	1:564
Leeds	c. 75/post 1736	16,380/1771	1:218
Liverpool	c. 30/1724–50	34,407/1773	1:1,147
Manchester	48/1773	27,246/1773–4	1:568
Sheffield	c. 40/post 1722	96, 95/1736	1:242

Note: Counts of almshouse places and population estimates are drawn from numerous urban histories; the population estimate for Oxford is based on my own calculation.[63]

old, well-established centres in 1700. Second, towns experiencing rapid growth as a result of their incipient industrial or expansive port and trading activities were not quite so well provided since they 'lacked the longstanding traditions of civic charity found in incorporated towns' but could still retain an important almshouse presence.[64] The elderly poor even had a fair chance of admission to an almshouse in a vibrant industrial centre like Sheffield before populations expanded rapidly in the later eighteenth century; it is perhaps more surprising that Chester's ratio was so low than that Liverpool's was almost of the same order. Crucially, numerous towns possessed multiple almshouses for the poor, old and sick of both sexes; when age and wealth are taken into consideration, to reduce the pool of potential applicants, the coverage of residential charity improves further. Eighteenth-century urban populations were likely to comprise no more than ten percent over the age of sixty, for example. Ratios of almshouse places to just ten percent of urban populations are startling; for instance, approximately one in six of the elderly in Gloucester might have been accommodated. Prosperity might have removed even more people from the prospect of ever having to apply to an almshouse, but given the wide variation in the likely status of almshouses (and the consequent perception of their suitability among the elderly) it would be unwise to estimate how far the wealth of urban populations reduced the pool of potential applicants. Still, numerous urban communities could clearly rely on a substantial provision of residential charities to alleviate the poverty of the elderly and the burden borne by parishes.

Also, table 3.1 does not attempt to account for cathedral bedesmen and it is worth observing that any consideration of cathedral charity has been slight until recently.[65] Cathedrals founded in the 1540s offered almshouse places as a condition of their post-Reformation foundations. Cathedral almshouses typically provided six or eight places to old or disabled soldiers but by the eighteenth century this rule was not always applied. In the 1760s and 1770s silk weavers were elected to Canterbury Cathedral almshouse and labourers to Ely.[66] Places were always allocated to men, but it was usual for married men to bring their wives and families to live in the almshouse, and for the families to remain there after the men died; for example, in the seventeenth century Gloucester Cathedral housed almsmen and widows in a range of buildings which included parts of the former Abbey infirmary and cloister.[67] Places in cathedral almshouses lay in the gift of the crown and were classed as Church appointments. Cathedral almsplaces were not strictly limited to the inhabitants of the immediate town so it is not appropriate to include them in the table above but it remains unlikely that successful applicants would be drawn from outside the county where the cathedral lay.

In 1986 Thomson estimated that the proportion of all elderly women who received free housing and possibly cash in almshouses might have been as high as five percent or more, especially in old, established urban settlements.[68] This suggestion proved a useful counterweight to research that denigrated the role of almshouses by finding them totally unequal to the task of alleviating poverty; their numbers were either too small to be thought significant, or the quality of the accommodation or value of pensions rendered the benefits for almspeople slight.[69] Table 3.1 confirms Thomson's thesis (in that one in six, or sixteen percent of all elderly people in Gloucester might have found their way to workhouses) and so provides a more nuanced picture of the reach of almshouse charity. It remains necessary, however, to flesh out this table with detailed work on individual charities, to test the quality of provision. What follows is a close investigation of two Oxford almshouses, their inhabitants, and the nature of almsmen's poverty.

St Bartholomew's Hospital

St Bartholomew's Hospital was founded in the twelfth century as a leper hospital and became a city almshouse in the mid-sixteenth century. Oriel College had control of the hospital but the town claimed the right to nominate poor men to vacancies. Rules of 1367 stated that eight almsmen would be paid 9d weekly and 5s per year for clothes and staggeringly these payments remained substantially unchanged until the 1890s. There is no evidence that the clothing money had to be laid out on distinctive almsman's dress, although it was common for other foundations to insist on a dark or 'sober' academic-style gown and cap for almsmen, sometimes with a distinctive badge or clasp.[70] The hospital was situated one and a half miles east of the town towards modern Cowley and comprised a chapel and two buildings of two storeys for accommodation.[71]

Accounts that describe elections of almsmen by town councillors in the first half of the eighteenth century depict closely fought contests and intense interest in the fate of candidates. John Webb was elected by a great majority 'there being a vast meeting'[72] on 17 January 1733, as opposed to John Acres[73] elected by a majority of only one vote on 31 January 1726. Webb's election was such an occasion of joy to his parish of St Peter in East that a peal was rung on the church bells. Nevertheless, this enthusiasm for the almshouse on the part of town and parishes may not have been matched by prospective almsmen. In 1762, *Jackson's Oxford Journal* advertised two vacancies at St Bartholomew's Hospital and appealed for applications.[74] Only two candidates had so far been found, John Buckingham and Richard Uzzel. At least one more man eventually came forward, Charles Scudamore, as he and Buckingham were later elected.[75] This apparent apathy on the part of the St Bartholomew's men may reflect a lack of publicity in a form which would reach the poor men who might be both eligible and desirous of an almsman's place, but it probably indicates that, although places continued to be filled throughout the century, the men elected were not quite so enthusiastic about their receipt of charity as their wealthier fellow townspeople were about its high-profile allocation.[76] There are two very good reasons why this may have been the case.

First, and most importantly, St Bartholomew's men did not tend to live in the almshouse. In April 1734, an Oxford Methodist Benjamin Ingham attempted to visit the poor at St Bartholomew's but found no almsmen to talk to, despite four separate visits.[77] In 1773, an Oxford historian claimed that the men 'generally reside at Oxford'.[78] Divine service was performed in the chapel only occasionally during the summer months when the almsmen could walk there. It cannot be automatically assumed that the hospital buildings were ruinous. They had been destroyed in 1643 but Oriel college had rebuilt the hospital and chapel in 1649, and college accounts show payments in the first half of the eighteenth century for upkeep and repairs.[79] Nevertheless, almsmen may have found an additional incentive to reject the accommodation if it was considered low quality or onerous by eighteenth-century standards despite periodic payments for upkeep.[80]

Second, almsmen's pensions were so low they could not afford to live on them. The stipend of 9d per week would not have been sufficient to buy even the minimum amount of food required to live, so almsmen must have combined their receipt of charity with some other form of income simply in order to eat. Local contemporaries knew that the men were 'obliged to get their living some other way', hence their non-residence at the almshouse; they needed to live in the town to gain access to work or other forms of income.[81] Therefore St Bartholomew's Hospital in the mid-eighteenth century had comparatively little to offer; a regular but tiny stipend could not hope to provide the necessaries of life, while its houses may have been technically habitable but too distant from town for the penurious inmates.

Even so, the charity continued to function and, eventually, to fill its vacancies. Thirty men held one of the eight places during the mid-eighteenth century (defined here as 1740–70).[82] The men chosen were usually elderly but were not all necessarily inactive, which was probably just as well given their tiny pensions. It was described as 'an Hospital of invalids'[83] in 1716. Yet when Isaac Earl died in January 1726, he was missed at Christ Church where he waited and went on errands.[84] Also, although men may have been considered old, this did not necessarily lead to a rapid turnover of inmates. Exactly fifty percent of these men survived ten years or fewer after their election, but twenty-seven percent managed terms of ten to fifteen years and some survived as almsmen for much longer. Matthew Jones carried on for thirty years after his election in 1718. This shows that the life expectancy of St Bartholomew's almsmen was quite unlike that of male workhouse inmates, who tended to enter workhouses as a result of serious illness for a short period before their death.[85]

Finally, it is possible that the impact of election to St Bartholomew's was one of status rather than material advancement. Public elections to the charity ensured that almsmen remained a distinct group among the otherwise undifferentiated urban poor (particularly for the town council) and as such the men received attention and attractive perquisites. Almsmen took money on some special occasions, for example payments to them were listed among the canvassing expenses of parliamentary candidates for Oxfordshire during the elections of 1780 and 1784.[86] These cannot have mitigated the small pension, but were possibly welcome acknowledgments of 'office', however lowly.

Christ Church almshouse

Christ Church almshouse, by contrast, was a more munificent and sophisticated establishment. Its foundation was planned by Wolsey but it was formally founded by Henry VIII as a cathedral almshouse. Whereas most cathedrals founded in the 1540s typically had six or twelve bedesmen, Christ Church in Oxford and its sister institution at Trinity College in Cambridge had twenty-four. Financially, Christ Church inmates were much better off than St Bartholomew's men. The almsmen were given £6 each per year in quarterly instalments, meaning that they received approximately 2s 4d per week. This amount would have represented a small but sufficient income for a single person in the mid-eighteenth century, and the majority portion of a poor family's income (though not enough on its own for a family's survival). This was significant because Christ Church men were not necessarily old; their precise ages are not given but their responsibilities were those of men with young or growing families (circumstantially confirmed by the baptisms of almsmen's children in St Aldate's parish church).

Men wishing to become almsmen at Christ Church had to set out their case in a petition. This was typically endorsed by the cathedral dean before being forwarded to the crown (since places in cathedral almshouses were in the royal gift). Royal approval meant that petitioners were issued with a patent authorising their admission to the almshouse when a vacancy occurred. It was then a matter of waiting for a place to become free. Some died before their turn came while others became impatient waiting. John Skillern was nominated by patent in 1749, and wrote to Christ Church in 1756 wanting to know if he was next in line. John Rogers wrote to contradict reports that he had died. On average, men had to wait three years and three and a half months for a vacancy in the mid-eighteenth century.

Applicants had typically served in the armed forces, and therefore continued to fulfil the brief that cathedral charity should be directed to wounded or elderly ex-servicemen. Surviving petitions from men asking to be elected to almshouse places often detail the nature of their military service including lists of successive commanding officers and catalogues of wounds sustained. For example James Keats of All Saints parish in Oxford, a blacksmith in peacetime, gave details of his military history mentioning his service in Flanders where he went lame in his left leg as a result of fever and ague.[87] He allegedly spent time in St Bartholomew's and Guy's Hospitals, and in the London and Westminster Infirmaries but without being successfully cured. He also cited in his favour his three small children and his dead wife.

Ironically the issue of almshouse accommodation was almost as vexed at Christ Church as it was at St Bartholomew's. Not all cathedrals possessed almshouse accommodation, so in some ways Oxford men were fortunate that the two-storey almshouse in St Aldate's parish existed at all. The almshouse stood opposite Christ Church (and the buildings have now been incorporated into Pembroke College), but the premises were a problem, because at most they could accommodate only two-thirds of the men. Anthony Wood described the buildings of Christ Church hospital as incomplete in 1662,[88] and drawings dating from the early nineteenth century depict the almshouse partly in ruins.[89] One Oxford historian confirmed that no lodging was ever provided for eight of the men and that parts of the building were let at times for use as a timber yard.[90] By the nineteenth century, men who could not live in the almshouse were termed 'out-pensioners'.[91] Even so, unlike St Bartholomew's, accommodation was jealously guarded by those who secured it. In the early nineteenth century Christ Church decided to demolish the building but met resistance from the occupants. Almsmen eventually had to be given £10 per year more in lieu of accommodation in 1868 when the building was transferred to other uses.[92]

Pressure on living space may have been heightened by the presence of the young families of almsmen who lived with him and who may have stayed on after his death. Elizabeth Crosier was described as a lodger in Christ Church almshouse when she married in 1761. Yet the only other Crosier known to have been living there in the eighteenth century had been John Crosier who had been buried in 1745. William Green must have completely filled his allotted living space, as his wife gave birth to four children in the almshouse in the 1760s and 1770s. The tensions of semi-communal living occasionally became too much. In 1745, Elizabeth Brickland was found guilty of swearing by the Oxford town quarter sessions on the evidence of Matthias Skillem. Brickland's husband Thomas had been a Christ Church man since 1720 and Skillem since 1742. Thomas Brickland must have attempted retribution as by October 1745, Skillem had bound him over to keep the peace.[93] Nonetheless, Christ Church, in common with other almshouses, rarely issued punishments. One expulsion of 1781 was precipitated only by the almsman in question being convicted of a felony.[94]

Men did not always come from Oxford, in that people from outside the city occasionally petitioned for a place; during the mid-eighteenth century, the majority of evidence points to men applying from Oxford, with one or two coming from Chipping Norton or elsewhere in the county. As Christ Church almsmen were younger than those in St Bartholomew's, they predictably enjoyed a longer tenure. Of the 129 men admitted between 1701 and 1800, only around seventeen percent enjoyed their place for ten years or less, while fully thirty-two percent of men admitted 1751–1800 remained for twenty-six years or more, including John Blundell's tenacious fifty-one years.[95]

Christ Church therefore presents a picture of a substantially different sort of charity to St Bartholomew's. It supplied some accommodation for beneficiaries, paid a much larger stipend, and was apparently more attractive to applicants (given that many successful petitioners had to wait for a vacancy before their admission); however, inmates at Christ Church did have more responsibilities, and higher outgoings, if they had young families.

Almshouse charity and poor relief

A comparison of these two groups of male almsmen with the identities of parish paupers in Oxford over the period 1740–70 reveals that the two cohorts experienced quite different levels of exposure to parish relief. St Bartholomew's men were found to retain close connections with their parishes of settlement while Christ Chuch men operated independently of parishes.

Fourteen of the thirty St Bartholomew's men received identifiable relief from parishes. Five were relieved even before they became almsmen but thirteen also took parish relief after their election to the charity.[96] Furthermore, as only half of the town's population were covered by surviving parish accounts, the number of St Bartholomew's men found to be paupers can be doubled to estimate the total number of almsmen who also took some relief. This suggests that St Bartholomew's were paupers to a man. Their tiny stipend (and the effective if not absolute barriers to almshouse occupation) certainly left them more in need of relief than almsmen elsewhere, but it is also worth suggesting that this was the kind of charity paupers were more able to exploit.

Information from parish accounts can help to clarify almsmen's accommodation. Two of the men had rents paid by their parish after they became almsmen. For example Thomas Corbett was elected in October 1758 and St Mary Magdalen parish paid for some of his lodging during 1763–66, meeting a full year's rent in 1765 of £1 6s. A further four of the pauper almsmen spent some time in a workhouse after their election. Michael Heathfield was buried from Cross's workhouse in 1752, and parish funds paid to carry Martin Wiggins to the same establishment in 1757. St Michael's parish paid £9 to keep Matthew Winkle in Cross's workhouse from 1754 until the year of his death in 1756.[97] Only one man is known to have spent any time at all at the almshouse. On 20 October 1752, St Peter le Bailey recorded 1s to bring Benjamin Showell from 'Batelmas', probably to bring his body from the almshouse to the parish to be buried.[98]

Three or four pauper almsmen came to receive a parish pension. Ben Showell received 9d per week for the year 1750, which was reduced to 6d for most of 1751. James Bolt received 1s rising to 1s 6d in 1758 up to his death in October and Martin Smith took 6d per week in 1757 which was raised to 1s three-quarters of the way through 1759. It may have been that the St Bartholomew's pension reduced the amount that parishes had to pay pauper almsmen. An average pension in Oxford[99] came to around 1s 9d but these three almsmen received consistently less than this. Barker-Read observed that pensioners receiving less than a shilling in Kent had resources aside from the parish while those receiving over two shillings had unusual needs,[100] and this assessment is borne out by St Bartholomew's men. Robert Clark was given a high pension of 2s 6d per week by St Peter in East because he had broken his leg and required nursing. After his recovery he took only 1s per week. Parishes also bought clothing for at least seven of the men, tending to buy shirts rather than external clothing.

Of the five men who became paupers before they became almsmen, John Carpenter, Robert Warren and Matthew Winkle had families who required substantial help. All three had children born at the expense of the parish. By contrast, Martin Wiggins combined receiving relief with working for the parish prior to his election. He was paid to work at the St Mary Magdalen workhouse in 1747. Most interesting is the way the St Bartholomew almsmen could all benefit from parish disbursements when a new man was elected. Warren had 9s 4d paid on his behalf by St Michael's for treating the almsmen on his election in November 1764 and a similar sum had been paid by St Peter le Bailey when Ben Showell was admitted as an almsman in 1740. It seems that the town councillors' excitement at almsmen's elections was infectious and inspired parishes to pay up for celebratory traditions (not just for material necessities).

As Christ Church almsmen were younger than those in St Bartholomew's and were also more likely to come from outside Oxford, one would expect that a comparison with paupers' names would reveal fewer overlaps. This was certainly the case. Only three of the seventy almsmen admitted 1740–70 can definitely be identified among town paupers and their level of need was markedly less pronounced than that of St Bartholomew's men.[101] Another four almsmen might well have been paupers given the identical occurrence of first names and relatively unusual surnames, but their status cannot be confirmed. This means that a maximum of ten percent of Christ Church almsmen may possibly have been paupers within the parishes with accounts, or that at most around twenty percent may have been paupers from the town as a whole. Obviously, with their higher stipend and a better chance of useable accommodation, Christ Church almsmen had less need of parish help. Furthermore, Christ Church paupers were not tightly enmeshed in parish relief systems. St Martin's parish paid Ralph Pettit's rent in 1730, but the £1 disbursed to him in 1755 was matched by a receipt in the accounts for the same amount (in other words, St Martin's loaned him the money until his quarterly pension payment was made). Edward Maiden was relieved by St Mary Magdalen only in 1766 and then received a total of just 15s. He was made seven payments from November 1766 to January 1767 in illness, but 7s of his parish money was to pay for a 'Patern', or in other words, to apply for his almsman's patent (which was issued in the same year).

Even so, the case of Henry Huntingdon illustrates that contact between almsmen and parishes was not necessarily benign, as he was possibly a victim of the contemporary practice of selling pensions; if people in receipt of some regular benefit like an almshouse pension or friendly-society payment needed to approach a parish for additional relief, the parish might insist on receiving the pension or payment to offset its costs.[102] In his satirical poem of 1740, John Woodman was heavily critical of the system that allowed Chelsea hospital pensioners to sell their pensions (also worth £6 per year at this time). At Chelsea, pensions could be paid a year or more in advance. The money was allegedly squandered in a fraction of the time it was supposed to last, leaving pensioners destitute as 'there is not the one Half of them who are inclined to be careful or frugal'.[103] Creditors would supply money until the pension was due and then demand all of this income in repayment. Woodman deplored the fact that from the pensions that they should have received from the hospital, 'their overseers and others may get above £6000 a year'.[104]

On 20 April 1756, St Mary Magdalen paid 2s 6d to have Hunting-don's pension made over to them. They were pursuing an ongoing policy of caution with this man. In 1755, he had apparently run away from his responsibilities (comprising a pregnant wife), whereon the parish had paid 17s 6d to follow him to Abingdon, apprehend him and commit him to one of Oxford's gaols.[105] It should be noted, however, that there were no entries on the credit side of overseers' accounts during Huntingdon's life to suggest that the pension was actually received; the legal right to requisition his pension was perhaps held over him to ensure his good behaviour, or at least his continued presence in Oxford.[106]

Any attempts to generalise about almshouses and the provision for the poor must be qualified by both the terms of their foundation and subse-quent evidence of their operation. Barker-Read pointed out some of the problems that could emerge in the ongoing administration of almshouse charities; after 1726, the almshouses in Tonbridge in Kent began to be let for rent.[107] Where no money was left for maintenance, houses could fall into disrepair and disuse, and non-residence from a variety of causes seems to have been a problem in Oxford. Yet the availability of almshouse places nationwide may have had a significant impact on the circumstances of poor people, particularly those on the margins of parochial relief. A munificent charity could remove the need to apply for any relief while a low-income charity may have compelled recipients to make other arrangements. Thus, where a living pension was provided, almshouse places formed a part of the total welfare safety net that inter-sected between independence and reliance; where funds were slight, they effectively compelled inmates to take small jobs or petition for regular relief. Ultimately, the relationship between almshouse charities and parish relief can be characterised only as varied, with evidence from different towns and at different times pointing in different directions. In 1738 the parish of St John in Chester gave one of its paupers, Thomas Haddock, a bed and some linen from the workhouse stock when he went into one of the city almshouses;[108] in contrast, in 1788 the guardians of the Shrewsbury house of industry agreed that Widow Whitefoot, in the St Mary or Drapers' almshouses, must have her pay stopped and come into the house if she could not do without.[109] Parishes and charities might work together or in opposition; the varied and flexible nature of the relationship implies that there was some scope for the poor to negotiate their own welfare bargains.[110] How else could we explain the decision of parishes to requisition some charity pensions but not others?

Non-residential charity from municipal endowments 1740–70

If work on substantial, residential charities has been patchy, research on more ephemeral handouts is positively scarce. The assumption has been that the total quantity of charity available was so inadequate that there could be little point in focusing on any one fund that conferred intermittent, uncertain benefits. In other words the quality of uncertainty for recipients, which was so appealing to eighteenth-century commentators, has made charity ostensibly unrewarding as a focus for study by historians. I think that this unwillingness to engage with charity on the part of welfare historians has been a mistake. The range of possible benefits and the numerous different ways in which charity was administered requires careful handling but this does not make them impossible to study.

A rich supply of accounts for municipal charities in Oxford survive for the mid-eighteenth century, disbursing sums from a few shillings to over five pounds per year. The corporation of Oxford was responsible for administering and disbursing a number of charities until the Municipal Corporations Act of 1835. The town was apparently conscientious in distributing and recording charity payments. Of the fifteen municipal charities operating in the eighteenth century,[111] the disbursements of thirteen were meticulously recorded.[112]

Four of these, Harris's, Reeves's, Toldervey's and Wall's benefactions, yielded long-term, dependable benefits in the form of pensions.[113] Toldervey's provided 30s per year for four poor widows, while Reeves's supplied £2 per year to six poor people from St Thomas's parish. Harris's and Wall's provided twenty-eight pensions between them, worth £4 per year each. The remaining nine charities paid one-off cash disbursements ranging between 10s and £5. They did not all make payments continuously throughout the century. Rowney's, Sweet's and Herbert's charities were paid from the interest which accrued on money given to the corporation for the purposes of building a new town hall. When the money was eventually needed to meet the costs of the new town hall, which was begun in 1751, no more money was available for disbursement. Boyle's charity may have been disbursed throughout the period but evidence survives only from 1751 onwards. Only Hawkins's, Whorwood's, Seyman's and Harris's dole charities were disbursed and recorded continuously, each benefiting two poor people per year.

The corporation book of elections to charities reveals 953 allocations of charity money relevant to the period 1740–70. These included the granting of pensions to people before 1740 who did not die until that year or later. Recipients are named for each of the thirteen charities and often it appears that the same person received two or more charitable disbursements; approximately 494 people shared the available charities.[114] When the charity recipients were compared with town paupers, 50 people emerged who probably had some connections with paupers (where such a connection was supported by additional information). Of these, 24 appeared to be receiving income at some time from both sources at the same time. As with calculations for almsmen among paupers, parishes with surviving accounts contained around half of the population of Oxford, requiring the number of identifiable paupers to be doubled to estimate the total diffusion of paupers throughout the cohort of charity recipients. This calculation indicates that 100 or twenty percent of people on town charity were also paupers at some time, and that 48 or ten percent of town-charity recipients were taking some parish relief in the same years when they received charity. If the probable connections are examined in terms of the numbers of charity allocations rather than the numbers of people involved, very similar results are reached, with some-time paupers taking a little over twenty percent of all charity allocations. Finally, it is important to recognise that fifty percent of the charities available were reserved for men, whereas the typical poor-relief recipient was an elderly woman, necessarily placing a limitation on the evident connections. This is not to discount the possibility that men might have taken charities and subsequently their widows could have received relief, but it would require family reconstitution to establish this kind of link.

The maximum potential overlap between paupers and charity recipients, denoted here as 'possible',[115] was more than twice as high. If the 126 possible paupers are doubled to find a total possible overlap for the town, it may have been that up to half of charity recipients were paupers at some time. An examination of the probables and possibles, broken down by the charities they received, can illuminate some of the relationships between paupers and charity. Parish poor were apparently able to secure some charities more readily than others. Some charities seem to have been virtually denied to some-time paupers. Whorwood's charity, for example, featured a one-off payment of £5 to maidservants, preferably the daughters of freemen, who had been in the same service for seven years. Therefore it would have been unlikely that the same woman would appear as a pauper in one of the seven years prior to eligibility for the charity. Yet it is striking that none of those servants were children in pauper families or became paupers some time after they received the money. Perhaps the time span of this study is too short to reveal overlaps between paupers and Whorwood's recipients; women in secure employment would not need relief until much later in their lives. Alternatively, Whorwood's charity was distributed to a slightly higher echelon among the Oxford poor, who rarely needed to resort to the parish. It is unlikely that the lack of additional information was solely to blame for

Table 3.2 *Charity disbursements to paupers*

Charity	Amount paid per person per year	No. of disburse- ments 1740–70	Disburse- ments to probable paupers (possible paupers)	% of charity disbursements taken by probable paupers (possible paupers)
Bogan	£5	31	6 (7)	19.4 (22.6)
Boyle	£1 10s	160	12 (36)	7.5 (22.5)
Harris #1 (pension)	£4	15	3 (5)	20.0 (33.3)
Harris #2 (dole)	£4	66	21 (22)	31.2 (33.3)
Hawkins	£4	63	11 (17)	17.5 (27.0)
Herbert	10s	56	5 (16)	8.9 (28.6)
Reeves[a]	£2	20	0 (0)	0 (00.0)
Rowney	10s	217	11 (59)	5.1 (27.2)
Seyman	£2 10s	62	8 (19)	12.9 (30.6)
Sweet	£1	107	8 (28)	7.5 (26.2)
Toldervey	£1 10s	19	3 (5)	15.8 (26.3)
Wall	£4	74	8 (14)	10.8 (18.9)
Whorwood	£5	63	0 (8)	0 (12.7)
Total		953	96 (236)	10.1 (23.8)

Source: ORO, Oxford City Archives, Q.4.9. Elections to charities 1715–1834.
Note: [a] Reeves's charity was specific to St Thomas's parish (with no surviving overseers' accounts), so it was inevitable that none of the paupers from other parishes would appear receiving this money.

the minimal overlaps with paupers, since even the possible overlaps with Whorwood's were among the fewest achieved for any of the charities.

The disbursements of Toldervey's pension to paupers deserves some comment. This charity was largely confined to three of the parishes possessing accounts namely, St Peter in East, St Mary Magdalen and St Michael. It was also specifically for widows and yielded a small stipend of £1 10s per year. Yet only three paupers emerged as recipients, and the picture is not vastly improved for paupers if the possibles are also included. If this charity was substantially cornered by poor women other than paupers, it proves that competition could exclude paupers from the charities most ideally suited to their stereotype. The pension charities of Toldervey, Wall and Harris had relatively low visible uptakes by probable paupers but were not necessarily the charities that provided least access to paupers. Sweet, Boyle and Herbert all display probable uptakes of under ten percent. The uptake of Toldervey's money by paupers was apparently in strict contrast with Harris's dole charity. This also named the parishioners of St Michael and St Peter in East as particular beneficiaries and probable paupers were able to secure twenty-one or over thirty percent of disbursements. Most telling is Hawkins's charity; this was supposed to be reserved for the non-parish poor, yet even here seventeen percent of disbursements went to paupers.

The twenty pensions provided by Wall's charity can be traced from person to person. Some thirty-three recipients both began to receive their pension and then died in the period 1740–70, and the brevity of their tenure compares very unfavourably with the experiences of either St Bartholomew's or Christ Church men. Only half of St Bartholomew's men died after ten years, but eighty-two percent of Wall's pensioners died within a decade.

The amounts received from charity by individuals can be tied up with parish payments to assess annual income based on the two sources. Twelve paupers took charity pensions, and a further twelve took one-off cash payments. As the town pension charities were granted for life, it is not surprising that connections with paupers are most discernible at the end of their lives. Two-thirds of paupers who were also charity pensioners died on the parish. For half of the people identified, the scale of the charity offered by the town was often broadly comparable with the scale of relief being paid; there was a good chance that if a pauper was receiving a town pension, the parish was paying one also. Six of these twelve people received parish pensions in the same years they received charity pensions and amassed some relatively tidy sums. Thomas Horn and William Nash could certainly have lived on the £7 to £9 they took in the years before their deaths. Nash's wife was living at this time as she continued to be a parish pensioner after his death, so this income was being used towards the support of two people.

The premise that individual paupers could construct a comparatively good income from their two pensions relies on their being allowed to receive the charity money. As with almshouse pensions, beneficiaries could be compelled to sign away their right to charity but evidence for confiscation was rare; there is only one example from this analysis. William Dye was a parishioner of St Peter in East and started to receive a town pension charity of £4 per year in 1751. He apparently enjoyed the fruits of this for twelve years until he required parish relief. On 5 December 1763, the parish paid 'Mr Bradley for writing Dye's resignation of his pay from ye City' so that a historian might presume that Dye took no charity and parish money simultaneously;[116] however, the parish accounts do not feature £4 or a part of £4 received from the town representing Dye's pension. It may be that (as with the case of almsman Henry Huntingdon, cited above) the parish prepared the assignment with a view to enforcing it only if Dye became a particularly heavy burden.

Chronologically, people applied successfully for town charity rather earlier than they became regular paupers. Town pensions slightly pre-dated parish pensions. Five of the six double pensioners received the town money first, while the sixth, Thomas Horn, came from St Peter in East, which has no overseers' accounts for the years 1752–57 so the start of his pension cannot be determined. The fact that they were not dependent paupers when they first received the charity may have worked in their favour; if any electors had an interest in excluding the parish poor, they could not easily have predicted the likelihood of future pauperism. Charity recipients who showed themselves unworthy after their election could be a problem. They may have troubled or annoyed those administering the charity, but were unlikely to be turned out or denied the charity in Oxford. In 1729, it was complained in council that if Alderman Harris's pensioners neglected their duty by failing to attend church or wear the designated clothing their pension should be suspended, but no further references were made to these sanctions.[117] The fact that all town pensioners appear to have received the money until their deaths during 1740-70 demonstrates the security of a successful election to charity.

The recipients of one-off charity payments formed a slightly different group. Only three of them were definitely parish pensioners. Also, their average payments per year from the parish were much lower. These people took only £1 7s 7d per year as opposed to the pensioners' £2 3s 11d. Again this suggests that the level of relief they received from charity was on the same scale as their parish relief; more extraordinary than regular. Thomas 'Farmer' Mason received only cash doles and a shirt during these years and Widow Jane Lines merely had her land tax paid by the parish. Ultimately, the differences between pensioners and occasional charity recipients are small. Pauper recipients of Oxford town charities fell into two subsets, those in need of regular parish relief and those needing occasional help, and the parish-dependent group was smaller. This examination proves that the members of the labouring poor who were parish paupers did have access to charity funds, if not in proportion to their numbers, and individuals pieced together satisfactory incomes from multiple sources. All charities seem to have embraced people from most levels of poverty, but paupers were more able to saturate some than others. Toldervey's charity demonstrates that the charities most open to paupers cannot necessarily be predicted from the terms of endowments.

Non-residential charity from parish endowments 1740–70

Contemporary commentators often had as jaundiced a view of parish-run charities as they did of parish relief. One writer cited only two explanations to account for the disappearance of charity money; the cash 'has been lost, or embezzled by the Parish Officers some time ago'.[118] Writers justified publishing the accounts of parish charities by observing that loss or corruption were more likely where the details of endowed charities were not widely known.[119] Twentieth-century historians (Jordan aside) have been all too ready to accept this judgement. A modern, more generous interpretation has been offered by Broad, who has rightly sought to adjust perceptions; 'Though some were undoubtedly inefficiently or corruptly used, far more were not only diligently maintained but flexibly applied to suit changing needs.'[120] It is high time that these general assumptions be put to the test, and particularly that a more sensitive investigation of the operations of parish charities be undertaken.

Very little research of this sort has been attempted, and none pertains to urban charity in the period 1723–82. In Whitkirk, Yorkshire, Richard Adair calculated that the one hundred recipients of the Lady Dole and Rush Dole in 1683 overlapped substantially with the parish pauper population; sixty were parish pensioners in the same year that they received the charity and another fourteen were pensioners before or after 1683.[121] This seems a high uptake of charity compared with the Oxford town examples, particularly as these connections were with parish pensioners, or people in need of regular relief, and exclude connections with those receiving only extraordinary relief. Sam Barrett has concluded from his study of kinship connectedness in West Riding townships 1780–1820 that the proportion of people able to access rate-based relief and other charity was always limited, comprising at most forty-five percent of paupers (and usually a lesser proportion).[122] Taking her evidence from the nineteenth century, Jean Robin found in mid nineteeth-century Colyton that between twenty-six and twenty-eight percent of all households listed in the 1861 census took relief from both the poor law *and* the town's charity feoffees at some time in the period 1851–81. Recipients of poor relief were barred from receiving help from the feoffees for three months, so there was a measure of explicit policing of access to the two welfare streams, but, these measures notwithstanding, fully a quarter of all inhabitants were able to utilise both resources; however, the two were not dispensing to an equal value since the expenditure of the poor law guardians 'far exceeded that of the feoffees'.[123] Like many eighteenth-century parish charities the value of the endowed charity was relatively small in purely monetary terms,

Table 3.3 *Oxford paupers and sundry parish charities*

Charity	Parish	No. of disbursements 1740–70	Recipients who were paupers in the same year they received the charity	Recipients who were paupers in a different year
Sambach (worth 1 guinea p.a. shared by all recipients)	St Peter le Bailey	70	28	24
Faulkner (by 1770s worth 3s 6d each p.a.)	St Michael	29	2	4
Snowe (worth £4 p.a. shared by all recipients)	St Michael	254	39	111
Blackford (worth 12 guineas shared by all recipients)	St Peter in East	96	10	19
Hody (worth 16–18s each in the 1760s)	St Mary Magdalen	56	12	20
Hody (a gown or a coat)	St Mary Magdalen	176	33	92
Hody (paid £2 to teach 2 girls to sew)	St Mary Magdalen	34	2	2
Hody (up to £10 to apprentice 1 poor boy)	St Mary Magdalen	15	2	3
Morris (up to £10 to apprentice 1 poor boy)	St Mary Magdalen	26	5	3

but was not administered in such a way as to permanently exclude the parish poor.

Parish charities in Oxford were more numerous than town funds, but evidence of their distribution is more spotty. Four parishes that possess overseers' accounts also have surviving charity accounts, which relate to ten different benefactions. Where payments totalled only a few shillings per person per year, as was the case with nine of the charities, it seemed more sensible to concentrate on the extent of pauper uptake only rather than look at the charities in terms of individuals' incomes; yet in St Mary Magdalen, Poole's charity disbursed £1 per person per year as a pension. For this charity the receipts of individual paupers have been traced, as with the town charities, to establish the kind of connections that occurred.

The nine non-recurrent charities offered a variety of benefits to men and women, adults and children. Faulkner's charity from a will of 1609 provided money to the poor fatherless children of three parishes, one of which was Oxford St Michael. Ann Sambach left a charitable estate by a will of 1657 that was to benefit apprentices and widows, again divided between three parishes. St Peter le Bailey received one-sixth of the income each year to relieve poor widows. Snowe's, Blackford's and Hody's money went to assist poor householders in St Michael, St Peter in East and St Mary Magdalen respectively, but only Hody's money was distributed in most years 1740–70. Snowe's money stopped after 1747 and was not distributed again until 1782, while Blackford's charity was a one-off payment in 1768. Hody's charity also comprised funds for clothing old men and women, teaching two poor girls to sew and apprenticing poor boys. Finally, Morris's charity was devoted to apprenticing poor boys.

The proportions of paupers qualifying for each charity are partly connected to the terms placed on distributions by benefactors. Blackford's 12 guineas had upper and lower limits on the amounts people could receive; no person was to have less than 2s 6d and no family more than 5s. The money was evidently spread very thinly throughout the parish and may have benefited some relatively well-off families. Snowe's money was similar in that it was spread between tens of families rather than a few, but whether this was in accordance with the terms of the will is not known. Sixty percent of Snowe's recipients were paupers at some time as opposed to just thirty percent of Blackford's. Faulkner's, Morris's and the children's portions of Hody's charities had the lowest visible uptake by paupers. This is quite surprising, particularly in the case of Faulkner's where the beneficiaries, fatherless children, were one of the classic life-cycle groups relieved by the parish. These comparisons may have been hampered by a lack of children's first names in overseers' accounts. Sambach's and the clothing portion of Hody's charity were the most likely to be available to paupers and again this may have been a result of the groups of people supposed to benefit (widows and the elderly).

Despite the potential importance of donors' wishes, distributors of charities did not always adhere to the specifications of their wills. All of the branches of Hody's charity were taken up by some people in the same years that they received parish relief, but the will intended the clothing and money for poor householders to go to poor people 'that do not receive Alms of the parish'.[124] This intention should not have faded from the memories of parish officers as the will was proved as late as 1736 and a copy was written out in a parish ledger. It was not even the case that people became paupers after the charity was allocated. Widow Warburton was a typically dependent pauper widow during 1757 to 1765, yet in 1766 she was still given Hody's cash charity.

The fact that paupers had access to funds which were technically denied to them is fairly significant. Historians have been compelled to assume that of all the wishes laid out by testators, those excluding paupers would probably have been observed (although in 1822 the Charity Commissioners were notably concerned when they discovered charities overlooking the instructions of testators, demonstrating that compliance was not universal).[125] Yet if it was commonplace for this rule to be ignored by other charities and in other places, the position of charity in paupers' economies of makeshifts may have been more prominent than has been previously thought. Even if this laxity was more characteristic of parish-controlled rather than trustee-run charities, paupers' opportunities for charity income would have been better than supposed.

John Poole's pension charity (established by his will of 1643) gave three pensions of £1 each to the parish of St Mary Magdalen; by the mid-eighteenth century the estate could afford to pay fourteen pensions of this sum. The charity did not set out to exclude parish poor and a full twenty-one out of fifty-nine pensioners for the period 1740–70 can be identified as paupers in the same years that they were charity recipients. Fifty-four percent of Poole's pensioners enjoyed their pension for only ten years or less, putting them on a par with St Bartholomew's men. Even so, eight percent exhibited considerable longevity and took their pensions for twenty-six years or more.

In the case of Poole's charity, though, the number of years spent receiving the charity did not automatically equate with life-expectancy after election. Most pensions still ended when recipients died but others were concluded differently. Widow Brewman disqualified herself from the pension list by remarrying to St Giles's parish. Widow Jarvis's pension stopped when she went 'on the parish'. This was in 1769 and as the parish had countenanced paupers receiving Poole's pension before this, the increased stringency may be attributable to the town's imminent union for poor-relief purposes. Perhaps when relief meant entry to the workhouse of the incorporated parishes, the poor were faced with an either/or situation over charity and relief that had not pertained before.

The paupers among Poole's pensioners received £2 1s 11.5d on average per year from overseers, less than paupers on town charity pensions; eight of the twenty-one people who overlap are known to have been parish pensioners in some of the same years that they were charity recipients. Poole's charity was only worth £1 per year, ten shillings below the smallest town charity pension, so recipients would certainly have needed income from other sources.

Unfortunately it is difficult to say whether Poole's pensions pre-dated relief in the same way that town charities did. Widow Bryan must have used the charity to defray her living costs in the period 1743–45 when she was relying on the parish for her rent only, but must have been earning or receiving income from some third source. Twenty years later the income from the charity was lower both in real terms and proportionately, while the parish loomed much larger (see appendix 3.1). Private charity may have assumed most significance for people in the transitional period between independence or full employment and reliance on the parish. Its impact would have been greatest in the period when income from earnings would have been declining or fragmenting and when relief remained 'extraordinary'. Unfortunately issues with the sources make it difficult to establish how representative Bryan was.

This chapter has focused on the incomes from charities where disbursements to individual beneficiaries are recoverable, and chronologically comparable to lists of parish paupers. Nonetheless, numerous charities survived throughout the eighteenth century which do not happen to leave disbursement lists, but which were clearly operational at the time of the Charity Commission report on the city of Oxford in 1822. Therefore it is technically possible to assess the total sum of money available in Oxford from endowed charity in any one year. The full list of operative charities suggests that £587 was distributed to the poor in cash, bread, clothing, apprenticeship premiums or loans in 1750, accounting for approximately 1s 4d for every man, woman and child in the city.[126] A comparison of this figure with the average *per capita* spending on poor relief surveyed in chapter one, five and a half shillings per person in 1776, shows that endowed charity amounted to approximately one quarter of poor-relief spending. This is a vitally important point, given Slack's estimation that endowed charity was worth perhaps a third of the amount spent on poor relief around 1700 (and implications from subsequent historians that the relative place of charity declined rapidly after this date). In Oxford and comparable towns the significance of charity monies was declining, but it still enjoyed an important position in the welfare spectrum in that it demonstrably accounted for at least a fifth of formal welfare disbursements during the mid-eighteenth century.

Even so, any enthusiasm about the extent of charity that was technically available must be tempered by the knowledge that individual attempts to live on a combined income from these sources were rarely successful. People who became paupers had variable success in garnering this welfare. A few individuals were able to gather incomes or other benefits from three or four known sources per year (see appendix 3.1 'Paupers receiving two or more charities'). It is clear that even with four incomes, the total received could be quite low. Widow Margaret West was the only person who definitely took money from four sources in the same year but the resulting £3 18s was probably insufficient on its own for a living. Widow Carpenter took the most money and a gown in 1764. In some ways the brevity of this list is sobering. When all known sources of charity are interleaved just thirteen people can be seen creatively combining parish relief, town charity and parish charity to construct an annual income. This is the economy of makeshifts in action, but challenges any easy generalisations about the incorporation of charity into the material economy of makeshifts, particularly for the parish poor. Doubtless this is in part attributable to the fiendish difficulty of identifying communities with full records of charity disbursements, but until an alternative picture is drawn the experiences of the Oxford poor must surely stand as testimony to the partial, halting and unreliable nature of living on these combined welfare resources.

Conclusion

Private charities typically catered for subsections of the poor more or less out of kilter with the typical parish definition of the deserving poor. A charity like Toldervey's for widows accorded fairly well with parochial intentions but both of the Oxford almshouses diverged in that they catered for men with long-term welfare requirements. The facilities provided by the different charities varied widely (in some cases, against the specific intentions of benefactors). In the case of the two almshouses the provision of accommodation and the level of their cash payments generated very different experiences of charity for their beneficiaries. St Bartholomew's men were forced to find additional support, eventually from their parishes, and some even ended their lives in workhouses. Christ Church men were able to get by on charity alone or by other means without turning to their parishes. Thus, where a living pension and accommodation were provided, almshouse places formed a part of the total welfare safety-net which intersected between independence for poor households and their reliance on parochial relief. The coverage of almshouse places must clearly take account of both the quantity and quality of provision. Nonetheless, Christ Church on its own provided twenty-four pensions that could cater for the equivalent of one percent of the eligible male population.[127] This seems paltry until considered alongside the statistic, quoted at the start of the chapter, that between four and eight percent of urban populations were entirely dependent upon poor relief. Christ Church almshouse's contribution to welfare in Oxford was therefore significant in the total welfare context even though numbers of beneficiaries and the percentage of the population concerned were small. The availability of high-quality almshouse places nationwide may have had a significant impact on the options open to poor people, particularly those on the margins of parochial relief. The picture is complicated by the fact that parish responses to almshouses and their inmates were varied. The evidence from Oxford suggests that strict divisions between charity recipients and parish paupers were not often threatened and were even less often enforced. Parishes and charities might work together or in opposition but the impact of all residential charities on poor households was still much greater than historians have appreciated to date.

People took up charity at all different stages of pauperism, but it is likely that most people began to receive it in a period between the two poles of full employment and parish dependency. Town charity pensioners and St Bartholomew's almsmen took the bulk of their poor relief after their election to charity. Those in workhouses were not necessarily excluded; however, their presence is more noticeable among St Bartholomew's men than beneficiaries of other, more munificent private charities.

Local knowledge of what was available enabled paupers to enter into negotiations for non-residential charity. Thereafter, their personal powers of persuasion or attributes which recommended them for generosity sifted the group of potential claimants into the group of actual recipients. The evidence available for Oxford demonstrates that around ten percent of town charity disbursements went to people who received parish relief at the same time. It is sometimes possible to account for paupers' success in receiving a charity by reference to the benefactor's intentions, but the same information cannot be used to guess the probability of paupers receiving the money since they could receive charity even when the terms of endowments tried to exclude them. Only rare individuals among the urban poor pieced together a sufficiency or the majority of their living from a combination of relief and charity.

Notes

1 Elements of this chapter were first published in my article 'Almshouse *versus* workhouse: residential welfare in eighteenth-century Oxford', *Family and Community History* 7: 1 (2004). I am grateful to the editor for permission to reproduce them here.

2 J. Innes, 'The "mixed economy of welfare" in early modern England: assessments of the options from Hale to Malthus (c. 1683–1803)', in M. Daunton (ed.), *Charity, Self-interest and Welfare in the English Past* (London, 1996), p. 155.

3 B. Croxson, 'The public and private faces of 18th century London dispensary charity', *Medical History* 41 (1997).

4 B. Howson, *Houses of Noble Poverty* (Sunbury, 1993), p. 110–11.

5 In relation to medical history for example see R. Porter, 'The gift relation: philanthropy and provincial hospitals in eighteenth-century England', in L. Granshaw and R. Porter (eds), *The Hospital in History* (London, 1989) and S. Cavallo, 'The motivations of benefactors: an overview of approaches to the study of charity', in J. Barry and C. Jones (eds), *Medicine and Charity Before the Welfare State* (London, 1991).

6 *Gentleman's Magazine* 9 (1739), 233.

7 D. Andrew, '*Noblesse oblige*: female charity in an age of sentiment', in J. Brewer and S. Staves (eds), *Early Modern Conceptions of Property* (London, 1995), p. 277.

8 Innes, 'Mixed economy of welfare', p. 157.

9 J. Innes, 'The state and the poor: eighteenth-century England in European perspective', in J. Brewer and E. Hellmuth (eds), *Rethinking Leviathan: The Eighteenth Century State in Britain and Germany* (Oxford, 1999), pp. 254–5; J. B. Baker (ed.), *Pleasure and Pain 1780–1818* (London, 1930), the reminiscences of Sir Thomas Bernard, p. 58; see also Sir T. Bernard, *Reports of the Society for Bettering the Condition and Increasing the Comforts of the Poor* 2 (London, 1800), p. 4.

10 A. Brundage, 'Private Charity and the 1834 Poor Law', www.class.csupomona. edu/his/Tonyart, accessed 4 October 2000, p. 4.

11 R. Tompson, *The Charity Commission and the Age of Reform* (London, 1979), pp. 57–60; Innes, 'Mixed economy of welfare'; for example see *An Act for the better relief and employment of the poor belonging to several parishes within the town of Shrewsbury and the liberties thereof, and in the County of Salop* (1783), p. 29.

12 Tompson, *Charity Commission*, p. 55; Innes, 'Mixed economy of welfare', p. 168.

13 M. van Leeuwen, 'Histories of risk and welfare in Europe during the 18th and 19th centuries', in O. P. Grell *et al.* (eds), *Health Care and Poor Relief in 18th and 19th Century Northern Europe* (Aldershot, 2002), p. 41. There is good evidence for guilds working in this way in Oxford, Shrewsbury and Chester. Regrettably there is not space to do justice to guilds' role in urban makeshift economies here.

14 M. Harris, 'Inky blots and rotten parchment bonds: London, charity briefs and the Guildhall Library', *Historical Research* 66 (1993).

15 T. Hitchcock, *Down and Out in Eighteenth-Century London* (London, 2004).

16 P. Slack, *Poverty and Policy in Tudor and Stuart England* (London, 1988), p. 169; *The Life and Times of Anthony Wood* 2, ed. Rev. A. Clarke (Oxford Historical Society 21 old series, 1892), p. 212.

17 C. Wilson, 'Poverty and philanthropy in early modern England', in T. Riis (ed.), *Aspects of Poverty in Early Modern Europe* (Florence, 1981), pp. 256, 268.

18 F. Heal, *Hospitality in Early Modern England* (Oxford, 1990); I am indebted to Steve King for confirmation of this point, based upon the experiences of the Browns of Troutbeck in Cumberland and the Cartwrights of Aynho in Northamptonshire.

19 M. J. D. Roberts, 'Head *versus* heart? Voluntary associations and charity organisation in England, c. 1700–1850', in H. Cunningham and J. Innes (eds), *Charity, Philanthropy and Reform* (London, 1998).

20 Innes, 'Mixed economy of welfare', pp. 144–5, 163, 166.

21 W. K. Jordan, *Philanthropy in England 1480–1660* (London, 1959).

22 W. G. Bittle and R. T. Lane, 'Inflation and philanthropy in England: a re-assessment of W. K. Jordan's data', *Economic History Review* 29 (1976); J. F. Hadwin, 'Deflating philanthropy', *Economic History Review* 31 (1978); M. Feingold, 'Jordan revisited: patterns of charitable giving in sixteenth and seventeenth century England', *History of Education* 8 (1979).

23 A. Wilson, 'Conflict, consensus and charity: politics and the provincial voluntary hospitals in the eighteenth century', *English Historical Review* 111: 442 (1996), 599.

24 T. Wales, 'Poverty, poor relief and life-cycle: some evidence from seventeenth century Norfolk', in R. M. Smith (ed.), *Land, Kinship and Life-cycle* (Cambridge, 1984), p. 359.

25 R. Smith, 'Relief of urban poverty outside the poor law, 1800–1850: a study of Nottingham', *Midland History* 2: 4 (1974), 224.

26 Wilson, 'Poverty and philanthropy', p. 267; Slack, *Poverty and Policy*, p. 163.

27 Bernard, *Reports of the Society* 2, p. 2.

28 P. Colquhoun, *A Treatise on Indigence* (London, 1806), pp. 60–1.

29 F. K. Prochaska, 'Philanthropy', in F. M. L. Thompson (ed.), *The Cambridge Social History of Britain 1750–1950* (Cambridge, 1990), p. 358.

30 D. Andrew, *Philanthropy and Police: London Charity in the Eighteenth Century* (Princeton, 1989).

31 M. Daunton (ed.), *Charity, Self-interest and Welfare in the English Past* (London, 1996).

32 H. Cunningham and J. Innes (eds), *Charity, Philanthropy and Reform* (Basingstoke, 1998).

33 L. H. Lees, *The Solidarities of Strangers: The English Poor Laws and the People, 1700–1948* (Cambridge, 1998), p. 7.

34 M. Gorsky, *Patterns of Philanthropy: Charity and Society in Nineteenth-Century Bristol* (Woodbridge, 1999).

35 Exceptionally see S. Lloyd, '"Agents in their own concerns"? Charity and the economy of makeshifts in eighteenth-century Britain', in S. King and A. Tomkins (eds), *The Poor in England 1700–1850: An Economy of Makeshifts* (Manchester, 2003).

36 S. J. Woolf, *A History of Italy 1700–1860* (London, 1991), pp. 25–6; S. J. Woolf, *The Poor in Western Europe in the Eighteenth and Nineteenth Centuries* (London, 1986), p. 6.

37 R. Canning, *An Account of the Gifts and Legacies that have been given and bequeathed to Charitable Uses in the town of Ipswich* (Ipswich, 1747), p. 159.

38 Ibid., p. 24.

39 *York Herald* 30 November 1833, quoted in P. M. Tillott (ed.), *The Victoria History of Yorkshire: The City of York* (Oxford, 1961), p. 266; a similar situation pertained in Lincoln, see J. W. F. Hill, *Georgian Lincoln* (Cambridge, 1966), p. 163.

40 Andrew, *'Noblesse Oblige'*; E. S. Larson, 'A measure of power: the personal charity of Elizabeth Montagu', *Studies in Eighteenth Century Culture* 16 (1986). Some Nonconformists kept diaries accounting for every donation they made, see for example R. P. Heitzenrater (ed.), *Diary of an Oxford Methodist Benjamin Ingham 1733–34* (Durham Carolina, 1985).

41 S. Hindle, *On the Parish? The Micro-politics of Poor Relief in Rural England c. 1550–1750* (Oxford, 2004), pp. 58–81, 97.

42 Shropshire Archives (hereafter SA), Shrewsbury Borough Records 3365/664, Mayor's accounts 1759 (vouchers); see also National Archive (hereafter PRO) C. 33/435, fo. 15 and C. 38/636 for Chancery papers relating to the regulation of the Shrewsbury charities; I am indebted to Bob Cromarty for these references.

43 SA, 83/1/309, Shrewsbury House of Industry directors' order book 1784–1808, minutes of 15 November 1784.

44 I am indebted to Mrs Rita Freedman, York City Archivist, for assistance with this point; York City Archives, CC.33–CC.63 for Chamberlain's account books 1722–82; Borthwick Institute Y/MB 36 St Michael le Belfrey church-wardens disbursements 1751–85, for example, gives totals of at least twelve parish charities disbursed in money or bread but not recipients.

45 H. Caffrey, 'The almshouse experience in the nineteenth-century West Riding', *Yorkshire Archaeological Journal* 76 (2004); S. Pinches, 'Women as objects and agents of charity in eighteenth-century Birmingham', in R. Sweet and P. Lane (eds), *Women and Urban Life in Eighteenth-Century England* (Aldershot, 2003), p. 75.

46 E. Prescott, *The English Medieval Hospital 1050–1640* (London, 1992).

47 M. Barker-Read, 'The Treatment of the Aged Poor in Five Selected West Kent Parishes from Settlement to Speenhamland 1662–1797' (PhD thesis, Open University, 1988), pp. 83–4.

48 M. D. Lobel (ed.), *Victoria County History of Oxfordshire 5* (London, 1957), p. 266; P. Broster, *The Chester Guide* (Chester [1780]).

49 J. S. Cox, *The Almshouse and St Margaret's Leper Hospital Ilchester* (Ilchester Historical Monographs 5, 1949), p. 111.

50 J. Roach, *The Shrewsbury Hospital, Sheffield 1616–1975* (Borthwick Paper York, 104, 2003), p. 7.

51 Hampshire Record Office, 40M83W/PR2 St Faith and St Cross parish register 1776–1812.

52 Caffrey, 'Almshouse experience', 242.

53 P. Slack, *From Reformation to Improvement: Public Welfare in Early Modern England* (Oxford, 1999), p. 48.

54 Caffrey, 'Almshouse experience', 242.

55 SA 1831/6/ Drapers' company book of minutes 1607–1740 fo. 271 rev.

56 E. Hird, *The Lady Margaret Hungerford Almshouse and Free School, Corsham, Wiltshire 1668–1968* (Corsham, 1997), pp. 80–1.

57 W. H. Godfrey, *The English Alms-House* (London, 1955); Prescott, *English Medieval Hospital*.

58 J. P. C. Roach (ed.), *Victoria County History of Cambridge and Ely* 3 (Oxford, 1959), p. 307.

59 *Caring: A Short History of Salisbury City Almshouse and Other Charities* (Salisbury, 1987).

60 *An Account of the Hospitals, Alms-Houses, and Public Schools in Bristol* (Bristol, 1775) p. 16.

61 Caffrey, 'Almshouse experience', 235–6, 239–40.

62 Ibid., 243.

63 Almshouse places have been calculated from PP *Abstract of the Returns of Charitable Donations for the benefit of poor persons, made by the ministers and churchwardens of the several parishes and townships of England and Wales. 1786–1788* (London, 1816), pp. 102–5, 156–64, 308–14, 624–5, 918–21, 1,034, 1,114–16, 1,290–3, 1,364–5, 1,400–8, 1,438–53; L. F. Salzman (ed.), *Victoria County History of Cambridge and Ely* 2 (Oxford, 1948), p. 307; Roach, *Cambridge and Ely* 3, pp. 146–7; B. E. Harris (ed.), *Victoria County History of Chester* 3 (Oxford, 1980), pp. 179, 182, 184; N. M. Herbert (ed.), *Victoria County History of Gloucestershire* 4 (Oxford, 1988), pp. 351–6; H. A. Doubleday and W. Page (eds), *Victoria County History of Hampshire* 2 (London, 1903), pp. 196, 200; W. Page (ed.), *Victoria County History of Hampshire* 5 (London, 1912), pp. 77, 79; W. Page (ed.), *Victoria County History of Northamptonshire* 3 (London, 1930), pp. 59–64; A. Crossley (ed.), *Victoria County History of Oxfordshire* 4 (Oxford, 1979); A. T. Gaydon (ed.), *Victoria County History of Shropshire* 2 (Oxford, 1973), pp. 110–14; W. B. Stephens (ed.), *Victoria County History of Warwickshire* 7 (Oxford, 1964), pp. 556–67; E. Crittall and R. B. Pugh (eds), *Victoria County History of Wiltshire* 3 (Oxford, 1956), pp. 353, 357; E. Crittall (ed.), *Victoria County History of Wiltshire* 6 (Oxford, 1962), pp. 168–71; W. Page and J. W. Willis-Bund (eds), *Victoria County History of Worcestershire* 4 (London, 1924) pp. 413–20; K. J. Allison (ed.), *Victoria County History of the East Riding of Yorkshire* 1 (Oxford, 1969), pp. 341–6; P. M. Tillott (ed.), *The Victoria History of Yorkshire: The City of York* (Oxford, 1961), pp. 420–40;

Reports of the Charity Commissioners (1831) volume 11 (Shrewsbury), pp. 213–92; *Caring*; R. Smith, 'Relief of urban poverty outside the poor law, 1800–1850: a study of Nottingham', *Midland History* 2: 4 (1974), 219; J. A. Langford, *A Century of Birmingham Life* (Birmingham, 1868), p. 462; A. D. Dyer, *The City of Worcester in the Sixteenth Century* (Leicester, 1973), pp. 169, 228; G. L. Fenwick, *A History of the Ancient City of Chester* (Chester, 1896), pp. 366–7; J. A. Picton, *Memorials of Liverpool* (Liverpool, 1907), p. 189; K. Grady, 'The Georgian public buildings of Leeds and the West Riding', *Publication of the Thoresby Society* 62: 133 (1989), 160–79; W. T. MacCaffrey, *Exeter 1540–1640* (Cambridge Mass., 1958), pp. 105, 113; G. B. Hindle, *Provision for the Relief of the Poor in Manchester, 1754–1826* (Chetham Society Manchester 22, 1975), pp. 143–5. Population counts are found in C. W. Chalklin, *The Provincial Towns of Georgian England: A Study of the Building Process 1740–1820* (London, 1974), pp. 9, 11, 18, 22, 36, 338–9; P. J. Corfield, *The Impact of English Towns 1700–1800* (Oxford, 1982), pp. 129, 183; A. McInnes, *The English Town, 1660–1760* (London, 1980), p. 6; R. Sweet, *The English Town 1680–1840: Government, Society and Culture* (Harlow, 1999), p. 3; *Abstract of the Answers and Returns made pursuant to 'An act for taking an account of the population of Great Britain 1801'* (London, 1802).
64 Pinches, 'Women as objects', p. 83.
65 A. Tomkins, 'Cathedral almsmen: a new prosopographical project', *History and Computing* 12: 1 (2000); Eileen McGrath's doctoral research on cathedral charity in Worcester is currently in progress.
66 *Calendar of State Papers, Home Office Series, George III 1760–65* (London 1878); *Calendar of State Papers, Home Office Series, George III 1766–69* (London, 1879); *Calendar of State Papers, Home Office Series, George III 1770–72* (London, 1881); *Calendar of State Papers, Home Office Series, George III 1773–75* (London, 1899).
67 Herbert, *Gloucestershire* 4, p. 286.
68 D. Thomson, 'Welfare and the historians', in L. Bonfield *et al.* (eds), *The World We Have Gained* (Oxford, 1986), p. 369.
69 Smith, 'Relief of urban poverty', 224.
70 This was a more common feature of post-Reformation foundations; P. Cunnington and C. Lucas, *Charity Costumes* (London, 1978), pp. 229–33.
71 Crossley, *Oxfordshire* 4, p. 472; Prescott, *English Medieval Hospital*, gazetteer.
72 D. W. Rannie (ed.), *Remarks and Collections of Thomas Hearne* 11 (Oxford Historical Society 72 old series, 1918), p. 148.
73 Rannie, *Remarks and Collections of Thomas Hearne* 9 (Oxford Historical Society, 65 old series, 1909), p. 87.
74 *Jackson's Oxford Journal* 24 April 1762.
75 Some charities required elections of this kind to be made from at least three or four people; see *A Short Account of the Two Charitable Foundations at Kings-Cliffe in the County of Northampton* (Stamford, 1755), pp. 16–18.
76 Charities in Bristol were advertised explicitly for the benefit of potential applicants; *An Account of the Hospitals*.

77 Heitzenrater, *Benjamin Ingham*, p. 27.

78 J. H. Deazley and J. T. Dodd, *Case Prepared on Behalf of the St Bartholomew's Committee of the Oxford City Council* (Oxford, 1896), p. 35.

79 *Wood's History of the City of Oxford* 2 (Oxford Historical Society 17 old series, 1890), pp. 517–18; *Appendices to the Assistant Charity Commissioner's Report on St Bartholomew's Hospital* (1896), pp. 50–2.

80 Dilapidated almshouses offering meagre pensions were visibly unpopular elsewhere; Caffrey, 'Almshouse experience', 236.

81 A. Wood, *The Antient and Present State of the City of Oxford* with additions by Rev. Sir John Peshall (London, 1773); Peshall quoted in Deazley and Dodd, *Case Prepared*, p. 35.

82 M. G. Hobson (ed.), *Oxford Council Acts 1702–1751* (Oxford Historical Society 10, 1954); M. G. Hobson (ed.), *Oxford Council Acts 1752–1801* (Oxford Historical Society 15, 1962).

83 Rannie, *Remarks and Collections of Thomas Hearne* 5 (Oxford Historical Society 42, old series, 1901), p. 276.

84 Rannie, *Hearne* 9, p. 87.

85 T. Hitchcock, 'The English Workhouse: A Study in Institutional Poor Relief in Selected Counties 1696–1750' (DPhil thesis, Oxford University, 1985), pp. 194–200.

86 Bodleian Library, Ms Top Oxon c.280, Miscellaneous papers including contributions of parliamentary representatives to Oxford charities 1765–96, fos 60, 116.

87 PRO, SO 8/52, Signet office, warrants for King's Bills series 1.

88 *Wood's History of the City of Oxford* 1 (Oxford Historical Society 15, old series, 1889), pp. 193–4.

89 J. Skelton, *Oxonia Antiqua Restaurata* 2 (Oxford, 1823).

90 D. Macleane, *A History of Pembroke College* (Oxford Historical Society 33, old series, 1897) p. 436.

91 J. Curthoys, '"To perfect the College …": the Christ Church almsmen 1546–1888', *Oxoniensia* 60 (1995), 381.

92 Macleane, *Pembroke College*, p. 439.

93 Oxford Record Office (hereafter ORO), Oxford City Archives, O.2.7, 8, Oxford town quarter sessions minutes 1735–45, 1745–50.

94 Curthoys, 'Christ Church', 387.

95 Ibid., 384.

96 Only one, John Carpenter, took all of his identified relief before he became an almsman.

97 See chapter two for details of the workhouse run by the contractor Solomon Cross. Heathfield and Wiggins were both paupers of St Mary Magdalen parish.

98 Benjamin Showell had been buried three days earlier on 17 October 1752.

99 An average based on parish pensions paid by seven town parishes 1760–65; this was comparable with the average pension found by Barker-Read in Kent of 1s 6d which she estimated to be the minimum required to buy food for one person for one week, see Barker-Read, 'Aged Poor', pp. 136, 175. It was also

comparable with pensions paid by rural Oxfordshire parishes (Whitchurch and Dorchester) which paid 1s 6s to 1s 10d in the eighteenth century, figures derived from R. Adair, 'Age Composition of Pensioners in Early Modern England', paper given at the Wellcome Unit for the History of Medicine, Oxford seminar (1993).

100 Barker-Read, 'Aged Poor', p. 175.

101 Christ Church Archives, Christ Church almsmen's patents boxes 1–3 LXI. a.1–374.

102 For example, in 1751 it was made a rule of the Leeds workhouse that anybody admitted who also received a pension must sign it over to the committee; P. Anderson, 'The Leeds workhouse under the old poor law: 1726–1834', *Publications of the Thoresby Society*, 56: 2 (1980), 90.

103 J. Woodman, *The Rat-Catcher at Chelsea College* (London, 1740), p. 24.

104 Ibid., p. vii.

105 The parish was justified in assuming that Huntingdon's family would be needy without him, because after his death in 1759 his widow was relieved extensively; for example in 1763, she was paid a total of £6 17s 9d.

106 In contrast the one St Bartholomew's man who lost his pension to his parish overseers was categorically deprived of the money; the income from Matthew Jones's charity pension was listed among overseers' receipts by St Peter in East.

107 Barker-Read, 'Aged Poor', p. 289.

108 Cheshire Record Office, P51/22, Chester St John poorhouse book 1731–56, 15 September 1738.

109 SA, PL2/2/3/1 Shrewsbury House of Industry minute book, minutes of 2 June 1788.

110 A sentiment echoed in Lees, *Solidarities*, 'Introduction'.

111 I am indebted for much of the basic information on charities to Crossley, *Oxfordshire* 4, pp. 465–6. The fifteen charities referred to exclude William Palmer's and Henry Cherry's charities which were not operative. Beneficiaries of Trinity Men's charity (benefactions by John Howell and Robert Linke) and the Berkshire Charity were not found; see also PP *Reports of the Charity Commissioners* (1822) volume 9, pp. 379–462 for Oxford's charities.

112 ORO Oxford City Archives Q.4.9. Elections to charities 1715–1834.

113 The two Harris charities are problematic. The charities of John and his son Charles Harris are dealt with as one pension charity and one dole charity, partly because Charles had a hand in redefining John's charity after his death and partly because the records do not distinguish whether pensioners were benefiting from John's or Charles's money. They seem to have provided eight pensions of £4 per year and two doles of £4 per year between them. The people named as recipients of Harris's charity can be classed as pensioners or otherwise by the fact that the doles were always allocated on 21 or 22 December each year.

114 Unless occupational or other labels suggested two different people, it was assumed that the same first and surnames indicated the same person.

115 That is to say the total number of probables plus those people whose names coincided but where no other information supported the connection.

116 Dye's name first appeared in overseers' accounts only twelve days before his pension was signed over.

117 Hobson, *Oxford Council Acts 1702–51*.

118 Canning, *Account*, p. 193.

119 R. Rouse, *A Collection of the Charities and Donations Given … to the Town of Market Harborough* (Market Harborough, 1768), pp. iiv, 58.

120 J. Broad, 'Parish economies of welfare, 1650–1834', *Historical Journal* 42: 4 (1999), 1002.

121 Adair, 'Age Composition'.

122 S. Barrett, 'Kinship, poor relief and the welfare process in early modern England', in S. King and A. Tomkins (eds), *The Poor in England 1700–1850: An Economy of Makeshifts* (Manchester, 2003), p. 218.

123 J. Robin, 'The relief of poverty in mid nineteenth-century Colyton', *Rural History* 1: 2 (1990), 193–7, 214.

124 ORO, Mss dd par Oxford St Mary Magdalen c.55 (rev. of volume).

125 Gorsky, *Patterns of Philanthropy*, p. 99.

126 For a list see Crossley, *Oxfordshire* 4; this does not include the £144 solely for Christ Church men.

127 Oxford's total population was around 9,000 in 1750. If we assume that half of this number were women, and that forty percent of the men were under twenty and therefore not of an age to qualify, then approximately one percent of all men in the town were admitted; this does not take account of exclusions on the basis of prosperity.

4

'Medical' welfare and provincial infirmaries[1]

Sickness and physical debility were familiar accompaniments to the experience of poverty. Maladies propelled people into poverty by the twin expedients of hindering earning power and demanding unwonted forms of expenditure. The vicious circle closed wherever the conditions of deprivation were so severe that they further engendered illness, whether via enforced mobility, unsanitary housing, inadequate diet or undue exposure to the elements. Therefore it is no surprise that the sick poor were a constant presence among parish paupers. Poor-law legislation singled out the 'lame, impotent, old, blind' as representatives of the deserving poor and assumptions about the impotent poverty in the eighteenth century took age and sickness as their immediate points of reference.[2] From the later seventeenth century onwards the nature of parish provision for the sick poor became increasingly complex (in terms of administrative arrangements) and varied (at the point of receipt by paupers). The range of practitioners' services and medicaments that overseers were willing to buy became very broad indeed in the eighteenth century.

In this way 'medical' relief formed an important category of expenditure, but some scholars have argued that there is little point in distinguishing between payments made for medical purposes and other forms of material relief.[3] Mary Fissell has observed that there is little reason to separate the two as qualitatively different, since all poor relief fell more or less into the general category of health care.[4] Nonetheless, it is still important to ask whether paupers or parish officers perceived intrinsic differences between explicitly medical resources and generally supportive provision. Did treatment of paupers alter when diagnoses shifted, or underlying or chronic conditions became acute? Kevin Siena's work on venereal disease in London suggests that attitudes and apportionment of relief varied with diagnoses, age and the marital status of sufferers, but in variable and unpredictable ways.[5] Therefore, is it possible to characterise the emphasis of 'medical' interventions by parishes? In her study of the south-east, Mary Dobson has supplied an invaluable collation of the range of medical treatments and practitioners available from parishes.[6] My interest lies in asking to what extent was any one type of treatment accessible by parish paupers? It is one thing to identify the types of items funded by parishes, but another to assess how likely paupers were to receive any particular benefit. It is important to get beyond the broad generalisation that the national picture was varied, and attempt to identify the subtleties that are recoverable for different localities.

The preferences of the very poor, and the practical limitations on their access to medicine which carried a price tag, are of particular interest because the comfort or harshness of experience must be partly gauged by the trials and alleviations of illness and treatment. Poverty is rendered more acute by awareness of a palliative that is financially out of reach, or by coercive tactics to ensure the take-up of unpalatable options. Steve King and Alan Weaver have emphasised the importance of the twin motivators, choice and constraint, in governing people's immersion in or avoidance of the medical market place in Lancashire.[7] Did the poor always suffer from extreme lack of choice owing to lack of money? The need to resort to assistance from another party would inevitably introduce other limitations (determined by the benefactor's priorities). In this context, when the character of medical welfare provision emerges, whose choices does it illustrate, paupers' or vestries'? Were medicines taken willingly or is there any reason to infer that they were forcibly administered? Where cures were effected by practitioners, was there any scope for resistance or coercion? Aside from parish provision, the broader economy of medical makeshifts offered a range of alternatives. The poor might persuade local practitioners to treat their ailments for free, or at a greatly reduced rate, or in exchange for non-financial payment. Furthermore, the poor might self-dose, or pay for lay treatments, by siphoning parish cash (or money raised by liquidation of material assets) into medicine. Finally, medical charities arose to make provision for the sick poor. In the mid-eighteenth century the subscription infirmary quickly became established as the most familiar new medical resource in the provinces. How did these hospitals become incorporated in existing systems of welfare? Infirmaries could straddle the parish/charity boundary wherever parish communities decided to subscribe to them. Can a distinctive urban economy of medical makeshifts be identified and assessed?

This chapter will address three aspects of urban 'medical' welfare provision. First, it will unpick the 'medical' relief provided to the sick poor in various towns to demonstrate the variety and typicality of treatments available from the parish, including the credentials of medical personnel, relief for the sick, and payments made at times of birth and death (occasions of physical challenge and defeat). These are at least indicative of local preferences on the part of the poor. Second, it will analyse the impact of infirmaries on urban populations and particularly on the poorest town dwellers by evaluating the extent of pauper uptake of infirmary facilities. The imperatives of parish policy and hospital attitudes (which varied subtly from town to town) could dictate that the experiences of infirmary paupers differed from those of the average patient, but in rather divergent ways. Third, an analysis of the parish relief given to people who were definitely both paupers and infirmary patients will illustrate the role of the infirmary in the experiences of paupers. The primary focus here is on Shrewsbury, with additional material from Oxford, Northampton, York, and occasionally Chester, concentrating on the period 1740–60.

Parish arrangements: 'medical' relief for the sick poor

Parishes' 'medical' relief was usually explained in overseers' accounts in very general terms (such as 'in their illness') with specific conditions or diagnoses being cited more rarely. Similarly, it is more common to encounter references to anonymous nurses or apothecaries, or even generalisations about 'physick' than named practitioners or identifiable drugs. Therefore it is tempting to give undue prominence to the more detailed entries that occasionally crop up. These details, however, while anomalous, provide a toehold for a characterisation of parish provision for the sick. By looking at the individuals employed to treat the poor, the medical and dietary supplies bought for paupers, and the relative frequency with which each resource was mentioned, it is possible to gain an impression of both the cures which may have been requested by the poor, or those bought by them in more prosperous times (as well as, of course, the level and type of treatment for which different parishes were willing to pay). The value of parochial care and the status of practitioners selected by parishes was called into question or directly attacked by promoters of new medical charities like infirmaries and (later) dispensaries.[8] This was naturally a rhetorical device to boost subscriptions for the charities but it does invite questions about the qualifications of surgeons, apothecaries and others who treated urban paupers, the depth of their commitment to pauper patients, their professional, part-time or amateur status, and their links with formal medical establishments like infirmaries.

Parishes occasionally chose to employ highly reputable practitioners. In Shrewsbury St Mary and St Alkmund's parishes paid for the services of Peter Blakeway, who was one of the three surgeons elected to the Shropshire (or Salop) infirmary on its opening in 1747; he could charge premiums of £100 for apprenticeships.[9] Blakeway had a long-standing relationship with St Mary's parish during the 1740s and 1750s, when he had a contract with the parish to treat all paupers for an annual fee of 4 guineas, charging extra for tricky or intractable cases; in 1752 or 1753 he was paid an additional 4 guineas to cure a tumour on Elizabeth Davis's shoulder.[10]

Nonetheless, the presence of a relatively high-status surgeon among overseers' payments should not obscure the fact that Blakeway embodied the most elite medical attendance paupers could expect (there were no parish physicians) and furthermore his employment was not necessarily representative.[11] Parish payments to apothecaries or for physic are more prevalent than references to surgeons. St Mary had another permanent arrangement, with the apothecary John Wood junior, who was working with the parish by 1740 and who was paid £4 a year between 1750 and 1752. St Mary also dealt with three further apothecaries in the period 1745–55 for a more casual supply of drugs. Similarly, Holy Cross made use of four different apothecaries in the relatively brief period between 1747 and 1752, including Samuel Winnell, the house surgeon (or apothecary) at the infirmary between 1750 and 1763.[12]

Procedures requiring specialist knowledge or equipment could also be provided but these were one-off instances; for example, in June or July 1744, St Mary paid £1 for William Cooke to be salivated (treated with mercury) for the pox. Lay cures were more typical, but still fairly rare. In 1752 Holy Cross paid Richard White's wife 10s 6d for curing a 'scald head'. Finally, people holding official posts related to the management of the poor, such as workhouse contractors or keepers of houses of correction, might be paid for services to the sick poor. John Langford, keeper of the Shrewsbury house of correction, was paid nearly £5 on behalf of Elizabeth Peet before she was sent to Bedlam in 1740 or 1741, presumably for her bed and board while under restraint.[13] By far the most frequent payments for personnel related to midwives and nurses, but as their names were often omitted it is not clear how often individual women were paid. St Mary called on midwives Mrs Birch, Mrs James and Mrs Powell; both St Mary and Holy Cross parishes paid midwives 5s for their services.

This delineation of 'parish' personnel, whereby occasional expert attention was underpinned by an array of less formal and less obviously qualified people, was mirrored in Oxford. There, the surgeon sought most frequently by parishes was Charles Nourse, another high-status practitioner. He charged £100 for an apprenticeship premium in 1743, but could command £200 or more from 1756.[14] He served the poor of at least five Oxford parishes during the mid-century, but not under a fixed contract. For example, in 1762, Holywell paid for sea water for members of John Green's family on Nourse's recommendation.[15] In 1770 Nourse was appointed as one of the surgeons at the Radcliffe Infirmary, where he remained until 1780, and was knighted in 1786.[16] Other qualified surgeons are mentioned by parishes much less frequently; Samuel Glass was approximately the same age as Nourse but did not become such an imposing figure if apprenticeship premiums are any guide.[17] A larger group of men were employed who were referred to as 'Doctor' or provided cures without their professional status being confirmed. In the 1740s Dr Franklin attended the poor of St Michael, particularly for salivation. In dealing with apothecaries, Oxford parishes tended to identify one or two preferred men and patronise them consistently. Mr Sayer was the choice of St Michael's parish, since he was conveniently local with a shop in Ship Lane, and St Martin preferred Mr Kenner in the early 1750s despite the fact that he was well over eighty years old. In contrast, when it came to employing midwives, it is clear that many different parishes repeatedly turned to the same people. Mrs Long and Mrs Shepherd both travelled all over the town to attend births in the 1750s, with John Wood the man-midwife attending occasionally up to his death in 1764, particularly for the birth of twins. The women were paid 5s for their services but Wood got a guinea for each birth (2 guineas for twins); both were typical levels of payment.[18] Oxford parishes did employ people in an entirely lay capacity to effect cures, particularly Solomon and Ann Cross the workhouse contractors, but non-specialists were more commonly used for miscellaneous nursing, sitting up with, or laying out the sick, dying or dead.

The evidence from York is limited but indicates a less extensive use of both professional and lay medical people for obtaining cures than was the case in Shrewsbury or Oxford. In 1769 the parish of St Michael le Belfrey sent two different paupers to Dr Hoggard, who seemingly ran a private mad-house, in Doncaster. Surgeons are notable only by their absence, while apothecaries Mr Smith and Mr Stillingfleet were each called upon once to supply physic to individual paupers. Other unnamed purveyors of drugs may have been drawn into the parish purview. In 1771 St Sampson bought a bottle of Godfrey's Cordial for Mrs Williamson who was dying but this was a far cry from the annual bills paid to the Oxford men. There are fewer references to the employment of midwives in York than in other towns although they received 5s per visit as elsewhere. These findings may be a function of parish accounting, but they may also indicate that regional influence militated against the use of doctors and drugs by York parishes.

Therefore what emerges from a close reading of Shrewsbury, Oxford and York is that urban parish overseers were not too shy to consult some fairly high-powered practitioners, and paupers clearly had access to the same professionals who acquired university degrees or status and became infirmary appointees; however, such access was not guaranteed, and may have been quite restricted in some places like York. This conclusion is not particularly surprising, but adds additional weight to the argument that parish relief could not always be relied upon to provide a particular service, or meet a need, in every case. This is not to discount the possibility that the poor in York might actively have rejected formal doctoring and preferred to manage without. There is good evidence that inhabitants of selected regions in the north-west of England, rich and poor alike, chose to consult doctors rarely.[19]

Medical relief, though, did not stop at doctors and drugs. Other measures could be taken and this is where a characteristic difference emerges between Shrewsbury and Oxford. In Shrewsbury, greater attention was paid to diet. Provision of drinks and foodstuffs was routinely a component of relief for the sick.[20] Alcohol and sweet foods were among the most common purchases, particularly for those about to give birth, those near to death and people who were sick in the workhouse. Adults were given brandy, wine and gin while children got biscuits, apples and tarts.[21] Among the workhouse accounts for both St Mary and Holycross parishes there are numerous purchases of white bread and sugar specifically for sick (if unnamed) inmates. Still, not all of these groceries were intended to be eaten; white bread was probably used in the application of poultices rather than as a dietary supplement.

What was the significance of these purchases? Was a reliance on diet a feature of attitudes to cures in Shrewsbury, among the more prosperous inhabitants as well as the poor, or was it just that dietary intervention was thought to be enough for the poor (whereas, under the same complaints, the rich sought 'physick')? These questions must remain unanswered but one important inference may be drawn; the foodstuffs and drinks bought by reason of illness were largely attractive consumables, being sweet, soft or potentially intoxicating. They could be characterised as the sorts of things people might actively request when ill, or certainly not refuse if offered. The purchases of overseers may therefore be said to consist of a list of pauper 'wants', granted in periods of physical stress.

Unfortunately for the sick poor, the evidence of these purchases is chronologically very widespread. Over a ten-year period, Shrewsbury St Mary and Holy Cross parishes listed purchases of sugar on sixteen occasions, bread or biscuits on twenty-four, and wine on seventeen. In other words, each commodity was bought only about once a year in each parish. Purchases of other groceries like apples or custards do not reach double figures. Despite caveats concerning miscellaneous bills (see appendix 1.1), this simple count of references to purchases is telling because it demonstrates how apparent variety may be misread as generosity of provision. Sweet foods and alcohol were by no means guaranteed to the sick poor and may have been distributed very sparingly, even if they did constitute the treatments at the forefront of the parish's battle against illness.

Unlike Shrewsbury, Oxford parishes did not obviously turn to dietary supplements (except in childbirth cases, described below) but the two towns were entirely at odds when it came to blood-letting. Oxford parishes made a point of bleeding their paupers. Mr Dennis bled the poor of St Peter le Bailey in the 1750s and Mr Douglas supplied leeches to St Michael at 6d each. Mr and Mrs Webb worked as a team and worked for at least three different parishes, with Mrs Webb bleeding the female paupers. This is in sharp contrast to Shrewsbury, where there are virtually no references to the poor being bled. Did the poor of Shrewsbury refuse to be bled and did Oxford paupers ask for such treatment? It seems that Oxford parishes confronted illness from a more formally medical stance.[22] Proximity to the professional medical training provided at Oxford University may almost certainly have exerted some influence over the practice of medicine in the town, whereas elsewhere distance apparently attenuated the influence of conventional medical preoccupations.[23]

Parish births

Births paid for by the parish have been neglected in contrast to the interest shown in pauper burials. Relatively little is known about what paupers in different places could expect in the way of maternity provision, once their parish had accepted responsibility. Fissell has commented that unwed mothers in Abson and Wick near Bristol were given 1s 6d per week and a lump sum of 25s for their month's lying-in.[24] Tim Hitchcock has described the use of the Chelsea workhouse to deal with illegitimate births, characterising the metropolitan workhouses as 'uniquely well designed for problems faced by unmarried, plebeian mothers'.[25] Outside London, large workhouses were able to offer similarly tailored services for pauper mothers; there was increasing demand for places in the lying-in ward of the Leeds workhouse;[26] however, few workhouses operated on a scale to permit such niceties in the division of available space. When Elizabeth Davies entered the St Mary parish workhouse in Shrewsbury to give birth in 1745, it is unlikely she even had a room to herself while in labour.

Over the course of the eighteenth century the number of charities which aimed to assist women at the time of lying-in proliferated; the British Lying-in Hospital for Poor Married Women was founded in London in 1740 and provincial copyists eventually subscribed for the same

Table 4.1 *Parish assistance with birth costs, 1747–55*

	Shrewsbury St Mary		Shrewsbury Holy Cross		Oxford St Peter le Bailey		Oxford St Michael	
	No.	%	No.	%	No.	%	No.	%
No. of births assisted	21	5	14	5	23	11	33	20
Midwife (named or specified)	14	67	7	50	18	78	24	73
Midwife only	5	24	0	0	9	39	8	24
Help during birth	11	52	10	71	7	30	20	61
Churching/dues	2	10	5	35	10	43	7	21
Christening assistance	6	29	3	21	6	26	11	33
Medical payments in same year	3	14	1	7	7	30	14	42
Average spent per baptism	4s 6d		6s 3d		8s 2.5d		11s 0.5d	

purposes.[27] Nevertheless, it took time for specialised medical charities to become established and even then both hospitals and the later charities which delivered women in their own homes required that women must be married.[28] This left parish authorities fulfilling a crucial role in the care of poor, unmarried mothers.

What goods and services would overseers and vestries countenance supplying to the urban parish poor on the occasion of childbirth?

First, the percentage of all births assisted from public rates was relatively low, but then expenditure was not confined to helping with the birth costs of illegitimate children. Overseers repeatedly referred to pauper women as 'Mrs' or as a named man's wife, suggesting that they were at least partners in a consensual union. In Oxford, such evidence from overseers' accounts implies that over seventy percent of births assisted by both parishes benefited married women. In Shrewsbury, the figure was lower but still significant at thirty-three to fifty percent. Notably though, a smaller percentage of people were helped with the costs of birth and baptism in Shrewsbury than in Oxford. The Shrewsbury parishes also paid less per birth than in Oxford. Further to this, mothers and children in Oxford seem much more likely to have taken other medical payments in the same payment year that the birth was assisted. If Shrewsbury did assist more unmarried mothers than Oxford, a stingy provision for birth costs might reflect an attempt to penalise single mothers (or an attempt not to place a premium on illegitimacy).

No 'package' for pauper mothers was used in any of these parishes but, as might have been anticipated, a midwife's services were the most common purchase in three out of the four parishes. In the fourth, the largest category of spending was general assistance in lying-in, which may conceal more payments to midwives. Under-specification of payments for midwife services in Shrewsbury Holy Cross may explain why this parish appears to have no births receiving only midwife services, whereas most parishes have thirty to forty percent of births helped only to this extent. Overseers in both towns helped between twenty and thirty-five percent of pauper births with christening costs. This may imply effective agreement between parishes regarding proportions of families needing birth assistance (being unable to provide this for themselves). The extent to which parishes helped with lying-in was more varied but the practice was also more prevalent. St Peter le Bailey was the only parish where under fifty percent of births were assisted in this way. As this was also the parish where midwives were most likely to be the only help people received, it may have been a reflection of the greater financial constraints on spending in this parish.

These variations may have been a function of the nature of help given at birth and christening; the latter was presumably not technically or medically necessary but nonetheless customary and desirable (from the pauper point of view). Payments in both the categories of help with lying-in and christening included, in both towns, cash doles, cloth and most frequently food and drink. The range of eatables purchased for lying-in is exemplified by Mrs Warren's receipts from St Michael in May 1750 of ale, bread, butter and tea 'at the groning'. Sugar and alcohol were sometimes part of this list, presumably as ingredients for a caudle.[29] At christenings, joints of meat (commonly mutton) were most frequently specified. Food purchased at the time of birth may have had a medical purpose but payments for caudle ingredients and christening hospitality conformed with those ritualistic aspects of birth which women wished to retain (feasibly, which custom would not allow to be stinted).[30] In these instances, parishes were effectively propping up female birthing traditions. Nonetheless, a relatively small proportion of births were assisted with all of these extras, accounting for between one-fifth and a third of all births that were paid for in any way by parishes. Once again, availability did not mean universal coverage. Are we to assume that families who turned to parishes to pay for midwives were able to provide their own caudles and christening feasts? It seems likely that parishes refused payment for extras to some women and families, but in other cases expenditure may not have been appropriate for either the parish or the family (such as where the labour was very brief, the mother was ill, or the child died).

Pauper burials

Death, like birth, was an occasion of physical challenge and defeat that might spur parishes into a variety of actions. Pauper burials have already been the focus of some sustained discussion among historians. Attention has centred on the development of the stereotypical nineteenth-century attitude of the poor and lower-middle classes, who expressed fear and horror at the threat of a parish burial. This was in marked contrast to earlier traditions; in the seventeenth century, there was some acknowledgement of the democracy of death, striking rich and poor alike. If people had any ambition in relation to their own demise, it was to 'make a good death' or behave appropriately in their last hours. This ambition therefore became transformed over time into the hope of achieving a good burial, a matter of social demarcation and material display.[31] Of course, change was neither sudden nor universal, and making a good death could still be critical in 1800, but at this date the concept of death as an occasion for conspicuous consumption was in the ascendant.[32] Laqueur dates the start of a shift in opinion around 1750 (when parishes began to implement more stingy burial provisions).[33] Gittings has cited both overcrowding and social dislocation as urban pressures that began to influence perceptions of burial and burial practices. The Anatomy Act has been seen as introducing dissection as the ultimate punishment for the 'crime' of poverty. By the early 1830s, burial had come to symbolise the summation of the individual's life achievement, with a pauper burial representing utter failure.[34] Poor, working people began to save money whenever possible to provide for their own burials.[35]

The question remains, what was the prevailing attitude to being buried on the parish in the mid-eighteenth century, essentially the start of the supposed transitional period? Laqueur's example of a relatively late but still generous provision being made for burials comes from the burial of a deaf mute from Oxfordshire bridewell in 1775.[36] The revulsion towards a pauper burial later in the period is partly explored in terms of what was provided at this burial but denied to people later. The deaf mute was sent off with bearers, ale, bread, cheese and bell-ringing, while the Poor Law Unions of post-1834 were forbidden to allow the ringing

Table 4.2 *Items purchased for pauper burials*

	Shrewsbury Holy Cross 1747–55		Oxford St Peter le Bailey 1747–55		York St Sampson 1770–77		York St Mary Bishophill senior 1762–87	
	Adult	Child	Adult	Child	Adult	Child	Adult	Child
No. burials	33	15	44	23	12	8	14	3
Laying out	11	2	30	2	2	1	0	0
Coffin	23	8	37	20	7	3	9	3
Wool/jersey	14	10	41	17	3	2	0	0
Bran	10	6	24	4	0	0	0	0
Affidavit	21	11	8	0	0	0	0	0
Clerk/dues	20	8	40	17	4	4	3	0
Parson/minister	16	6	3	0	0	0	0	0
Sexton	21	8	0	0	0	0	3	0
Ale	17	6	41	12	1	1	3	0
'Funeral only'	7	3	2	1	5	4	5	0
Face cloth	6	0	0	0	0	0	0	0
Cap	6	1	0	0	0	0	0	0
Bread	0	0	5	1	1	1	2	0
Cheese	0	0	5	1	1	1	0	0
Other	8	5	16	3	4	3	1	1

of bells at pauper funerals. We should certainly be wary of assuming that burial on the parish was regarded with universal horror in the eighteenth century, but what could the paupers of eighteenth-century traditional towns expect from their parishes? Was the provision for Laqueur's deaf mute the exception or the rule?

One general point that emerges is that the provisions for children's funerals were not so varied as those for adults. This might have something to do with the likely wealth of families who lost a child (still probably in the young-family phase of their life-cycle) against the wealth of families who lost an adult, or lone individuals who died. The death of a child might come at a time when some of the cost could be borne by the family. This is probably the case when it seems that the parish did not pay for a coffin, as it was common practice to use coffins for the vast majority of burials (including those for children) by the mid-eighteenth century. On the same theme, the parish probably did not pay for laying out so many children as it did adults, because the children more frequently had surviving relatives (parents) willing or desiring to do the job themselves.

The parishes in Oxford and Shrewsbury seemed willing to furnish ale for the 'drinking', found to be an integral part of what was understood by a decent adult burial in early modern England.[37] This usually took place after the burial and, from the sums expended by both parishes on ale, the provision was not mean. As a quart (two pints) of ale had cost only sixpence at the birthing of a woman in Holy Cross in 1749, presumably around a gallon of drink was available at most adult funerals when two shillings was laid out for the purpose. St Peter le Bailey purchased ale for ninety-three percent of adult burials and ale is among the five items most likely to be purchased for adults by either of the Oxford or Shrewsbury parishes. By contrast, it was rare for ale to be specified among the funeral provisions in York, another suggestion of limitation of the reach of parish relief in this town. In Oxford, parish-bought bread and cheese was not unheard of but was rare, suggesting that Laqueur's deaf mute may not have been so representative of the generosity of local practices as he hoped.

Aside from the wool or jersey used to shroud the body, the parishes in Oxford and Shrewsbury bought bran for thirty or forty percent of burials. This was a post-Restoration practice whereby the coffin was filled with bran to a depth of about four inches. Purportedly for the easier lying of the corpse, it was really soundproofing against the mourners hearing the body shift in the coffin when it was being carried. Bran was used elsewhere, for example in Chester, but York's parishes of St Sampson and St Mary Bishophill senior never mentioned it.[38] Gittings calls the use of bran a 'refinement'[39] (and as such it would probably have been deemed an unnecessary expense by administrators under the New Poor Law).

Little is known about pauper coffins. These may have been built to a standard design. Adults' coffins in Oxford cost around nine shillings, which included handles; on single occasions St Martin's paid for 'a parish coffin' and a 'wanscoat' or wooden panelled coffin.[40] Adult coffins in York twenty years later cost between 7s and 9s 6d. As styles of coffin altered over time, the mid-eighteenth century design may well have been different from the only surviving examples of parish coffins that date from the mid-seventeenth century.[41] These were made of half-inch oak, unlined, and featured iron-ring handles so that the coffin might be padlocked against body-snatchers.

Overseers' vouchers in Oxford contain itemised bills for 'dues', which appear to have paid for six distinct services; grave-digging, the use of cords to lower the coffin into the ground, a small gratuity for registering the burial, the minister's and clerk's dues for conducting the service and the ringing of the bells on two separate occasions. The passing bell was rung when a person died and the warning bell was sounded at the time of the funeral. In York dues or 'fees' were paid in the majority of cases where the costs of burials were itemised, but it is not clear what this term could encompass in that town. In Shrewsbury, money paid to the sexton was separated from the more miscellaneous category of 'dues', and traditionally a sexton's duties often included grave-digging and bell-ringing. If the paupers in these parishes put much store by the bell-ringing so ruthlessly denied to their successors, they were not disappointed by their parishes of settlement in this period.

None of these findings constitute proof that the indignity of a pauper burial was felt any less in the mid-eighteenth century than in the mid-nineteenth. Even if parishes bought coffins, paid for ale and rang bells, paupers may have felt the lack of other things bought for higher-status corpses or they may have resented the poor quality of the parish provisions. But it does seem worthwhile to point out that, whatever perceptions of parish funerals were to become, it is unlikely that the same intense feelings of bitterness and degradation attended them in the mid-eighteenth century. Overseers in Oxford and Shrewsbury paid regularly for a limited range of 'extras' that maintained aspects of the communal and consolatory elements of burial practices. These levels of provision were not always matched in York, which may point (once again) to differences in regional practices among the independent poor and may suggest that this was a period ripe for the development of hostile feeling towards pauper burial in that town.

It would be instructive to compare the goods and services provided by parishes with the provisions made by the independent poor when paying for their own or near relations' burials at this time. Burial clubs provide tantalising but incomplete evidence on this score, since they tended to quote the sum provided to pay for total costs rather than describe what that sum was expected to buy. There is rare evidence of the funeral provisions made by other welfare agencies, such as almshouse charities. The example of one almsman's burial at Ilchester in Dorset suggests that parishes might have been supplying all the right consumables for a good or appropriate send-off but not necessarily in sufficiently satisfying quantities. When George Cheney was buried in 1767 the charity found money for a coffin, shroud, bell-ringing, bread, cheese and ale but the total amounts spent outstripped the parish provision. Over 4s was spent on buying bread and cheese, and a substantial 11s 2d went on ale (constituting a third of the total cost of the burial).[42] This was much more than contemporary parishes spent on ale and must have given the bearers of the coffin, the almspeople and possibly the charity trustees the opportunity to drink to the dead man.

Paupers in Shrewsbury began to experience a change in attitude towards parish burial in the 1780s. The town's house of industry opened in 1784 and a new burial ground was provided for pauper inmates. Town paupers became uneasy about the fact that they were to be buried away from their parish churchyards in land that had not been consecrated. In an attempt to set their minds at rest, the Reverend Thomas Stedman, vicar of St Chad's parish, preached and later published a sermon, addressed to the poor of Shrewsbury.[43] He encouraged them to think that the new burial ground was a proper place for interment, and mentioned that the town churchyards were crowded; however, his message was diluted if not completely nullified by his eagerness to explain that easy access to the new burial ground would also save the house of industry trouble and expense. He asserted that the land was effectively consecrated if only because the new burial ground was approved by the bishop, adding that only the form of consecration had been omitted! He clinched his argument with the claim that 'your superiors ... are thoroughly satisfied with what we are about, and you should be so too'.[44] Even in comparison with other sermons of the period, this tract reeks of self-congratulation, and it seems highly unlikely that the inmates of the house of industry would have been reassured.

Thomas Laqueur has pointed to population pressure as one of the factors that encouraged parishes to economise on pauper funerals, but this simple and sweeping generalisation must be qualified by detailed reference to the additional factors. In this example from Shrewsbury, a town where population was increasing but pressure had not become acute, a change in administrative structure provided the opportunity for the town parishes to relieve some of the strain on their churchyards at the expense of native paupers. Marginalisation of the poor and their preferences was achieved in a number of ways and ratepayers were not necessarily forced by financial and population pressures to restrict pauper provision; instead they may have used any form of change as an excuse to enforce constraint.

Short-term crises versus regular relief

All forms of 'medical' relief, whether designed to treat a condition, manage a birth or effect a burial, took place in the context of a population of poor people with varying long- and short-term needs. So far this chapter has only considered these episodes of relief in isolation from individual people's broader neediness but, in order to acknowledge the justice of Fissell's injunction (to see medical relief as connected to welfare generally) it is necessary to restore a sense of context. To what extent were the people who needed relief due to a sudden medical crisis in need of regular relief at the same time? The well-known bands into which most regular relief recipients fell – the elderly, one-parent families and those overburdened with children – were presumably among those who also needed short-term assistance but in what proportions? Tim Wales's research implied that pensioners took a significant amount of extraordinary relief in seventeenth-century Norfolk, but is this borne out by the eighteenth-century urban evidence?[45] According to the theory of life-cycle poverty, which has linked acute financial need to certain stages in families' and individuals' lives, there should have been some families, already overburdened with children and in receipt of regular relief, who also needed to turn to the parish for help with birth costs. Perhaps only a similar number needed help with child burials. It should be a safe assumption that a higher proportion of adult burial costs would relate to those habitually dependent, as the elderly were commonly the largest dependent pauper group.

Few parishes possess sufficiently full, detailed records to permit a study of this sort, since it requires full listings of parish pensioners and workhouse inmates in successive years. Fortunately, for Oxford St Peter

Table 4.3 *Medical payments to those on regular relief, 1747–55*

	Oxford St Peter le Bailey	
	No.	%
Births assisted	23	
Regular relief previous year	3	13
Regular relief same year	1	4
Regular relief next year	3	13
Child burials assisted	23	
Regular relief previous year	3	13
Regular relief same year	2	9
Adult burials assisted	44	
Regular relief previous year	17	39
Regular relief same year	5	11
Medical relief	71	
Regular relief same year	32	45

le Bailey it was possible to compare all people who received payments made for medical reasons, from the ubiquitous 'in their illness' to the more specific diagnoses, with those receiving regular relief in the form of a workhouse place or a year-long pension.

The assumptions based on the life-cycle theory are, broadly speaking, borne out by the findings. A tiny proportion of families needed regular relief in the same year as a birth. The only instance in this period involved John and Jane Showell. In March 1752, their son John was christened, the overseers paying for the midwife and for churching Jane. During the same payment year, the couple received a pension of between 1s 6d and 2s.

As anticipated, adults buried by the parish were much more frequently dependent on a regular dole. As dependency is defined here as receiving a pension for a full year, this is seen to best effect in families on a pension in the previous year; if a pensioner died they may not have received a full year's pension. Thirty-nine percent of adults who were buried by the parish came into this category. Perhaps the most interesting way to look at it is to turn this perspective on its head. As sixty-one percent of adults buried by the parish were not habitually dependent, adult parishioners of St Peter le Bailey who were barely independent when all other things were equal must have been aware of the distinct possibility of meeting this end.

This analysis of parish arrangements for 'medical' relief has shown that while the range of provision could be extensive the extent was much more limited; an extreme example, such as the provision of custards for a terminally ill man, seems generous and sensitive until this relief is seen in its proper context. Only Shrewsbury Holy Cross made this provision, for one pauper, as opposed to thirty-three pauper burials undertaken by the same place in the same period, 1747–55. The rich variety of potential parish measures for paupers during times of physical challenge or defeat must not obscure the equally significant fact that very few paupers could command the full range. Disbursements were sparing, and may have been extremely finely judged.

An economy of medical makeshifts? Medical hospitals for the provinces

Parish provision in times of illness was one element of the medical economy of makeshifts. The poor potentially had recourse to a wide range of assistance other than the poor law. This could include direct reference to doctors who might be persuaded to treat the poor gratis. Robert Waring Darwin, for example, who practised as a physician in

Shrewsbury from 1786, was said to have offered free treatment to the poor.[46] The poor could also have self-dosed (depending on local expertise and custom). Drugs and treatments might be purchased in a shop or market, or made up at home, since Fissell cautiously suggests 'even the rural poor had access to commercial remedies' and receipts for domestic medicine comprised an important form of social currency at all levels.[47] Informal medical charity was also a possibility, from employers to workpeople, or landlords to tenants. Evidence for such strategies is naturally slight but it is best to be cautious before accepting the verdict of educated opinion, which condemned the recourse to 'mercenary and pernicious Empirics' as fatal or desperately injurious.[48]

Institutional charity for medical purposes received an enormous boost in the eighteenth century. Winchester Infirmary opened in 1736 with the specific objective of admitting the sick poor, providing access to trained personnel, relevant drugs or other specifics, and (for in-patients) appropriate diet and accommodation.[49] Numerous provincial towns eventually followed suit and made some provision, via subscription raised among local elites, for the care of the sick poor. Out-patient numbers were technically unlimited but in-patient capacities can speak to the institutional reach of infirmaries among local populations.

Table 4.4 *In-patient capacity of selected provincial infirmaries*

	Year/beds	Year/population	Beds:town population
Birmingham	1779/40	1775/c. 49,000	1:1225
Chester	1761/100	1774/14,713	1:147
Hull	1782/70	1792/22,286	1:318
Leeds	1769/36	1775/c. 36,000	1:1000
Liverpool	1749/30	1750/c. 22,000	1:733
Manchester	1760/60	1750/c. 18,000	1:300
Northampton	1744/30	1746/5,136	1:171
Oxford	1775/94	1770/c. 10,000	1:106
Shrewsbury	1747/40	1750/8,141	1:204
York	1745/58	1730/10,800	1:186

Source: Infirmary histories;[50] for precise population totals see Sources table 3.1. Approximate populations extrapolated from R. Sweet, *The English Town 1680–1840: Government, Society and Culture* (Harlow, 1999), p. 3.

Coverage of the local urban population was often far from comprehensive, particularly in rapidly expanding urban centres, yet even the level of provision in traditional market and county towns is deceptive since infirmary rules frequently specified the availability of beds to poor people from outside the hospital's home county. Similarly, rules could privilege patients who had travelled long distances to seek admission over those whose homes were nearby. For example, the rules of the Shropshire Infirmary stated that in the event of two cases of equal need being presented at a time when only one admission was possible, the person living furthest away was to be given preference over the local.[51] To counterbalance this, it is important to remember that beds did not always equate to in-patient places, since beds might be shared. The Shrewsbury hospital accommodated two patients per bed, potentially halving the ratio of inhabitants to places.[52] Also, this table must be viewed very differently from that demonstrating the capacity of almshouse charities (employed in chapter three) because infirmaries aimed at rapid turnover. An almsperson might hold their place for years until their deaths but hospitals wanted to cure as many people as possible and not devote too much time or too many resources to any one person. Rules often forbade the admission of chronic cases and sometimes specified a maximum length of stay in the hospital. In this way the ratios for county towns in particular could be read very favourably.

Technical permission for people to be admitted from beyond county boundaries gave rise to a variety of typical origins for the patients actually admitted. In other words, some hospitals appear to have catered fairly exclusively for the population of the town and neighbouring countryside, whereas in others the patients were more likely to have been drawn to the hospital from a distance. Fissell found that eighty-four percent of the patients in Bristol came from the town or its close environs,[53] while at the other end of the spectrum it was thought in September 1784 that two out of every three patients in the Chester Infirmary had come from north Wales.[54] Nonetheless, hospitals were particularly useful for urban populations as regards their admission of accident cases. The majority of people injured by accidents were of necessity from the town or its immediate surroundings, since distance from the hospital would have increased the likelihood that the victim of an accident would seek more immediate attention.

If infirmaries were geographically inclusive, their rules rendered them medically exclusive. Typically infirmaries were closed to children under six or seven (unless they required surgery), pregnant women, the mentally ill, people suffering from consumption and epilepsy, infectious cases including smallpox (for fear of an institutional epidemic akin to gaol fever),[55] venereal disease and the itch, chronic ulcers, inoperable cancers, the incurable and the dying.[56] Kent and Canterbury hospital went further, excluding those who had not had either cowpox or smallpox and those not free from vermin.[57] Consequently only a narrow range of complaints were admitted to eighteenth-century infirmaries for treatment, particularly accidental injury, rheumatism, ulcers and fevers.

These admissions policies were formed with a view to returning the curable poor to health and therefore to work. Anne Borsay has interpreted the behaviour of the Bath Infirmary's managers as an attempt to render the hospital an instrument of mercantilism. By returning numerous patients to the community, infirmaries were boosting the number of capable labourers, who formed a key economic resource. The pamphlets which originally proposed the foundation of a hospital in Shrewsbury certainly suggested that, ideally, the infirmary should treat short-term, non-contagious illness or disability with a view to setting the labouring poor back to work, and this sentiment was repeated elsewhere.[58] The result was a mismatch between conceptualisations of the parish poor, particularly the 'deserving' poor, and the poor thought to be eligible for infirmary treatment. While paupers tended to be predominantly (but not exclusively) female, and to be either young or elderly, hospital patient records all demonstrate a bias in admissions towards men and working-age adults.[59] It was common for fifty-five to sixty-five percent of patients to be male, with a very high proportion of accident admissions being for men.[60] Men presumably suffered more accidents than women, and curable injury was precisely the kind of complaint that infirmaries aimed to treat. Hospitals could congratulate themselves on restoring bread-winners to their families. It also seems likely that women who were victims of accidents were not so eager to obtain hospital attention on the grounds that they did not want to risk admission as an in-patient.[61] The charities founded from mid-century onwards to provide lying-in facilities for poor women give contemporary confirmation of this, since it was thought that a woman's continuous presence at home was crucial for family stability.[62] The 'dangerous consequences of hospitalising women'[63] were emphasised by the founders of dispensaries towards the end of the eighteenth century. It seems likely that the views of charity founders coincided with those of poor women themselves, that women should not be removed from their family context wherever possible. The average ages of patients (where determinable) also indicate institutional preoccupation with working-age adults. The best-represented age group in most if not all hospitals was the fifteen to thirty-five age group, with younger adolescents and the elderly comprising much smaller proportions of patients.[64]

Infirmaries certainly sent out contradictory messages about the prosperity or relative poverty of their clientele. Many employed the rule that only those incapable of providing medicines for themselves could legitimately claim the resources of the charity. At the same time, though, they frequently required patients or their sponsors to pay a deposit or 'caution money' upon admission, to defray the costs of burial or removal in the event that the patient died or was found to be incurable. This stipulation effectively excluded anyone who could not raise the money. More problematic for charity promoters, it also made prospective patients apprehensive about the likely outcome of entering the hospital. The trustees in Shropshire effectively acknowledged this problem when they repealed the rule requiring the payment of 12s deposit after the hospital had been open for fifteen months and thereafter paid for some burials from

Table 4.5 *The discharge records of selected infirmaries*

	Shrewsbury 1755		York 1745–46		Norwich 1772–79		Edinburgh C. 18th	
	No.	%	No.	%	No.	%	No.	%
Cured	436	70.8	334	67.3	319	60.3	2,155	70.7
Relieved	37	6.00	63	12.7	96	18.1	319	10.4
Sub-total 1	473	76.8	397	80.0	415	78.4	2,474	81.1
Incurable	6	1.0	13	2.6	17	3.2	122	3.9
Dead	33	5.5	14	2.8	22	4.2	125	4.1
Subtotal 2	39	6.5	27	5.4	39	7.4	247	8.0
Improper	2	0.3	0	0.0	0	0.0	0	0.0
Own request	35	5.7	0	0.0	0	0.0	169	5.5
Irregularity	8	1.3	0	0.0	0	0.0	40	1.3
Non-attendance	44	7.1	27	5.4	75	14.2	0	0.0
Other	2	0.3	0	0.0	0	0.0	117	3.7
Unrecorded	13	2.0	45	9.0	0	0.0	0	0.0
Subtotal 3	104	16.7	72	14.4	75	14.2	326	10.5
Total	616	100.0	496	99.8	529	100.0	3,047	99.6

Source: SA, 3909/1/1 Royal Salop Infirmary trustees' minute book 1747–56; *An Account of the Publick Hospital*; Risse, *Hospital Life*, p. 230; Cherry, 'The role of a provincial hospital', 298.

charity funds, but other institutions were not so flexible. York retained its 20s fee, as did Northampton which required a 15s deposit until the end of the eighteenth century.[65] One way for hospitals to limit post-mortem costs was to acquire a burial ground (Oxford's Radcliffe Infirmary apparently conducted internal burials from the outset),[66] but this introduced another worrying possibility about the handling of bodies, for patients apprehensive about post-mortem dissection. At Newcastle-upon-Tyne Infirmary, dissections were carried out on deceased patients before burial.[67] At least one contemporary thought the requirement for caution money 'fraught with cruelty and inhumanity', if a charity which aimed to assist the partially distressed could, via its own rules, preclude people who were wholly so (in other words, those who were both sick and poor).[68] Nonetheless, infirmary places were frequently oversubscribed, suggesting that caution monies were forthcoming from somewhere and that the desire for medical attention was more pressing than fear about death or dissection.[69]

The poor were apparently not coerced into infirmaries, if discharge records are any guide, nor were undue fears about death justified. Eighteenth-century hospitals were often over-optimistic about the proportion of cases they had cured, given their powerful incentives to do so. Risse has observed that the label 'cured' was applied very liberally even in cases where a cure was partial, or discharge was swiftly followed by readmission.[70] Even so, such impressive advertised cure rates probably exerted an influence over potential subscribers and patients alike. If the categories of 'cured' and 'relieved' are amalgamated, to give the total of people who (it was claimed) found the experience of being a patient in some way beneficial, then the four hospitals had a similar success rate.

The acquiescence of patients to their treatment can be inferred from their propensity to remain on the hospital books. Very few were accused of misbehaviour after admission ('irregularity') and relatively small proportions voted with their feet, either by requesting a discharge or failing to attend. Even if all categories of discharge other than cured, relieved, incurable, or dead are amalgamated (subtotal three), then only between ten and fifteen percent of patients were discharged for broadly non-medical or social reasons. This means either that hospitals did not terrify their patients into flight, or that patients were so subdued, by illness alone, by gratitude, by apprehension or by isolation from their habitual support systems of family and friends, to be rendered quite tractable. Infirmaries certainly liked public acknowledgment of gratitude; Shrewsbury managers distributed copies of the pious Dr Stonehouse's *Letter to Patients in an Infirmary* to the literate when they were admitted to promote such expressions, but did they extract thanks from a brow-beaten clientele? [71] Shreds of evidence suggest that patients were not entirely cowed by their institutional contact with medicine.[72] For instance, one Shrewsbury patient whose paralysis was treated with electrical shocks stood up to doctors and insisted she would 'rather ... remain paralytic than undergo such operations any more' and so was presumably relieved to be discharged.[73] At Chester the nurses were specifically instructed to treat the patients with tenderness, and opinion is divided on the alleged manipulation of patients in Bristol for the benefit of medical science.[74] Aggressive exploitation of patient vulnerability would arguably have been as damaging to infirmary reputations as an elevated death rate. But death rates of around three to six percent were moderate; reassuringly, most caution monies must have been safely returned.

So the medical benefits on offer by infirmaries were apparently accepted with alacrity. For in-patients there was also the issue of domestic care. Improved living conditions, 'in respect of fresh air and cleanliness' and also diet might have been a sufficient improvement on a labourer's home to ensure recovery.[75] Contemporaries certainly placed a high value on the restorative powers of the right environment and the harm which might be taken from the wrong one; a letter of 1790 written in support of the proposed Canterbury hospital contrasted the salubrity of the future hospital with 'the want of convenient ... beds, the disturbance and anxiety occasioned by a numerous family, ... improper articles of diet, irregularity in the administration of drugs' in labourers' own homes.[76] The historian might not take quite such a sanguine view, if only as a result of the references to infestations of 'bugs' found in trustees' minutes.[77] Yet it does seem logical, even allowing for exaggerations in discharge statistics, that hospitals were of material assistance in relieving if not curing the poor-sick, and contributing to the long-term welfare of families by promoting the health of working adults.

Provincial infirmaries and the parish poor

Mary Fissell's work on the Bristol Infirmary has established the similarity of circumstances that pushed people on to poor relief or into an infirmary, but not whether there was a substantial overlap of people who used both options at the same time.[78] Individuals may theoretically have been in- or out-patients in an eighteenth-century infirmary at the same time that they or their families received a parish pension or other forms of poor relief, but was there realistic scope for overlap given the different age and sex profiles of paupers versus infirmary patients (not to mention the differing priorities of parishes and charities)? Additional research on Bristol suggests that differences in the social origins of infirmary patients and workhouse inmates are distinguishable;[79] Amanda Berry has characterised the subscription charities as catering for the 'non-pauperised poor', particularly in towns where the workhouse possessed its own infirmary, but this is too sweeping a generalisation (and workhouse infirmaries were not common outside the largest institutions).[80] The remainder of this chapter will tackle these questions for paupers in Shrewsbury 1747–55, via comparisons with pauper patients in Northampton and York.

Promoters and initial sponsors of infirmary charities frequently couched their publicity in terms of the limitations or shortcomings of parish relief. One commentator for Exeter condemned 'the superficial Care that is taken of them in the Parish Way'.[81] Similarly, an account of the York Infirmary published six years after its opening alleged that the poor were provided with 'Necessaries' by their parishes but that when ill, appropriate nursing care, food and other benefits were 'scarce ever to be had' (but went on to emphasise that the hospital was not intended solely for paupers).[82] A puff for the Radcliffe Infirmary in Oxford went further and ignored parishes altogether, alleging that 'our civil Police has made none, or at least no adequate Provision for the Poor labouring under these Calamities'.[83] The author of the pamphlet proposing the foundation of the Shropshire Infirmary also had a low opinion of the quality of parish provision in cases of illness; 'the little money that is in such cases to be expected from parish officers is seldom sufficient to provide them with a proper diet, much less to pay for their medicines, attendance etc'.[84] These claims could perhaps be dismissed as the enthusiastic and very natural exaggerations of a supporter for a new (and in some ways rival) project. In the case of Shrewsbury this judgement initially seems rather unfair, given the evidence from the parishes of St Mary and Holy Cross, since medicines and special dietary provisions were made available for the sick, and paupers in St Mary were used to being treated by the same surgeon as infirmary patients; but given the infrequency of evidence that drugs and services were paid for (and the unknown frequency with which cures were needed and sought by, but denied to, the parish poor) perhaps infirmary promoters had a point. Nonetheless, criticism of parochial relief was disingenuous, given that infirmary charities consciously and rigorously limited the potential range of their activities by excluding key groups of people, and sufferers from certain types of complaint. Parishes did not have the same scope for discrimination; if a person was legally settled somewhere, the responsibility for providing some form of relief, no matter how unpalatable the format of relief might prove to the pauper themselves, could not be avoided.

Undoubtedly, the opening of an infirmary increased the options open to poor labouring people, assisting some who would have received no formal medical attention, others who would have struggled to pay for treatment and a rump who would have gone to their parish officers. The poor presumably made decisions about which agency to approach on the basis of familiarity with parish options versus eventual acquaintance with those offered by charities. Even so, in both cases applicants might be offered in-patient or out-patient care, if parishes used workhouses to this end.

A third possibility was that the parish itself would act as a conduit to the infirmary, although unlike London parishes, provincial equivalents had no history of working in tandem with hospitals.[85] As people with local knowledge about poor individuals, overseers would have been well placed to facilitate links between subscribers, who could nominate people to places on the infirmary's books, and prospective patients. In Birmingham parish officers clearly anticipated this sort of role, since in 1765 the town's overseers were responsible for initially suggesting the establishment of a hospital in imitation of the neighbouring county of Staffordshire.[86] Once a hospital was in existence, overseers were relatively unlikely to be subscribers personally, but they could have known whether parish clergy, town magistrates or prominent ratepayers were subscribers. It is unclear, though, how far the 'hierarchy of belonging' in each place permitted or denied overseers the chance to use this knowledge in explicit negotiation with subscribers who were their social 'superiors'.[87] Parish vestries or overseers might also have initiated a collective subscription, which would have entitled parish officers to nominate poor patients in their official capacity. Parish subscriptions (or the active promotion of requests by paupers to be nominated) would have been in the interests of the ratepayers, assuming that paupers would be receiving residential care or at least medical assistance (as out-patients at an infirmary would lighten the burden to be borne by the poor rate). Some hospital supporters thought a parish subscription so advantageous that they could not understand why they were not universally adopted, while others calculated the cost of in-patient care (and therefore the amount to be saved by parishes).[88]

Hospital policy was often instrumental in determining the extent of parishes' involvement as subscribers. In some places parochial subscriptions were explicitly barred, or hospital rules forbade the admission of paupers. The Norfolk and Norwich hospital excluded paupers on the grounds that those on relief already had access to medical treatment, while the Radcliffe Infirmary in Oxford took parish money but refused admittance to paupers until parishes had subscribed for at least three months, and barred workhouse inmates entirely for fear of the spread of infection.[89] The Northampton Infirmary may have been fairly unusual in that it actively sought parochial funding from the time it opened and had raised forty-eight parish subscriptions in the decade 1765–74.[90] Worcester Infirmary initially had fourteen parochial subscribers but the hospital's relationship with parishes was chequered. After 1752 the hospital rejected parish subscriptions, and although a few Warwickshire parishes found their way on to the list of subscribers by the 1760s, the governors considered rejecting them again in 1792 because they tended to fall into unacceptable arrears with their subscription payments.[91] Furthermore, subscriptions by poor-relief authorities might be contested even after they had been accepted by the infirmary. In the 1760s, Leeds town council objected to the workhouse committee's subscription of 12 guineas to the new infirmary on the grounds that it was unfair to other subscribers because workhouse patients would take up too many places.[92] Clearly there were various relationships pertaining between infirmaries and parishes in the eighteenth century that were rarely simple and often tense.[93]

In Shropshire, for example, parishes were not among the early subscribers to the Salop Infirmary and this was partly a result of the hospital's failure to solicit parish subscriptions. In 1757, ten years after the infirmary had opened, there was only one parochial subscription. The urban parish of St Mary's did not subscribe but had earned the right to nominate two in-patients and unlimited numbers of out-patients following a decision in 1754 to exempt the infirmary from all parochial taxes.[94] Shropshire parishes remained largely impervious to the advantages of an infirmary subscription until 1773, when the infirmary trustees woke up to the fact that parishes represented an untapped source of income. The annual report of that year urged the Shropshire clergy to promote parochial subscription. By 1780, the number of parish subscribers had risen somewhat, to twelve, but relations worsened again in the 1780s when it became apparent that parishes were not always willing to remove a pauper from the infirmary once he or she had been cured. In 1788 the hospital introduced an admission deposit of a guinea for patients nominated by parish officers.[95]

Even when parishes did subscribe or acquire rights to nominate patients to hospitals, they did not necessarily exercise those rights. Northampton Infirmary had between two and four parishes subscribing throughout the 1740s but from 1746/47 to 1750/51 they nominated no patients at all. The number of parish nominations crept up during the 1750s, but even in 1760/61, the nineteen subscribing parishes sent only thirty patients between them, accounting for just six percent of the patients seen in that year. In the period 1768–71, only half of the parishes which subscribed took advantage of their entitlement to nominate patients.[96] Similarly, parish subscriptions in Chester were responsible for the admission of between one and five patients in the period 1756 to 1763, at most a paltry two percent of all patients. The number of Cheshire parishes whose paupers technically had access to the infirmary increased dramatically when the house of industry (managing the poor of twenty-seven parishes) subscribed; the majority of such paupers were treated as out-patients and typically accounted for twenty-five to thirty-five percent of all patients annually.[97]

Consequently, parish officers were sometimes instrumental only in mediating between sponsors and patients, or in transporting suitable infirmary patients to the doors of the charity without having nominated them. In Shrewsbury, the infirmary trustees' minutes of 14 July 1750 record that the board heard the complaint of Thomas Beale Esquire who had been charged 15s 10d for the burial of a patient he had recommended. There had apparently been a breakdown in communications between the sponsor and the deputising parish officer, as the patient 'was buried in the manner directed by the parish officer who brought her and that he was acquainted what the price would be'. Of all the references in Shrewsbury overseers' accounts to infirmary patients in the period 1747 to 1755, nearly half are in terms of carrying or taking people to the infirmary.

Pauper patient experiences at Shrewsbury

A comparison of the names of in- and out-patients being treated by the infirmary with the names of paupers in town parishes who were referred to in overseers' accounts as ill has the potential to reveal the extent to

Table 4.6 *Pauper patients in the Shropshire Infirmary in selected years, 1747–55*

	St Mary definite: possible	Holy Cross definite: possible	St Julian definite: possible	Total definite plus possible	Maximum % of all admissions
1747	0:4	0:3	No info	7	3.5
1748	0:9	0:4	No info	13	5.5
1749	0:11	5:4	No info	20	4.1
1750	0:7	3:4	No info	14	2.2
1755	2:19	0:1	2:12	36	4.7
Total	2:50	8:16	2:12	90	3.9

which town paupers made use of the infirmary charity at the same time that they received parish poor relief (see appendix 1.1 for definitions of 'possible' and 'definite').

Paupers from these parishes accounted for a maximum 3.9 percent of admissions. Holy Cross sent the largest number of paupers who definitely gained admission to the hospital. It is possible that either paupers themselves or parish officers developed a relationship with parish residents who subscribed to the hospital and used the connection to secure nominations. Nominations were not forthcoming from the vicar of Holy Cross who did not subscribe in these years. The largest number of possibles from any parish came from among paupers in St Mary, which may reflect the fact that the parish itself had some rights of nomination.

It is also likely that there was a fairly small amount of overlap between patients in the infirmary and paupers from the town as a whole. The three parishes of Holy Cross, St Mary and St Julian contained forty-one percent of the town's population at this time, so the maximum 3.9 percent of admissions deriving from pauper patients in these parishes translates into a maximum of ten percent for town paupers from all parishes. Having said this, it is likely that these three parishes were home to fewer than forty-one percent of all patients from Shrewsbury. St Chad was notably the poorest parish in the town and may have been home to proportionately more patients than other parishes. The figures available from the Shrewsbury house of industry in the 1780s suggest that fifty or fifty-five percent of the poor in the house came from St Chad and only thirty-seven or thirty-eight percent came from the three parishes in table 4.6.[98] If these percentages also applied to infirmary patients in the 1750s, then at most eleven percent of infirmary places were taken by Shrewsbury paupers. Thus the maximum possible overlap between Shrewsbury paupers and infirmary patients was limited and definite overlap was minimal. As predicted, the infirmary's stated interests in returning people to work, the age structure of patients and the gender division between patients militated against the admission of the parish poor.

Alternatively, this small amount of overlap represents pauper choice as much as hospital policy. Paupers may have tended to go to a relief agency they knew rather than one they did not (particularly in the early years of an infirmary's operation), meaning that a short-term crisis occasioned by illness in the life of a dependent pauper was much more likely to be met by a short-term increase in parish spending rather than by a resort to other agencies. Conversely, people not habitually or previously dependent on parish money may have been more willing to turn themselves over to the care of a charity which may have been seen as more appropriate to their circumstances than turning to the parish.

Table 4.7 *The experience of pauper patients in the Shropshire Infirmary compared with that of all patients*

	All patients (1755)		Pauper patients (1747–56)	
	No.	%	No.	%
Admissions				
In-patients unknown sex	4	0.5	1	
Out-patients unknown sex	2	0.3	0	
Women in-patients	116	15.2	2	
Women out-patients	189	24.7	1	
Women both in- and out-patients	45	5.8	3	
Men in-patients	155	20.3	4	
Men out-patients	218	28.5	2	
Men both in- and out-patients	36	4.7	3	
Total women	350	45.8	6	37.5
Total men	409	53.5	9	56.2
Total[a]	765	100.0	16	
Discharges				
Cured	436	70.8	6	
Better/relieved/supposed cured	37	6.0	1	
Incurable	6	1.0	1	
Dead	33	5.4	8	50.0
Other	104	16.8	0	
Total	616	100.0	16	

Note: [a] The discrepancy between total men plus total women and total patients arises because some patients' gender was indeterminable.

A close examination of the overseers' accounts for three Shrewsbury parishes and the infirmary patient lists 1747 to 1756 produces a list of sixteen people who were definitely in the infirmary and receiving poor relief. It is instructive to compare this set of people with the profile of all infirmary patients to see in what ways they differed.

Perhaps the most telling difference between the average patient and the pauper patient was the vastly increased likelihood of dying while a pauper patient. The death rate among all patients was only five percent in 1755 and never rose above ten percent in the period 1747–56 yet pauper patients had a fifty percent chance of dying. What is more, one of the men discharged 'cured' died less than two months later. As paupers in Shrewsbury habitually received help from their parish during illness it is probable that fewer paupers would have been admitted to the infirmary with minor illnesses, since parishes would have assisted and effectively cured some paupers without the infirmary becoming involved. If it was only cases of illness which were more problematic, serious or conditions requiring surgery which were eventually referred to the hospital, this would explain the higher death rate among pauper hospital patients and may also account for pauper patients' greater propensity to become in-patients.

Although women feature more prominently than men among all paupers in Shrewsbury, male paupers are more numerous among these hospital patients (taking nine of the sixteen places). Therefore the gender split between pauper patients mirrors that among all patients, making pauper men more likely to secure an admission than pauper women. Significantly, the two people carried to the infirmary by their parishes in the period 1747 to 1755 who were rejected by the charity were both women.[99] Nevertheless, this did not prevent the admission of pauper men who later died. Half of the eight deaths among pauper patients occurred among the men.

The differences between the experiences of the average patient and pauper patients may be clarified by a closer look at the parish relief that pauper patients received in the period before and then during their time in the hospital, from 1740 to 1755. Edward Cartwright is a good example of someone who required parish help only occasionally. All of the payments he received from Holy Cross in 1749, the year he went into the infirmary, were made in the month he became a patient, and his need for relief was a result of his illness; he was bought sugar and given small doles of money. The other distinct time when Cartwright needed help was during February and March 1754, the last months of his wife's first pregnancy in the parish. Cartwright was clearly independent except during periods of unusual expense, and five other pauper patients fell into the same category.

Around half of the pauper patients spent some time as a workhouse resident in the years 1740–55. This is unusual given the infrequency with which the names of workhouse inmates occur among the Shrewsbury workhouse accounts and suggests that a combination of illness and workhouse residency could indicate serious bad health. This was probably not the fault of the workhouse conditions but rather the result of parish policy, to use the workhouse specifically for the care of the sick.[100] None of the Shrewsbury workhouses technically had an infirmary of its own, but this did not stop parishes using workhouses for residential, medical care that could be quite temporary. John Howle only appears in the Holy Cross overseers' accounts during one month, August 1751, when he was ill in the workhouse. He was bought ale and wine before being carried to the infirmary. He was admitted as an out-patient but died later the same month. John Harris, also of Holy Cross, endured a similar experience. His family experienced some unspecified difficulty in October and November 1748 when they received numerous cash doles and the parish paid for a midwife and other birth costs when John and Margaret's son Samuel was born in June 1749. John became an out-patient in September 1749 and was made an in-patient in October. The parish bought him a shirt while he was in the hospital and he was returned to being an out-patient in November. At some time after he became an out-patient for the second time he was taken into the workhouse and given extensive 'medical' relief in the form of special foods before his death in May 1750. He was bought sack and other drink, mutton, eggs, sugar and white bread each on several occasions, and finally custards were bought for him four times in the month immediately before his death.

Edward Tudor was cared for in St Mary's workhouse between spells in the infirmary. On 30 August 1755, Tudor was both discharged as an in-patient apparently 'cured' and paid 6d in St Mary's workhouse 'Being ill'; he was readmitted as an in-patient just seven days later on 6 September 1755. Tudor rented his own house under normal circumstances. He was listed in the poor rate assessment of 1754 living in Castle Hill and the parish paid for a lock for his door in August 1755, the same month when he apparently spent time in the workhouse. This means that the workhouse was being used specifically as a place of temporary residential care during his sickness.

In contrast to workhouse usage, which could be temporary or long-term, only two pauper patients took a regular pension, and even then their regular support was slight; for example, Gilbert Davis's pension in 1749 amounted to only 6d per week. He was admitted to the infirmary as an in-patient in November 1750 and was discharged cured in December; however, the cure was not permanent and his relief shot up when Holy Cross parish paid for his lodging (somewhere other than the workhouse) and washing in the run-up to his death in February 1751.

The experience of the workhouse by pauper patients, particularly by those who were dying such as John Howle and John Harris, shows that the workhouse was being used to provide temporary residential care that included a specialised diet. This appears to have been true for both St Mary and Holy Cross, although some of the most detailed evidence for these pauper patients relates to Holy Cross. In Harris's case, the workhouse was operating like a hospice.[101] This also implies that the infirmary was admitting paupers who may have been very ill but were not among the long-term dependent. This may have been the practical result of hospital policy, or because the sick poor in the workhouse received sponsorship more frequently than other paupers when parishes subscribed or when they were able to influence the nomination of patients by individual subscribers.

It is not possible to make a direct comparison between Shrewsbury and the other traditional provincial towns studied in this book, since the nature and content of the records which survive for provincial infirmaries and infirmary towns are rarely comparable between different places. Nonetheless, the rest of this chapter will be devoted to a brief summary of the information available for two other towns, Northampton and York, and an examination of the substantial differences between Shrewsbury paupers' infirmary experiences when compared with the experiences of their counterparts in these other towns.

Northampton

The Northampton Infirmary opened in 1744 following efforts to raise a local subscription by Dr James Stonehouse (a medical practitioner who was eventually ordained in the Church of England) and Phillip Doddridge (a Nonconformist divine). The hospital initially opened in an existing building in George Row which accommodated thirty beds; after an extension was built in 1753 this total doubled but it took another forty years for the first purpose-built hospital to open in Northampton (in 1793).[102] The detailed admissions books kept by the Northampton infirmary trustees reveal some aspects of the experiences of their parish-nominated patients. Unfortunately, these admission registers are not complemented by sets of surviving overseers' accounts. Consequently, the information for Northampton relates to patients sponsored by one of the three urban parishes, without reference to the extent of people's parish dependency. They may have approached the parish only for the favour of a nomination to the hospital or they may have been long-term paupers.[103]

Silverstone was the first parish to subscribe to the Northampton Infirmary, joining the first printed list of the charity's supporters in 1744. The Northampton town parishes were slower to subscribe; All Saints nominated its first patient in 1753 and it had been joined on the subscription list by St Sepulchre and St Giles by 1756. Between 1753 and 1766, sixty-seven different men, women and children from the town of Northampton were admitted one or more times to the infirmary by means of a parish nomination, accounting for a total of eighty-one admissions.

'Pauper patient' status here is determined by infirmary records of nominations rather than entries in overseers' accounts, and Northampton made particular efforts to encourage parish subscriptions, so it is not surprising that the two different groups of pauper patients in Shrewsbury and Northampton had rather different experiences of hospital life. On most points where it was possible to make a comparison, Northampton pauper patients differed from their counterparts in Shrewsbury. Most noticeably, the death rate among pauper patients in Northampton was dramatically lower than was demonstrable for Shrewsbury. Only two parish-nominated patients died, or three percent of parish people admitted. This was a far cry from Shrewsbury's fifty percent. Furthermore, Northampton patients were not often transferred between in- and out-patient status. Over fifty percent of cases were dealt with solely as out-patients and were not admitted to a hospital bed. The greater involvement of Northampton parishes with the infirmary provided scope for a wider range of cases to be treated; the Shropshire infirmary operated as a last resort for indigenous paupers whereas the Northampton parish poor did not have to be so desperately ill to secure a nomination. Consequently, Northampton was able to discharge eighty-two percent of pauper patients claiming that they had been cured or relieved, with only three percent adjudged incurable or no better; these statistics compare rather favourably with the discharge records of all patients from numerous provincial infirmaries.

Having said this, not all of Northampton's parishes were equally eager to use the infirmary for paupers. There was clearly a strong relationship between St Giles and the hospital, since it was home to a disproportionate number of the pauper patients. In the absence of any surviving indications of policy by the St Giles vestry, the possible explanations for this connection can only be guessed. Perhaps the parish perceived that its best interests lay in obtaining hospital care for as many sick paupers as possible, and the restrictions placed on admissions by the hospital did not hinder this ambition. It is possible that hospital managers were not checking nominations against the limits for each subscriber; in 1811

Table 4.8 *Pauper patients admitted to the Northampton Infirmary*

Parish	% pop. 1801	% pauper patients 1753–66
All Saints	57	40
St Giles	19	49
St Peter	5	0
St Sepulchre	18	10

Note: St Peter did not subscribe to the infirmary.

parish subscribers to Northampton were able to nominate more patients than their subscriptions technically permitted.[104] There may have been personal connections between men holding parish authority and the managers of the hospital that facilitated the entry of paupers from St Giles. It may be relevant that when the infirmary was reopened in new buildings in 1793 it stood on a site near to St Giles church (although not technically in the parish), so the intimacy between the parish and the institution continued and was geographically strengthened somewhat by the end of the century.[105]

Additional information about pauper patients in Northampton gives an impression of their ages, the length of time they had suffered before hospital admission, the duration of their time as in-patients and the variety of complaints they endured. Parish nominators enjoyed a limited but noticeable ability to disrupt the concentration on curing the working-age population. Northampton paupers tended to stretch infirmary services to the younger and older age groups, as fully forty-five percent of pauper patients were under twenty-four or over sixty. The information can therefore be used to posit a rare, democratising role for parish nominators, in opening up a medical resource to a wider range of the population than would have been the case with only private subscribers.

Northampton tried to keep track of how long people had suffered from a complaint before they were admitted to the infirmary. The lengths of time quoted were presumably the result of direct enquiries made of the patients rather than the evidence of a third party (such as a medical practitioner). Therefore, there is the risk that durations of illness might have been exaggerated in order to elicit sympathy or admission. Alternatively, the exaggeration may have taken the form of shortening the alleged period of suffering, to discourage the idea that they might be incurable and therefore not admissible. Still, it is interesting to note that approximately a third of all pauper cases had been suffering for a month or less, one-third for between one and five months and a final third for six months or more. Berry estimated that the evidence of pauper patients between 1771 and 1791 suggested that parishes were actively choosing to refer cases that had become, or were likely to become, a long-term burden on the poor rate.[106] I would argue instead that, from the evidence from Northampton between 1753 and 1766, paupers were able to secure nomination and admission whatever the alleged duration of their illness if duration was the only criterion being considered. It is entirely likely that infirmaries weighed both duration and nature of complaint before making a decision about admission.

The nature of the complaints endured by pauper patients in Northampton presented the infirmary with a wide range of conditions. The main reasons identified for prompting general admission in Bristol, Exeter and Northampton (ulcers, rheumatism and fevers)[107] were represented among paupers, accounting for twenty of the sixty-seven poor patients treated. Yet fully forty-seven others were diagnosed with alternative maladies ranging from the perennially familiar coughs and colds (five patients) through to 'foul bones in hand' (one patient), a feature of venereal co-morbidity.[108] A number of distempers may have been, like ulcers and fevers, secondary symptoms of consumption (dropsy and worms fell into this category).[109] Diseased, inflamed and otherwise sore eyes accounted for six admissions. Given the wider age range of pauper patients in comparison with the patients nominated via other routes, it seems reasonable that they would have presented a wider range of complaints than was usual. Yet for all the bewildering variety of the complaints endured, the evidence indicates both the range of work undertaken by the infirmary and also its limits, helping to account for the low death rate among paupers (in comparison with their Shrewsbury counterparts); pauper patients in Northampton were sick and uncomfortable but were no more at risk of losing their lives than other patients.

York

The infirmary at York was opened in 1740 at a house in Monkgate, following a bequest of £500 by Lady Elizabeth Hastings for the purpose of providing a city hospital in 1739. A purpose-built infirmary was opened on the same street in 1745.[110] In York, the only information available about infirmary patients is contained in the overseers' accounts because admissions registers do not survive. Nonetheless, the insistence of the York hospital on the payment of caution money meant that all parishioners too poor to pay the necessary money were forced to approach some other agency to supply it, frequently the parish. In consequence, overseers paid when paupers were admitted and received any balance when they were discharged. The hospital demanded £1 in caution money

Table 4.9 *Paupers sent by parishes to the York infirmary*

Parish	Years	Individuals assisted to Hospital [a]
St Mary Bishophill senior	1760–86	6
St Michael le Belfrey	1764–9, 1773–81	12
St Sampson	1762–80	6

Note: [a] Assistance in this context means carriage to the hospital or, more usually, payment of the £1 caution money.

until 1787, when the amount was reduced to 10s for nominated patients and to nothing for accident cases.[111] Hospital policy initially curtailed access by denying admission to anyone from the parish of St Maurice, which had had the temerity to assess the hospital for poor rates, but this slightly ungenerous order was repealed in 1746.[112]

Three of the twenty-eight York parishes that have overseers' accounts surviving from the mid to late eighteenth century reveal a steady if rather slight use of the hospital by pauper patients. St Michael le Belfrey parish in York sent or was concerned with twelve pauper patients in the hospital during the periods 1764–69 and 1773–81, in other words fewer than one pauper per year. Over half of these individuals did not occasion more than £1 of parish expenditure over and above the £1 needed for caution money. Robert Burgess, admitted with parish assistance in 1767, took relief only in 1767 and 1768; his frugal lodgings cost 6d per week and additional money was sometimes granted. Just four pauper patients either were a constant presence in the overseers' accounts or were admitted to the workhouse. Jane Derby and her sister Judith, for example, were relieved in 1764, 1780 and most years in between. They were often parish pensioners, given money for rent, assisted with child burial costs, clothes and shoes. It is not clear whether they ran separate households but between them they received calculable relief of £44 17s 5d over the fifteen-year period of good overseers' accounts. Jane was probably admitted to the infirmary in 1775 while Judith was in the hospital in 1780. One of them may also have been admitted briefly in 1779.

St Mary Bishophill senior's parish was even less active in sending paupers to the hospital; six people between 1760 and 1786 were admitted with caution money supplied by the parish. Once more, the beneficiaries of parish nomination or support were divided between the occasional paupers, like Susy Rudd who needed a chair to hospital in 1762 or 1763 but no caution money, and those living in dependency like Robert Brown. He was allocated a pension of 2s per week in 1780 that was continued during and after his hospital admission in 1783 (for a broken leg). Similarly, Grace Stott needed continual support from 1778, the year when she was first taken into the workhouse and then carried to the hospital. She returned to hospital in 1779 and experienced heavily dependent poverty until 1783 when she may have (re)married.

The involvement of St Sampson is puzzling, since this parish apparently paid no caution money at all, but did make payments for paupers to be washed at the hospital (in other words they were definitely admitted as in-patients) and for gratuities to nurses. The parish was also unusual in sending two-thirds of its patients in the two years 1779 and 1780, and in sending a majority (five out of six people) who were heavily dependent on parish relief. Martha Stead took only 4s in total, in 1769 when she was a patient, but the remaining four women and one man were given (in various combinations) pensions, rent, clothing, additional medical costs and workhouse accommodation.

As in Shrewsbury, paupers in York who can be identified as pauper infirmary patients were not all long-standing paupers with chronic complaints; there were noticeable variations between parishes. There was a spread of dependency between those whose illness had itself occasioned poverty receiving short-term parish attention and those more noticeably reliant on parish support. In another similarity with Shrewsbury, there are surprisingly frequent references to pauper patients in the context of workhouse admissions or occupation. This is significant, since only one of the York parishes possesses surviving lists of workhouse inmates. The workhouse seems to have been operating in York in a similar way to houses in Shrewsbury, where interim care (before and after periods in hospital), treatment and dietary supplements were granted to paupers via the medium of the workhouse.

Different parishes might come into contact with the infirmary less than once each year, but there was a continued awareness of the charity's presence and a willingness to organise or support admission for paupers under certain circumstances. What is interesting about access to the infirmary for paupers in York is the apparently sustained nature of the hospital's use, not being characterised by significant use by just one parish, nor by the kind of famine and flood fluctuation in use as seen in Chester and, to a lesser extent, in Northampton. Given the large number of small parishes in York, steady usage of the hospital by all of them would have offered the greatest chance of access to the total population of town paupers.

Conclusion

It is possible to draw four conclusions from this study. First, paupers enjoyed technical access to some sensitive, customised treatments and reputable medical personnel because parishes are seen to have paid for them but this access was limited. If the infrequency with which each resource is mentioned is a genuine reflection of the infrequency of purchase, then the regularity of varied and imaginative medical provision was much less impressive than its range. This analysis of parish arrangements, though, does emphasise the utility of studying 'medical' relief as a discrete variety of parish relief, and provides the basis for some generalisations about birth and death on the parish that are thus far missing from the pre-1834 literature. Second, paupers from Shrewsbury apparently did not comprise the majority or even a significant minority of patients in the Shropshire Infirmary during its first years of existence. Despite criticisms of parishes by the founders of the hospital, it certainly did not remove much of the responsibility for the medical relief of the sick poor from the parish. Therefore in the economy of medical makeshifts the infirmary supplied a new source of welfare; it did not displace all earlier forms. Third, people who were receiving some poor relief at the same time as their encounter with the Shrewsbury hospital charity had a markedly different experience to that of most patients and particularly suffered a much higher death rate. This disparity was probably the consequence of Shrewsbury parishes having treated paupers' minor illnesses, and using the workhouse to provide residential care. A place in the infirmary was sought (by parishes or paupers) in cases of serious illness and acted more as a last resort than as a first port of call. Fourth, this sort of use was typical to Shrewsbury, and not the typical nature of pauper patient experiences nationwide (although there were apparently similarities with pauper experience of the infirmary in York). In other towns, admissions of paupers were not confined to the seriously ill; in Chester the infirmary treated paupers as out-patients en masse and parish patients in Northampton suffered proportionately fewer deaths than other patients.

Despite initial copying among hospital managers, who reproduced rule lists without concern for local circumstances, hospitals quickly developed their own practices in relation to parishes. Pauper patients were evidently problematic for managers, since they were one of the few groups to be judged by economic status rather than age, sex or medical history. Therefore their access to hospitals was partly controlled by the overt or tacit policy towards paupers. Given that parish authorities also had their own agendas, what emerges is a picture of care for the sick poor in mid-eighteenth century urban society being a delicate balance between what hospitals would offer, what parishes preferred to undertake in-house (specifically in the workhouse), and what was requested (by overseers or directly by paupers) in the way of hospital involvement.

The only measure of pauper choice or satisfaction in this equation must be derived from their willingness to participate in hospital treatment (gauged from the fact that they were no more likely to run away than other patients, and that escapes from infirmaries nationwide were rare). The rate of pauper use of infirmaries was as much a reflection of pauper choice, a request for admission, as it was the imposed decision of a vestry or overseer. The relief administered and dispensed by parishes is often characterised as reactive, responding to requests (sometimes with refusal, or a counter-offer). Therefore it is possible to argue that the rate of pauper admissions to infirmaries from urban parishes (aside from places like 1770s Chester, where out-patient admissions were clearly wholesale rather than individual) is a direct reflection of pauper requests for admission when parish facilities had either been exhausted or were unpalatable.

Even so, the unpredictable and sometimes infrequent role played by parish paupers as patients in these new infirmary charities confirms the conclusions of chapter three, that the experience of some form of dependent poverty was more pervasive and varied in mid-eighteenth century urban society than has been assumed so far. If parishes, hospitals and other relief agencies catered for substantially different subsets of the population who could conceivably have been described as poor, this implies a further-reaching but more fragmented coverage of the collective needs of 'the poor'. These agencies formulated different criteria for entitlement and either engendered or responded to different patterns of reliance by their users. Infirmaries offered a more specific and limited form of relief than parishes, could make careful selections of people to benefit from the charity while scorning the poor quality and high cost of poor-law provisions, and were much more tightly controlled than municipal or parish charities (as indeed was the intention of subscription charity). Thus for the very poor, the infirmary was an awkward resource to incorporate into an economy of medical makeshifts.

Notes

1 Parts of this chapter were published in my article 'Paupers and the infirmary in mid-eighteenth-century Shrewsbury', *Medical History* 43 (1999), copyright of The Trustee, The Wellcome Trust. I am grateful for permission to reproduce portions of that article in this revised and expanded treatment.

2 39 Eliz c. 3 (1597–98); 43 Eliz c. 2 (1601).

3 M. Fissell, *Patients, Power and the Poor in Eighteenth-Century Bristol* (Cambridge, 1991), p. 98; J. Andrews, '"Hardly a hospital, but a charity for pauper lunatics"? Therapeutics at Bethlem in the seventeenth and eighteenth centuries', in J. Barry and C. Jones (eds), *Medicine and Charity Before the Welfare State* (London, 1991), p. 63.

4 Fissell, *Patients, Power and the Poor*, pp. 99–100.

5 K. Siena, *Venereal Disease, Hospitals and the Urban Poor: London's 'Foul Wards', 1600–1800* (Rochester, 2004), chapter 4.

6 M. J. Dobson, *Contours of Death and Disease in Early Modern England* (Cambridge, 1997), chapter 5 especially p. 273; S. King, *A Fylde Country Practice: Medicine and Society in Lancashire, circa 1760–1840* (Lancaster, 2001).

7 S. King and A. Weaver, 'Lives in many hands: the medical landscape in

Lancashire, 1700–1820', *Medical History* 45 (2000).

8 For example, see *An Account of the Publick Hospital for the Diseased Poor in the County of York* (York, 1746), p. 1; *Gentleman's Magazine* 11 (1741), 653.

9 R. R. James, 'Medical men in practice in Shropshire, 1779–1783', *Transactions of the Shropshire Archaeological and Natural History Society* 40 (1920), 210; National Archive (hereafter PRO), IR 1/50 Board of Stamps apprenticeship book, p. 194.

10 Shropshire Archives (hereafter SA), P257/L/3/4 Shrewsbury St Mary overseers' accounts 1748–53; Shrewsbury Borough Records 3365/725, St Alkmund's Overseers' Accounts 1729–52.

11 For the relative status of physicians, surgeons and apothecaries see P. J. Corfield, *Power and the Professions in Britain, 1700–1850* (London, 1995), pp. 149–55.

12 H. Bevan, *Records of the Salop Infirmary* (Shrewsbury, 1847).

13 SA, Shrewsbury Borough Records 3365/725, St Alkmund's Overseers Accounts 1729–52.

14 P. J. Wallis and R. V. Wallis (eds), *Eighteenth-Century Medics* (Newcastle upon Tyne, 1988).

15 Oxford Record Office (hereafter ORO), Mss dd par Oxford St Cross or Holywell b.14 overseers' accounts 1757–72.

16 *Jackson's Oxford Journal* 13 September 1770, 9 November 1780; *Alumni Oxoniensis 1715–1886* (Oxford, 1888).

17 Wallis and Wallis, *Eighteenth-Century Medics*.

18 D. N. Harley, 'Provincial midwives in England: Lancashire and Cheshire, 1660–1760', in H. Marland (ed.), *The Art of Midwifery: Early Modern Midwives in Europe* (London, 1993), pp. 34, 39.

19 King and Weaver, 'Lives in many hands'.

20 This has also been identified elsewhere; J. Lane, *The administration of an eighteenth-century Warwickshire parish: Butler's Marston* (Dugdale Society Occasional Paper 21, 1973), p. 20; Dobson, *Contours of Death*, pp. 263, 266.

21 For example, see St Mary's overseers' accounts, 18 February 1744, 31 March 1744, 11 June 1748, 22 March 1755, 3 April 1755.

22 See Fissell, *Patients, Power and the Poor*, chapter eight, for the emphasis that the medical profession placed on bleeding at this time.

23 Lane, *Butler's Marston*, p. 19.

24 Fissell, *Patients, Power and the Poor*, p. 98.

25 T. Hitchcock, ' "Unlawfully begotten on her body": illegitimacy and the parish poor in St Luke's, Chelsea', in T. Hitchcock *et al.* (eds), *Chronicling Poverty: The Voices and Strategies of the English Poor, 1640–1840* (Basingstoke, 1997), p. 75.

26 P. Anderson, 'The Leeds workhouse under the old poor law: 1726–1834', *Publications of the Thoresby Society* 56: 2 (1980), 90.

27 S. Pinches, 'Women as objects and agents of charity in eighteenth-century Birmingham', in R. Sweet and P. Lane (eds), *Women and Urban Life in Eighteenth-Century England* (Aldershot, 2003), p. 71.

28 D. Andrew, 'Two medical charities in eighteenth-century London', in J. Barry

and C. Jones (eds), *Medicine and Charity Before the Welfare State* (London, 1991), pp. 84–5.

29 A. Wilson, *The Making of Man-Midwifery: Childbirth in England 1660–1760* (Cambridge Mass., 1995), p. 26.

30 Ibid., p. 27.

31 R. Houlbrooke, 'Introduction', in R. Houlbrooke (ed.), *Death, Ritual and Bereavement* (London, 1989).

32 R. Porter, 'Death and the doctors in Georgian England', in Houlbrooke (ed.), *Death, Ritual*, p. 94.

33 T. W. Laqueur, 'Bodies, death and pauper funerals', *Representations* 1 (1983).

34 C. Gittings, *Death, Burial and the Individual in Early Modern England* (London, 1984), pp. 60–5; R. Richardson, *Death, Dissection and the Destitute* (London, 1987), pp. 266–81.

35 P. H. J. H. Gosden, *Self-Help: Voluntary Associations in the Nineteenth Century* (London, 1973), pp. 115–19.

36 Laqueur, 'Bodies'.

37 See Gittings, *Death, Burial and the Individual*, p.155.

38 Cheshire Record Office, P29/11/1–6 St Oswald overseers' accounts 1747–54, 24 July 1749.

39 Gittings, *Death, Burial and the Individual*, p.115.

40 ORO, Mss dd par Oxford St Martin c.29 miscellaneous papers including overseers' receipted bills 1601–1768.

41 J. Litten, *The English Way of Death* (London, 1991), pp. 97–8.

42 J. Stevens Cox, *The Almshouse and St Margaret's Leper Hospital Ilchester* (Ilchester Historical Monographs 5, 1949), pp. 111, 121.

43 Rev. T. Stedman, *An Address to the Poor Belonging to the Several Parishes within the town of Shrewsbury* (Shrewsbury [c. 1787]).

44 Ibid., pp. 15, 18–19

45 T. Wales, 'Poverty, poor relief and life-cycle: some evidence from seventeenth-century Norfolk', in R. M. Smith (ed.), *Land, Kinship and Life-cycle* (Cambridge, 1984), p. 357.

46 J. Bowlby, *Charles Darwin: A Biography* (London, 1990), p. 51.

47 Fissell, *Patients, Power and the Poor*, pp. 37–41.

48 J. Bromehead, *An Oration on the Utility of Public Infirmaries* (London, 1772), pp. 11–12.

49 The provinces took their lead from metropolitan and Scottish institutions, under a complex set of motivations; see P. Slack, *From Reformation to Improvement: Public Welfare in Early Modern England* (Oxford, 1999), pp. 135–41, and D. Andrew, *Philanthropy and Police: London Charity in the Eighteenth Century* (Princeton, 1989).

50 W. B. Stephens (ed.), *Victoria County History of Warwickshire* 7 (Oxford 1964), p. 339; J. Reinarz, *The Birth of a Provincial Hospital: The Early Years of the General Hospital, Birmingham, 1765–1790* (Dugdale Society Occasional Papers, 2003), p. 22; H. E. Boulton, 'The Chester Infirmary', *Chester and North Wales Architectural, Archaeological and Historical Society Journal* 47 (1960), 10, 15; G. Jackson, *Hull in the Eighteenth Century* (London,

1972), p. 282; S. T. Anning, 'The General Infirmary at Leeds 1767–1967', *University of Leeds Review* 10 (1966); G. McLoughlin, *A Short History of the First Liverpool Infirmary 1749–1824* (London, 1978), p. 22; J. V. Pickstone, *Medicine and Industrial Society* (Manchester, 1985), p. 14; W. Page (ed.), *Victoria County History of Northamptonshire* 3 (London, 1930), p. 39; A. H. T. Robb-Smith, *A Short History of the Radcliffe Infirmary* (Oxford, 1970), p. 214; SA, 3909/1/1 Royal Salop Infirmary trustees' minute book 1747–56, 30 May 1747; *Medical Register* (London, 1780); P. M. Tillott (ed.), *The Victoria History of Yorkshire: The City of York* (Oxford, 1961), p. 467.

51 The Salisbury, Exeter and Northampton infirmaries were some of the other institutions to cite this objective; A. Berry, 'Patronage, Funding and the Hospital Patient, c. 1750–1815: Three English Regional Case Studies' (DPhil thesis, Oxford University, 1995), p. 169.

52 SA, 3909/1/1 Salop Royal Infirmary trustees' minute book, 8 December 1750; see chapter two for a discussion of bed-sharing.

53 Fissell, *Patients, Power and the Poor*, p. 96.

54 Boulton, 'The Chester Infirmary', 15.

55 Chester was the first infirmary to provide isolation wards for fever patients; Boulton, 'The Chester Infirmary', 11–12.

56 See among many *The Statutes of the General Infirmary at Chester* (Chester, 1763), p. 18; *An Account of the Publick Hospital*, p. 24; Robb-Smith, *Radcliffe Infirmary*, pp. 25–6; *Gentleman's Magazine* 11 (1741), 474; Berry, 'Patronage', p.163; S. Cherry, 'The role of a provincial hospital: the Norfolk and Norwich hospital, 1771–1880', *Population Studies* 26 (1972), 295; S. T. Anning, *The General Infirmary at Leeds volume 1: The First Hundred Years, 1767–1869* (Edinburgh, 1963), p. 81; Reinarz, *The Birth of a Provincial Hospital*, p. 24.

57 Dobson, *Contours of Death*, p. 277.

58 A. Borsay, *Medicine and Charity in Georgian Bath: A Social History of the General Infirmary c.1739–1830* (Aldershot, 1999), pp. 211–13; SA, 3909/6/2, Royal Salop Infirmary Proposals and Annual Reports 1745–1847; Anning, *General Infirmary*, pp. 3–4; Andrew, 'Two medical charities', p. 94.

59 Echoed by Siena's finding for venereal patients in London, where workhouses treated women and hospitals treated men; Siena, *Venereal Disease*, p. 165.

60 Berry, 'Patronage', pp. 218–20.

61 Ibid., p. 219.

62 Andrew, 'Two medical charities', p. 88.

63 B. Croxson, 'The public and private faces of 18th century London dispensary charity', *Medical History* 41 (1997), 137.

64 Berry, 'Patronage', pp. 221–5.

65 3909/1/1 Royal Salop Infirmary trustees' minute book 1747–56, minute of 30 July 1748; *An Account of the Public Hospital*, p. 9; YCH 1/1/1/1 County Hospitals Trustees' Court Book 1742–1889; Bury, 'Patronage', p. 170.

66 Robb-Smith, *Radcliffe Infirmary*, p. 27.

67 A. Chamberlain, 'Teaching surgery and breaking the law', *British Archaeology* 48 (1999).

68 W. Nolan, *An Essay on Humanity: or a View of Abuses in Hospitals* (London, 1786), pp. 21–2.
69 Berry, 'Patronage', pp. 171–2; A. Tomkins, 'The Experience of Urban Poverty: A Comparison of Oxford and Shrewsbury 1740–1770' (DPhil thesis, Oxford University, 1995), p. 167.
70 G. B. Risse, *Hospital Life in Enlightenment Scotland* (Cambridge, 1986), pp. 230–1.
71 SA, 3909/1/1 Royal Salop Infirmary trustees' minute book 1747–56, 24 December 1748, 22 April 1749.
72 Anning, *General Infirmary*, p. 82 .
73 'Part of a letter from Cheney Hart, M.D. to William Watson F.R.S. giving some account of the effects of electricity in the county hospital at Shrewsbury', *Philosophical Transactions of the Royal Society* 48 (1754), 786–8.
74 Boulton, 'The Chester Infirmary', 14; B. Boss, 'The Bristol Infirmary 1761–2 and the "Laborious Industrious Poor"' (PhD thesis, Bristol University, 1995).
75 E. G. Thomas, 'The Old Poor Law and Medicine', *Medical History* 24 (1980), 5; for diets see Anning, *General Infirmary*, pp. 87–90; *An Account of the Publick Hospital*; B. C. Turner, *A History of the Royal Hampshire County Hospital* (Chichester, 1986), pp. 14–16.
76 Quoted in Dobson, *Contours of Death*, p. 277.
77 For example, Boulton, 'The Chester Infirmary', 10; Anning, *General Infirmary*, p. 13; H. C. Cameron, *Mr. Guy's Hospital 1726–1948* (London, 1954), p. 66.
78 Fissell, *Patients, Power and the Poor*, pp. 94–5.
79 M. Gorsky, *Patterns of Philanthropy: Charity and Society in Nineteenth-Century Bristol* (Woodbridge, 1999), p. 122.
80 Berry, 'Patronage', p. 182; A. Berry, 'Community sponsorship and the hospital patient in late eighteenth-century England', in P. Hordern and R. M. Smith (eds), *The Locus of Care: Families, Communities, Institutions and the Provision of Welfare Since Antiquity* (London, 1998), p. 134.
81 *Gentleman's Magazine* 11 (1741), 653.
82 *An Account of the Publick Hospital*, pp. 1–2.
83 Bromehead, *An Oration*, p. 10.
84 *A Proposal for Erecting an Infirmary for the Poor-Sick and Lame of this County and Neighbourhood* (Shrewsbury, 1737), p. 1.
85 Siena, *Venereal Disease*, p. 144.
86 A. Wilson, 'The Birmingham General Hospital and its public, 1765–79', in S. Sturdy (ed.), *Medicine, Health and the Public Sphere in Britain, 1600–2000* (London, 2002), p. 92.
87 K. Wrightson, 'The politics of the parish in early modern England', in P. Griffiths *et al.* (eds), *The Experience of Authority in Early Modern England* (Basingstoke, 1996), p. 19.
88 Berry, 'Patronage', p. 100; *An Account of the Rise, Progress and Present State of the County Infirmary at Northampton* (Northampton [1775]), p. 22.
89 Cherry, 'The role of a provincial hospital', 295; Thomas, 'The old poor law',

5 for the Radcliffe Infirmary; *Rules and Orders for the Government of the Radcliffe Infirmary* (Oxford, 1770), p. 12.

90 J. Woodward, *To Do The Sick No Harm: A Study of the British Voluntary Hospital System to 1875* (London, 1974), p. 17; Berry, 'Patronage', pp. 99–100.

91 J. Lane, *Worcester Infirmary in the Eighteenth Century* (Worcester Historical Society, 1992), pp. 20–1.

92 Anderson, 'Leeds workhouse', 97.

93 Berry, 'Community', pp. 131–4.

94 SA, P257/B/3/4 Shrewsbury St Mary churchwardens' accounts book 1753–83, 21 April 1754.

95 W. B. Howie, 'The administration of an eighteenth-century provincial hospital: the Royal Salop Infirmary 1747–1830', *Medical History* 5 (1961), 51.

96 Berry, 'Patronage', p. 191.

97 Chester Archives, H1/51, 52 Chester Royal Infirmary journals of patients 1755–63, 1772–78.

98 SA, 83/94/374 Shrewsbury House of Industry daily figures of the poor in the house 1784–88.

99 St Mary paid Jane Tudor 6d 'infirmary' on 19 July 1755 and Holy Cross paid for Widow Murphy to be taken to the infirmary on 6 April 1753. Neither woman appears listed as a patient.

100 Also found elsewhere; Dobson, *Contours of Death*, p. 267–8.

101 S. Ottaway, *The Decline of Life: Old Age in Eighteenth-Century England* (Cambridge, 2004), p. 253 found a similar situation in Terling.

102 Page, *Northamptonshire* 3, p. 39.

103 Northampton Record Office, Northampton General Hospital Annual Reports 1743–80; Northampton General Hospital Journals of patients volumes 1 (1744–53), 2 (1753–59), 3 (1759–65), 4 (1765–69) and 5 (1769–74).

104 Berry, 'Patronage', p. 202.

105 Page, *Northamptonshire* 3, p. 39.

106 Berry, 'Patronage', pp. 232–3.

107 Ibid., p. 233.

108 Siena, *Venereal Disease*, p. 152.

109 Dobson, *Contours of Disease*, p. 252.

110 Tillott (ed.), *City of York*, pp. 467–8; P. Wallis, 'Charity, politics and the establishment of York county hospital: a "party job"?', *Northern History* 38: 2 (2001).

111 Borthwick Institute YCH 1/1/1/1, County Hospital Trustees' Court book 1742–1889, minutes of 8 May 1787.

112 *An Account of the Publick Hospital*, p. 24; Borthwick Institute YCH 1/1/2/1 County Hospital General Court Book 1742–1820, minutes of 9 December 1746.

5

Charity schools and the treatment of poor children[1]

Eighteenth-century charity schools bore a number of similarities to infirmaries as regards their origins, funding and links to the wider community. Both were expressions of the contemporary trend for philanthropy that ran on donations from the living rather than endowments from the dead. This entailed fostering considerable support and goodwill among local people to ensure that subscriptions and donations continued to flow. Both schools and infirmaries had links with religious leaders and more or less aimed at moral instruction. Schools laid a heavy emphasis on reading and catechising in order to give pupils a grounding in Protestantism and the ability to benefit from printed religious works, whereas hospitals could compel in-patients to follow a behavioural code while inculcating religion via visits from chaplains, or by handing out copies of pious publications. Anglican and dissenting ministers were involved in both types of establishment as subscribers, deliverers of sermons and general advocates. Both schools and infirmaries came to fill a visible and important role in community life, usually though not exclusively urban life. Children in charity school uniforms were a continual reminder of the effects of philanthropy. Both institutions acquired physical premises that acted as focal points and sometimes provided facilities for other purposes.

Yet schools and hospitals were different types of charitable ventures in several crucial respects. On a financial and organisational level, infirmaries were much more expensive and complex to establish and run. Infirmaries provided residential care for their patients, and required numerous members of staff and varied items of domestic and medical equipment to function properly. By comparison, schools needed only to rent a large room and appoint a single master or mistress; equipment such as horn books and testaments were relatively inexpensive and durable. Also, patients on an infirmary's books changed weekly while pupils commonly stayed in schools for a number of years. This necessitated a greater commitment on the part of infirmary trustees to oversee the running of infirmaries. Another difference lay in their relationship to their allied professional groups. Infirmaries quickly developed a recognised function in training medical professionals. Teachers and the science of education were not viewed in a similarly professional light until much later.

Most importantly, charity schools were much more controversial institutions than infirmaries. In the early eighteenth century, schools attracted some fairly wild accusations of political and religious bias, as some people feared that schools could be used to indoctrinate pupils. Yet there were also more enduring reasons why some contemporaries could countenance hospitals but not schools for the poor. There were clear biblical and traditional precedents for assisting the sick that the poor laws had reinforced. Infirmaries had well-established forerunners in the form of almshouses and mediaeval hospitals which had provided relief to the aged poor and poor travellers; 'the promoters of eighteenth-century hospitals were rediscovering the past'.[2] The new eighteenth-century charities carefully called themselves 'infirmaries' to try to distinguish themselves as new medical charities but the familiarity and tradition of the older hospitals may have helped to give the impression that infirmaries were not controversial. The influence of the older institutions may also have served to keep the new infirmaries for the sick poor as opposed to the sick in general.[3] Infirmary founders and organisers could pour scorn on poor-law provisions for medical care and claim to be more cost-effective than statutory relief while simultaneously making very careful selections of people to benefit from the charity. Medical charity for the sick poor could be represented as both demographically prudent, since saving lives would combat the perceived decline in the population, and scientifically advantageous, if it enabled physicians and surgeons to train more effectively.[4]

Both charities appealed to the self-interest of the subscribing public but the infirmaries enjoyed more success in this respect. If people were employers of labour, in either the domestic or industrial spheres, they would perceive a very direct way in which they might benefit from the availability of local hospital places. Their servants or labourers might be restored to health and work without any further trouble or expense. The attractions of educating the poor with a view to long-term benefits such as crime prevention were pressed quietly and persistently by commentators but had a less immediate and less certain appeal for the public.[5]

Porter has argued that the publicity used to promote infirmaries was bland and reassuring, stressing the unifying role of a medical charity as it brought rich and poor together,[6] and these claims were not necessarily spurious. In other ways, hospitals proved cohesive rather than divisive; in Bath the general infirmary acquired the support of both Anglican and dissenting individuals and congregations.[7] Of course, consensual propaganda did not rule out relationships between hospitals and political groupings, or prevent local conflicts since hospitals could become the focus of party political disputes, emphasising divisions within the community of potential subscribers or governors.[8] But hospitals did not attract 'the same socio-political anxieties as schemes to teach the poor to write'.[9] Schools fell into this trap; they highlighted the gulf that could exist between the uneducated poor and their employers, and apparently threatened to narrow the gap.

A lack of education was neither so visible a problem as illness nor was it a need traditionally or extensively met by charitable activity or the poor-law authorities. Schools prior to the subscription-charity schools had provided free places for poor scholars but on a fairly small scale, to the benefit of people 'who were able to spare their children from the exigencies of the daily grind of keeping alive to acquire the inessential fripperies of education'.[10] The new schools appeared to aim at 'that greatest of evils, a general diffusion of learning'.[11] This might encourage ambition among poor children who would seek a position in life 'above their station'.

Just as there was contemporary debate about the merits of educating the (undifferentiated) poor, so there has been more recent confusion about the groups of poor who benefited from the establishment of charity schools. Joan Lane has argued that paupers were invariably excluded from charity schools while Joan Simon suggests that schools were designed almost exclusively for the children of the dependent poor.[12] Recent research has come down on the side of Lane; Deborah Simonton's analysis of schools in Essex and Staffordshire found that limits were placed on access to charity schooling by the poorest, while charity schools might be utilised by relatively prosperous tradesmen's children.[13] This kind of dispute can be resolved only by comparing the pupils of individual schools with concurrent lists of local paupers.

Concern for the welfare of children, as a discrete group of the poor with specific needs, was drawn to public attention by the opening of the Foundling Hospital in London in 1739. Whereas charity schools were designed to provide education and an opportunity for apprenticeship, the Foundling aimed at more comprehensive, residential care of children from their earliest infancy. Babies would be cared for by nurses (in the nurses' own homes) until they reached three or five years old when they were taken into the hospital. Initially the Foundling charity, like infirmaries and schools, relied largely on the continued goodwill of subscribers, collections at charity sermons and other donations to survive financially.

In the 1750s, however, Parliament agreed to support the charity with public money, providing the hospital operated a policy of unrestricted admissions from 1756 onwards. The London hospital did not have the capacity to cope with a general admissions policy so another parliamentary requirement was that the Foundling open country branches. It was thought that living conditions would be healthier outside London, and that the lower price of food and wages outside the capital would make the charity more cost-effective. As a result, the charity established five hospitals in provincial locations including one at Shrewsbury in 1758 and one at Chester in 1762. Committees of local gentlemen, townspeople and clergy were set up to direct the leasing, building and running of the country hospitals, but matters of policy, including fine details such as the pattern of clothes to be worn by children, were decided in London. The unrestricted admission of children ended in 1760, bringing an end to parliamentary subsidy. Consequently, the country hospitals were wound down and closed between 1767 and 1773. The Foundling achieved greater nationwide publicity and influence than other London foundations via these provincial branches.

This chapter will start by surveying contemporary views of charity schools, particularly their perceived role in teaching pauper children. It will go on to review the availability and character of charity school places in Oxford, attempting to quantify the level of pauper involvement with charity schools, and in particular comparing the nature of charity school provisions with parish treatment of children. Finally, the chapter will look at a provincial manifestation of the Foundling Hospital, namely the facilities offered by the Shrewsbury branch hospital, to contextualise this relatively proscriptive, national charity against urban parochial measures.

Contemporary thoughts on charity schools

Most contemporary printed sources for eighteenth-century charity schools are either promotional sermons or annual accounts of schools' income and expenditure. Sermons were preached when schools opened, and more frequently on a yearly basis to raise funds. As a result, they were a steady source of both income and propaganda for the schools. They had to be competitive given the increasingly long list of other charities that also tried to raise money using sermons over the course of the eighteenth century.[14] Opposition to education for the poor found an early champion in Bernard Mandeville, but his stinging essay on charity schools fairly summed up the main objections which were to be levelled for the rest of the century, particularly the accusation that charity schools would educate the children of poor families beyond what was thought to be their station in life; published denials of this phenomenon were rare, and people continued to question the wisdom of educating the poor.[15] Soame Jenyns, commenting in the 1750s, thought the poor lived in blissful ignorance.[16]

Early in the eighteenth century the clergy who gave charity sermons in support of schools were forced to become apologists for the movement. There were two main reasons for this. First, the early strident criticisms of the schools from Mandeville took the initiative and put supporters on the defensive. Second, the role and attitude of the Society for the Promotion of Christian Knowledge (or SPCK) changed between the founding of the first schools at the start of the century and the 1720s. The society was initially at the forefront of the campaign to establish charity schools for poor children, sending advice to people wishing to open schools and publishing statistics relating to the success and spread of the new charities. Nevertheless, problems soon arose. In the early years of the charity school movement, criticisms were directed at schools to the effect that they were subject to party bias or were nurseries of Jacobitism. Also, charges that schools would educate children beyond their station in life made a profound impact on the SPCK, which then cast around for an extenuating factor to justify support of schools. The contemporaneous rise of the workhouse movement in England gave the society the new angle it required. If simple work tasks were introduced in schools then children would be trained to fill their perceived role in life, not be educated above it. In 1712 the SPCK recommended that children receive schooling only on alternate days between days of work and in 1722, the secretary Henry Newman wrote, 'a working school is in all respects preferable to one without labour'.[17] The introduction of work presented some schools with intractable problems, so work was not universally adopted (or continuously maintained) but promotional rhetoric was adapted to retain the ideal of preparation for work; one sermon of 1782 advertised on its title page that the school in Warrington was designed to instruct children 'until they are fitted for business'.[18]

Eventually, the SPCK withdrew from the vigorous promotion of charity schools to pay more attention to less controversial projects such as the advancement of Christianity overseas and a reprint of the Welsh Bible. Nonetheless, interested clergymen could remain in close contact with the SPCK and charity sermons were often printed under the auspices of the society, or bound together with the society's annual reports. As a result, sermons also advocated 'a narrower outlook and a more restricted curriculum'[19] as time went by. The strength and persistence of the conservative point of view, however, meant that English charity school campaigners remained on the defensive throughout the eighteenth century and into the nineteenth.[20]

Charity sermons were rather formulaic in both their texts and their arguments, particularly as regards the religious education of the poor. Numerous preachers used the biblical exhortation 'Train up a child in the way he should go: and when he is old, he will not depart from it' as the springboard for their argument.[21] Childhood was claimed to be the best opportunity for inculcating religion and piety into the poor, before corruption or immorality took root. Also, a translation of the Bible was useless without the ability to read, but literacy would enable the poor to discover for themselves the truths of Protestantism and reject Catholicism. Many souls would be saved who would otherwise have been lost. The children themselves would be brought to God and their innocent influence would be disseminated to their parents and possibly throughout whole congregations. The clergy also stressed the redeeming nature of alms-giving to children. God had a special relationship with children due to their inherent innocence. Support of children's charities was therefore particularly worthy and would all but ensure the salvation of the giver. The defensive position of most sermon writers compelled them to be firmly optimistic about the likely effects of a charity school education.

Fears that charity schools would disrupt the social order were confronted in two ways. It was stressed that schools taught the poor their duty and did not irresponsibly raise their expectations. Some looked forward to the specific effects of a religious education, like the writer who anticipated that charity boys could not become pickpockets as they would have the eighth commandment too firmly impressed upon them.[22] The other way to distract opposition was by referring to a recognised social ill as a problem which would be reduced if only the poor were better taught. Swearing, vagrancy, prostitution and gin-drinking were all mentioned in this context. The most popular device of this sort was to juxtapose the education of the poor with the death penalty as the two motivators needed to encourage people to live in a moral and law-abiding fashion.

A characteristic fear of eighteenth-century charity trustees was that resources would be wasted on improper candidates, in other words the undeserving poor. More than one contemporary writer blithely ignored such concerns, believing all the recipients of a children's charity would be inherently deserving, rendering it 'liable to no perversion'.[23] Yet the education of the poor presented a particular problem; the children may have been innocent but their parents might not be thought to qualify. This gave rise to a discrepancy between the way the SPCK envisaged schools and the way the same schools were described in sermons and pamphlets. The SPCK wanted to provide schooling for children but make access to it contingent on parental good behaviour. In editions of their *Methods Used for Erecting Charity Schools* the society advised trustees to devise orders that were to be read to parents and then given to them in printed form. The gist of these orders was that parents should send their children to school every day, clean and tidy, ensure that they prayed morning and evening, and that parents take care to set a good, sober, religious example. If parents were seen to neglect these orders, their children could be expelled.

In contrast to the SPCK's stance, sermon writers took particular care to point out the faults of parents, in order to give greater justification for sponsoring schools. It was argued that 'the Parents of these poor Children are generally very great Reprobates'[24] and implied that most displayed a perverse refusal to take some responsibility for the advancement of their children. This group was mentioned in the same breath as those who could not help their children due to their own ignorance or poverty, but prominence was given to the wicked rather than the pathetic. Bishop Butler accepted that the practicalities of poverty meant that a poor child 'must be an Eye and Ear witness of the worst Part of his Parents Talk and Behaviour'[25] but did not think this a sufficient excuse for not trying to counteract a corrupting influence.

In practice it seems very doubtful that trustees or teachers of schools would always have been prepared or able to act on any apparent breach of rules by parents. It was not usual for provincial schools to issue rules specifically for observance by parents.[26] The SPCK may have carried some weight with London schools at the start of the century but its influence was probably significantly diluted elsewhere and at other times.[27] It has been claimed that parents very often confronted teachers with hostility and aggression, without wholesale expulsions being the automatic result. The parents and children are instead described as having 'the whip hand of masters and mistresses'.[28] At St Anne's Soho, one parent summoned to a school trustees meeting for sending her child to work in the brick-fields responded with spirit 'yt she did not owe ye Trustees so much service'.[29] Things were no better at Nonconformist establishments; Richard Hutton, the steward of the Quaker workhouse and school at Clerkenwell reported in July 1726 'It very much [harms] us in the managing affairs in the family when the children's parents treat us not only with disrespect but also abusively and that in the presence of the children.'[30] It seems that sermon writers may have held the more realistic opinion, and that 'the poor [parents] had limited but effective power to obstruct, constrain or redirect charitable intentions'.[31]

Nevertheless, Jonathon Barry has observed that children of the respectable poor were more likely to be attracted by the long-term advantages which formal schooling (and promises of apprenticeship) could offer; 'Non-compulsory charitable education could never attract the people it most wanted to reform' because the very poor were compelled to take a short-term view.[32] School rules potentially cut across the domestic economies of the very poor, by insisting on prompt and regular attendance of pupils on pain of expulsions for truancy.[33] Yet poor families might reasonably need the child's earnings, which may in turn have been irregular and dependent on the child's opportunistic availability for casual work. Sarah Lloyd has pointed out that economic opportunities grasped by children (with or without parental direction) made perfect sense but ran counter to the imperatives and concerns of charity managers; 'Contrary to school propaganda, therefore, charitable assistance and labour were frequently at odds in practice.'[34]

Charity school sermons constituted one subset of the larger body of literature concerned with the organisation of statutory, rate-based relief and the balance that should be struck between this relief and voluntary efforts such as charity schools.[35] Charity school sermons include scattered references to the parish poor. Bishop Butler made the most firm connection between the two. His contention was that children have as much right to education as to life. The poor laws covered the maintenance of children, but legal provision for schooling was lacking. Other parents, although able to feed their children, were similarly unable to educate them but as ignorance was not so evident a deficiency as hunger the problem went unnoticed.[36] Earlier, Hendley had scorned parish provisions for children in general, one writer who followed a trend for castigating the 'tricks and cabals' of parish officers and their mismanagement of parish funds.[37] Allowances were so small people were forced to either beg or starve, while concern for children on the part of parish officers extended only 'to get them off from their Hands, as soon and upon as easy Terms as they can'.[38] Other writers referred to education for the poor only as a way to reduce the cost of poor relief. If the poor could learn to work hard in their youth, they might 'rise up towards Manhood … no longer chargeable, nor eat any Man's Bread for nought'.[39] The expense of an education was small compared to the charge of a man and his family on the parish.[40]

Unfortunately, there is only conflicting and imprecise evidence about the likely social origins of the majority of pupils in charity schools from these sources. While some sermon writers stressed the idle and dissolute nature of most parents, Chapman said that charity managers approached 'poor people of the better sort' and most referred to the poor only as opposed to the rich.[41] Therefore, it is fortunate that the sources permit a comparison of scholars with paupers in Oxford, to test the power of pauper children to make use of charity schools. Only close investigation of specific cases can determine the level of pauper participation in schools and allow some assessment of schools' clientele.

Charity schools in Oxford

In eighteenth-century Oxford, education was available free from most or all expenses in up to eight charity schools.[42] There were three principal charities. Nixon's free school had been established by endowment in 1658 and aimed to teach forty sons of freemen to read, write, cast accounts and learn some Latin. The founder, Alderman John Nixon, rather spitefully circumscribed the likely pool of entrants when he specified that the sons of University employees should not be taught in the school.[43] Nixon's operated throughout the eighteenth century but reputedly suffered considerable decline in the mid-eighteenth century. This was blamed at the time on a lax headmaster, James Croney, who had control of the school from 1744 to 1755. The trustees accused him in March 1755 of having 'grosly neglected his duty and that by his neglect the school is almost ruined'.[44] The Bluecoat and Greycoat schools were funded by subscription from 1708 onwards. The Bluecoat was supported by the corporation and the inhabitants of Oxford and was established to teach fifty boys but in the years 1748–67 the number of charity pupils was kept down to thirty.[45] The trustees also ran a Bluecoat school for girls that ran from 1708 until at least 1722, but this failed and had to be refounded in 1756. After this date the school catered for around thirty-six girls. The Greycoat school taught fifty-four boys and was funded exclusively by subscriptions from University colleges;[46] however, not all Oxford academics were equally enthusiastic about charity education. Dr Conybeare made it no secret 'that he hoped to live to see Charity Schools put a stop to or quite obstructed'.[47]

There were a number of other, smaller schools with free places. Endowments of 1702 and 1714 provided a schoolhouse and part of a master's salary for a school in St Thomas's parish. The salary supplement of £1 was supposed to pay for ten poor boys who would be taught alongside paying pupils; however, in the mid-eighteenth century, this school was reported to be teaching only four to eight pupils.[48] Ann Alworth left money in 1721 for a school to teach twenty children, boys and girls, in St Michael's parish and the charity survived in 1784.[49] Another endowment, for Salman's charity school, is referred to only between 1710 and 1720 and was probably very short-lived. A Methodist school run by the Wesleys existed in St Ebbe's parish from 1726 to 1739 which catechised and taught knitting and spinning.[50] Lastly a small school to teach reading and catechising by 'a prudent matron' was supported in St Giles's parish by offertory money and this continued throughout the century.[51]

Charity schools were founded to benefit 'the poor', but the larger schools at least were not closed to others since they also took on paying pupils. This was common practice and was looked upon by masters as a way of supplementing their income. In the case of the Oxford Bluecoat school 'it is probable that the master ... rented the house and paid for it by taking private day scholars'.[52] The charity accounts did not include any payments for rent between 1748 and 1781, and it was not until 1804 that the trustees raised the master's salary on condition that the paying pupils were dismissed. Barry found that the trustees of charity schools often allowed the numbers of paying pupils to be between ten and twenty.[53]

Elementary education from charity schools was supplemented by privately run establishments, but before 1765 there is evidence for only a handful of formal schools and these were run as purely commercial ventures.[54] John Brickland, for instance, taught in a tenement in Catte Street with his son William as an assistant. He probably offered writing and arithmetic and these were the subjects his son advertised when John had died. Brickland senior was said to have been a teacher for fifty years, and he was certainly in Oxford for at least thirty-five.[55] A second school was run by Robert Stratford, a writing master. When Stratford died in 1778 he was said to have been teaching for forty years. A third school was for girls. Mrs Lanyon kept a boarding school for young ladies in St Aldate's by 1755, which lasted until around 1769. Between 1765 and 1780, twenty-three further academic enterprises were advertised in the town. Most were short-lived and the availability of private education was probably an ever-shifting scene.

The range of elementary schooling was completed by dame schools. These too were run as money-making concerns, in that the women charged a few pennies per week for their services, but charges this low enabled some rather poor families to consider paying for their children's education. The extent of dame school provision is unknown, as are any details about the nature of the learning opportunities they comprised. In the past historians have been tempted to castigate all dame schools as merely providing a cheap child-minding facility.[56] Such criticisms echo the disapproval of nineteenth-century educational reformers and thereby risk being anachronistic; for example, it was said of the dame schools in Manchester in the 1830s that 'no instruction really deserving the name is received in them'.[57] Yet it is likely that dame schools did teach pupils rudimentary literacy skills, given the testimony of dame school pupils who wrote their memoirs in adulthood.[58]

Table 5.1 *Access to charity schools in selected towns*

	Number of school places: estimated school-age population	Children in school over a decade		Boys in school over a decade	
		No.	%	No.	%
Chester	65: c. 2,900	162	6	100	7
Northampton	100: c. 1,100	250	23	175	32
Oxford	200: c. 1,800	500	28	375	42
Shrewsbury	177: c. 1,600	442	28	Not known	
York	100: c. 2,200	250	11	150	14

Given the obvious difficulties with enumerating the elementary school 'places' available in Oxford, it would be impossible to gauge the extent of educational provision in Oxford in relation to the school-age population. Yet if the investigation is confined to charity school places for poor children only (where the number of available places is most readily confirmed) it is clear that in mid-century Oxford charity schools were able to cater for a significant if minority group of children. Furthermore, a comparison with other 'traditional' towns shows that this coverage was not unique.

It is certain that there were at least 200 free charity school places in Oxford in this period.[59] The population of Oxford was approximately 9,000; if the national average of twenty percent of the population were aged between five and fourteen then 1,800 children were potentially of charity school age.[60] It has been pointed out that as charity schools often did not accept children below seven or eight years old and as pupils frequently attended for four years or less, the number of available places can be multiplied two and a half times to give a more realistic calculation of the children who received some schooling in any ten-year period.[61] The Oxford evidence relating to pupils' ages fits this pattern. Age data for boys at the Bluecoat school confirms that most children started school at nine and had an average stay of four to four and a half years (giving a leaving age of thirteen or fourteen). Similarly, the rules at the Greycoat school admitted boys from eight to twelve years old and did not apprentice them before thirteen.[62] Therefore it is reasonable to multiply the number of school places by two and a half to find the number of effective places over the course of a decade. By this reckoning, 500 or twenty-eight percent of all children in Oxford received some charity school education. Even so, the provisions for girls were much more sparse than for boys. If it is assumed that half of all children were girls, then only seventeen percent of girls could possibly have attended charity schools. Boys were much better off with approximately forty-two percent having access to a charity place over a decade. A gender imbalance in the number of available school places is unsurprising, since the situation is repeated across the towns studied here and echoes findings for Essex, Staffordshire and Norwich.[63]

Of course, not all children in Oxford would have been permitted to take up a charity place as some parents would have been too prosperous to qualify (or to desire a place for their child). Yet estimating the number of people who were sufficiently poor to qualify is a thorny problem. Hume used the Hearth Tax assessments of 1664 to determine this for a study of education in Kent, assuming that households exempt from the tax or having only one or two hearths were the social group who corresponded with families who could make use of charity schools.[64] Whatever questions might be raised about this use of the hearth tax, there is no equivalent evidence from the mid-eighteenth century from which to calculate the eligible population. Nevertheless, it is reasonable to suggest that forty-two percent of all Oxford boys constituted more than half of all boys from families that were sufficiently poor to be eligible. Also, the overall extent of educational provision did not deteriorate up to 1780 as a consequence of population growth. Oxford's population appears to have remained relatively stable, with sustained growth occurring only towards the end of the eighteenth century.

A comparison with other towns reveals a similar picture, which is telling since charity school places were sought more assiduously in Oxford than elsewhere, although coverage was notably less full in York and Chester. In Shrewsbury, the extent of provision was apparently identical to Oxford. The 177 places were available in three big charity schools. A subscription charity school was started in 1708, called the Brown school since that was the colour chosen for the children's clothing. The pupils were to be between eight and thirteen and in 1763 there were 107 children in attendance.[65] Thomas Bowdler founded a school by endowment in 1724 for thirty children from St Julian and Holy Cross parishes to be taught to read and write. Millington's hospital supplied a further forty school places when opened in St Chad in 1749.[66] All three schools were co-educational, suggesting that girls were particularly well provided for in Shrewsbury, but the numbers of places reserved for boys and girls respectively is not clear.

In the 1760s, Northampton was also well provided with free school places but like Oxford the majority of places were for boys. The fifty or more places for boys at three Anglican schools (Dryden's Free or Orange school from 1710, the Bluecoat school from 1755, and the Greencoat school from 1761) were augmented by twenty places at a free-church charity school from 1738 until about 1772. Facilities for girls were limited to a Bluecoat school from 1738, which took thirty pupils.[67]

Yet children in York were significantly less likely to receive any instruction at a charity school. A handful of small, endowed charities founded between 1647 and 1729 provided for the free education of up to thirty-seven children but did not found schools, so it is not clear how the charity benefits were delivered.[68] The subscription charity schools which opened in 1705, Bluecoat for boys and Greycoat for girls, catered for forty pupils each but were more ambitious than the schools mentioned elsewhere because they supplied bed and board to children in addition to education. The addition of a Greencoat school in 1717 added twenty more places for boys but no other charity schools were then founded until the 1770s. Therefore schools alone could have reached only eleven percent of town children in each decade (although the testamentary charities may have boosted educational access to sixteen percent).

Mid-century Chester possessed just two Bluecoat schools, one for boys and one for girls, founded by Bishop of Chester Nicholas Stratford and his wife. The schools taught forty boys and twenty-five girls, but achieved relatively slight educational provision for the poor.[69] This picture pertained until the later eighteenth century when the foundation of Nonconformist schools, Sunday schools and particularly the adaptation of the Bluecoat boys' school to increase the number of scholars improved coverage considerably; by 1809, there were allegedly no poor boys in the town without the opportunity to attend school for two years.[70]

So far this discussion has considered the potential reach of charity schooling. Unfortunately, the mechanism by which specific children were recruited to school vacancies is rarely explained. Rules tended to delineate sponsors' rights of nomination, not children's access to sponsors. Schools worked in much the same fashion as other subscription charities. Personal recommendations from subscribers who paid more than a certain sum were required to promote a particular child. According to the SPCK's *Methods Used for Erecting Charity Schools* the school would be started by subscribers casting their votes to choose children from a previously compiled list. Vacancies would be filled by subscribers nominating in turn.[71] Rules fifteen to twenty-two of the Oxford Greycoat school describe a similar procedure. The preacher of the annual charity sermon could nominate a boy and the vice chancellor and proctors could each have a turn every five years. The remainder of turns would be decided by the subscribers (i.e. University colleges) drawing lots. At the Bluecoat school subscribers also took turns, but occasionally people jumped the queue, nominating 'in somebody else's turn'.

None of this really explains how a boy like James Hutt born in St

Thomas's parish in Oxford in 1756 came to enjoy the sponsorship of a man like William Blackstone, jurist and author of *Commentaries on the Laws of England*, to the Bluecoat in 1766. One writer has claimed that children were expected to know their sponsors.[72] Alternatively, at some charity schools, parents who wished their children to attend had to apply to gain the interest of a subscriber. If sponsors and pupils were brought together by the joint agencies of parents and school managers, then parental behaviour may have been a deciding factor. This is one way that an informal weeding-out process may have excluded the 'undeserving' if not the parish poor. Apathetic parents would never have approached trustees: those who were idle and troublesome might have failed to find a sponsor or been vetoed by trustees. Hanway was possibly the first writer to observe that parish overseers were well placed to recommend children as fit objects of a school charity, a thought that rarely occurred to school trustees or did not appeal to them.[73]

The extent or reach of charity education was important, but the benefits offered to poor pupils were another matter. The most serious gap in the Oxford records is the lack of information about the academic life of schoolboys. Little is known beyond the probability that they were taught reading, writing and how to cast accounts at all three principal charity schools. It seems highly unlikely that any of the Oxford schools introduced work in the way recommended by the SPCK. None of the circumstantial evidence suggests that boys undertook any kind of craft or manufacture (unlike the Leeds charity school, for example[74]). Historians have tended to be critical of the educational facilities offered by charity schools.[75] This springs partly from schools' overt intention to teach poor children to read the scriptures for the good of their souls, rather than to teach them the skills of reading and writing *per se*, and partly from the dilution of any educational effort by the limits placed on learning, usually by the imposition of work. Children at some schools had to leave after they had satisfactorily acquired certain skills, and girls in most schools were not taught to write or cast accounts. There was also the issue of how children were taught to read, another aspect of charity schooling that was attacked during the eighteenth century and has been criticised subsequently. In 1786 one writer thought that a charity school child spent nine-tenths of their time 'kicking its heels or picking its fingers', since he or she was employed usefully only when it was their turn to stand up and read.[76] Nonetheless, it is overstating the case to say that education received at charity schools was 'minimal'.[77] Joan Lane described their impact on literacy as 'widespread' by 1760 given that an estimated 30,000 children were attending them.[78] Once poor people had acquired the ability to read they could choose how to use their skill. One of the schools' opponents unconsciously outlined some of the possibilities when he asserted that teaching the poor to read 'would enable them to read seditious pamphlets, vicious books and publications against Christianity'.[79] Nonetheless, Laqueur has argued that the quantity of basic literacy transmitted by charity schools probably could not compete with that supplied by the proliferating private day schools. He contends that in the early nineteenth century, parents preferred to pay to send children to private schools, and pay the 4d or 8d per week demanded, rather than make use of the free schooling available at the local National school.[80] This was possibly the case in Oxford. In 1818 the vicar of St Peter in East claimed that of the children of the poorer classes 'many are educated at a moderate price by masters and mistresses in the city'.[81] There is no evidence by which to judge parental preferences in eighteenth-century Oxford, but the motives which Laqueur ascribes to poor parents generally for the later period could plausibly have pertained earlier. Families could choose to opt in to private schooling sporadically, when they could afford the fee and the child could be spared from family or work duties. Private schools did not have rules governing truancy and they certainly did not try to impose rules on the conduct of parents. These are convincing reasons why even the poorest families might have preferred to pay for children's education when they could, rather than receive charity schooling.

As a counterweight to possible disincentives, schools did offer the material advantages of free clothing and reliable access to an apprenticeship. Contemporaries writing about charity schools seemed to accept that it was necessary to offer some inducements to ensure that parents co-operated with their children's continued attendance. Clothing children, for example, took some of the burden off parents, for 'without some advantages of the latter sort, poor People would not send their children to our charity schools'.[82]

These criteria can form the basis of a comparison between the three largest Oxford charity schools, and it seems that the quality of the services they offered were quite divergent. Take clothing: the SPCK calculated that a complete suit of charity school clothes would cost approximately 16s. This sum would have bought a coat, breeches, waistcoat, cap, shirt, stockings, shoes with buckles and a pair of gloves.[83] Two of the Oxford schools scored highly against this template. Both the Bluecoat and Greycoat schools bought clothes and shoes annually for their pupils, and from 1763 onwards the Bluecoat bought a second pair of shoes and stockings for all of the boys at Easter. Also both spent more than 16s. The Greycoat spent an average of £1 2s on each pupil every year, slightly less than the £1 5s spent at the Bluecoat. Nixon's school, however, offered no clothes at all.

Clothing could be crucial in determining attitudes towards a charity, but responses by beneficiaries were not always predictable. The provision of clothing was a feature of the older, 'hospital' types of charity that bought gowns and coats for inmates. Clothing for charity recipients may have been as much tradition as it was an apparent incentive. Schools may have hoped that such traditions assisted in binding the child more closely to the school, and inspired a sense of belonging, allegiance and other positive if intangible outcomes. Pupils and their families may have taken a more pragmatic and less upbeat view.[84] Indeed there is evidence that uniforms which had to be worn to attend free schools were not necessarily viewed as a benefit by children's families but rather as a disadvantage, a mark of poverty which carried stigma rather than status.[85]

The short-term access to free clothing had to be weighed against the longer-term view of apprenticing opportunities.[86] Boys at the Greycoat could expect guaranteed admission to an apprenticeship when they left school, and that a premium of £10 would be paid to their master, which made this easily the most munificent school scheme. Nixon's school offered less money, £5 or £4 10s per pupil, and apparently secured apprenticeship places for only twenty-seven percent of boys. The Blue-coat school changed its apprenticing policy in the middle of the century to become the least generous establishment. From 1748 to 1755 boys could be confident of being apprenticed with £5 on leaving school, but by the 1760s it had become the rule to apprentice boys or put them out to service with only £2.

But schoolboys benefited from school membership in other ways, when parish officers, parents and others supplemented the apprentice-ship premium offered by the school.[87] This information can be obtained in Oxford only when boys were apprenticed to freemen.

Some boys from all three schools obtained extra apprenticing money, but Greycoat boys received this money from parents whereas Bluecoat and Nixon's boys acquired most of their supplements from other charities such as town apprenticing charities. There was a neat synergy here; the Bluecoat and Nixon's schools were run principally by the corporation, either as a body or as individual trustees, and the same men were respon-sible for the disposal of town charity money. Boys were beneficiaries of Bogan's and Thomas's charities and received between £3 and £8 more towards their premiums. Two boys at the Bluecoat were also appren-ticed by Hody's parish charity, although in these cases boys did not also receive school money. In effect, the apprenticing part of the charity was failing, a common fault of charity school finance, but was being propped up by other charity money. The greater tendency of parents to contribute

Table 5.2 *Supplements to Oxford charity school apprenticeship premiums*

	No. of boys for whom information available	No. receiving school money only	No. receiving extra money	No. taking money from parents	No. taking money from other relatives	No. taking money from charity funds	No. taking money from parish funds	No. taking money from other sources
Blue-coat	25	11	14	4	1	8	0	1
Grey-coat	69	54	15	12	1	1	0	1
Nixon's	48	35	13	2	0	9	1	1

Source: Graham, *Oxford City Apprentices.*

to Greycoat premiums may suggest that a marginally wealthier cohort of the town's population managed to exploit the slightly better facilities at the Greycoat school. If parents were able to contribute £5 or £10, this money may have been saved for the purpose or be evidence of former prosperity. These people were the very 'respectable' poor.

Even when supplemented, these premiums were not sufficient to threaten the established social order; contrary to the fears of schools' opponents, pupils in Oxford were definitely not being educated beyond their station in life. The range of occupations followed by boys' fathers can be compared with the occupations to which boys were later apprenticed; over sixty percent of both groups were given one of ten job labels.

It is relatively self-evident that boys would not have been apprenticed to unskilled labourers but might well have had labourer fathers. To this extent, charity apprenticeships might conceivably have spared boys a life of unskilled labour, but did not give them a decisive boost up the social ladder. Tailors and cordwainers were the two trades most commonly followed by fathers and masters. Both typically attracted high proportions of charity and poor boys, had low average premiums and suffered similar occupational illnesses related to close indoors work and a static, bent posture. They did not necessarily have very good employment prospects but were sufficiently successful as groups to have their own companies in Oxford.

Occupations best represented among fathers include barge and boatmen, butchers, coopers and gardeners. The absence of bargemen and

Table 5.3 *The occupations of fathers and masters of charity school boys*

	Fathers		Masters	
	No.	%	No.	%
Barber	7	2	19	6
Barge/boatman	10	3	0	0
Butcher	28	7	9	3
Carpenter	18	5	29	9
Cooper	14	4	7	2
Cordwainer	30	8	60	19
Gardener	15	4	5	2
Joiner/cabinetmaker	9	2	25	8
Labourer	53	14	0	0
Tailor	64	17	43	14
Total	248	66	197	63

boatmen from the list of masters is not particularly surprising. Watermen may have been trained by their fathers without a formal apprenticeship, given their stereotypical 'dynastic tendencies'.[88] Similarly, butchering was often a family trade.[89] Gardeners may well have been virtually unskilled labourers who worked in the market gardens around Oxford and so have been in a similar position to labourers. Coopers were among the freemen most frequently taking apprentices into the woodworking trades in Oxford prior to 1750 but numbers declined after this date. This may indicate a shrinking of Oxford coopering business due to external competition in the second half of the century.[90] In contrast, barbers, carpenters and joiners were all better represented by masters. Barbers were in an interesting position in Oxford; they were matriculated tradesmen, which meant that they depended heavily on the custom of the university and did not have to take up the freedom. Their apparent prominence may simply derive from the good information on masters supplied by the records of the Greycoat school; 17 of the 19 apprenticeships to barbers were arranged by the Greycoat. Alternatively, tradesmen who were already connected with the university may have been more keen to take university school apprentices (or the school may have been better able to persuade them to take boys).

Boys were predominantly apprenticed inside the town of Oxford rather than being sent to masters elsewhere. Of all boys apprenticed by the Greycoat school, for example, seventy-two percent were bound to Oxford masters, while the thinner information from the other two schools still echoes this emphasis on the town. Apprenticing charities were compelled to be a little sensitive to the issue of placement because a term of apprenticeship was one means of acquiring a new settlement, and this became explicitly contentious is some places.[91] It is not clear, though, whether this inadvertent power on the part of charity schools was resented by poor-law authorities; individual parishes can occasionally be found reprimanding inhabitants for taking apprentices from outside the parish, but such shreds of evidence are scanty and I have never yet encountered reproaches directed specifically at schools.[92]

The reputations of these three schools, within the town and specifically among poor parents, depended upon all of these aspects of school management; the range of the curriculum, enforcement of school rules, or neglect of the master (as was alleged of Mr Croney at Nixon's), had to be weighed against the benefits or otherwise of compulsory uniform (where the Bluecoat invested most money) and the opportunities for apprenticeship (demonstrably superior at the Greycoat). Two ways to test parental preference relate to repeat custom (were families prepared to send more than one son to the same school?) and withdrawn custom (did families remove boys from school?).

Repeat custom ~~can be measured~~ by the ~~propensity of sib~~lings to secure a nomination to the same school. Some boys were plainly brothers, where they shared the same father's name or some other identifying label, but the maximum number of children potentially involved can be signified only by an overlap of surnames. This reveals an interesting difference between the schools.

The percentage of boys who definitely attended Nixon's free school with brothers is striking. This must partly be a testament to parental preference, but is also a function of the school's policy to prefer the sons of freemen (and omit the children of university employees). The number

Table 5.4 *Siblings at Oxford charity schools*

	Definite siblings		Additional boys potentially related
	No.	%	No.
Bluecoat	29	16.0	33
Greycoat	8	4.3	74
Nixon's	133	55.9	0

of families who were also poor enough to qualify for entry presumably reduced the number of eligible boys still further. Most families whose applications were successful sent two sons but others like Thomas Walker, a tailor from St Peter le Bailey, sent four of his sons to the school between 1733 and 1739. Therefore the number of families benefiting from this educational charity was far fewer than the total number of pupils because certain families established a long-term relationship with a school. Once the family was known to the trustees and the subscribers, it was presumably easier for another younger brother to be drawn to their attention.

Yet the evidence of withdrawn custom shows the three schools enjoying different sorts of allegiance. Access to three schools for boys of eight to fourteen years old in the same town gave rise to a little movement between them, as parents transferred sons from one school to another; five percent of boys attended two of the schools successively. There was a decided flow of boys away from Nixon's and the Bluecoat school in favour of the Greycoat; all four of the boys who moved from the Bluecoat and twelve out of the twenty who moved from Nixon's went there. The university school obviously had a cachet not matched elsewhere. The small number of definite siblings attending the Greycoat can now be seen in a different light; perhaps competition for places meant that brothers were less well placed to attend the same school.

The extent of pauper involvement in charity schools

At least one school promoter lamented his inability to 'trace minutely the Progress and Issue in Life of all the former children from these Schools'.[93] Fortunately some of the charity school boys in Oxford can be traced or identified in other contexts, specifically relating to parish relief. How many children were in school and on parish relief at the same time, and what was the relationship between the experience of pauperism and access to schools? Were people more likely to be paupers before, during or after their time at school?

None of the three main charity schools in Oxford denied entry to pauper children; paupers or workhouse inmates were sometimes excluded under the terms of endowment or rules.[94] Therefore the names of all charity school boys were compared with the names of all paupers listed by overseers in five selected Oxford parishes between 1740 and 1770 (see appendix 1.1, 'Prosopographical methodology').[95] Of the 641 schoolboys whose names were known, probable connections with paupers were found for 48 and possible connections for a further 76. Both probable and possible connections with paupers were made least often with boys at the Greycoat school. In the case of probable connections this might be wholly attributable to problems with the source but this cannot explain the infrequency of possible connections. As the Greycoat school was probably the most desirable educational option of the three charity schools, this is further evidence that places tended to be secured by slightly wealthier families.

As with similar exercises conducted in earlier chapters, this comparison exercise used the overseers' accounts of only selected Oxford parishes. These parishes between them contained around half of the population of the town at this time, so the findings of this comparison can be doubled to give the likely connections between charity boys and paupers from the town as a whole. This would mean that around fourteen percent of all charity boys were probably paupers at some time, and that a further twenty-four percent would have possible connections with paupers.

The range of contacts between boys, their families and the parish, was highly varied. Not all probable connections with people mentioned in overseers' accounts were long-term paupers or pensioners. Some families received only extraordinary or occasional relief payments. Also, not all boys or their families were paupers in the same years which boys spent at school. Only twenty-one or under half appear in overseers' accounts and school records simultaneously. It was quite common for families to be relieved only in years before boys went to school. This may have been a result of the life-cycle aspect of poverty. If families struggled to cope with very young children but were increasingly able to cope as children got older, particularly if some left home, were apprenticed or started earning, they may have regained full financial independence before the charity school child reached school age. Another fairly large group were those who needed relief well after their time at school. This included the likes of Jonathon Hughes who was at Nixon's in the 1730s but whose young family became needy in the 1760s. He was buried by the parish of St Peter le Bailey in 1765. Similarly, Abel Gold was apprenticed by the Greycoat school in 1741 but he needed relief only as a married man, after his family fell ill during 1758. In 1764 his rent became an annual charge on the parish and by August 1766 he had run away, a 'rascal' in the eyes of the parish.

Although relatively few families had children who were paupers and pupils simultaneously, at least one boy received a parish pension in his own right. John Goodgame of St Peter in East was paid a pension of at least one shilling per week, sometimes more, from 1758 until May 1764 when he was apprenticed by the Greycoat. He also received payments for clothes (in addition to school-bought clothes), and when he contracted smallpox in 1759. Another boy, James Nichols, did not receive a pension from St Peter le Bailey but was maintained for the parish by Mrs

Woodward, a parish equivalent of a foster mother, after his own mother died in 1765. His family was still on relief when he went to the Bluecoat in 1766. Some charity school boys saw the inside of a workhouse. Simon Bowers was born in one and may have returned to the same house with his mother for six months in 1754 shortly before he was admitted to Nixon's. Boys even had definite connections with the unruly poor. John and William Ensley were admitted to Nixon's in 1755 and their parents were both admitted to the Oxford town house of correction in 1758.

It seems that school children and the adults they became experienced all levels of involvement with the parish. Payments to them ran the usual gamut from pensions and workhouse places to occasional payments for illness. Yet behind this breadth of experience very few boys were definitely being supported by parishes while they were in school. Perhaps only two or three boys at any one time in a charity school of thirty to fifty boys had families who were substantially reliant on parishes. Thus it is not fair to generalise that 'children from workhouses would often be sent to local charity schools'.[96] The close investigation of Oxford shows that there was no link between schools and workhouses. On balance, charity schooling was a benefit to the poor who did not need parish relief.

Paupers in schools

If the available evidence is scrutinised in the opposite direction, starting with the parishes rather than the schools, then the direct involvement of parish officers with charity schools in Oxford is even more scanty. When the three subscription schools first opened in 1708, some parishes subscribed to the Bluecoat girls' school.[97] Overseers' accounts made only one clear reference to a pauper pupil, when in 1764, St Peter in East parish gave Mrs Tay 1s to pay for her son's entrance to the Bluecoat. Another payment can be inferred for the same parish; during 1762–64 St Peter in East paid Mr Bradley 2s each year for schooling Goodgame's boy when Mr Bradley was the master of the Greycoat. This money represented the small contributions required by charity schools from pupils for firewood or books.

More interesting are the payments by St Mary Magdalen parish in 1747 to Mr Croney for the quarterly schooling bills of children called Ives, Roberts, Boddington and Wiggins. Mr Croney was the master of Nixon's who proved so unpopular with the trustees. The implication is that charity school masters may have been teaching paupers, but as paying pupils not as charity boys. The parish paid around 4s per quarter for each of these boys' educations, considerably more than the 1–2d per quarter which rule 17 of the school estimated would be the cost to children for candles. In addition, none of these four boys' names are among the names in the school register. It may be that the register is faulty, but it is more likely that Croney was taking them as paying pupils. If he charged 4s per quarter per pupil, his income from each child would have been comparable with that of the mistress of the Bluecoat girls' school who was paid 15s per girl per year in the late 1750s.[98] There is even fragmentary evidence that parishes might be prepared to pay for paupers' education at non-charity schools. St Michael's parish paid for two boys to attend Brickland's private school in Catte Street, one during 1744–45 and the other 1758–59.[99]

Other pauper children were educated in dame schools in Oxford, and in the process overseers provide the best information available for the identities of women working in this way. Mrs Tubb was teaching pauper children in the 1740s. In 1745 St Peter in East paid her for children's schooling and in 1747 St Mary Magdalen paid her to teach Day's children. Mrs Brown taught in the 1760s and charged 2d per week per child, whereas a Mrs Franklin charged 4d per week. These children in dame schools at the parish cost were aged between three and twelve. Individual boys received some education of this type before entering a charity school. William Day, a Bluecoat boy, was probably one of Day's children educated by St Mary Magdalen at dame school in 1747. This is not intrinsically surprising, since some charity schools tried to ensure that pupils had basic literacy skills before they were permitted to attend. In Leeds, the rules of the subscription charity school included the stipulation that children must already know the letters of the alphabet.[100] What is significant is the exposure of one pauper boy to two different forms of elementary education, at least one of which was supported by the parish. Perhaps more characteristically, the children taught at dame school by St Peter in East included Robert Kite and Frances Simpson who were both later apprenticed by the parish. This shows that parish officers did not always assume apprenticeship to be the only appropriate training for the children of the poor; other forms of outlay were also legitimate or desirable.

Yet far from all children named in overseers' accounts in any of the urban parishes examined in this book were educated at the expense of the parish, even where parishes made a habit of paying for some schooling. How did overseers decide who to send to school, and how many children were left out? Unfortunately there are no grounds on which to surmise or infer parochial strategy. It may have been that some parents asked for schooling to be paid for and vestries complied. Alternatively, schooling may have been a way to deal with children drawn to parish officers' attention as unoccupied or troublesome. Child unemployment was likely to have been a problem in Oxford, since the town had no obvious manufacturing industry in which to place them.[101] Urban parishes were potentially forestalling the evolution of juvenile crime as a discrete problem and responding with this rather spotty attention to educational provision. Peter King has ascribed the high profile of juvenile delinquency in the early nineteenth century to a 'movement from diversion to discipline', whereby measures to control unruly children were shifting from informal discipline imposed by parents and schoolteachers to formal indictment.[102] Certainly in the 1820s 'the Prison Discipline Society saw the education of the poor as a preventative measure' but others remained concerned about the deleterious effects of education if it was not swiftly followed by arduous employment.[103] Fears of raising people 'above their station' were highly persistent. Doubtless different ideas and practices prevailed in different parishes. Financial considerations will have played some part in determining parish attitudes towards paying for schooling. It is telling that in Oxford, children educated at Brickland's school came from St Michael, one of the wealthier town parishes. Still, it would be heartening to think that parishes also paid some attention to the children themselves; what was deemed appropriate in the way of education and training may have been based in part on perceptions of the abilities and dispositions of different children.

Charity versus pauper apprenticeships

In Jones's study of the charity school movement, it is claimed that the schemes for apprenticing or placing out charity children at the end of their schooling were designed at the time to save them from the unenviable fate of parish apprenticeships. A combination of low premiums paid by parish officers and the practice of apprenticing to a different parish (in order to secure a new settlement for the child) were responsible for their placements in the lowest unskilled positions and consequently for the cruelty and neglect they suffered.[104] It is not difficult to find evidence that Oxford parish apprentices suffered their share of unhealthy and cruel circumstances. In 1745 Ann Green was bound to Jane French, only to be discharged from her indentures two years later after French beat her. Charles Low who was apprenticed to John Timothy of Thame by St Michael's parish in 1757 was found dead in a field in 1761.[105]

Nevertheless, it is not clear that charity schools provided intrinsically better places than parishes. A comparison of the apprenticeships secured in Oxford by schools with those arranged by parishes reveals that although some of the stereotypes apply, the role of charity schools may have been to supply more of the same type of places. It has been seen that the premiums offered by schools ranged between £5 and £10 when unsupplemented by parents or other charities. Parishes managed to provide broadly comparable premiums for the majority of children even when they came from impoverished parishes. Of sixty-three pauper apprentices[106] found by reference to parish records, forty-one had cash paid by the parish while another twelve received money from a town or parish charity either on its own or in addition to overseers' contributions. This leaves only ten for whom no money can be found to have changed hands.

The sums paid with parish children ranged from £2 2s to £12, although very few payments of less than £3 were made. Most received around £5. This means that some children's masters received more than was paid by the Greycoat school, and all received more than was paid by the Bluecoat after 1763. Even the children of St Peter le Bailey, one of the poorest town parishes, were not neglected. These payments compare well with the average premiums required by many trades in Warwickshire in the eighteenth century. The average premiums paid to tailors, hatters, cordwainers, bricklayers and numerous other trades on behalf of paupers and non-paupers alike were all under £10 for the period 1700–1834.[107] Of course, not all occupations which demanded a premium of £10 or less enjoyed the same prospects but the evidence from Oxford suggests that poor children were not excluded from places simply because they lacked appropriate premiums.

Another similarity between parish apprentices and charity boys was the way parish premiums were supplemented from other sources. The example of the two children Mary and William Bignell in 1756 must have been fairly unusual. They had been in the workhouse for two years yet their father contributed to their premiums. In addition to the £2 10s spent by St Michael's parish on each child, he gave £7 10s for his daughter to learn spinning and housewifery and also £2 10s for his son to learn husbandry. Extra money came more often from charities. Richard Edmonds was bound to Oxford freeman Edward Bowers in 1758 with £8 10s of Thomas's charity money. In the same year St Peter in East agreed at a vestry meeting to pay Bowers a further £5 in two payments. It was not only wealthy parishes which could afford to do this. St Peter le Bailey supplemented £5 of town charity with another £5 to apprentice Francis Stapler in 1752. This is all the more surprising as town apprenticeship charities (aside from the schools) were not extensive. Town charity was allocated to apprentice up to thirteen children per year, or fewer than one child per town parish per year.[108]

Age data, where available, also puts the parish apprenticeships in a favourable light. Of the sixty-three parish apprentices studied, an age or baptism date could be found for a third. On average, as elsewhere, Oxford parish apprentices were bound out marginally younger than non-pauper children but not when they were very small.[109] The vast majority of Oxford apprentices were over ten, and over half were indentured at eleven to thirteen years. The fact that some children were fifteen or sixteen before being placed out suggests that parishes did not always hustle them into an apprenticeship and a new settlement to save the rates.

One way in which parish apprentices did conform to type was they were almost exclusively bound outside their parish of residence. The destination is unknown for twenty-six of the sixty-three apprentices, but only fourteen were decisively bound to other Oxford city parishes; the remaining twenty-three went to masters elsewhere, principally towns and villages in Oxfordshire and Berkshire. This tendency to place children outside their parish of origin cannot have been true for all parish apprentices. It is possible that some children were apprenticed to parishioners without formal indentures or a premium. For example, in St Mary Magdalen parish in 1757, the vestry announced that anyone could have a child out of the workhouse. The child would be clothed but would not be given with money;[110] however, parishioners did not find this an attractive offer, since no children were taken out of the house on this basis. Parishes could even choose to compel parishioners to take apprentices in turn (under the Statute of Artificers), but there is no evidence for this occurring in mid-century Oxford.[111]

The number of parish apprentices whose masters' occupations are known is small. Obviously the charity schools studied here contained no girls but twenty-five percent of these parish apprentices were girls. In Warwickshire it was found that ninety-nine percent of all apprentices to housewifery were parish girls and Oxford overseers also seemed to favour this type of placement.[112] Leather trades were favoured by both parishes and charity schools; nine parish boys went to cordwainers or shoemakers. It is striking, however, that no parish children seem to have been apprenticed to tailors. This is in contrast to the charity boy masters and to the proportion of all town apprentices to freeman tailors. Tailoring and clothing accounted for fifteen to seventeen percent of all apprentices to freemen throughout the eighteenth century.[113]

From the large number of trades which took one parish apprentice each it is clear that the same broad sweep of occupations were open to both types of apprentice, from the parish and from charity schools. In some instances they even shared the same masters. Richard Edmonds was apprenticed to a farrier Edward Bowers in 1758 by St Peter in East parish. He joined another boy, Henry Sellar, who had already served four years of his time with the same master having been placed with Bowers in 1754 by the Greycoat. It is improbable that much overlap of this type occurred, where the same master took charity and parish boys, because the numbers of parish children bound away from the town militate against it. Still, this evidence suggests that the gap between charity school and pauper apprenticeships was probably much smaller than schools would have liked to think.

For the majority of poor children in the eighteenth century, parish or charity school provisions for education and apprenticeship provided an opportunity to escape child unemployment and a life of unskilled labouring but the mid-century saw the arrival of a new style of institution. The Foundling Hospital was at first a purely metropolitan charity initiative but the country branches of the hospital, opened in response to parliamentary funding (and the struggle to maintain an open-door policy in the face of huge demand) provided an alternative model for the maintenance of children's welfare. The surviving records of the Shrewsbury experiment allow some interesting comparisons to be made between the treatment of local children and the experience of London foundlings who were transplanted to Shropshire.

The Shrewsbury branch of the Foundling Hospital

The Foundling had a branch hospital in Shrewsbury for fourteen years, and the treatment of children by this essentially metropolitan charity forms a useful contrast with both charity schools and parish provisions for children. Essentially the Foundling aimed to combine the residential welfare function of parish workhouses with the educational and apprenticing policies that were broadly shared by schools and parishes and additionally with the some-time interest of schools in employing poor children.

The domestic arrangements made for housing children in Shrewsbury were fairly complex. The local committee both received older children from London who were immediately installed in the country hospital and sent nurses to London to collect small babies. The women who travelled to London in this capacity caused something of a scandal by begging their way to London, despite having been paid in advance for their journey.[114] The hospital opened in 1759 in leased premises in Dog Lane but the committee also ordered new premises to be built. The new hospital was swiftly constructed in Kingsland to the south-west of the town, on a rise above the south bank of the River Severn, and the children were installed there around November 1761. The hospital was staffed by a master, matron and numerous nurses and maids.[115] There was probably accommodation for around eighty children at Dog Lane but, at its height, the new building held 400 foundlings.[116] While the hospital cared for eighty children, it was comparable in size or capacity with the St Chad's workhouse or the infirmary. When the charity expanded its role to fill the new building, it became by far the largest charitable or relief venture in the town.

Material conditions inside the Shrewsbury Foundling Hospital (at both
Dog Lane and Kingsland) appear to have borne some superficial similarities to workhouse life. These might be attributable to the joint needs
of workhouses and the Foundling charity to provide residential care for
large numbers of people. In Dog Lane all of the children of each sex slept
in the same room. In the girls' ward there were fifteen beds and in the
boys' eighteen suggesting that, as 'Two Children lye in a Bed', thirty to
thirty-six children were sleeping in each room.[117] Another similarity to
workhouse organisation related to the serving of food. The hospital also
favoured a combination of trenchers and spoons to feed their inmates.

Yet the hospital achieved some touches of relative sophistication not
mentioned in any of the workhouse inventories. The children's wards
boasted two or three close stools with pewter pans, and bars to prevent
the children from accidentally falling into the fire. The Foundling was
much more lavishly equipped than any of the workhouses studied. The
inventories taken in 1759, 1767 and 1772 reveal more in terms of quantity and variety of kitchen utensils, soft furnishings and bedding than
in any of the workhouses. Also the size of the new building allowed a
complexity of organisation that was not an option for many individual
parishes. Separate lodging rooms for all of the residential staff were
matched by more numerous rooms for children to sleep in than had been
available in Dog Lane. They continued to be divided by sex but also by
age bands (for example, for sleeping in the big boys' dormitory).

The diet provided at the Shrewsbury Foundling Hospital shared many
similarities with workhouse diets.[118] Three meals were served per day.
Breakfast was either bread, gruel or milk pottage. Supper was always
bread, with a portion of cheese three times per week. Dinners were based
on the same dishes of roast or boiled meat, stew or pudding which were
suited to any institution which tried to feed large numbers of people. Yet
there were differences between this and other institutions based on the
age profile of the inmates. Specifically, the foundlings were not given small
beer to drink; presumably they received milk or whey instead. Their diet
may have been more rich in vitamin C than some workhouse diets since
the recommended dietary always stipulated greens to be served with the
meat at dinner. Like workhouse paupers, foundlings could look forward
to treats of plum pudding and gooseberry pie on special occasions.

Unlike most charity schools and some workhouses, the Foundling
consistently tried to put the poor children in their charge to work. In
Shrewsbury, this came to involve carding, spinning and weaving, although
initial difficulties had to be overcome to achieve regular working practice.
In 1760, the Shrewsbury committee wrote to London for advice, as the
type of spinning wheel then used 'in this country'[119] was thought to be

too difficult for children to manage. A visit to the Foundling Country Hospital at Ackworth to learn how work was conducted there had to be postponed, but eventually a Mr Mostyn of Denbigh sent a boy and girl from his own manufacture to instruct the children in Shrewsbury in scribbling (coarse carding) and spinning. Woollen cloth was sold from the Shrewsbury hospital in 1767.[120]

Foundlings were given rudimentary schooling in addition to being set to work; the first schoolmaster was appointed on 1 January 1761. Thereafter, masters and mistresses taught the children to read and may have taught the boys to write. In London some boys were taught to write from 1759 onwards. There was a considerable turnover in educational staff at Shrewsbury, with eighteen masters and mistresses being employed between 1761 and 1767 but their continued recruitment and the provisioning of two schoolrooms demonstrates the sustained commitment of the charity to basic schooling.[121]

The Shrewsbury and London committees alike were evidently concerned with the general health of their charges and made more obvious attempts than any of the parishes studied to prevent illness. The Foundling made a concerted effort to inoculate against smallpox, not a policy pursued by any of the parishes in this study. This was certainly attributable to the influence of the London committee.[122] A house was rented on Clerimont Hill to house the sick and those recovering from inoculation. In 1764 a sedan chair was acquired to carry sick children there.[123] Early links with the Salop Infirmary also helped the Foundling to establish its own health care arrangements. The infirmary let the Foundling have medicines at 'prime cost'[124] until the children's charity acquired its own dispensary, and representatives of the infirmary's medical staff agreed to act as physician, surgeon and apothecary for the Foundling.[125] The medical aspect of child care could be quite hazardous for Foundling employees. Five died as a result of illness contracted at the sick house. Both committees also recognised the importance of fresh air to children's health. In November 1758 London had expressed the hope that the hired house would provide the children with the opportunity 'of being in the Open Air, without which they cannot be in any tolerable State of Health'.[126] The new building at Kingsland had an area of ground set aside for play. In addition, work was curtailed or modified if it was thought to threaten health. The matron reported on 7 May 1759 that if the little girls were made to spin, it would 'prejudice their shapes' so thereafter only the larger girls were expected to spin.

The unrestricted admissions policy was supposed to apply to London foundlings only. Children would be taken in by the London hospital and transported to the country branches for the duration of their infancy and

childhood. As adolescents they would be returned to London for apprenticing. In practice, the system worked a little differently. Many children hailed from the provinces; their presumably desperate parents (or
parental intermediaries) travelled to London with the specific design of
surrendering them to the Foundling. The local committee in Shrewsbury
was apparently fearful that Shropshire parish officers would persuade
parents to part with their infants and then foist the children directly on
to the country hospital. In April 1759 (two months after the first children
arrived from London), the committee decided to publish a warning in the
Birmingham, Chester and Worcester newspapers and in 300 handbills
that 'if any Parish Officers or others shall presume to take any Child
from its Parents by Force to send to the Foundling Hospital they shall be
prosecuted at the Expense of the Hospital'.[127]

Yet in subsequent (if infrequent) encounters with local children, the
committee seemed either reluctant to surrender responsibility or actively
keen to keep local children once they had been taken into the Foundling.
One Mary Lamb made a complaint against a parish officer in Westbury
for having removed her son to the Foundling. Yet close investigation
seemed to reveal that Lamb was more eager to 'Extort' money from her
parish to travel to her husband than she was to complain against the
loss of her child. In a letter, she announced herself to be 'contented now
she knew her Child was safe in the Hospital'.[128] Indeed in 1763, it was
decided that the hospital would *try* to gain possession of one particular
child, who was reported to be 'secreted' at the house of a Catholic. This
was achieved within the month. The only instance when the hospital
refused to care for local children arose in relation to the Williams girls.[129]
These unfortunates had either been abandoned by their parents or were
orphans who were maintained from county funds in one of the Shropshire county houses of correction from the late 1750s until at least 1764.
The county rather than any individual parish may have been forced to
take responsibility if the children's legal settlement was unknown. The
eldest girl Martha was apprenticed (again from county funds) in 1760
but Catherine and Susannah remained in bridewell. In April 1762, the
county tried to negotiate a place for them at the Foundling and the two
girls did go and stay at the hospital for two months. Yet the county
was not prepared to pay the 2s per girl per week that the Foundling
demanded, so in June they were returned to the bridewell. The timing of
these examples suggests that the apparently contradictory attitude that
the Shrewsbury committee demonstrated was not wholly explained by
the duration of the unrestricted admissions policy. Varied responses to
local children may have been the result of a complex set of pressures
including instructions from London, local and religious sympathies or

prejudices and financial concerns.

Like charity school pupils, foundlings were dispatched by their charity to an apprenticeship. The characteristics of these apprenticeships echoed parish arrangements. Most foundlings were supposed to be apprenticed in London but some children were apprenticed directly from the Shrewsbury hospital to midlands tradesmen.[130] Between 1759 and 1767, thirty-nine children were apprenticed in Shrewsbury, other Shropshire towns, Birmingham and Kidderminster and this practice continued until the hospital's closure in 1772. This geographical range was entirely consistent with the experiences of Shrewsbury pauper children.[131] There did not appear to be any great local outcry against foundlings being apprenticed in Shropshire, despite the fact that most had come from London but would gain a settlement locally. The Foundling Hospital had to place apprentices where they would gain a settlement because, as foundlings, they had no recourse to their parents' parish of settlement. Perhaps the limited numbers involved in local apprenticeships (the equivalent of around five per year) did not seem to pose a threat to the local poor rates. Letters kept with the Shropshire records were generally requests for apprentices not complaints. Occupationally, experiences of foundlings placed out in the midlands were more akin to those of local paupers than to their London counterparts'. In London before 1763, most girls from the Foundling were put out to service and most boys sent to sea. After the end of the Seven Years War, places in the merchant marine were given to ex-Navy boys so the London Foundling had to place boys in trade and was even forced to consider mass apprenticeships to manufacturers.[132] Shrewsbury foundlings by contrast went to farmers, weavers, carpenters and other places familiar to parish children. Similarly, the age distribution of apprentices from the Foundling at Shrewsbury is identical to that found for parish apprentices in Oxford. A sample of 702 children ranged in age from just six to eighteen, but less than five percent were apprenticed before the age of ten. The average age at apprenticeship was 11.8.[133] Therefore it is not clear that the majority of foundlings experienced substantially better conditions as apprentices than either parish or charity school children.

In two respects, however, the financial conditions of a foundling's apprenticeship were substantially different to those of either a parish pauper or a charity pupil. First, the London hospital had decided that no premiums would be paid with their apprentices (whereas Shrewsbury pauper children could expect an average premium of £2 5s 6d).[134] The London committee feared that poor people would be tempted by the money to take an apprentice and then be forced to seek parish relief for themselves and the foundling when the premium ran out. Instead the charity reasoned that their children would make desirable apprentices without a fee, and insisted that the circumstances of potential masters be investigated. As a result, masters needed a recommendation from their clergyman or another authority to confirm their suitability, but as pressure increased to find apprenticeship places, these checks became more burdensome and less stringent. Second, foundlings' indentures stipulated that masters should pay their apprentices £5 per year in the last three years of the contract. In March 1760, the Shrewsbury local committee wrote to London proposing to excuse masters from providing clothes for apprentices in the same three years, as a requirement for both clothes and wages might prove an obstacle to placing apprentices; unfortunately, London's reply was not recorded.

Also there is circumstantial evidence that foundling apprentices may have found more emotionally satisfying places than might have been possible for pauper children. Numerous foundlings who were boarded out with local women effectively became foster children. Adults and foundlings alike found it very difficult to part when the child was taken into the hospital. For example, in September 1767, Ann Stoaks wrote to the Shrewsbury committee asking if she and her husband could take back the child Bernard Harris.[135] They had cared for him since he was one month old and they missed him. Ann added persuasively that her husband earned ten or eleven shillings per week as a papermaker and would teach Bernard the same trade. Many children in Shropshire and from the other country hospitals were eventually apprenticed to the husbands of their former nurses.[136]

Finally, the Foundling in Shrewsbury had an important impact on poor working adults in the town. The hospital must have given a significant boost to the town's market economy. It employed builders and labourers to construct the new hospital in Kingsland and a new road up the hill from the Severn to the new hospital. It made contracts with tradesmen to supply the furniture, clothing and foodstuffs required for the day-to-day running of the hospital and the sick house on Clerimont Hill. It was also a large employer of domestics. In the decade 1758 to 1767 it employed 116 people, mostly women as nurses, maids and cooks.[137] This was a mixed blessing, as the working conditions were quite challenging; a reliable salary of £3 10s or £4 per year for the majority of these women was insufficient to prevent high staff turnover, with over a third leaving as a result of resignation.

The Shrewsbury branch of the Foundling hospital had a relatively short-lived impact on the town, in the sense that it operated for just fourteen years, from 1758 to 1772, and made a difference only to individual local children. Still, its primary and longer-term role in the locality may have been instructive rather than direct. The hospital was the largest institution in Shrewsbury at the time, larger than any of the parish work-houses and more imposing than the Shropshire Infirmary. It required the active involvement of local elites to staff the Shrewsbury branch committee (including the Lord Lieutenant of Salop, Members of Parliament for Shrewsbury and other boroughs and Shrewsbury gentlemen such as the Reverend Orton).[138] The charity consequentially exposed these men to metropolitan methodology, scale of working and rules. It is plausible that the example set by the Foundling in these years became useful or influential in inspiring the controlling committee of the Shrewsbury House of Industry, which was opened just twelve years after the Foundling abandoned Shrewsbury (and in the same premises which the charity had built).[139]

Conclusion

Charity schools offered a controversial model of long-term welfare for most of the eighteenth century, and their supporters were compelled to fight a rear-guard action against accusations that they would educate children 'beyond their station'. This was ironic in the sense that this was precisely the desired aim, to improve the life chances of children otherwise destined (it was feared) for dependent poverty. A close analysis of school operation and clientele finds that opportunities for social elevation were present but marginal. Two boys who were at the Oxford Bluecoat together in 1758 illustrate the extremes of children's experiences. Steven Kinsill prospered, and his son established the firm of Kinsill and son that in turn supplied the Bluecoat with books for many years.[140] By contrast Charles Hargrave wasted his prestigious apprenticeship to the Attorney Mr Taylor by misbehaviour, which resulted in the cancellation of his indentures in April 1759.[141] Opportunities occasionally arose for advancement as a result of the liaison by schools between poor but able boys and the town or county elite but these rarely allowed poor boys to climb the social ladder. The majority simply advanced incrementally, from their father's status as an unskilled labourer to a semi-skilled but still low-paid occupation.

Parental attitude was key to securing a charity school place, and maximising the potential benefits. This was at odds with school promoters, who saw their task as the removal of children from a baneful domestic influence. Parents in Oxford were not an obstreperous group, so their voices are never directly heard, but they did take advantage of vacancies to move their boys between schools and optimistically position their children for meagre advancement. The vigour of competition for places, and the emotional involvement of parents, is elusive in Oxford; did they, like James Howell of Ely, petition their parishes for assistance with charity school apprenticeships arguing 'how Can we posibley miss such an Opportunity – for the Benifit of our poor Boy'?[142] The perceived value of a charity school place could be higher than its material advantages would, with hindsight, suggest.

Eighteenth-century contemporaries were confused about the relative roles of the parish and charity schools in the education and training of poor children and adolescents. This has led to some doubt over who benefited from the establishment of such schools. The evidence from Oxford shows that the children of paupers did not tend to occupy a school place at the same time that their family needed regular parish payments or support, largely vindicating Joan Lane's view. Families were more likely to need relief before their child went to school; however, paupers were not wholly excluded. Moreover, the apprenticeship opportunities offered by schools were comparable with provisions paid for by parishes. Charity schools cannot be seen as having rescued children from the terrors of a parish apprenticeship, but may have ensured that more of the same apprenticeship places were available. In some cases parish apprentices were better resourced.

The country branches of the Foundling Hospital witnessed the injection of metropolitan philanthropy into provincial communities. The result in Shrewsbury was a translation of London principles to fit local opportunities and constraints. Metropolitan ideals survived in aspirations for child health, education and in-house work training, but broke down when it came to apprenticeship. Once again, charity offerings were largely comparable to parish provision, rather than a marked improvement. The legacy of the Foundling though was institutional, governing the experiences of the Shrewsbury poor a dozen years after the hospital's closure, since it provided a theoretical model and the physical premises of the town's celebrated House of Industry.

The real benefits to individuals at schools, and at the Foundling Hospital, may have been the greater access to formal education and literacy, and the slim opportunity these offered for the cultural if not material improvement of one's lot. Attempts to gauge the impact of schools on literacy are notoriously fraught, and while the history of education is potentially unbalanced through concentration on formal schools which have left institutional records, these are often patchy enough. The curricula of the Oxford schools are confined to a couple of aspirational remarks, while the kind and extent of informal learning in the town can only be guessed. Assessment of the perceived significance of scholarship, both during and after school years, offers one way forward.[143]

Notes

1 Parts of this chapter were published in my article, 'Charity schools and the parish poor in Oxford, 1740–1770', *Midland History* 22 (1997). I am grateful to the editors for permission to reproduce portions of that article in this revised and expanded treatment.

2 P. Slack, *From Reformation to Improvement: Public Welfare in Early Modern England* (Oxford, 1999), p. 138.

3 D. Owen, *English Philanthropy 1660–1960* (Oxford, 1965), p. 38.

4 A. Borsay, *Medicine and Charity in Georgian Bath: A Social History of the General Infirmary c.1739–1830* (Aldershot, 1999), pp. 211–13.

5 Sir T. Bernard (ed.), *Reports of the Society for Bettering the Condition and Increasing the Comforts of the Poor* 3 (London, 1802), p. 32.

6 L. Granshaw and R. Porter, *The Hospital in History* (London, 1989), pp. 151–3.

7 Borsay, *Medicine and Charity*, pp. 307–8.

8 A. Wilson, 'Conflict, consensus and charity: politics and the provincial voluntary hospitals in the eighteenth century', *English Historical Review,* 111: 442 (1996), 605; P. Wallis, 'Charity, politics and the establishment of York county hospital: a "party job"?', *Northern History* 38: 2 (2001), 249.

9 Granshaw and Porter, *Hospital in History*, p. 152.

10 M. Spufford, *Contrasting Communities* (Cambridge, 1974), p. 173.

11 *Considerations on the Fatal Effects to a Trading Nation of the Present Excess of Public Charities* (London, 1763), p. 47.

12 J. Lane, 'Apprenticeship in Warwickshire 1700–1834' (PhD thesis, Birmingham University, 1977), p. 197; J. Lane, *Apprenticeship in England 1600–1914* (London, 1996), p. 69; J. Simon, 'Was there a charity school movement? the Leicestershire evidence', in B. Simon (ed.), *Education in Leicestershire 1540–1940* (Leicester, 1968), p. 62.

13 D. Simonton, 'Schooling the poor: gender and class in eighteenth-century England', *British Journal for Eighteenth-Century Studies* 23 (2000), 190.

14 D. Andrew, 'On reading charity sermons: eighteenth-century Anglican solicitation and exhortation', *Journal of Ecclesiastical History* 43: 4 (1992), 582.

15 B. Mandeville, *The Fable of the Bees or Private Vices Publick Benefits* with commentary by F. B. Kaye (Oxford, 1988). *Gentleman's Magazine* 28 (1758), 475–7 carried a letter ostensibly from a former charity-school girl 'Betty Broom' who denied that her education had disqualified her from menial work.

16 V. E. Neuberg, *Popular Education in Eighteenth Century England* (London, 1971), p. 3.

17 F. Smith, *A History of English Elementary Education 1760–1902* (London, 1931), p. 42; M. G. Jones, *The Charity School Movement: A Study of Eighteenth Century Puritanism in Action* (Cambridge [1938] 1964), p. 92.

18 E. Owen, *A Sermon upon the Occasion of Opening a Charity School in Warrington* (Warrington, 1782).

19 W. E. Tate, 'The charity sermons 1704–1732 as a source for the history of education', *Journal of Ecclesiastical History* 9 (1958), 64.

20 C. F. Kaestle, '"Between the Scylla of Brutal Ignorance and the Charybdis of a Literary Education": elite attitudes toward mass schooling in early industrial England and America', in L. Stone (ed.), *Schooling and Society: Studies in the History of Education* (Baltimore, 1976), p. 180.

21 Proverbs 22:6.

22 W. Hendley, *A Defence of the Charity Schools* (London, 1725), p. 16.

23 Owen, *A Sermon*, p. 17; see also Hendley, *Defence*, pp. 46–7.

24 Hendley, *Defence*, p. 52.

25 J. Butler, *A Sermon ... Yearly Meeting of the Children Educated in Charity Schools* (London, 1745), p. 18.

26 For example, rules survive for two of the three Oxford boys' charity schools, but neither specifies conditions for parents.

27 Simon, 'Was there a charity school movement?', p. 88.

28 Jones, *Charity School Movement*, p. 105.

29 J. H. Cardwell, *The Story of a Charity School* (London, 1899), p. 16.

30 T. Hitchcock (ed.), *Richard Hutton's Complaints Book: The Notebook of the Steward of the Quaker Workhouse at Clerkenwell, 1711–1737* (London Record Society, 1987), pp. 75–6.

31 S. Lloyd, '"Agents in their own concerns"? Charity and the economy of makeshifts in eighteenth-century Britain', in S. King and A. Tomkins (eds), *The Poor in England 1700–1850: An Economy of Makeshifts* (Manchester, 2003), p. 113.

32 J. Barry, 'The Cultural Life of Bristol 1640–1775' (PhD thesis, Oxford University, 1985), p. 36.

33 D. Wardle, 'Education in Nottingham in the age of apprenticeship 1500–1800', *Thoroton Society Transactions* 71 (1967), 50.

34 Lloyd, 'Agents in their own concerns', pp. 111–13.

35 J. Innes, 'The "mixed economy of welfare" in early modern England: assessments of the options from Hale to Malthus (c. 1683–1803)', in M. Daunton (ed.), *Charity, Self-interest and Welfare in the English Past* (London, 1996).

36 Butler, *A Sermon*, pp. 10–11.

37 *Gentleman's Magazine* 14 (1744), 654.

38 Hendley, *Defence*, pp. 94–5.

39 P. Bearcroft, *The Wise and Useful Institution of Our Charity Schools* (London, 1748), p. 11.

40 H. Stebbing, *Of Charity to the Poor and the Religious Education of Poor Children* (London, 1732), p. 25. Paupers had to wait for Sunday school supporters before their position was considered more fully.

41 J. Chapman, *The Ends and Uses of Charity Schools for Poor Children* (London, 1752), p. 16.

42 Education was also largely free at the three grammar schools (associated with Magdalen, New College and Christ Church), but this chapter is concerned only with elementary education.

43 A. Crossley (ed.), *Victoria County History of Oxfordshire* 4 (Oxford, 1979), p. 444.

44 Oxford Record Office (hereafter ORO), Oxford City Archives Q.5.1. Nixon's

School deeds, rules and order 1658–1825.

45 ORO, Oxford City Archives JJ.4.1. Bluecoat Boys' School subscribers and accounts 1748–81.

46 Bodleian Library (hereafter Bod. Lib.), Gough Oxf 138 (15, 16), Greycoat charity school accounts 1740–47, 1752–58; Gough Oxf 103 (8), Greycoat charity school accounts 1759–65.

47 D. W. Rannie (ed.), *Remarks and Collections of Thomas Hearne* 11 (Oxford Historical Society 72 old series, 1918), p. 418.

48 *Articles of Enquiry Addressed to the Clergy of the Diocese of Oxford at the primary Visitation of Dr Thomas Secker 1738* ed. Rev. H. A. Lloyd Jukes (Oxford Record Society 38, 1957), p. 38: ORO, Mss Oxf dioc. Papers d.556, d.559, d.562 and d.565, visitation returns 1759, 1768, 1771 and 1774.

49 Bod. Lib., Ms Top Oxon e.371. A history of the Bluecoat school 1710–1892 by Henry Hughes, fo. 13 rev.

50 R. P. Heitzenrater, *Diary of an Oxford Methodist Benjamin Ingham 1733–34* (Durham Carolina, 1985) p. 28 and diary 14 May 1734.

51 ORO, Mss Oxf dioc. Papers d.559 visitation returns (for St Giles) 1768.

52 Bod. Lib., Mss Top Oxon e.15. Selections from the annual records of the Bluecoat school.

53 Barry, 'Cultural Life of Bristol', p. 61

54 Bod. Lib., R Top 731. Typed index to *Jackson's Oxford Journal 1754–1780* ed. E. C. Davies (1967); typed index to *Jackson's Oxford Journal 1781–1790* ed. E. H. Cordeaux (1976).

55 ORO, transcript of St Michael's parish register, baptism of 18 February 1734; Bod. Lib., R Top 731. Typed index to *Jackson's Oxford Journal 1754–1780* ed. E. C. Davies (1967), 17 January 1769.

56 Lane, *Apprenticeship*, p. 70.

57 *Report of a Committee of the Manchester Statistical Society on the State of Education in the Borough of Manchester in 1834* (London, 1835), pp. 7–9.

58 J. Burnett, *Destiny Obscure: Autobiographies of Childhood, Education and Family from the 1820s to the 1920s* (London, 1984), pp. 144–6.

59 Namely at the Bluecoat Boys', Bluecoat Girls', Greycoat, Nixon's, Alworth's, St Thomas' and St Giles's schools.

60 Children aged five to fourteen may have represented less than twenty percent of the population in towns due to the numbers of young adults who migrated to them; see J. Landers, *Death and the Metropolis* (Cambridge, 1993), pp. 98–100 and J. De Vries, *European Urbanisation 1500–1800* (London, 1984), chapter nine.

61 R. Hume, 'Educational provision for the Kentish poor 1660–1811: fluctuations and trends', *Southern History* 4 (1982), 142n.

62 Bod. Lib., G.A. Oxon c.261 Greycoat charity school rules 1766.

63 Simonton, 'Schooling the poor', 190–1; W. M. Jacob, 'The eye of his master: children and charity schools', in D. Wood (ed.), *The Church and Childhood: Studies in Church History* 31 (Oxford, 1994) p. 368.

64 Hume, 'Educational provision', 131.

65 Shropshire Archives (hereafter SA), DO4 1167.31 Shrewsbury charity school

1763, two reports and lists of subscribers.

66 H. Owen, *Some Account of the Ancient and Present State of Shrewsbury* (Shrewsbury, 1808), pp. 328–30, 401–2.

67 W. Page (ed.), *Victoria County History of Northamptonshire* 3 (London, 1930), p. 62; PP *Digest of Parochial Returns made to the Select Committee on the Education of the Poor* (1819), volume 9b.

68 *Report of a Committee of the Manchester Statistical Society on the State of Education in the City of York in 1836–7* (London, 1837), p. xii; P. M. Tillott (ed.), *The Victoria History of Yorkshire: The City of York* (Oxford, 1961), pp. 427–8, 433.

69 D. Robson, *Some Aspects of Education in Cheshire in the Eighteenth Century* (Chettam Society Manchester 13, 1966), pp. 23, 109, 143, 170; C. P. Lewis and A. T. Thacker (eds), *Victoria County History of Chester* 5: 2 (Woodbridge, 2005), p. 277.

70 Lewis and Thacker, *Chester*, p. 277; Sir T. Bernard, *Of the Education of the Poor* (London [1809] 1970), p. 231.

71 *Methods Used for Erecting Charity Schools* (London, 1717), p. 6.

72 H. Stone, 'The Ipswich charity schools of Greycoat Boys and Bluecoat Girls 1709–1809', *Proceedings of the Suffolk Institute of Archaeology* 25 (1952), 175.

73 J. Hanway, *A Comprehensive View of Sunday Schools* (London, 1786), p. 55. Overseers' opinions were, however, consulted in Leeds; see C. P. Johnston, 'The charity school, the Church and the Corporation: aspects of educational provision for the poor in eighteenth-century Leeds', *Publications of the Thoresby Society* 3 (1993), 11.

74 Johnston, 'The charity school', 21.

75 Jones, *Charity School Movement*, p. 73.

76 Rev. J. Acland, *A Plan for Rendering the Poor Independent on Public Contribution* (Exeter, 1786), p. 52.

77 B. Hill, *Servants: English Domestics in the Eighteenth Century* (Oxford, 1996), p. 138.

78 Lane, *Apprenticeship*, p. 69.

79 Ibid., p. 74.

80 T. W. Laqueur, *Religion and Respectability: Sunday Schools and Working Class Culture 1780–1850* (New Haven, 1976), pp. 158–60.

81 *Digest of Parochial Returns made to the Select Committee on the Education of the Poor* (1819), volume 9b.

82 Butler, *A Sermon*, p. 12.

83 Jones, *Charity School Movement*, appendix I.7.

84 Lloyd, 'Agents in their own concerns', pp. 108–11.

85 P. Cunnington and C. Lucas, *Charity Costumes* (London, 1978), pp. 55–8 cite as much evidence for humiliation in charity uniforms as they do gratitude; T. W. Laqueur, 'Working-class demand and the growth of English elementary school education, 1750–1850', in L. Stone (ed.), *Schooling and Society: Studies in the History of Education* (Baltimore, 1976), p. 199 identifies this sentiment in relation to the later National schools.

86 For apprenticeships in Oxford see throughout M. Graham (ed.), *Oxford City Apprentices 1697–1800* (Oxford Historical Society 31, 1987).

87 Stone, 'The Ipswich charity schools', 179.

88 M. Prior, *Fisher Row: Fishermen, Bargemen and Canal Boatmen in Oxford 1500–1900* (Oxford, 1982), pp. 159, 162.

89 Lane, *Apprenticeship*, p. 118.

90 Graham, *Oxford City Apprentices*, p. xiii.

91 W. G. Briggs, 'Records of an apprenticeship charity 1685–1753', *Derbyshire Archaeological Journal* 74 (1954), 60.

92 S. R. Broadbridge, 'The Old Poor Law in the Parish of Stone (Staffs) 1691–1834', unpublished typescript in the William Salt Library, Stafford, p. 32.

93 Chapman, *Ends and Uses*, p. 22.

94 Simonton, 'Schooling the poor', 190.

95 St Martin, St Mary Magdalen, St Michael, St Peter in East, and St Peter le Bailey.

96 Hill, *Servants*, p. 139.

97 ORO, Mss dd par Oxford St Peter le Bailey b.12 overseers' accounts to 1722; St Michael c.27 overseers' vouchers 1663–1759.

98 A. Wood, *The Antient and Present State of the City of Oxford* with additions by Rev. Sir John Peshall (London, 1773), p. 87.

99 ORO, Mss dd par Oxford St Michael c.27 and c.28 overseers' vouchers 1663–1759 and 1761–72.

100 Johnston, 'The charity school', 23.

101 H. Cunningham, 'The employment and unemployment of children in England 1680–1851', *Past and Present* 126 (February 1990).

102 P. King, 'The rise of juvenile delinquency in England 1780–1840: changing patterns of perception and prosecution', *Past and Present* 160 (1998), 160–1.

103 H. Shore, *Artful Dodgers: Youth and crime in early 19th-century London* (Woodbridge, 1999), pp. 38–9.

104 Jones, *Charity School Movement*, p. 48.

105 ORO, Mss dd par Oxford St Peter in East b.28 overseers' accounts 1740–52; ORO, Oxford City Archives O.2.8. Oxford town quarter sessions minutes 1745–50; ORO, Mss dd par Oxford St Michael b.31 overseers' accounts 1751–58; ORO, handwritten transcript of Oxfordshire County Quarter Sessions Rolls, coroner's inquest of 4 January 1761.

106 These included all apprenticeships where the overseers had some part in meeting the costs in the five Oxford parishes studied 1740–70.

107 Lane, 'Apprenticeship', pp. 382, 401, 413, 430, 433, 437, 443, 446, 448, 457, 461.

108 The apprenticing portion of Thomas's, Bogan's, Nicholl's and Wall's charities benefited a maximum of thirteen boys per year.

109 I. K. Ben-Amos, *Adolescence and Youth in Early Modern England* (London, 1994), p. 59.

110 ORO, Mss dd par Oxford St Mary Magdalen b.74 vestry minutes 1714–1849.

111 Lane, *Apprenticeship*, p. 3.

112 Lane, 'Apprenticeship', p. 172.

113 Graham, *Oxford City Apprentices*, p. x.

114 Greater London Record Office (hereafter GLRO), Shrewsbury Foundling Country Hospital, Committee minutes 1758–72, 4 June 1759.

115 GLRO, Shrewsbury Foundling Country Hospital, Servants' entry and discharge register 1758–67.

116 Owen, *Some Account*, pp. 333–46.

117 GLRO, Shrewsbury Foundling Country Hospital, Committee minutes 1758–72, 30 October 1758; see chapter two for a discussion of bed-sharing.

118 Ibid., 27 February 1759.

119 Ibid., 19 May 1760.

120 R. K. McClure, *Coram's Children: The London Foundling Hospital in the Eighteenth Century* (New Haven, 1981), p. 185.

121 Ibid., p. 221; GLRO, Shrewsbury Foundling Country Hospital, Committee minutes 1758–72, 30 October 1758; Servants' entry and discharge register 1758–67.

122 GLRO, Shrewsbury Foundling Country Hospital, Committee minutes 1758–72, 23 June 1759. The London Smallpox Hospital had been established in 1746; P. Razzell, *The Conquest of Smallpox* (Sussex, 1977), p. 54.

123 Owen, *Some Account*, pp. 328–30, 401–2.

124 GLRO, Shrewsbury Foundling Country Hospital, Committee minutes 1758–72, 5 March 1759.

125 Ibid., 19 February 1759, 5 March 1759, 1 October 1759.

126 Ibid., 20 November 1758.

127 Ibid., 5 April 1759.

128 Ibid., 25 February 1760.

129 SA, Shropshire County Quarter Sessions Records, QS/1/4 Order book 1757–72; QF/1/1/1 Treasurer's account book 1666–1764.

130 Similarly, children at Ackworth were apprenticed in Yorkshire; B. Scott, 'Ackworth Hospital 1757–1773', *Yorkshire Archaeological Journal* 61 (1989), 162–6.

131 Information relating to the addresses of Shrewsbury parish apprentices is admittedly sparse, but local children were sent to masters in Wolverhampton, Walsall, Birmingham or Kidderminster.

132 McClure, *Coram's Children*, p.128.

133 I am indebted to Alysa Levine for this information.

134 Shrewsbury pauper children could therefore expect a much smaller premium than was paid in Oxford, but most children did have a premium; in both towns, only sixteen to eighteen percent apparently took no money into an apprenticeship.

135 GLRO, Shrewsbury Foundling Country Hospital, Applications for apprentices 1767–70.

136 Scott, 'Ackworth Hospital', 160.

137 GLRO, Shrewsbury Foundling County Hospital, Servants' entry and discharge register 1758–67.

138 GLRO, Shrewsbury Foundling Country Hospital, Committee minutes

1758–72, 4 October 1758.

139 F. M. Eden, *The State of the Poor* (London [1797] 1928), pp. 296–301.

140 Bod. Lib., Mss Top Oxon e.371. A history of the Bluecoat school 1710–1892 by Henry Hughes fo. 17.

141 ORO, Oxford City Archives, O.2.9. Oxford town quarter sessions minutes 1750–61.

142 T. Sokoll, *Essex Pauper Letters 1731–1837* (Oxford, 2001), pp. 437–8.

143 Lloyd, 'Agents in their own concerns'.

6

Pawnbroking and the use of credit[1]

Uncertainties of income and occasional urgency for expenditure made retail credit a necessity for the labouring and poor population in the eighteenth century. Shopkeepers routinely extended credit to their customers, and while the trader needed to balance their offers of credit against the likelihood and timing of repayment to avoid becoming debtors themselves, the system broadly operated to the advantage of both parties. Grocers and chandlers were either favoured for their sympathy towards people with cash-flow problems or they were guilty of exploiting the poor and imprisoning them in a cycle of debt repayment but in both cases they supplied customers' wants at times when money was short. The provision of retail credit was widely tolerated and it is possible that as many as half of all retail transactions involved promises of future payment.[2] Therefore it is not surprising that David Davies found 'most families in debt to little shopkeepers' in 1795.[3]

Credit advanced on pledges or pawns had become an element of this delicately balanced system by the end of the eighteenth century. Pawnbroking emerged as a discrete trade (rather than existing simply as a sideline for bankers, goldsmiths or jewellers) in London over the second half of the seventeenth century. By 1750 there were around 250 large pawnshops in London and countless smaller ones, with individual shops opening in larger provincial towns. Between 1750 and 1850 English pawnbroking underwent its most rapid period of growth.[4] Yet the majority of work on pawnbroking has concentrated on the nineteenth century when the proliferation of pawnshops and the survival of manuscript sources has required and enabled a thorough investigation of their role. The position for the urban poor over the course of the eighteenth century is much less clear, owing to a paucity of records giving detailed insights into the clientele and usage of early pawnshops. The lucky survival of a pledge book from a pawnshop in York from the 1770s makes it possible to examine the status and function of the provincial pawnbroker, and evaluate the significance of the pawnbroker for some of the poorest inhabitants of

York, as defined by receipt of poor relief. Therefore this chapter will look first at public perceptions of eighteenth-century pawnbrokers and their likely clientele from contemporary printed sources, and will go on to conduct a detailed consideration of strategies used by customers of one specific shop to exploit pawnshop credit to the full.

Public perceptions of pawnbroking

Public opinion of pawnbrokers in the early and mid-eighteenth century was low; descriptions ranged from 'not very reputable'[5] to 'the chief agents of corruption ... the wretches by whom all wickedness is encouraged'[6] or 'Monsters in the Shape of Men'.[7] The bulk of published opinion was concentrated at the extremely critical end of this spectrum. Individual practitioners were perceived as inherently dishonest, in business 'to cheat both friend and foe',[8] while collectively they allegedly held meetings 'to invent new Schemes to grind the Face of the Poor'.[9] Doubts about the legality and propriety of living by moneylending, combined with anti-Semitism (given the image of pawnbrokers as typically Jewish), created a virulent, anti-pawnbroking press.[10] Brokers were accused of allying with other dubious characters including tally-men,[11] or of using intermediaries such as the servants at bawdy houses, gambling dens and gin palaces to generate business and ruin families; the consequence was allegedly 'the loss of life in many cases'.[12] There was even suspicion of diabolical association, given the epithet 'old Nick's warehouse keeper'.[13] One satirical epitaph summoned some suitably damning verse ("Tis by his customers allow'd, That Satan took him in his shroud'[14]), but a more lasting judgement was supplied by Hogarth's 'Gin Lane' engraving of 1751. This powerful, derogatory and enduring image of pawnbrokers remains a popular way to represent the terrors of eighteenth-century London life and poverty.

Henry Fielding, in common with many others, characterised pawnbrokers as the receivers of stolen goods, an anxiety sharpened by the difficulties associated with convicting receivers in the eighteenth century.[15] He referred to pawnbrokers' shops as 'fountains of theft', while numerous writers alleged that thieves were encouraged or instructed and employed by pawnbrokers.[16] Furthermore, pawnbrokers were accused of corrupting the legal system to ensure they were not convicted, via private association,[17] or of manipulating the established channels for the recovery of stolen goods in order to maximise their own profits. Abuses apparently included raising an outcry and driving away thieves 'for Fashion-sake, to keep up a seeming Reputation of Honesty' while keeping a firm hold on suspicious pledges. Pawnbrokers' knowledge of the criminal underworld was thus second to none, since even thief-catchers could be counted among the pawnbroker's 'pensioners'.[18] A final piece of sophistry required the advertisement of suspected stolen goods, in a facsimile of civic responsibility, but with erroneous details to prevent the items being recognised by their original owners.[19]

Writers also took issue with the rate of interest earned on pawns. A satirical writer in 1745, posing as a discounter, who loaned money against promissory notes, wrote to a pawnbroker addressing him with the epithet 'Brother Use' (usurer) and confiding 'both you and I know the sweets of thirty percent'.[20] Pamphlet writers engaged in both mathematical calculations and resentful declarations to convince readers that pawnbrokers charged extortionate rates, rendering customers 'more poor, wretched and distressed'.[21] Particular concern was expressed about pawnbrokers' ability to charge two months' interest on a loan of only a few days which happened to span the end of one month and the start of the next.[22] Subsidiary anxieties focused on the broker's failure to lend even half of the value of the pledge, and on the use that pawnbrokers might make of the goods in their charge; they were accused of wearing the clothing pledges, or making more money by renting out items of clothing left in pawn.[23] Solutions to these evils circled vaguely around the panacea of legislation, although one creative opponent of extortionate earnings published a plan to tax pawnbrokers and jewellers to fund financial rewards for army recruits.[24]

Pawnbrokers were popularly considered to be personally culpable for the uses to which their customers put them. If pawnbrokers were guilty of knowingly lending money on stolen goods then the accusation that they acted as receivers was just, but the practices of the poor in seeking credit were varied and opened up much greyer areas regarding the moral culpability attached to both borrowers and lenders. Writers questioned the honesty of a trader who would lend money to a servant or prostitute on valuables without enquiry, implying that their guilt lay in their unwillingness or inability to check the provenance of pawns; 'men, who trust at random, cannot mean honestly'.[25] Gin-drinking or gambling with money obtained on credit was held to be the fault of the moneylender. A milder but repeated accusation was that brokers accepted pawns from children without their parents' knowledge;[26] however, it is not impossible that the adult poor actively used children as their intermediaries and messengers. It was in the interest of opponent commentators to imply that the broker rather than the parent was 'at fault'. One writer highlighted some injustice with this type of criticism by pointing out that other trades were not held accountable for their customers' actions, citing the example of vintners who are free to sell wine even though people become drunk on it.[27] Another acknowledged that other traders' prosperity might depend on the supply of ready money to the labouring poor,[28] but this was a rare reflection in a period when the necessity for pawnbrokers was so often rejected.

Individual critics of pawnbrokers did not necessarily maintain a consistent opposition to their trade and existence; they might be criticised but also utilised as occasion required. The author of a legal advice manual distained the 'unreasonable' and 'usurious' behaviour of pawnbrokers but grudgingly admitted that 'many times they do a greater kindness by lending upon pawns than a pretended friend will, and that without any upbraiding or murmuring'.[29] Horace Walpole expressed his distaste for moneylenders in 1776 when he wrote 'Our Jews and usurers contrive to lounge at home and commit as much rapine as Lord Clive!'[30] But in 1749 his eagerness to have stolen goods returned to him overcame his scruples. He inserted an advertisement in the *Daily Advertiser* to the effect that if his watch, stolen by highwayman James Maclean, was brought to Mr Cates the pawnbroker in Chandos Street 20 guineas would be paid for it without further enquiries being made.[31] Ironically, this use of pawnbrokers as conduits for the recovery of stolen goods did not go without comment or criticism either; a plan for the better prevention of robberies suggested that victims like Walpole should not be permitted to advertise for the return of goods with no questions asked.[32]

Despite this lack of internal consistency in some publications, public (published) opinion of pawnbrokers and moneylending altered very little over the course of the eighteenth century; only Jeremy Bentham's *Defence of Usury* (1787) asserted that 'no man of ripe years and of sound mind ... ought to be hindered ... from making such bargain, in the way of obtaining money, as he thinks fit: nor ... anybody hindered from supplying him, upon any terms he thinks proper to accede to'.[33] In contrast Patrick Colquhoun spoke for many in 1797 when he railed against the practice of weekly pawning; typically a working family might pledge tools or other goods on Saturday to redeem their Sunday best, which would be pawned again on Monday morning (a long-established custom, since as early as 1729 it was sufficiently familiar to be an object of satire). Colquhoun concentrated his attention on the apparently unreasonable profits made by pawnbrokers from this practice (and the folly of 'insuring' in lottery tickets) without considering the alternatives open to the poor who continued to require some 'temporary accommodation'.[34] In the early nineteenth century, the author of *Pawnbrokers Detected and Dissected* bundled together 'usurers, receivers of stolen goods, Jews, and men of the worst principles' as would-be deceivers of the poor.[35] There was no concession here to the idea that the poor in question might legitimately consider pawning to be in their own best interests in the absence of alternative strategies.[36] The writer viewed the high rate of interest endured by people who frequently resorted to pawning as evidence that 'It is not the really industrious poor that make the most frequent use of these shops.'[37] The consequences of 'easy' credit were still considered to be drunkenness, crime and suicide. Also pawnbrokers continued to be criticised for the use made of them, especially by people who pawned several times a day (given the proportionately high rate of interest that was charged). The accusation that pawns were taken from children was modified to include the knowledge of parents and complicity of brokers so that the children grew 'lost to all becoming modesty', and this may have been an aspect of growing fears concerning juvenile crime.[38]

Contemporary perceptions, however, are not a reliable guide to the practice of pawnbroking. There appears to have been a discrepancy between the type of pawnbroking that attracted intense, vocal opposition and the 'honest' trade. The quality of the service provided and the wealth of the clientele who used the shop, the 'tenor of the trade',[39] were determined by the goods which were considered to be acceptable collateral and the permanency or ad hoc nature of the business. There may have been pawnbrokers who organised theft and burglary but they were not necessarily the majority, or the same as the substantial pawnbrokers who wrote in defence of the practice of moneylending. One alleged convert to the necessity for pawnbrokers claimed in 1745 that people said to be pawnbrokers were really 'people of different professions'. 'Pawnbroker' was a label which could be applied to any individual who lent money on material security, however slight, and the disreputable 'pawnbrokers' caught up in criminal proceedings were claimed to be first and foremost those who took pawns as a sideline (including gin sellers or keepers of disorderly houses).[40] Another less reputable variation of the pawnshop was the 'dolly shop' that took low-value goods which pawnbrokers would not accept.[41] Also, James Lackington claimed that some establishments which advertised as pawnbrokers were in fact simple shops, where customers were overcharged (when they thought that they must be getting a bargain in the form of an unredeemed pledge).[42] Many people might be called 'pawnbroker' in official sources who did not pursue the business full-time. Williams judged that in Exeter, receivers of stolen goods used the label 'pawnbroker' to secure a cover of legitimacy.[43] Similarly, John Styles has found that criminal cases involving people who were described as pawnbrokers were few in comparison to those of tradespeople who accepted pawns informally, such as the owners of public houses;[44] however, this may simply be testimony to pawnbrokers' close knowledge of the law. One writer asserted in 1703 that 'they are so wise as to make no usurious contract before hand' and those prosecuted for offences against the usury laws 1763–73 were not labelled as pawnbrokers.[45]

A pamphlet of 1744 rehearsed the arguments or 'apologies' of the 'honest' pawnbroker.[46] The writer commented on the then relatively recent example of the failure of the Charitable Corporation to assert that pawnbrokers were the most proper people to fill the role of supplying the poor with small sums. They were represented as substantial businessmen with stock of at least £2,000. Also, the pamphlet put the unusual view of the difficulties that pawnbrokers faced in honest trading. If pledges were left for a long time, they were dead stock bringing no return. When sold, they may not bring in the value of the money loaned especially if the clothes had gone out of fashion; there was some legitimacy in this claim, since towards the end of the eighteenth century breeches made of leather, for instance, were entirely replaced by cloth alternatives such as corduroy meaning that there was no domestic market for second-hand leather trousers.[47] Also, if the goods were sold and the customer later returned to redeem their possessions, the pawnbroker might face a lawsuit for their full value, 'aided and abetted by pettifogging attorneys'.[48] If only honest traders were relieved of such threats they could afford to charge lower interest, which (it was alleged) would constitute a genuine benefit to the poor. Furthermore, it was argued that pawnbrokers needed to make enough to live and support a family. In fact, the writer of the *Apology* asserted that the interest charged was not an unreasonable reward for the service provided since if the poor person had had to sell their goods instead of pawning them, they would not have been able to replace them without considerable loss, much greater than the interest charged by a pawnbroker. Also, it was claimed that pawnbrokers' return for their investment was modest in relation to the profit made by other traders for smaller outlay and over a shorter time. Many tradesmen had preserved their trade and credit via use of brokers. The pamphlet drew attention to the language routinely used when writing about pawnbrokers, that they 'incur infamy' as a result of the 'opprobrious language freely bestowed'.[49]

In response to accusations that pawnbrokers were in the habit of receiving stolen goods, and thereby gave encouragement to thieves, the *Apology* asked why more pawnbrokers were not convicted. It was alleged that pawnbrokers became receivers only by accident and even then they were often the one to expose the thief. The writer's resort to hyperbole is some indication of the impact made by past criticism, since they claimed that other traders might more easily steal a horse than a pawnbroker might look over a hedge; indeed, as the takers of valuable goods, pawn-brokers were themselves liable to be the victims of thefts.[50] Anxious to prove their probity, the London pawnbrokers announced their intention in 1753 to take the daily newspaper the *Public Advertiser* to try to iden-tify any stolen goods advertised within if they were presented as pledges and return them to their lawful owners.[51]

Customers of pawnbrokers who felt cheated in some way by their transactions (and who could afford it) could technically choose to seek legal redress. If the pawnbroker refused to return goods, either because they had been sold or because the customer refused to pay the interest that had accrued, then the customer could bring a suit of trover to recover the value of the goods. This explains the complaint by one pawnbroker that people were likely to bring malicious suits to recover the value of the goods without returning the advanced loan.[52] There seems to have been some justice in the pawnbrokers' complaint in that they were punished for the wrongdoing of others. In 1752 a jury found against a pawn-broker, who had refused to return goods without the payment of money advanced. The fact that the goods had been pawned not by the owner of the goods but by his laundress suggests that the laundress was guilty of theft but it was the pawnbroker who suffered since he lost both the money loan and the goods.[53] This example helps to account for their need to associate, to meet the costs of defending such cases (and prob-ably for mutual support in the face of public suspicion and hostility). The legal position of pawnbrokers and their customers was somewhat clari-fied by an act of 1757.[54] This required pawnbrokers to keep a register, detailing the goods pledged, money lent, date and the name and address of the customer. If a person pledged goods on behalf of someone else, the owner's name was also noted. The customer could choose to pay for a ticket comprising a duplicate of the register details. The pawnbroker was obliged to take care of the goods and compensate customers for any loss of value resulting from neglect or wear and tear; however, it also gave pawnbrokers eventual rights over the goods, since items securing a loan of up to £10 were forfeited after two years. There were also clauses to control illegal pawning, such as pledging stolen goods or piecework materials which were the property of an employer. Subsequent acts sought to define the legitimate activities of pawnbrokers further, for example by stipulating in 1784 the interest that might be charged on loans of varying sums over different durations.[55]

There was clearly room for a significant gulf between the public, printed opinion of pawnbrokers and the practical relationships that existed between pawnbrokers and their fellow tradesmen, between pawnbrokers and customers, or between pawnbrokers and the law. The opprobrium to which pawnbrokers were subjected in the press was not necessarily a feature of their everyday experience, particularly where the shop was long established and the business well regulated. The interactions between pawnbrokers and others can be tested via an examination of cases reported in the Old Bailey Proceedings.[56] Cases covering the calendar years 1777 and 1778 (to render a sample chronologically consonant with my research on York, below) required the involvement of 102 pawnbrokers as witnesses to criminal trials, including 94 men and 8 women. All but one of these people gave evidence in cases of theft, or were called upon to produce stolen goods, but the character of their involvement is varied. A very few pawnbrokers fulfilled the fears of their vociferous opponents and attracted adverse comment (or even threat of prosecution in court) as a consequence. William Knight, for example, had taken in cloth and clothing proffered by Sarah Davidson, even though she had shadily asserted 'the person they belonged to was at the door but did not chose to come in'. Knight protested at the trial that he did not suspect Davidson because she was a familiar customer, but the court reproached him 'she told you enough to make you suspect her'.[57] Even more forcefully the unnamed male pawnbroker who had received pledges from Margaret Pearce (but had refused to attend her trial) was ordered to surrender the goods to the prosecutrix under pain of indictment for receiving.[58] But for all that they fitted the popular stereotype, these examples are not representative of pawnbrokers' appearances at the Old Bailey. The majority made statements rather neutrally and presumably with some readiness, while an important minority actively endeavoured to cut across contemporary presupposition and gave every impression of probity and credibility. They questioned customers about the provenance of their pledges, recognised stolen goods from their advertised descriptions, called constables, and ensured that suspects did not escape (as testified by both the pawnbrokers themselves and the relevant constables).[59] John Lane and his son, who had pawnbrokers' shops in Holborn and Drury Lane respectively, were particularly reputable. They worked in concert with constables to effect the arrest and conviction of Richard Oldgate when they realised that goods he had pledged were stolen, despite the fact they had known Oldgate 'a great many years'. Furthermore, the word of Lane senior carried some weight with the court; he provided a character witness for Mary Yates and she was acquitted.[60] In these ways the demeanour and public activity of pawnbrokers in London as revealed at the Old Bailey belied their caricature.

Also, all published commentary focused on London pawnshops. In the capital, facilities for pawning were ubiquitous and contemporaries recognised that there was considerable scope for anonymity and evasion of the law; in 1794, London was described in one novel as 'an inexhaustible reservoir of concealment'.[61] The situation was different in the provinces. Opportunities for anonymity were fewer, and established pawnshops were more sparsely distributed. By the end of the eighteenth century there were allegedly 431 pawnbrokers in the provinces throughout the country who bought licences,[62] principally located in substantial towns (pawnbroking being 'an urban phenomenon').[63] In contrast to their London counterparts, provincial pawnbrokers are not known to have featured constantly in town and county quarter sessions cases; this is not surprising if Williams's conclusion for Exeter is valid elsewhere, that thieves often did not know how to dispose of their stolen goods.[64] Nevertheless, people could plausibly be guilty of theft and consequent business with pawnbrokers without being brought to trial; in the early years of the nineteenth century, Benjamin Shaw's wife stole his clothes and his watch to pawn them but he did not subject her to prosecution.[65]

There were also provincial equivalents of the casual or part-time moneylender.[66] It was claimed in 1809 that the practice of pawning was familiar in towns throughout England 'except the Universities of Oxford and Cambridge, where no pawnbrokers whatever are allowed'.[67] The universities had historically tried to stand between students and moneylenders; in mediaeval Oxford and Cambridge, loan trusts or 'chests' provided cheap loans to prevent Christian texts being pledged with Jewish pawnbrokers.[68] By the eighteenth century students in the university towns were 'in all their Matters of Bargain and Expense under the Direction of the respective Tutors … and ought not to be trusted or dealt with for any sum'[69] which meant that traders could not enter bargains with students, and tavern-keepers in particular were forbidden to allow students to run up debts. Furthermore, the universities were able to discommon tradesmen, preventing them from trading with anybody connected with the university.[70] Prohibitions of this sort upon traders and students alike did not rule out the possibility that students flouted the rules when in need of money, no matter how draconian the threatened punishment. Also, even if the universities were able to prevent pawnshops being established in their respective towns, they could not have eradicated all forms of moneylending; in the 1770s someone called Haynes took pawns at the sign of the Lamb in Oxford.[71]

This array of opportunities for formal and informal borrowing has been treated more kindly by historians than by contemporaries, as an indispensable 'financial tool' in the makeshift economy.[72] The predominance of women among pawnshop customers has seen them valued for their role in women's credit networks, for instance.[73] The flexibility and measure of independence offered by pawning means that it could be considered a variety of self-help. People could take decisions about the timing and means by which credit was sought, which goods they would risk by offering them as pledges, and when or whether to redeem them.[74] But too little is known about the workings of the trade, particularly before 1800. The unique nature of the pledge book compiled by George Fettes in York 1777–78 therefore presents a rare opportunity to witness a pawnbroker in action. The problem, as with other one-off sources, is typicality. Melanie Tebbutt has demonstrated that in the 1870s, pawn-shops were most prevalent in industrial, manufacturing areas,[75] and this pattern was already evident by the end of the eighteenth century when pawnbrokers outside London were clustered in the north-west and the midlands.[76] Therefore the evidence of a pawnbroker working in the almost anti-industrial atmosphere of 1770s York cannot be used confi-dently as a proxy for patterns of pawning in general. Nevertheless, there was probably little uniformity in the practices of different populations in different regions; 'industrial pawnbroking was itself hardly uniform'.[77] The pledge book remains enormously valuable for the light it sheds on the situation in York.

George Fettes

George Fettes, a pawnbroker in York from the early 1770s to the 1820s, was one of the 'honest' pawnbrokers whose protests of innocence were occasionally heard above the general din of disapproval. He had an estab-lished shop in Lady Peckett's Yard off Pavement in the town centre.[78] The surviving pledge book of 1777 and 1778 is the earliest evidence of his business, which was the only pawnbroking firm in York to be listed in a town directory of 1781. George Fettes was listed with a second pawn-broker, Thomas Palmer of Swinegate, in 1798.[79] Fettes carried on trading until he sold the business at some time between 1823 and 1827. On at least one occasion he acknowledged the public's perception that pawn-brokers were liable to be offered stolen goods and attempted to position himself as a trader of honesty and discretion. In 1788, in an advertise-ment publicising the sale of unredeemed pledges, he promised 'Infor-mations, respecting lost or stolen Goods, attended to with the strictest fidelity'.[80] In 1793 he even identified himself in the press as an auctioneer rather than as a pawnbroker; he was possibly distancing himself from the occupational label that attracted so much printed distain, or alterna-tively he was selling the pledges from other pawnbroking businesses in addition to his own.[81]

George Fettes had been born into a family of substance; his father was an Edinburgh merchant and his cousin Sir Willliam Fettes later founded the Edinburgh school of the same name. He was a young man in his early twenties during the years for which the pledge book survives; in later years he came to be well regarded by his fellow traders and citizens in York. He was elected a commoner to the city council by 1798, served as sheriff for the city in 1802 and thereafter was one of the twenty-four city aldermen. His financial and trading experience was presumably influential in his being appointed one of the first directors of the York savings bank, established in 1816. He obtained a reputable apprenticeship for his son Richard with John Hepworth, a member of the city's Company of Merchant Adventurers.[82]

He and his wife Elizabeth were both Wesleyan Methodists and were valued members of the congregation. George was a 'President of the prayer leaders' and fellow Methodist John Pawson remembered his 'great kindness' at the time of his (Pawson's) marriage in 1785.[83] Fettes was a friend of John Wesley who stayed with him on his visits to York. The pawnbroking trade clearly did not stand in the way of this relationship, although it may have been the subject of some friendly raillery between the two men. In Wesley's only recorded letter to Fettes he wrote 'Prove these two points – first that pawnbroking is necessary, secondly that it is lawful (in England) - and you will satisfy your affectionate brother John Wesley.'[84]

Pawnshop customers

George Fettes kept a pledge book recording customers and their pledges in accordance with the law of 1757. He or his shop assistants recorded the date, the name and address of customers, the goods pledged and the sum advanced. If the items were redeemed the date of redemption was commonly entered but notes of redemptions become more rare towards the end of the volume. On the last day when the book was used to enter pledges, 26 December 1778, no redemption dates were written down, presumably because it was too much trouble to look up the initial entry in an old book once a new book was in use in the shop. A couple of dates of redemption or sales of goods were noted after December 1778; George Parrott pledged his silver watch during York's race week on 22 August 1777, and on 27 May 1780 it was redeemed or sold.[85]

Fettes received a total of 10,917 pledges in the eighteen months July 1777 to December 1778. The pace of business fluctuated according to the weekly, monthly and annual requirements of customers but also according to Fettes's willingness to loan money. The number of recorded customer visits (which can be used to infer the number of pledges accepted) fell from an average of 33 a day in February 1778 to a low of 17 in July 1778. The possible causes of this downturn in trade include the

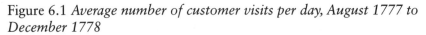

Figure 6.1 *Average number of customer visits per day, August 1777 to December 1778*

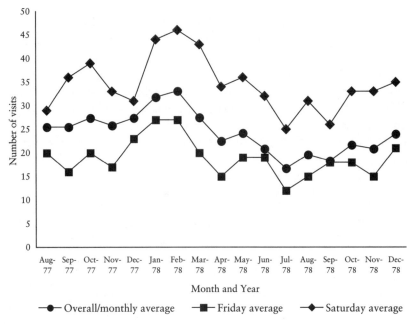

appearance of a trading rival or an improvement in the financial fortunes of York's labouring poor.[86] Nevertheless, the economic complexion of the two years 1777 and 1778 was very different and it is likely that increasing hardship had some part to play in making Fettes more reluctant or less able to accept pledges.[87] In 1777 England enjoyed a boom; the Yorkshire woollen cloth industry enjoyed considerable prosperity, with the output of broadcloth increasing.[88] Admittedly the harvests were good in both years but the crucial difference between them was caused by the entry of the French into the American War of Independence. Britain had been at war with the American colonists since 1775 but French involvement raised the stakes and intensified the British effort. Consequently, there was a hike in taxation rates, and financial crisis threatened. The construction industry suffered a serious depression 1778–84, a common feature of wartime in the eighteenth century, and the Yorkshire cloth industry experienced a sudden depression. It was said that 'trade of every kind seems to be at a perfect stand owing to an uncommon great and general scarcity of money' and there were 623 bankruptcies in 1778 as opposed to 471 in 1777. Therefore England experienced a peak of prosperity in 1777, with signs of decline in late 1777 and sudden crisis in the first months of

1778.[89] The rate of custom at Fettes's shop shows that pledges accepted reached a peak in the early months of 1778 then slackened off after April 1778 to below what had been usual in the summer of 1777. This suggests that Fettes initially responded to this sudden demand for money by meeting customers' requirements but was limiting his advancement of credit later in the year. Either he was suffering himself from the shortage of money, or he became more cautious about making loans, fearing that if redemptions were sluggish he would be left with a large, unprofitable, perishable 'dead stock'. In was not unknown for pawnbrokers to over-stretch themselves; it was said of Glasgow pawnbrokers in 1819 that they had advanced all their capital and were nearly in the same distress as their poor customers.[90]

The weekly pattern of pawning is clearly visible from the pledge book. Customers were most keen to pledge their property on Saturday or Monday, with these days seeing twenty-three percent and twenty-one percent of pledges deposited respectively. In other words, 'the Monday morning pilgrimage to the pawnshop' witnessed by Rowntree in York over a hundred years later was a feature of the trade but perhaps not the most prominent characteristic of the pawnshop's use in the eighteenth century.[91] The remaining pledges each week were shared between the other four working days. This broad pattern conceals a wide variety of usage by different customers. Some people entered the shop only once during the eighteen months covered while others periodically visited several times a day. One strategy employed by customers was to pledge several items at the same time but in separate lots and redeemable on separate tickets. This meant that goods could be redeemed one at a time although it did mean buying a ticket for each pledge. On 2 October 1777 Henry Richardson made eight pledges of individual items of clothing for between 3s and 6s each; he redeemed them over the next ten months, between 1 November 1777 and 22 August 1778. Predictably, the pawn-broker's services were in great demand during the week of York races, in August, when visitors to the town needed to raise ready cash.

The record of all redemptions in the period July 1777 to December 1778 is incomplete, since goods pawned before July 1777 could have been redeemed at any time without a record being made in the surviving pledge book; however, there is no particular reason to suppose that the pattern of redemption for goods not listed in the surviving book was different from any sample of redemptions that are listed.[92] Saturday was by far the most popular day for redemptions, with forty-one percent of pledges being collected. Monday was the next most popular day, but only accounted for fourteen percent of redemptions. This is what might have been expected. Presumably, Saturday was pay day for many of the working population in York and therefore the day when people were most likely to be able to redeem pawned goods. Another twenty-five percent of pledges were never redeemed.[93]

The average time-lapse between pledge and redemption (calculated from a sample database for the first two weeks in September 1777) was fifty-six days but this bland average reveals a very wide variety of practice with the emphasis on speedy redemption. A quarter of pledges that were destined to be redeemed would be collected within one week, while another quarter would be collected within four weeks. The remaining items occasionally stayed in the shop for much longer periods; on 3 September 1777 Frances Smith pawned a brown calamanca gown for 4s and returned for it nearly a year later on 31 August 1778.

The amounts of money advanced for pledges were usually considerably below their 'value' to their owners but may have represented little less than the pawnbroker could have hoped to make by their sale; 'The pawnbroker derived the vast bulk of his profits from redeemed pledges, not from the sale of forfeited articles.'[94] Fettes only occasionally recorded the sale of goods in the pledge book; there were two lone entries of goods sold during the first two weeks of September 1777 out of 236 pledges. Where he also recorded the amount he received for the sale, it does not seem to indicate a particularly high profit margin. In November 1777 he sold a gown for 10s 6d which had been pledged for 9s; he may have gained less from this sale than he would from the payment of interest by the owner. This position is confirmed by later evidence from another pawnbroker; in the 1820s an unidentified London pawnbroker kept a record of the amounts loaned on goods and the sums they fetched at sale, demonstrating that profits from this source were not always assured. Of the thirty-four pledges sold by Machin and Debenham on 19 August 1822, for example, fifteen made no profit or a net loss. The sale brought in a total of £103 2s 10d but only £4 14s 7d constituted profit on the original loans.[95]

The smallest sum Fettes lent in 1777 and 1778 was 2d and the greatest 10 guineas.[96] The average loan over the whole period was 3s 9d but the majority of loans totalled 2s or less.[97] The average amounts loaned rose significantly in August each year at the time of the races; in the seventeen months August 1777 to December 1778 the average amount loaned was between 3s and 4s during twelve of the months but rose to 5s 5d and 4s 10d in August 1777 and 1778 respectively. Visitors to the town were among Fettes's wealthier clients, able to pledge more valuable goods. William and Thomas Bradley of Newton on Derwent both pledged their watches in August 1777 and Thomas also pledged his greatcoat, coat and waistcoat. Thomas literally lost the coat from his back and the Bradleys both had to wait until a return trip to York in November to redeem their property.

The pledge book inevitably records only the pledges that Fettes accepted; we cannot know which customers and goods he turned away. Nevertheless, there is some reason to suppose that he was open to persuasion from customers eager to obtain money. On individual occasions he lent money on goods of very little value and even made loans without security. The advance of 1s on a worm-eaten waistcoat risked the damage of his other clothing stock.[98] The requirements of trade must have led Fettes to refuse some pledges but he was clearly willing to take chances to satisfy certain customers.

The majority of goods which Fettes accepted as pledges could be characterised as items of adults clothing (seventy-five percent) but he also routinely lent money on soft furnishings, household metalware such as irons and cutlery and more valuable pieces such as watches and jewellery.[99] This pattern is repeated in evidence of nineteenth-century pawnbroking and is an aspect of pawnbrokers' business that has been used to illustrate the vibrancy of the second-hand clothing trade in the eighteenth century.[100]

The predominance of women's clothing, particularly aprons and gowns, reflects the gender balance of Fettes's clients. Women represented the majority of his customers, and made more repeated visits than men. During the sample two weeks in September 1777, the most frequent male customers each visited the shop three times. By comparison, twelve women visited the shop on four or more occasions and Sarah Beeforth made pledges at fifteen different times (more than one pledge per working day). A database of customers' names[101] was edited and condensed to derive a guesstimate of the number of individual customers who visited Fettes's shop between 18 August 1777 and 26 December 1778 (see appendix 1.1: 'Prosopographical methodology'). This guesstimate gives 2,200 people of whom 1,349 or sixty-one percent were definitely women. This is a somewhat lower figure for female customers than might have been expected given that women were more likely than men to be counted twice in making the guesstimate. Women who married and therefore changed their name during the eighteen months of the pledge book would inadvertently have been counted twice. An informal money-lender in seventeenth-century London, for example, obtained eighty-four percent of his custom from women.[102]

The pledging of clothing and household goods by women to raise credit supplies circumstantial evidence for an overlap between the pawning poor and those guilty of theft. The same sorts of goods were the most popular targets for both male and female thieves but were disproportionately stolen by women who were also more active in pawnshop transactions than men. It is likely that this overlap (which may or may not have arisen from a causal connection) exacerbated public suspicion of pawnshops. Confusingly, in late eighteenth-century London the connection between pawnshops and theft was drawn explicitly when women pleaded *not* guilty to theft, on the grounds that they had pawned goods on behalf of others or with permission rather than as a strategy for converting stolen property into cash; 'these were instances of women's borrowing networks gone wrong'.[103]

The York evidence can show only that overt borrowing, or pawning on behalf of others, was not very common. The law of 1757 required Fettes to keep a record when goods were pawned by one person on behalf of another. There are only 114 instances of this practice accounting for only one percent of all pledges. Also there is no discernible pattern to these pledges for others. People may have been acting on behalf of friends, relatives, employers or tourists staying locally. On four occasions pledges from John Hare were brought by Nurse Hare, presumably a relation, whereas items belonging to Mrs Wood of North Street were brought by Mrs Aspinall of Petergate (addresses at some distance from each other). Catherine Woodhall of Thursday Market sent her apprentice to the shop with four silver teaspoons on 29 August 1777 but never came by to redeem them. Robert Hepworth, who was staying at Judges Lodgings, persuaded (or paid) Widow Aldridge, an almswoman who was otherwise a stranger to the pawnbroker's, to take a coat, waistcoat and silk gown to be pledged. Presumed cases of borrowing (by arrangement or without the owner's knowledge) are occasionally discernible, where the same item (such as a watch identified by a manufacturer's number) was pledged more than once by two or more different people, or where the owner arrived to redeem them, but it would be impossible to trace anonymous items (such as most clothes) moving between pawnshop customers.[104]

Customers were mainly drawn from the city of York itself, with tourists being the exception rather than the rule. Assuming the list of 2,200 people to provide a fair reflection of the individuals involved, the largest contingent came from Walmgate and North Street, locations on the south side of the city a little way distant from the centre.[105] Between two and five percent of customers were drawn from each of Fossgate, Goodramgate, Petergate and Micklegate, large thoroughfares leading into the city centre, and from the Water Lanes and Skeldergate, poor areas on the banks of the Ouse.[106] Other addresses accounted for fewer than two percent of all customers, suggesting that people were drawn to the shop regardless of its distance from their homes. They may have been drawn in by its proximity to their place of work or to places where ready money might be spent such as gambling dens or alehouses (one of the greatest fears of the anti-usury pamphleteers) but it is more likely that the need for cash drove people to walk any necessary distance to obtain it. Also, people would have needed to have relevant items with them in order to pledge spontaneously for immediate spending.

Finally, the most startling aspect of this research on customers relates to the implied prominence of Fettes's business within York. He possessed a customer base of approximately 2,200 in a town of 12,000 or 14,000 people. Discounting tourists (some 150 customers), this one shop catered to between fifteen and seventeen percent of townspeople over a period of less than two years. This was a significant proportion of the urban population, and would have comprised an even higher percentage of adults in York, suggesting a central role for pawnshop credit in the calculations of townspeople.

Poverty, the pawnshop and parish paupers

The importance of cheap credit for the very poor was appreciated as early as the 1570s. In 1571, amidst the plethora of sixteenth-century schemes for relieving the poor which pre-dated the codified poor laws, there was a plan for the establishment of seven 'Banks for the Relief of Common Necessity' to co-ordinate state-run moneylending. The banks would be run from London and six provincial towns including York, Chester and Exeter, and would lend money on pawns at the rate of six percent.[107] This project was never brought to fruition but in the eighteenth century the Charitable Corporation was set up in London to make government-funded loans on pledges. The corporation collapsed in 1731 amidst allegations of corruption and embezzlement; corporation functionaries were later imprisoned and a lottery was held to reimburse some of the people who suffered losses.[108] Thereafter, commercial pawnbrokers and dolly shops were once again the only resorts open to the poor who wished to secure loans against pledges.

Treble found that in the nineteenth century, credit was obtained from pawnbrokers for four different types of need; access to short-term (often weekly) credit, seasonal pawning to cover longer periods of difficulty, pawning to pay for costs associated with sickness such as doctors' bills or loss of earnings, and steady pawning in periods of unemployment. Yet it is important to distinguish between all people who had desperate need of credit and the individuals best placed to obtain it specifically from pawnbrokers, who were most accommodating for clients with regular wages and were wary of unemployment.[109] Beverley Lemire has observed that pawning in the eighteenth century 'was not restricted to the indigent, to the destitute, or to the recipients of charity'.[110] In fact the services of the reputable, established pawnshop were virtually denied to the destitute because, as in the nineteenth century, 'there were certain sections of the working classes who were treated as unacceptable risks'.[111] There was a reduced chance that they would be able to redeem their goods and pay the interest, leaving the broker with their (typically) low-value goods. The destitute were presumably compelled to turn to dolly shops, or moneylenders requiring little or no security, where the rate of interest was even higher.[112]

The process by which individuals or households fell into utter destitution (a state partly defined by a scarcity or absence of any goods to sell or pawn) could be lengthy and the pawnshop could be crucial to this experience. In addition to providing access to credit, pawning without redemption was an obvious way for people's material stock to decline. Yet parishes could intervene at different points in the process for different people. Any group of people on parish relief might encompass a wide range of material wealth, from those rich in goods to those who had reached destitution.[113] This means that very few assumptions can be made about people identified as paupers without additional information about the point they have reached in the process of destitution. The only thing that can be said about them is that they are sufficiently needy and insistent to have attracted the attention of the poor-law authorities, for which the threshold could be relatively or surprisingly high in terms of material wealth.

Contemporaries assumed that the clientele of pawnbrokers lay 'chiefly among the industrious poor, and working part of mankind, who have little or no credit at all, and who, for want of some such assistance, must come upon the parishes they belong to, or be starved'; pawnbrokers were characterised providing much-needed assistance in the period between the onset of a crisis and a resort to the parish.[114] Anecdotal evidence has indicated that this view was correct, and that pawning was typically an alternative expediency to parish relief, not an auxiliary service. In nineteenth-century Northumberland, for example, some women 'pawned all but their clothes before seeking relief', while letters from paupers to their parishes of settlement in Essex make the same point.[115]

This picture is confirmed by the York evidence; the number of customers who were simultaneously paupers is few. In order to find paupers among the pawnshop customers, I compiled the names of the poor receiving parish relief during the years 1777 and 1778 in the parishes where overseers' accounts survive. The five parishes with good accounts are St Michael le Belfrey (the parish with the largest population in York in 1801), St Sampson, St Mary Bishophill senior, St John Delpike and Holy Trinity

Goodramgate. These parishes contained twenty percent of the town's population in 1801, so if pauper customers were drawn from parishes in proportion to the total population, any overlap between known paupers would represent twenty percent of the total number of pauper customers. Unfortunately, it is unlikely that paupers were drawn from parishes in proportion to the total population because some areas of the city were poorer than others and more likely to be home to customers; the number of pauper customers found is likely to underestimate the total because some of the most popular addresses for customers fall in parishes with no surviving overseers' accounts.

A total of 201 paupers were found receiving parish relief in 1777 and or 1778, of whom 16 were probably Fettes's customers from a correspondence of names and addresses. A further 38 paupers may possibly have been customers but there was some inconsistency between the pauper's and the customer's name or address. This gives a total of 54 people who might have been both paupers and customers. Taking only probable individuals, and assuming they represent twenty percent of all probable pauper customers, then only four percent of Fettes's customers belonged to the parish poor. If the possibles are included then the total rises to twelve percent. Even if this underestimates the total extent of overlap between paupers and pawnshop customers by half, then over three-quarters of Fettes's customers were not paupers at approximately the same time they made use of his shop. However, it is likely that many more customers would technically become paupers over the course of their life-cycle, given the gradual, incremental nature of the process of decline into destitution. Calculations of this sort for other times and places are rare, but tend to echo the situation in York. In Glasgow towards the end of 1820, it was thought that of 2,043 heads of families who pledged goods, 1,375 had never applied for charity (presumably meaning the help given by public Relief Committees or Kirk Sessions); 474 (twenty-three percent) took occasional relief and 194 (just over nine percent) were paupers.[116]

Overseers (particularly in urban parishes) make direct if infrequent references to paupers' pawning activity. There are a couple of references in York to goods redeemed by parishes. In 1778 the overseers of St Michael le Belfrey paid to redeem from pawn clothes belonging to Mary Wilson's child, and paid twice to redeem the clothes of Elizabeth Gleddill's child. These clothes may have been placed with Fettes before the start of the surviving pledge book, because there is no record of them being pawned. Alternatively, this is a fragment of evidence that paupers had access to credit from another moneylender, who may have required less security and charged more interest.

Parish officers had an interest in monitoring the disposal of goods by paupers because parishes occasionally decided to appropriate material possessions when paupers entered the workhouse or died.[117] Parishes varied in the degree to which they attempted to exert this sort of control over the material lives of the poor. It was presumably easier for parishes to assume ownership where a pauper died without dependants or local kin to assert a claim to whatever scanty goods remained. Claiming pauper goods for the parish may have been only an occasional strategy to defray some of the costs of keeping a person over the preceding or succeeding years but it suggests an element of self-interest in parish scrutiny of pauper possessions and their disposal by pawning or other means.

An associated problem for parishes (and also for charities and other agencies which supplied free clothing or access to household goods, such as infirmaries) was the illegal pawning of goods by paupers for their own private gain. In some places, the parish 'mark' was fixed to clothes, household wares and even furniture to prevent or inhibit their theft and subsequent disposal. Charities which involved gifts of cloth or clothing were in the habit of marking them with a badge or indelible ink, both to prevent the poor from liquidating the asset and 'so that pawn-brokers – cannot plead ignorance' (of the origin of the item).[118] Such a strategy presumably made it easier to identify goods and for reputable pawnbrokers to avoid the charge of receiving stolen goods; it was not a guarantee, however, that theft or illegitimate pawning would not occur. In 1780s Birmingham, where poor relief was distributed by means of tickets given to the entitled poor, overseers complained of the impropriety of the tickets themselves being left with pawnbrokers as pledges, and announced that in future no tickets would be paid more than three months in arrears in an attempt to limit the practice. The overseers also opined 'many abandoned wretches have been detected in pawning and selling the Parish Apparell'.[119]

Benjamin Shaw, whose own wife stole his clothes, books and other possessions to pawn them, attributed her cavalier attitude towards possessions and credit to the extremity of her poverty in her youth. He described her use of credit drapers, and the way she would run up credit at one shop, and pay it off only to 'score on' at another. She stole his money and lied to him but his autobiographical notes comment stoically 'this was allways her way, for when she was young She never had any thing, Scarce any thing of her Back'.[120] He assumed that early experience of destitution itself could be the cause of a shift in attitude towards material possessions, making a person ruthlessly acquisitive regardless of technical ownership or consequent theft.

Individual people used the pawnshop in different ways but the variety of their usage was not decidedly conditioned by whether they were paupers at the same time. All types of customers employed a number of different strategies in maximising their use of the pawnshop. The only identifiable difference between pauper customers and all customers was that paupers redeemed their goods much more quickly; on average customers repaid their loan after fifty-six days whereas paupers took an average of only twenty-five days. It is difficult to know what to make of this given that each average conceals such a wide range of behaviour. It may possibly suggest that the poorer people became, the more short-term their strategies or the more central the pawnshop became to their survival. Notably this is at odds with evidence from elsewhere; in Amsterdam poor widows were likely to leave their goods in the pawnshop for longer than other groups.[121]

The main obstacle to determining patterns of use by different types of customer lies in the difficulty of categorising individual customers as representatives of the labouring poor or as parish paupers; I could not be certain that a customer who was not a pauper in one of the five parishes studied was not a pauper in one of the other twenty-three city parishes. Individuals are similarly indistinguishable as members of a particular trade or as domestic servants since there are very few occupational labels recorded against customers' names. Also, there was virtually no overlap between the tradesmen listed in the York directory of 1781 and the pawnshop's customers.[122] It was said in 1745 that it would be injurious for the reputation of a trader even to enter a pawnbroker's shop; tradesmen who were tempted to pawn were advised instead to admit their virtual insolvency.[123] If there was a stigma for tradesmen in approaching a pawnbroker they might have tried to use intermediaries, but if such a practice was widespread, it is not disclosed by a study of the few items reported to have been brought on someone else's behalf. If the customer Thomas Percival of Jubbergate was the same man who was admitted a member of the York merchant adventurers in June 1764, he was probably trying to conceal his use of the pawnshop by sending a pledge in the hands of 'Fentiman's youngest daughter' on 28 October 1777. His boots and coat were redeemed a month later and he did not need to use the shop again before the end of the pledge book, either in person or using a go-between. Percival was one of only a very few merchant adventurers who were even conceivably connected with the pawnshop, so it does not appear that notable but desperate traders formed a significant group among Fettes's customers.

One of the few identifiable groups of customers is the almsmen and women who lived in one of the many almshouses or 'hospitals' in York; at least nineteen almshouses were operational in the 1770s.[124] Almspeople are recorded amongst Fettes's customers by virtue of their address being given as the almshouse; however, only thirteen men and women are listed in this context, seven of whom used the pawnbroker just once or twice and none of whom visited more than thirteen times. A number of the almshouses paid a stipend to inhabitants in addition to providing accommodation, so these charity recipients could rely on a regular 'wage' or income. The infrequency of their custom suggests either that this rendered them less liable to the sudden need for credit, or that the regularity of their income did nothing to persuade Fettes to accept their pledges. The few charity customers there were seemed to use the pawnshop for very long-term credit, since their average time before redemption was sixty-seven days, much longer than paupers and even longer than the average for all customers of fifty-six days.

It is not feasible to compare the use made of Fettes's shop with Treble's categories of the reasons why credit was sought; it is possible to look at some patterns of custom. There were people who used the shop only once or twice during the period covered by the pledge book. Pendock Vane or Vame, apprentice to the barber-surgeon John Firth of Coney Street, pawned a silver watch on 18 July 1777 and redeemed it on 4 November of the same year but did not place any further pledges before the end of the volume.[125] Similarly, Philip Watts, apprenticed to a York merchant tailor called Thomas Richardson, pawned a waistcoat and handkerchief on 7 September 1778, redeemed it three weeks later on 26 September and did not reappear.[126] Others came in periodically over the eighteen months, perhaps on a monthly basis but not necessarily to a predictable pattern. Ann Plaister's address was 'Mr Telford's Nurseryhouse'; she was presumably an employee of John and George Telford, seedsmen who worked in Tanner Row.[127] She made eight pledges in September 1777, a further three in October and she reappeared periodically over the following months. She can be found pawning twice in the final week for which book applies in December 1778.

Some customers used the shop intensively over one or two months and then slackened off, or did not reappear in the book. An example of this sort of usage, which might best be characterised as episodic, is provided by the Beeforths who lived in the Shambles. Sarah Beeforth visited the shop fifteen times during the first two weeks in September 1777, pledging various items of clothing and shoes. One pledge was redeemed the day after it was pawned, while another remained in the shop until the following March. She visited the shop between three and six times each week for the following seven weeks. During the fifth week Elizabeth Beeforth also of the Shambles and possibly Sarah's adult daughter appeared as a customer.[128] In the seventh week Richard Beeforth of Shambles made

Figure 6.2 *Pledges and redemptions by Beeforths*

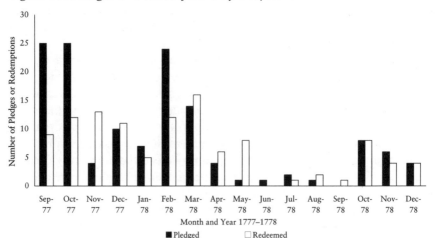

pledges. Richard was probably Sarah's husband; their close connection is circumstantially confirmed since they both pledged items used in patten-making.[129] On 8 October Sarah pawned a patten-maker's knife that remained unredeemed in December 1778 while Richard pawned four pairs of patten irons on 1 November and redeemed them on 8 November. After the end of the seventh week (Saturday 1 November), the Beeforths were obviously better off, redeeming more goods than they pledged in November. They remained occasional customers until their next period of particular difficulty in February 1778. From March to May they were net redeemers, and then made only a handful of visits to the shop until October; up to December 1778 the shop experienced a small concentration of custom from them, which was trailing off by the end of the year.

The sheer number of customers, and the difficulty in determining the continuity of individual, family or household custom, collectively make recovery of more complex patterns of credit-seeking in York's poorer households unfeasible. Nevertheless, the broad picture of pawnshop use illustrates these three patterns at work. There were many people who visited the shop only once or twice, but the majority of pledges are accounted for by people who either pawned periodically throughout the months covered by the pledge book, or who needed to pawn intensively over a shorter period of weeks or months.

The advantage in identifying people who were quite probably both pawnshop customers and paupers lies in the use of the two sets of accounts to observe the combination of the two sources of income. A close examination of overseers' accounts in conjunction with the pledge book reveals that nine of the sixteen paupers used the parish and the pawnbroker consecutively; most pawned goods up until the point they received parish relief but a couple worked the other way round and pawned once they were off the parish. The remaining seven obtained money from both sources concurrently. The evidence points to a situation where people might make extensive use of one facility or the other since there were no instances which could be found of paupers receiving regular relief who routinely made pledges.

Mary Budd and Mary Prince are both examples of customers who used the pawnshop energetically, if in very different ways. Mary Budd used the shop before she took relief. She worked systematically, pledging a large, fairly fixed bundle of goods on a monthly basis. She pledged her four gowns, her two black satin cloaks and a long list of other goods on the same ticket, left them with Fettes for about a month, and redeemed them only to pledge them again later the same day or the next day. She did this ten times between September 1777 and July 1778 (and made smaller pledges on four other days). She usually received between £4 and £5 for her bundle; £5 in September 1777, which dropped down to a low of £3 15s in July 1778. Fettes was shrewdly reducing the amount he would advance; he also began to insist that the bundle would be forfeit if she did not redeem it within one month. Whatever resources she was able to utilise monthly to redeem her clothes ran out after July 1778. The bundle was pledged for the last time on 31 July 1778 and shortly before Christmas she became a pensioner in the parish of St Sampson receiving 2s per week. Mary Prince, in contrast, was a much more frequent visitor to Fettes's shop, pawning between one and thirteen times a month, making 112 visits between 19 August 1777 and 5 December 1778. She pawned adults' and childrens' clothes, flat irons and a Bible on one occasion for small sums ranging between 4d and 3s 6d. A handful of items remained unredeemed by December 1778 and some items were left for long periods of three months or more but the majority of her pledges were redeemed within ten days. She fell into difficulty towards the middle of November 1778, went to St Sampson's parish for help and was given a shilling a week for four weeks.

The Armitages of St Michael le Belfrey parish were relatively unusual because they received their relief first, before they needed to pawn, but Joseph Armitage and his wife were only on the fringes of pauperism since they received just a single handout of 3s in 1777 and no relief in 1778. They pledged clothes and bedlinen with Fettes on seven occasions between January and September 1778 and redeemed the earlier pledges between March and September 1778 but by December 1778 their last three pledges, including a gold ring, remained unredeemed. An alternative picture is presented by Robert Turner. He was a pensioner in St Mary Bishophill senior parish receiving 4s per week from November 1777 onwards; he only visited the pawnshop once, on 9 April 1778, to pledge a green silk waistcoat for 4s 2d. He collected it on 2 July and apparently did not return again.

Conclusion

In the eighteenth century few were prepared to defend the trade of pawn-broking. Published opinion repetitively insisted on pawnbrokers' financial rapacity and criminal inclination, but unsurprisingly even a brief analysis of London pawnbrokers finds them operating along a much more realistic spectrum from the shady to the upstanding. Historians, meanwhile, have long supposed that in a world of restricted credit opportunities the pawnbroker offered a vital resource, but have been compelled to confine themselves to speculation for the period prior to 1800. The case of George Fettes provides the opportunity to test the operation of provincial, eighteenth-century pawning in the context of public opinion that tarred all pawnbrokers with a metropolitan brush. He was a respected businessman with a vibrant trade that stretched from the tourist visitors who came for the races to the poorest inhabitants of York's streets and alleys. He did not, however, attract the open custom of other substantial tradesmen.

Furthermore, the pledge book supplies vital information about the experience of poverty in York. The routine finding that approximately five percent of urban populations stood in need of parish relief is given context by the fact that between fifteen and seventeen percent of the town's inhabitants made use of this one pawnbroker in the relatively short period August 1777 to December 1778. Thus where pawning was an option it became deeply embedded in the survival economies of many working people. Different styles of usage can be identified among Fettes's clientele. Customers might use the shop once, possibly pawning a single valuable item, to help them cope with a particular crisis. Others used the shop persistently but not necessarily frequently to deal with periodic, recurrent problems or shortfalls. Brief periods of intense pawning followed by a lull in activity or disappearance from the pledge book can be labelled episodic, emanating from a period of crisis which either permitted short-term recovery or signalled an important stage in absolute material decline into destitution (and thereafter an absence of goods to pawn). The role of the pawnshop in the process of either inde-pendent survival or decline into dependency is particularly clear in the case of individuals who went on to receive parish relief. The strategies employed by the poor who dealt with Fettes's pawnshop were limited by whether he was willing to accept their pawn, by the amount he advanced, and by their ability to redeem their goods. Nonetheless, individual people exploited the essential flexibility of pawning to cover routine expenses, regain their financial equilibrium following a crisis, or stave off deeper destitution for so long as their material wealth would allow.

Notes

1 A version of this chapter was published as 'Pawnbroking and the survival strategies of the urban poor in 1770s York', in S. King and A. Tomkins (eds), *The Poor in England 1700–1850: An Economy of Makeshifts* (Manchester, 2003); I am very grateful to Manchester University Press for the opportunity to offer a revised version here.

2 P. H. Haagen, 'Eighteenth-century English society and the debt law', in S. Cohen and A. Scull (eds), *Social Control and the State* (Oxford, 1983) p. 229; J. Hoppit, 'Attitudes to credit in Britain 1680–1790', *Historical Journal* 33: 2 (1990), 313–14.

3 D. Davies, *The Case of Labourers in Husbandry Stated and Considered* (London, 1795), p. 6.

4 K. Hudson, *Pawnbroking: An Aspect of British Social History* (London, 1982), pp. 32–5.

5 R. Campbell, *The London Tradesman* (London, 1747), p. 296.

6 *Gentleman's Magazine* 15 (1745), 410.

7 J. Stow, *Survey of the Cities of London and Westminster ... Corrected, Improved, in the Year 1720 by John Strype* 1 (6th edn, London, 1754), p. 474 quoted in B. Lemire, 'Consumerism in preindustrial and early industrial England: the trade in secondhand clothes', *Journal of British Studies* 27 (1988), 14.

8 R. L'Estrange, *The Devil and Broker or a Character of a Pawnbroker in a Merry Dialogue* (London, 1677), p. 2.

9 *A Plain Answer to a late pamphlet intitled The Business of Pawnbroking Stated and Defended* (London, 1745), p. 4.

10 *A Letter from a Discounter in Bishopsgate Street to a Pawnbroker in Long Acre* (London, 1745), p. 34, where the author signs himself "'your brother in iniquity" Abraham Ben Little Wright'.

11 *The Mistery of Iniquity luckily Discover'd* (London, 1708).

12 *A Plain Answer* p. 8.

13 *The Honest London Spy: exhibiting the base and subtle intrigues of the town* (Dublin, 1793), p. 72.

14 *Mother Midnight's Comical Pocket-Book: or, a Bone for the Criticks* (London [1753]) p. 32.

15 J. M. Beattie, *Crime and the Courts in England 1660–1800* (Oxford, 1986), pp.189–90.

16 H. Fielding, *Amelia* (London, 1751) quoted in H. Fielding, *An Enquiry into the Late Increase of Robbers* [London, 1751] edited by M. Zirker (Oxford, 1988), pp. 125–30.

17 *A Plain Answer*, pp. 3–4.
18 *Mistery of Iniquity*, p. 6.
19 *The Life and Real Adventures of Hamilton Murray* (London, 1759), pp. 210–11; *Memoirs of the Noted Buckhorse* (London, 1756), pp. 53–4.
20 *A Letter from a Discounter*, p. 2.
21 *Reasons Against Licensing Pawnbrokers* (London, 1745), p. 31.
22 *Proposals for a Regulation or an Entire Suppression of Pawnbrokers* (London, 1732), p. 13.
23 *The Devil and Broker*, pp. 3–6; *Mistery of Iniquity*, p. 5.
24 *A Plan for Recruiting the British Army* (London [1780]).
25 *A Dissertation on Credit* (n. p., [c.1750]), p. 1.
26 *A Plain Answer*, pp. 11, 27.
27 *An Apology for the Business of Pawnbroking* (London, 1744), p. 57.
28 *Gentleman's Magazine* 15 (1745), 699.
29 *The Tradesman's Lawyer and Countrey-man's Friend* (London, 1703), pp. 110–11.
30 W. S. Lewis (ed.), *Correspondence of Horace Walpole* 24 (New Haven, 1967), p. 231, quoted in Hoppit, 'Attitudes to Credit', p. 314.
31 W. S. Lewis (ed.), *Correspondence of Horace Walpole* 20 (New Haven, 1960), p. 169; W. S. Lewis (ed.), *Correspondence of Horace Walpole* 40 (New Haven, 1980), p. 65n.
32 *Gentleman's Magazine* 22 (1752), 30.
33 J. Bentham, *Defence of Usury* (London, 1787), p. 2. Even so, there could be worse offenders in the eyes of the public; at a debate held in 1786 to consider 'Which contributes most to impoverish the lower class of people, the Publican, the Pawnbroker, or the Trading Justice?', the majority voted against the justice; D. Andrew (ed.), *London Debating Societies 1776–1799* (London Record Society 30, 1994), p. 182.
34 Report of Colquhoun's publication of *An Account of the Meat and Soup Charity established in the Metropolis* contained in *The Times* 20 March 1797 and *Gentleman's Magazine* 67 (1797), 856–7; *Hell upon Earth: or, the Town in an Uproar, &c* (London, 1729), pp. 2, 8.
35 *Pawnbrokers Detected and Dissected: or the poor man's adviser* (London, 1809) p. 4.
36 Bentham, *Defence*, pp. 1–2.
37 *Pawnbrokers Detected*, p. 8.
38 Ibid., p. 44; P. King, 'The rise of juvenile delinquency in England 1780–1840: changing patterns of perception and prosecution', *Past and Present* 160 (1998).
39 M. Tebbutt, *Making Ends Meet: Pawnbroking and Working-Class Credit* (Leicester, 1983), p. 3.
40 *Gentleman's Magazine* 15 (1745), 700.
41 Tebbutt, *Making Ends Meet*, p. 13.
42 J. Lackington, *Memoirs of the forty-five first years of the life of James Lackington* (London, 1795), pp. 226–7.

43 R. Williams, 'Stolen goods and the economy of makeshifts in eighteenth-century Exeter', *Archives* 31: 112 (2005), 86.

44 J. Styles, 'Clothing the North: the supply of non-elite clothing in the eighteenth-century north of England', *Textile History* 25: 2 (1994).

45 *Tradesman's Lawyer* p. 110; *Calendar of State Papers, Home Office Series, George III 1760–65* (London, 1878), *1766–69* (London, 1879), *1770–72* (London, 1881), *1773–75* (London, 1899), see annual tables of licences to plead.

46 *An Apology*; some of the views expressed in this pamphlet had apparently been aired earlier, in the *Daily Post Boy* 26 April 1731.

47 Lemire, 'Consumerism', 17.

48 *An Apology*, p. 16.

49 Ibid., pp. 16, 26.

50 *Gentleman's Magazine* 54 (1784), 711; a pawnbroker's apprentice stole jewellery in his master's keeping.

51 J. Black, *The English Press in the Eighteenth Century* (London, 1987), p. 60.

52 *An Apology*, pp. 15–16.

53 *Gentleman's Magazine* 22 (1752), 284.

54 30 Geo 2 c. 24.

55 24 Geo 3 c. 42.

56 *Old Bailey Proceedings Online* [hereafter OBP] (www.oldbaileyonline.org, accessed 24 August 2005).

57 OBP, July 1778, Sarah Davidson (t17780115–62).

58 OBP, June 1778, Margaret Pearce (t17780603–47).

59 OBP, February 1778, Robert Grace (t17780218–60); April 1778, Robert Crosby (t17780429–6); December 1778, William Jones and Richard Baker (t17781209–2); December 1778, Mary Clarke (t17781209–20).

60 OBP, January 1777, William Davis and Richard Oldgate (t17770115–2); February 1777, Thomas Turner and Mary Yates (t17770219–21).

61 W. Godwin, *The Adventures of Caleb Williams* (Oxford [1794] 1982), p. 254.

62 B. Lemire, 'Peddling fashion: salesmen, pawnbrokers, taylors, thieves and the second-hand clothes trade in England c.1700–1800', *Textile History* 22: 1 (1991), 82.

63 Hudson, *Pawnbroking*, p. 31.

64 Williams, 'Stolen goods', p. 94.

65 A. G. Crosby (ed.), *The Family Records of Benjamin Shaw Mechanic of Dent, Dolphinholme and Preston 1772–1841* (Publications of the Record Society of Lancashire and Cheshire 130, 1991), p. 77.

66 Informal opportunities existed in most communities; see S. Hindle, *On the Parish? The Micro-politics of Poor Relief in Rural England c. 1550–1750* (Oxford, 2004), pp. 76–81.

67 *Pawnbrokers Detected*, p. 60.

68 M. Rubin, *Charity and Community in Medieval Cambridge* (Cambridge, 1987), p. 283.

69 Bodleian Library (hereafter Bod. Lib.), GA Oxon b.19 fo. 141, printed orders of the Vice Chancellor 30 March 1763.

70 J. P. C. Roach (ed.), *Victoria County History of Cambridge and Ely* 3 (Oxford, 1959), p. 84; A. Crossley (ed.), *Victoria County History of Oxfordshire* 4 (Oxford, 1979), p. 155.

71 Bod. Lib., R Top 724 H. E. Salter (ed.), *Survey of Oxford 1772* (Oxford, 1912) with manuscript notes by W. P. Ellis identifying Haynes as a pawnbroker.

72 L. Fontaine, 'Women's economic spheres and credit in pre-industrial Europe', in B. Lemire *et al* (eds), *Women and Credit: Researching the Past, Refiguring the Future* (Oxford, 2001), p. 25.

73 B. Lemire, 'Introduction. Women, credit and the creation of opportunity: a historical overview', in B. Lemire *et al.* (eds), *Women and Credit.*

74 In many respects pawnbroking offered a route to self-help inverse to that available from friendly societies which, like pawnbroker's shops, were established in provincial industrial towns in increasing numbers in the second half of the eighteenth century. Contemporary commentators, unsurprisingly, perceived the two options to be in direct opposition; see Sir T. Bernard (ed.), *Reports of the Society for Bettering the Condition and Increasing the Comforts of the Poor* 3 (London, 1802), p. 186 and T. B. Hughes, *The Advantages of Friendly Loan Societies contrasted with the ruinous effects of pawning* (London, 1841).

75 Tebbutt, *Making Ends Meet*, pp. 3–4.

76 Lemire, 'Consumerism', 12.

77 Tebbutt, *Making Ends Meet*, p. 6.

78 I am indebted for much of the information contained in this paragraph and the next to the work completed by Alison Backhouse; see her *The Worm-Eaten Waistcoat* (York, 2003), pp. 62–5; figure 1.3, map of York.

79 *Universal British Directory* (London, 1798).

80 *York Courant* 25 November 1788 quoted in Backhouse, *Worm-Eaten Waistcoat*, p. 56.

81 *York Herald* 9 March 1793, given in Backhouse, *Worm-Eaten Waistcoat*, p. 50.

82 D. M. Smith (ed.), *The Company of Merchant Adventurers in the City of York: Register of Admissions 1581–1835* (Borthwick List and Index 18, 1996) pp. 21, 27; however, Richard himself became a bankrupt.

83 J. Telford (ed.), *The Letters of the Rev. John Wesley* 7 (London, 1960), p. 77.

84 Ibid., letter of 3 August 1781.

85 York City Archives, Pawnbrokers' pledge book, 1777–78. The contents of the pledge book are ideally suited to conversion to a computer database and the enormous task of converting the entire book has been undertaken by Alison Backhouse. In addition I have compiled some smaller, sample databases of my own to extract specific types of information; findings here are based on both analyses.

86 Backhouse, *Worm-Eaten Waistcoat*, p. 52.

87 This conclusion is supported by trade fluctuations for German pawnbrokers, whereby every economic downturn also hit the pawnshops, and the number of new pledges decreased significantly; see K. C. Fuhrer, 'Pawning in German working-class life before the First World War', *International Review of Social*

History 46 (2001), 40.

88 T. S. Ashton, *Economic Fluctuations in England 1700–1800* (Oxford, 1959), p. 130.

89 Ibid., pp. 23, 40, 100, 105, 130, 161–2, 172–3.

90 P. Holt, 'Scottish pawnshops 1792–1820: a note on a neglected index of the condition of the working class', *Journal of the Scottish Labour History Society* 8 (1974), 32.

91 B. S. Rowntree, *Poverty: A Study of Town Life* (London, 1901) pp. 25, 88.

92 My conclusions about redemptions are based on my sample database drawn from two weeks in September 1777. It seemed appropriate to select a period towards the start of the book where redemptions or details of sale were likely to be fullest (but not during August, when race week affected the composition of clientele and the value of pledges).

93 Backhouse, *Worm-Eaten Waistcoat*, p. 48.

94 R. J. Raymond, 'Pawnbrokers and pawnbroking in Dublin: 1830–1870', *Dublin Historical Record* 32: 1 (1978), 23.

95 National Archive, C110/134 Chancery exhibits, pawnbrokers' books 1822–34, auction sale book.

96 Backhouse, *Worm-Eaten Waistcoat*, pp. 46–7.

97 Based on my sample of two weeks in September, but coinciding with Backhouse's findings for the whole period.

98 Backhouse, *Worm-Eaten Waistcoat*, p. 26.

99 For a detailed breakdown of pledges see ibid., chapter 3.

100 B. Lemire, *Dress, Culture and Commerce* (London, 1997), pp. 105–12.

101 My own, rather than that compiled by Mrs Backhouse.

102 Lemire, 'Introduction', pp. 4, 9–10.

103 L. MacKay, 'Why they stole: women in the Old Bailey, 1779–1789', *Journal of Social History* 32: 3 (1999), 625, 628, 630–4.

104 Backhouse, *Worm-Eaten Waistcoat*, pp. 36–9.

105 Walmgate was identified by Rowntree a century later as the poorest district in the city; Rowntree, *Poverty*, p. 236 and *passim*.

106 In the nineteenth century the Water Lanes area became known as 'the most notorious and criminal district in the city'; F. Finnegan, *Poverty and Prostitution: A Study of Victorian Prostitutes in York* (Cambridge, 1979), pp. 35–6.

107 *Calendar of State Papers, Domestic Series, Edward VI, Mary, Elizabeth 1547–1580* (London, 1856), p. 410; I am indebted to Ian Atherton for this reference.

108 *Gentleman's Magazine* 1 (1731), 517; 2 (1732), 630, 783; 4 (1734), 235; for state-managed pawning in continental Europe see C. Jones, *Charity and Bienfaisance: The Treatment of the Poor in the Montpelier Region, 1740–1815* (Cambridge, 1982), p. 90.

109 J. H. Treble, *Urban Poverty in Britain 1830–1914* (London, 1979), p. 132.

110 Lemire, 'Consumerism', 23.

111 Treble, *Urban Poverty*, pp. 131–3.

112 Ibid., p. 133.

113 P. King, 'Pauper inventories and the material lives of the poor in the eighteenth and early nineteenth centuries', in T. Hitchcock *et al.* (eds), *Chronicling Poverty: The Voices and Strategies of the English Poor 1640–1840* (Basingstoke, 1997).

114 *Gentleman's Magazine* 15 (1745), 578, 698; F. M. Eden, *The State of the Poor* (London [1797] 1928), p. 191.

115 J. Long, *Conversations in Cold Rooms: Women, Work and Poverty in 19th-century Northumberland* (Woodbridge, 1999), p. 128; T. Sokoll, *Essex Pauper Letters 1731–1837* (Oxford, 2001), pp. 146, 285, 429, among others.

116 J. Cleland, *Enumeration of Glasgow* (Glasgow, 1831) p. 139 quoted by Holt, 'Scottish pawnshops', 31.

117 See chapter two for a discussion of this point.

118 G. B. Hindle, *Provision for the Relief of the Poor in Manchester, 1754–1826* (Chetham Society Manchester 22, 1975), p. 135.

119 M. McNaulty, 'Some Aspects of the History of the Administration of the Poor Laws in Birmingham between 1730 and 1834' (MA dissertation, Birmingham University, 1942), pp. 92–3, 98.

120 Crosby, *Family Records of Benjamin Shaw*, p. 77.

121 A. McCants, 'Petty debts and family networks: the credit markets of widows and wives in eighteenth-century Amsterdam', in B. Lemire *et al.* (eds), *Women and Credit: Researching the Past, Refiguring the Future* (Oxford, 2001), p. 46.

122 *Bailey's Northern Directory* (Warrington, 1781).

123 *Gentleman's Magazine* 15 (1745), 460–1.

124 P. M. Tillott (ed.), *The Victoria History of Yorkshire: The City of York* (Oxford, 1961), pp. 422–6.

125 Backhouse, *Worm-Eaten Waistcoat*, p. 36; British Library, Egerton 2572 Guild book of the Barber Surgeons of York, fifteenth to eighteenth centuries.

126 D. M. Smith (ed.), *The Company of Merchant Taylors in the City of York: Register of Admissions 1560–1835* (Borthwick List and Index 16, 1996), p. 101.

127 *Bailey's Northern Directory*, p. 317.

128 Elizabeth Beeforth, the daughter of one Sarah and Richard, was baptised on 26 June 1755 in Holy Trinity Goodramgate; Familysearch genealogy resource, www.familysearch.org, accessed 6 September 2005.

129 One Richard Beeforth was married to Sarah Hart on 25 June 1754 in St Maurice; Familysearch genealogy resource, www.familysearch.org, accessed 6 September 2005.

7

Conclusion

This book has sought, in the words of Barry Reay, to place the paupers of selected urban parishes 'under the microscope' in order to 'see and explore the complexity of the social interaction and social and economic processes'. While it could not realistically take *Microhistories* as a methodological model, given that work's emphasis on oral history, it has endorsed the philosophy and conviction that such small-scale work can both reveal hidden complexities and in some ways supersede a broader approach.[1] This study originated from a desire to decipher information about small groups of the urban poor, and particularly to evaluate the role of parish relief (in both its long-term and temporary forms), different varieties of charity, and pawnshop credit in individual and household economies. In this undertaking an innovative methodology, involving a measure of record linkage between overseers' accounts and other sources containing name lists (but without tackling urban parish reconstruction), has permitted some minute observations in the form of prosopographical compilations. It has also given a more holistic impression of experiences of poverty than is usually offered and has given rise to some broad new conclusions. In other ways, however, the tone and direction of this book fits in with some established trends and advances debate to a new level. It coincides with the current preoccupation of revising early twentieth-century verdicts on the old poor law and subscribes to the life-cycle explanation of poverty. Some sections contribute to debates that are already relatively vigorous, such as interest in pauper death and burial, while others tap into more recent concerns such as patterns of distribution of extraordinary relief.

The potential of the prosopographical device, namely using multiple sources to establish partial biographies for a small subset of the poor and supplying detailed histories of some people or families, can best be illustrated using the fullest examples available. These examples all involve paupers in Oxford where the wealth of source material, including legal records not used elsewhere in this study, allows the most comprehensive set of links. Take the Simms family: Philip Simms was born in St Mary Magdalen parish in 1739. His father Ralph stood surety for his mother Sarah in 1741 when she was bound over for assault but like Nack Wheeler (whose story is told in the introduction) rumours of troublemaking did not bar the family from parish relief; the family were relieved by St Mary Magdalen parish during 1743–46 with occasional doles of money and purchases of meat. Philip went to the Bluecoat school from at least 1748 (aged nine) but was taken out by his parents and transferred to the Greycoat in 1751 (aged eleven or twelve), exemplifying the importance of parental choices. In 1749 Ralph was given Hody's 20s charity by the parish and in 1750 he took Rowney's 10s charity from the town. Philip was apprenticed by the Greycoat in 1755 (aged about fifteen) and appeared again only in 1769 when he stood surety for another man. His mother Sarah received Hody's clothing charity four times in the 1760s and 1770s.

The family progressed from needing extraordinary relief when Philip was a small child to independence from the parish, although it continued to benefit from numerous private charities. The Simms family must have been one of the families on the margins of poverty who could remain independent at most times but who required relief at key crisis points. These are the very people whose experiences tend to be most inaccessible, who fell between ratepayers and relief-users for most of their lives.

Other partial biographies involve people or families who became more persistently in need of parish relief. The labourer Thomas Gadney was named as a pauper in Oxford St Michael in most years from 1745 to 1765. He received a variety of relief including payments for the birth of a child in 1751–52, numerous doles in his wife's illness in 1753 and rent of £2 per year from 1757 to 1759. Gadney had his legal settlement in St Michael but lived in St Mary Magdalen. As a result, he was clearly the same Thomas Gadney who received payments from Snowe's charity (a St Michael parish charity) in every year from 1740 to 1747 and also the Thomas Gadney from St Mary Magdalen who sent three sons to Nixon's school in 1755 and received town charity money from Rowney's, Harris's and Boyle's benefactions in 1750, 1757 and 1770.

Matthew Winkle eventually needed long-term relief. He received disbursements from Snowe's charity in 1740, 1742 and 1746 and took Rowney's 10s charity in 1744 but was not named in St Michael's overseers' accounts until 1749; however, he became a St Bartholomew's almsman in the same year. The parish paid a pension for his child for thirty-seven weeks in 1752 and Matthew entered the workhouse some time before April 1754. He left the workhouse in March 1756 and received a pension until his death in June of the same year. His wife Janet was buried from the workhouse in 1757.

Two generations of the Wildgoose family clashed with the law and the parish in this period. There were two branches of the family in St Peter le Bailey in the mid-eighteenth century and both took some parish relief. James and Thomas Wildgoose were brothers whose children were born in the parish. Thomas's family was to prove the poorer of the two and the overseers called him by his nickname, 'Gib', to distinguish him from his son and namesake in their accounts. Thomas senior (or 'Gib') and his family were relieved by the parish in 1741 but they were not mentioned specifically again until 1747. Then in 1750 tragedy struck; Thomas's wife Sarah died, leaving him with four children: Thomas junior aged fourteen, Valentine aged ten, Elizabeth aged six and John aged only one year. Father and children were heavily dependent on the parish during the early and mid-1750s. St Peter le Bailey spent over £40 on them during the period 1752–57, but by the end of the decade, only the youngest child John (or Jack) was still burdensome to the parish. Their responsibility for him did not end until his (relatively late) apprenticeship in 1765.

The Wildgooses collectively were somewhat given to running away from their responsibilities, and they were also prone to connections with property crime. At the Epiphany town quarter sessions of 1738/39, Thomas Wildgoose was indicted for four thefts but was acquitted on all counts. He did not appear again until 1752 when a recognisance included in the town records specified that Thomas Wildgoose was bound over (with James as one of the sureties) to appear at the Berkshire assizes. He was suspected of collaborating with John Castle to steal a parcel of check linen from Daniel Pitts's waggon. This case may have involved the father or the son as Thomas junior would have been sixteen at this point; however, it is likely that neither was transported or hanged as 'Gib' returned to contest another case and the parish were paying to lodge his eldest boy in Oxford during the early months of 1754. In 1753, the parish paid to keep one of Gib's boys in bridewell from July to September, but the reason for this punishment is not known.

In 1754, the elder Thomas Wildgoose was (finally) successfully accused of theft. On 4 October 1754, William Tranter was bound over to prosecute Thomas for stealing a rump of beef valued at 3s. On 10 October Thomas was found guilty to the full value and sentenced to transportation for seven years. This was certainly Thomas senior as *Jackson's Oxford Journal* described him as an old offender 'Job' Wildgoose (presumably a variant of Gib). This left the parish responsible for at least three children, now effectively orphaned. Thomas's two youngest children were taken into the workhouse but his second son Valentine was more of a problem. At fourteen years old he was suitable for apprenticing but he remained in the parish and his lodging was paid for at the Widow Mary Evelin's house. In 1757, an opportunity arose for the parish to dispose of him creditably. On 14 April it was reported that thirty-three stout parish boys were to be sent to London to be put to sea. The parish optimistically bought Valentine all the necessaries for going to sea and conveyed him to London in June. Yet he must have either run away or refused to co-operate, as soon after the constable was paid to apprehend him, and he spent part of July 1757 in bridewell.

The two youngest children were initially too small to be troublesome but both drew the attention of the authorities during their youth. John Wildgoose was apprenticed to Abingdon but in 1767 he apparently followed the example of his brother and ran away from his master. St Peter le Bailey had to pay 5s to take him back. Finally, Elizabeth went before the Trinity town quarter sessions in 1770 as the mother of James Young's bastard. As she had been apprenticed to St Thomas's parish in the 1750s, St Peter le Bailey was not responsible for a third generation.

These life histories provide fascinating, instructive and hitherto undetectable information on the lives of the Oxford poor, but they also betray one of the weaknesses of this approach (where parish reconstruction is lacking). With the exception of Sarah Simms, Janet Winkle and Elizabeth Wildgoose, they do tend to privilege male stories. This is not a negligible problem, given that the majority of urban papers (identified exclusively from overseers' accounts and workhouse inmate lists) were female in this period. This bias springs from the emphasis of contemporary mores and source compilation; there were after all more boys' charity schools than girls' establishments, only the men's almshouses in Oxford have surviving name lists (and elsewhere infirmaries took more male patients than female). Only the pawnshop pledge book (of course, for York rather than Oxford) puts the female poor in the foreground and even that reveals more male customers than might have been expected. Despite their copious appearances among overseers' accounts, details about the female poor frequently remain elusive.

Furthermore, although individual biographies may be composed in the case of peculiarly needy, criminal or uniquely named families (where a poor person's ill luck becomes a historian's good fortune), the vast majority of Oxford's poor population are not susceptible to tracing in this way. This exercise gave rise to name lists referring to hundreds of people, where the majority of connections between individuals on separate lists generate just a small part of their biography (perhaps comprising only two points of contact with welfare or other agencies). Added to the paucity of links between paupers and most other groups, it is not surprising that stories even so full as the examples given above are rare. Poor people were born, made ends meet, and died without being substantially traceable.

Nonetheless, the disappointing nature of these fragmentary biographies must be seen in the light of the meaningful alternatives; in other words, they are not dependent on the survival of pre-existing narrative sources (that are notably sparse before the late eighteenth century).

From this undeniably partial picture, the poor in mid-eighteenth-century England were a disparate bunch. It is difficult to find any two forms of institutional welfare where the cohorts benefiting at any one time overlapped substantially with one another (aside from the notorious St Bartholomew's almshouse). Despite the fact that records of poor relief were placed at the heart of this study, this finding serves to point up the centrality of the contingent and shifting 'economy of makeshifts' for the English poor in this period. Of course, it was not their lives that were fragmented but their institutional contacts and their incomes, attenuated across work, crime, welfare and credit (and this book has attempted to grapple only with selected aspects of the latter two forms).

Nonetheless, it is possible to offer a generalised compilation of the range of experiences undergone by mid-eighteenth-century urban paupers, represented in terms of a life-cycle. Babies born in town parishes had between a five percent and twenty percent chance that their parents would need relief to meet the costs of their birth. If born in a workhouse, their chances of survival may have been slim, but this was as much a factor of genetic problems, birth trauma or their mother's nutrition as a reflection on workhouse conditions. If families were overburdened with children the parish might have decided to target workhouse relief by taking some children from each family into the house. Outside the work-house the parish might maintain an interest in children's welfare and on rare occasions pay for a child to attend dame school but elementary education might also have been provided by relatives or paid for from parental income.

Boys from labouring-poor families may have had a statistically good chance of securing a place in a charity school, with up to half of all boys in towns being provided with free places. Girls had fewer opportunities for a formal education, but the foundation of charity schools in towns meant that both urban boys and girls had more likelihood of schooling than their rural counterparts. Neither charity school children nor their families were likely to be receiving parish relief, and so schools were decisively not catering for the children of the dependent poor; on rare occasions, however, parishes paid for the private education of pauper children. The lack of apprenticing opportunities in towns, even where schools and other charities boosted the money available to provide premiums, meant that most poor children must have taken unskilled work or entered domestic service. Urban parish apprenticeships were relatively infrequent in this period: on average, parishes put out one child every one or two years. Adolescents and young adults were unlikely to need any parish relief in their own right unless they were disabled or became unmarried mothers.

The adult poor in urban society could anticipate a variety of official contacts with their neighbours. Between the ages of twenty-five and fifty, they were unlikely to receive regular parish relief but could expect that short-term crises such as illness or cash-flow problems might necessitate an application for relief. Around sixty percent of medical payments by parishes went to those who were otherwise self-supporting. In a hospital town, alternative help might have been forthcoming in the form of a hospital bed or free medicines. The working-age population was most likely to benefit from such provisions. The sparsity of hospital places potentially available at any one time in the mid-eighteenth century was probably counterbalanced by the proportions of local populations which found their way into a hospital at some time.[2] Few people were able to exploit both hospital and parish resources at the same time; those who did were probably seriously ill, and in some places experienced an unusually high death rate. Paupers could have a distinctively different experience of hospitals compared with the average patient.

The adult poor were also among the clientele of England's provincial pawnshops; however, the evidence from York is striking in the sense that it implies that pawnshops in the late eighteenth century might cater to a much wider section of the population than previously supposed. One single shop saw fifteen percent or more of the town's population within one eighteen-month period. The pawnshop acted as petty banker for the urban population generally rather than being confined to the urban poor (as has been assumed for pawnshops in the later nineteenth century). Customers were predominantly but not exclusively adult women. Few people appear to have used pawnshops at the same time that they received parish poor relief. Goods lost to pawnbrokers or taken in distress for unpaid rent might be redeemed by the overseers but this was not a frequent occurrence, and people certainly could not have relied on parish intervention for the restoration of their property.

The onset of aging and consequent reductions in earning-ability forced people to look for more extensive relief. Yet people were not confined to receiving income from parishes alone. Around ten percent of town charity disbursements and up to one hundred percent of elections to some almshouses involved people who were on relief at the same time, and paupers were evidently not disadvantaged in encounters with formal charity. Some paupers even benefited from foundations where the benefactor had tried to exclude those who were already in receipt of alms. Even so, the place of charity in the economy of makeshifts was demonstrably problematic. Only a tiny minority of paupers were able to receive charity in the same years they took relief; once again, the extent of charity that was ostensibly available should not blind us to the difficulties of piecing together a living from two or more such sources at once.

Dependency at any age could precipitate entry into a workhouse, but old age was frequently the spur towards indoor relief. Workhouse life entailed sharing bedrooms and beds with others and enduring a bland but sufficient diet characterised by occasional props and comforts (especially in smaller houses). Poor people were probably used to bed-sharing in their own homes but in workhouses they may have been compelled to share with strangers. Workhouses disrupted the foodways of local poor people somewhat, but probably retained characteristics of diets outside, and in smaller houses routinely included nutritional comforts that are not obvious from formal dietaries. Needs for additional relief such as clothing and medical help were probably heeded, even when paupers were in a contractor's workhouse.

Finally, poor people were quite often buried by their parish in these decades. If forty percent of parish burials were for people who had been dependent on the parish in life (in other words a substantial proportion but still a minority), this would suggest that death posed another short-term financial crisis for people or families who were otherwise independent of relief. In the mid-eighteenth century this may not have been the humiliation it became in the early nineteenth century. If dying people or their relatives knew in advance that a parish funeral entailed the bell-ringing and ale-drinking considered proper in early modern society, their distress or grief might not have been tinged with the degradation felt later.

The life-cycle options outlined above confirm some current assumptions about the poor under the old poor law, but the findings of this research require some important adjustments to be made. The evidence suggests that old age rather than childhood was the more critical stage in the life-cycle for suffering acute financial hardship, but this may be more a reflection of how parish relief and other welfare was targeted than an indication that suffering was less severe for children and young families. One feature which emerges strongly is the balance that typically pertained between temporary and permanent forms of parish relief. Extraordinary relief in these urban settings most typically did not go to long-term paupers but was used to augment the household economies of largely independent (or gradually failing) poor.

A key question for historians of welfare, posed again in the introduction to this book, concerns the inclusiveness and reliability of parish relief for the poor. Did the old poor law provide systematic and comprehensive benefits to most applicants or was observance and implementation of the law so patchy as to be no system at all? One aspect of parish relief which this research could not evaluate was the extent to which urban paupers were turned away and denied the relief they had requested (since none of these parishes possessed vestry minutes or other sources which offered to address such a question). Nonetheless, the experiences of paupers from Oxford, Shrewsbury and York are consistent with the conclusion that relief was broadly accessible and inclusive, but this is not to say that the whole range of the much vaunted varieties of relief was open to all comers; on the contrary, the range of relief has probably been deceptively advertised when historians should have been stressing the infrequency with which each type of benefit was dispensed. The insecurity of pauperdom rested on the potential discretion exerted by parishes in the forms that relief usually took, but in this period the contextual attitude of ratepayers was not averse to sufficiency or occasional generosity. The fatal dangers of discretion were only made apparent to the poor after the end of this period, when attitudes became more harsh and the flexibility of the law allowed its interpretation in some ways and in some places to fulfil a much more restricted or even punitive role.

Sarah Lloyd has recently cautioned 'We diminish our historical understanding of the poor … if we reduce them to a set of objects in search of objects' and this is a particularly sobering injunction given the main methodology of this book.[3] Use of financial and administrative documents to explore the experiences of the poor provide at best an indirect view of such experiences and at worst a range of possibilities which are difficult to prioritise. Poor people may have been subjected to certain types of treatment by others or have been able to manipulate a given situation to their own ends. Yet by focusing on systems of relief and patterns of interaction, the character of some relationships emerges. As poverty is a process as well as a condition, the relationships and interactions of the poor with the wider community inevitably help to illuminate that process.

Notes

1 B. Reay, *Microhistories: Demography, Society and Culture in Rural England, 1800–1930* (Cambridge 1996), pp. 258, 260.
2 J. Reinarz, *The Birth of a Provincial Hospital: The Early Years of the General Hospital, Birmingham, 1765–1790* (Dugdale Society Occasional Paper, 2003), p. 30 implies that by 1800 the equivalent of thirty percent of Birmingham's population had spent some time in the hospital. In reality, as Reinarz acknowledges, this constituted a lesser proportion of the regional labouring

population but the figures are still striking.

3 S. Lloyd, '"Agents in the own concerns"? Charity and the economy of make-shifts in eighteenth-century Britain', in S. King and A. Tomkins (eds), *The Poor in England 1700–1850: An Economy of Makeshifts* (Manchester, 2003), p. 129.

Appendices

Appendix 1.1: Prosopographical methodology

The core research for this book involved some basic prosopographical work on overseers' accounts, charity accounts and a pawnshop pledge book. A simple Microsoft Works database was used to collect payments to individual paupers over time, and flat tables were constructed for the different source-types; comparisons of names between two or more tables were undertaken manually rather than via any automatic, SQL (Structural Query Language) function. Historiographically, research into masses of ordinary people has typically been tackled using the relational database as the tool of choice.[1] The analysis of demography and poverty undertaken by Steve King, and Samantha Williams's analysis of poor relief and medical welfare, both employ relational software to illustrate the potential of computerised nominal linkage.[2] In contrast, this research made use of computer technology at a relatively low level, simply for the speed it offered in organising information in new ways; most practitioners, though, employ a combination of computer applications and manual analysis.[3]

Manual comparisons of names gave rise to several problems.

1 Overseers' use of first names or other labels was rarely consistent meaning that the same individual might be called, for example, William Nash, Old Nash and Mr Nash. Sometimes it becomes obvious that these are all the same person but at other times the assumption cannot be made. Furthermore, name comparisons are not proof against contemporary mistakes. For example, in Oxford St Mary Magdalen in 1742 the overseers refer to one pauper who died as John Cornwall, yet in the burial register he was called James.

2. Comparisons had to take account of overseers' accounting years. Overseers' accounts do not cover a calendar year but run from 25 March to 24 March, or for around fifty-two weeks covering these dates approximately. Therefore, in order to ensure the fullest possible coverage of overlapping names in the comparison with infirmary patients in 1755,

for instance, the overseers' accounts for 1754–55 and 1755–56 were scanned for the names of sick paupers.

3 Studies of overseers' accounts must recognise the obstacle presented by miscellaneous bills. In each year the parish paid named tradesmen 'as per bill' where in most cases the original vouchers no longer survive. This means that the precise benefit to paupers as a result of this expenditure remains hidden. Both the nature of the bill (i.e. whether for medical, clothing or other relief) and the individual beneficiaries are unknown. The result is that no particular stress can be laid on the overseers failing to pay for a particular item without qualification by reference to miscellaneous bills.

4 A similar problem relates to the use of workhouses. Unless overseers assiduously noted the names of people in the house in every year, then the list of paupers technically relieved over the year is probably incomplete. Most of the workhouse paupers discussed in this book lack firm dates of entry and exit (except where 'admitted' by birth or 'discharged' by death). Chapter two demonstrates that people in the house may have been named among those receiving extraordinary relief, but not all workhouse inmates will have been so named each year. As a result, no undue stress can be placed on individuals' failure to be named in any particular year.

5 Name comparisons have been undertaken with the aim of establishing three categories of overlap. Where a pauper was named in overseers' accounts as receiving a particular charity, the overlap was deemed to be definite. Similarly, where peoples' approximate date of death was the same in two sources they were regarded as definitely the same person. These instances were rare, and cropped up most frequently in relation to paupers in St Bartholomew's almshouse in Oxford and paupers in the Shropshire Infirmary. Where the same first and surnames were found, and some supporting information or label suggested that the pauper was the same person to appear in another list, the connection was considered probable. Suitable information included occupational or parish labels. Either 'probable' or 'definite' was employed to discuss the character of an overlap but these terms were rarely used in relation to the same comparison to avoid confusion. The word used in each case accurately characterised the majority of overlaps in any given comparison. Finally, where first and surnames or some distinctive titles and surnames overlapped between sources but no additional information was available, the connection was described as 'possible'.

The extent to which groups 'possibly' overlapped is often unhelpfully large. Some sources did not contain any occupational or other labels rendering most name overlaps merely possible. In other cases, first and surnames continually overlapped; for example, there were three separate paupers with the name Elizabeth Davies in Shrewsbury who may all have been the Elizabeth Davies in the infirmary. The result was that all of these paupers were possible overlap cases but none were probable.[4] Where only surnames overlapped between sources there was no basis for anticipating connections between individuals.

6 Specific problems relate to the pawnbroker's pledge book. There are two reasons why the guesstimate of the total number of customers is likely to be an overestimate, arising from changes in customers' circumstances and variation in the pawnbroker's notation. A number of Fettes' female customers probably married during the seventeen months under study and changed their surnames meaning the same individual would be pledging under two different names. Also, both men and women were able to change address during the same period, but every variation of address in the pledge book might indicate a different person. Therefore Dorothy Batty, for example, has been counted four times because a woman or women with this name were listed at four different addresses. This is an extreme example but demonstrates how the number of both men and women are somewhat overestimated.

Glennie has observed that formulating rules for judging when two or more pieces of information relate to the same person 'requires sensitive, but inevitably subjective, interpretation'.[5] A name comparison exercise can aim to be as objective as possible given problematic sources, but this research coincidentally confirms that ideally all connections in record-linkage exercises should be confirmed manually.[6]

Notes

1 P. Hudson, 'A new history from below: computers and the maturing of local and regional history', *Local Historian* 25 (1995), 217.

2 S. King, 'Reconstructing lives: the poor, the poor law and welfare in Calverley, 1650–1820', *Social History* 22: 3 (1997); S. Williams, 'Poor Relief Welfare and Medical Provision in Bedfordshire: The Social, Economic and Demographic Context 1. 1770–1834', (PhD thesis, Cambridge University, 1998).

3 Williams, 'Poor Relief Welfare', p. 75; M. P. Gutman, 'The future of record linkage in history', *Journal of Family History* 2 (1997).

4 The difficulties posed by homonymy crop up in most prosopographical projects; J.-M. Carrié, 'The contribution of papyri to the prosopography of the ancient world: evaluation and prospects', in A. Cameron (ed.), *Fifty Years of Prosopography* (Oxford, 2003), p. 84.

5 P. Glennie, *Distinguishing Men's Trades: Occupational Sources and Debates for Pre-Census England* (Historical Geography Research Series 25, 1990), p. 111.

6 I am grateful to Katherine Keats-Rohan for confirmation of this point.

Appendix 2.1 Food per person per day in two workhouses, 1742, 1745 and 1751

Shrewsbury St Mary Workhouse Provision 1742

Period	Days	People	Spent on beef	Beef per capita in ounces
24/4 to 4/6	42	29	£2 6s	3.2
5/6 to 16/7	42	22	£1 12s 8s	3.4
17/7 to 27/8	42	16	£1 11s 9d	4.6
28/8 to 8/10	42	16	£1 8	4.0
9/10 to 19/11	42	14	£1 11s 8d	6.0
20/11 to 31/12	42	15	£2 3s 5d	6.6
1/1 to 11/2	42	15	£1 16s 8d	5.0
12/2 to 25/3	42	14	£1 11s 7d	5.2
26/3 to 16/4	22	11	£0 15s 8.5d	5.6
Year average				4.8

Period	Days	People	Spent on cheese	Cheese per capita in ounces
24/4 to 4/6	42	29	£1 0s 7d	1.1
5/6 to 16/7	42	22	£0 16s 7d	1.1
17/7 to 27/8	42	16	£0 18s 1.5d	1.6
28/8 to 8/10	42	16	£0 16s 7.5d	1.6
9/10 to 19/11	42	14	£0 11s 1.5d	1.5
20/11 to 31/12	42	15	£0 15s 10.5d	2.2
1/1 to 11/2	42	15	£0 11s 10d	1.5
12/2 to 25/3	42	14	£0 10s 8.75d	1.6
26/3 to 16/4	22	11	£0 3s 5.5d	1.2
Year average				1.5

Period	Days	People	Spent on corn	Corn per capita in pence
24/4 to 4/6	42	29	£2 6s 2d	0.5d
5/6 to 16/7	42	22	£1 19s 1d	0.5d
17/7 to 27/8	42	16	£1 12s 2d	0.5d
28/8 to 8/10	42	16	£1 7s 5d	0.5d
9/10 to 19/11	42	14	£1 3s 11d	0.5d
20/11 to 31/12	42	15	£1 9s 9d	0.5d
1/1 to 11/2	42	15	£0 17s 11d	0.5d
12/2 to 25/3	42	14	£1 2s 7d	0.5d
26/3 to 16/4	22	11	£0 7s 11d	0.5d

Shrewsbury St Mary Workhouse Provision 1745

Period	Days	People	Amount	Per capita in ounces
49 weeks	343	21	1,009 lb cheese	2.2
49 weeks	343	21	£7 4s 11.5d beef	2.6
49 weeks	343	21	£0 16s 9.5d mutton	0.3
49 weeks	343	21	£1 7s 1d veal	0.5
49 weeks	343	21	£0 5s pork	0.1
49 weeks	343	21	£0 19s 4.5d bacon	0.2
Average ounces of all meat per capita per day				3.7

Period	Days	People	Amount	Corn per capita in pence
49 weeks	343	21	£8 15s	0.25d

York St Michael le Belfrey Workhouse Food Provision 1751

Period	Days	People	Spent on beef	Beef per capita in ounces
1/5 to 1/6	32	8	£0 9s 4.5d	4.1
1/6 to 23/6	23	10	£0 12s 9d	6.2
23/6 to 27/7	34	6	£0 8s 6d	4.6
27/7 to 19/8	23	6	£0 8s 1d	6.5
19/8 to 16/9	29	6	£0 7s 7.5d	4.9
16/9 to 14/10	29	8	£0 8s 6d	4.1
14/10 to 11/11	29	8	£0 9s 3.5d	4.4
11/11 to 9/12	29	9	£0 10s 3.5d	4.4
9/12 to 7/1	30	9	£0 10s 10d	4.5
7/1 to 2/2	27	12	£0 10s 10d	3.7
2/2 to 2/3	29	12	£0 14s 4d	4.6
2/3 to 4/4	29	12	£0 17s 3d	5.5
Year average				4.8

Period	Days	People	Spent on corn and flour	Corn and flour per capita in pence
1/5 to 1/6	32	8	£0 9s 0.5d	0.5d
1/6 to 23/6	23	7	£0 9s 2d	0.75d
23/6 to 27/7	34	6	£0 9s 7d	0.5d
27/7 to 19/8	23	6	£0 6s 10d	0.5d
19/8 to 16/9	29	6	£0 2s 7d	0.25d
16/9 to 14/10	29	8	£0 6s 9.75d	0.25d

14/10 to 11/11	29	8	£0 7s 5d	0.5d
11/11 to 9/12	29	9	£0 9s 3d	0.5d
9/12 to 7/1	30	9	£0 8s	0.25d
7/1 to 2/2	27	12	£0 9s 9d	0.25d
2/2 to 2/3	29	12	£0 16s 8d	0.5d
2/3 to 4/4	29	12	£0 12s	0.5d
Year average				0.5d

Appendix 2.2 Inventories of workhouses, 1730–67

	Oxford St Peter le Bailey 1730	Chester St John 1737	Oxford St Martin 1742	York St Michael le Belfrey 1744	Shrews-bury Holy Cross 1750	Oxford St Michael 1767	Total
Bedding							
Bed	8	16	8	6	3	24	65
Bedstead	6	20	8	8	10	15	67
Cradle		2					2
Valance	2						2
Blanket	9	23	7	6	12	44	101
Rug	11	5	10			17	43
Cover/lid	1	10			7		18
Pair sheets	6	18	8	6	10	23	71
Bolster	3	8	8	5	4	13	41
Pillows	5	6	2	1			14
Tickings						4	4
Quilt						5	5
Warming pan		1	1				2
Misc linen	3	28		3	7	6	47
							482
Furniture							
Table	5	5		2	1	4	17
Chair	15	20	6	6	4	10	61
Bench/form	3	4	1	2	4	4	18
Stool	6	17		7	1	10	41
Cupboard/drawers	4	6				2	12
Trunk/chest	3	9	1	1	2		16
Box	1	8	2	1	4		16
Shelf				11+		5	16+
							186
Fire, light and heat							
Tongs/shovel	4	4	1	1	2	2	14
Bellows	1	1			1	1	4
Grate/fender				3	3	1	7
Furnace/boiler					1		1
Tinder box	2						2
Gridiron/box iron	2	1			1		4
Smooth iron	2	4					6
Candlestick			1		2		3
Candle box		1					1

	Oxford St Peter le Bailey 1730	Chester St John 1737	Oxford St Martin 1742	York St Michael le Belfrey 1744	Shrewsbury Holy Cross 1750	Oxford St Michael 1767	Total
Coal Scuttle						1	1
Misc metal		2					2
							45
Workhouse work							
(Spinning) Wheel	6	3		1	4	4	18
Pair cards				1	2	9	12
Card stocks						3	3
Reels				1	2	1	4
Scales						1	1
							38
Cooking utensils							
Pot	4	5	2	6	1	3	21
Pot lid		2			2	3	7
Pot hooks	3	4			2	2	11
Measuring pot	5		2	1	7	18	33
Kettle	3	3	1			1	8
Saucepan	1		1				2
Frying pan	1	1			1		3
Salt/pepper	2				1	2	5
Chopping block/ board	1			2		1	4
Hatchet/knife	1	1		1		2	5
Toasting iron		1					1
Sieve	1	2			2		5
Fish pan		1					1
Baking pan			1		1	1	3
							109
Crockery/cutlery							
Dish	12	3	2	4	2	20	43
Plate/platter	1						1
Trencher	11	36		18	12	24	101
(Flesh) Fork		2			3	13	18
Knife				12	1	12	25
Spoon			12	12	10	24	58
Pestle		1					1
Bowl/mortar	1			4	1		6
Ladle				3			3
							256

	Oxford St Peter le Bailey 1730	Chester St John 1737	Oxford St Martin 1742	York St Michael le Belfrey 1744	Shrewsbury Holy Cross 1750	Oxford St Michael 1767	Total
Household goods							
Barrel/large tub	1				3		4
Small tub/tub	3		3	1			7
Clothes line	1					1	2
Bucket/pail	1		1	1	3	1	7
Broom/brush				2		3	5
Specific tub		8		2	4	5	19
Basket			1			6	7
Trough					1		1
Misc container		1		26		4	31
Funnel/skimmer			1			1	2
Steps						1	1
Chamber pot/ close stool		3		6			9
Clock						1	1
Lock				5			5
							101

Sources: ORO, Mss dd par Oxford St Peter le Bailey b.13; Mss dd par Oxford St Martin b.19; Mss dd par Oxford St Michael b.38; SA, Shrewsbury Borough Records, 3365/727; Borthwick Institute, Y/MB 53, 54, 55; CRO, P51/22.

Appendix 3.1: Paupers receiving two or more charities

Name	Surname	Parish	Year	Source	Amount	Source
Widow	Carpenter	MM	1757	Poole	£1	Toldervey
Widow	Carpenter	MM	1758	Poole	£1	Toldervey
Widow	Carpenter	MM	1759	Poole	£1	Toldervey
Widow	Carpenter	MM	1764	Poole	£0 15s 10d	Toldervey
Widow	Carpenter	MM	1765	Poole	£0 15s 10d	Toldervey
Widow	Carpenter	MM	1766	Poole	£0 18s	Toldervey
Wid Mary	Lawrence	MM	1743	Poole	£1	Toldervey
Widow	Pavior	MC	1741			Wall
Wid Marg	West	MM	1742	Poole	£1	Toldervey
Widow	Viner	PleB	1740	Sambach	£0 3s 6d	Wall
Widow	Bryan	MM	1759	Poole	£1	Boyle
Widow	Bryan	MM	1764	Poole	£0 15s 10d	
Widow	Bryan	MM	1765	Poole	£0 15s 10d	
Widow	Mabbot	MM	1747	Poole	£1	
Wid Mary	Piesley	MM	1741	Poole	£1	
James	Cornwall	MM	1741	Poole	£1	
Widow	Warburton	MM	1766	Poole	£0 18s	
Widow	Whetnell	MM	1764	Poole	£0 15s 10d	
Widow	Wise	MM	1765	Poole	£0 15s 10d	
Ralph	Cox	PinE	1768			Hawkins

* Evidently a one-off disbursement by the town Alderman, revealed in overseer's accounts.

DCD = died same year; + = Possibly received more from overseers that year; Pension = receiving parish pension same year; Rent = bulk of parish money for rent.

Amount	Source	Amount	Parish relief	Total	
£1 10s			£1 8s 6d	£3 18s 6d	
£1 10s			£3 12s 6d	£6 2s 6d	
£1 10s			£0 3s	£2 13s+	
£1 10s	Hody	Clothing	£5	£7 5s 10d+	Pension
£1 10s			£2 11s	£4 16s 10d	Pension
£1 10s			£3 3s	£5 11s	Pension
£1 10s			£1 16s	£4 6s	DCD
£4	Snowe	£0 1s	£0 9s	£4 10s	
£1 10s	Hody	£1	£0 8s	£3 18s	
£4	Nicholes*	£0 3s 6d		£4 7s	
	Hody	Clothing	£2	£3+	Rent
£1 5s				£2 5s	
	Hody	Clothing	£3 18s 6d	£4 14s 4d+	Pension
	Hody	Clothing	£4 2s	£4 17s 10d+	Pension
	Hody	Clothing	£1 5s	£2 5s+	Rent
	Hody	Clothing	£0 6s 6d	£1 6s 6d+	
	Hody	£1	£1 0s 6d	£3 0s 6d	DCD
	Hody	£1	£1 15s	£3 13s	Rent
	Hody	Clothing	£3 15s	£4 10s 10d+	Pension
	Hody	Clothing	£3 19s 4d	£4 15s 2d+	
£4	Blackford	£0 2s 6d	£1 10s	£5 12s 6d	Rent

Bibliography

Manuscript sources

Bodleian Library

Gough Oxf 138 (15) Greycoat charity school accounts 1740–47

Gough Oxf 138 (16) Greycoat charity school accounts 1752–58

Gough Oxf 103 (8) Greycoat charity school accounts 1759–65

G.A. Oxon b.19 printed orders of the Vice Chancellor

G.A. Oxon c.261 Greycoat charity school rules 1766

G.A. Oxon b.77 (1) Rules and orders of the Bluecoat girls' school 1769

Ms Blakeway 16 T. Phillips' *History and Antiquities of Shrewsbury* (Shrewsbury, 1779) with mss notes by J. B. Blakeway

Ms Blakeway 4 Account of streets and non-ecclesiastical buildings in Shrewsbury

Ms Top Oxon b.126 Oxford St Peter le Bailey overseers' accounts 1766–71

Ms Top Oxon c.280 Miscellaneous papers including contributions of parliamentary representatives to Oxford charities 1765–96

Ms Top Oxon e.15 Selections from the annual records of the Bluecoat school

Mss Top Oxon e.371 A history of the Bluecoat school 1710–1892 by Henry Hughes

Mss Morrell 7 Election book of the Oxford company of tailors 1711–1833

Mss Morrell 12 Elections and accounts of the Oxford company of cordwainers 1646–1758

R Top 724 H. E. Salter (ed.), *Survey of Oxford 1772* (Oxford, 1912), with mss notes by W. P. Ellis

R Top 731 Typed index to *Jackson's Oxford Journal* 1754–1780 six volumes ed. E. C. Davies (1967); typed index to *Jackson's Oxford Journal* 1781–90 five volumes ed. E. H. Cordeaux (1976)

Oxford University Archives

MR/3/5/1–3 Clerks of the market corn books 1733–53, 1751–67, 1767–78

Borthwick Institute

YCH 1/1/1/1 County Hospital Trustees' Court book 1742–1889

YCH 1/1/2/1 County Hospital General Court Book 1742–1820

Y/HTG 16 Holy Trinity Goodramgate constables' accounts 1735–1834 and overseers' accounts 1777–94

Y/HTG 19 Holy Trinity Goodramgate parish accounts for bread and school money 1740–95

Y/HTG 18 St John Delpike overseers' accounts 1754–1821

Y/MB 36 St Michael le Belfrey churchwardens' disbursements 1751–85

Y/MB 53 St Michael le Belfrey accounts of the workhouse master 1744–56

Y/MB 54 St Michael le Belfrey overseers' book of workhouse admissions 1744–62

Y/MB 55 St Michael le Belfrey accounts of poorhouse 1744

Y/MB 56 St Michael le Belfrey abstracts of accounts 1764–92

Y/MB 91 St Michael le Belfrey overseers' accounts 1767–83

Y/MBpS 22 St Mary Bishophill senior overseers' accounts 1759–91

Y/MC 104 St Mary Castlegate overseers' accounts 1744–89

Y/MC 105 St Mary Castlegate overseers' accounts 1776–96

Y/SAM 33 St Sampson overseers' accounts 1763–1806

British Library

Egerton 2572 Guild book of the Barber Surgeons of York, fifteenth to eighteenth centuries

Add Mss 5832 fo.189 account of houses in Oxford 1737

Cheshire Record Office

CLA/6 *An Act for better regulating the poor* (1762)

EDD 9/2 Dean and Chapter records accounts of Abbey Court with the House of Industry 1759–72

EDD 3913/1/8 Cathedral muniments treasurers' accounts 1725–47

G/Mc 18 A report of the house of industry in the city of Chester 1781–82

P16/6/1 St Martin churchwardens' accounts and vestry minutes 1682–1816

P20/22 St Mary overseers' book 1700–90

P20/23/1, 2 St Mary workhouse agreement 1743

P20/23/3 Expenses of the in and out poor of the several parishes in the city of Chester 1759–1760

P29/11/1–6 St Oswald overseers' accounts 1747–54

P51/12/2 St John churchwardens' accounts 1684–1744

P51/22 St John poorhouse book 1731–56

Chester Archives

HI/1 Chester Royal Infirmary minutes of meetings 1755–58

HI/51 Chester Royal Infirmary Journal of Patients 1755–63

HI/52 Chester Royal Infirmary Journal of Patients 1772–78

Christ Church Archives

Christ Church almsmen's patents boxes 1–3 LXI.a.1–374

Greater London Record Office
Foundling Country Hospital at Shrewsbury (uncatalogued)
Committee minutes (one volume) 1758–72
Servants' entry and discharge register (one volume) 1758–67
Register of children at nurse (one volume) 1759–64
Applications for apprentices (two bundles) 1767–70
Inventory of furniture and utensils (one volume) 1759, 1767, 1772

Hampshire Record Office
40M83W/PR2 St Faith and St Cross parish register 1776–1812

National Archive (Public Record Office)
Assi2/12 to Assi2/21 Oxford Assize Circuit crown minute books (10 volumes)
    1739–71
Assi5/71/11, Assi5/72/8 and Assi5/80/11 Oxford Assize Circuit indictments
    Oxon lent 1751, Oxon lent 1752, Salop summer 1760
C.33/435/fo. 15 and C.38/636 Chancery papers relating to the regulation of Sir
    Thomas White's and other charities controlled by Shrewsbury Corporation
C110/134 Chancery exhibits, pawnbrokers' books 1822–34, auction sale book
IR 1/50 Board of Stamps apprenticeship book
SO 8/52 Signet office, warrants for King's Bills series 1

Lichfield Record Office
B/V/5, Salop Shrewsbury St Chad, St Julian and St Alkmund visitation returns
    1772
P/C/11 Will of Edward Podmore (1741)

Northampton Record Office
223p/25 All Saints vestry minutes 1736–82
223p/192 All Saints agreement with Richard Agar Wellingborough weaver for
    the farm of the workhouse 1742
233p/247 St Giles churchwardens' accounts poor matters 1717–1821
241p/43 St Sepulchre churchwardens' and overseers' accounts 1707–1835
241p/57 St Sepulchre vestry minutes 1692–1748
241p/153 St Sepulchre overseers' accounts 1759–60
241p/162 St Sepulchre correspondence

Northampton General Hospital:
    General court and weekly committee volumes 3 (1752–58), 5 (1763–69) and
        6 (1769–74)
    Annual Reports 1743–80
    Journals of patients volumes 1 (1744–53), 2 (1753–59), 3 (1759–65), 4
        (1765–69) and 5 (1769–74)

Oxfordshire Local Studies Library

OXFO 361.7 SBAR (outsize) Papers relating to the charity commissioners enquiry into St Bartholomew's Hospital (1896) 2 volumes

Oxford Record Office

Mss dd par Oxford:

St Aldate b.22 settlement papers; e.1 accounts of Faulkner's charity 1733–1836

St Cross or Holywell b.14 overseers' accounts 1757–72; b.1 and c.21 settlement papers; c.6 churchwardens' accounts 1741–81

St Ebbe b.8, c.3, b.9, b.10 and b.11 overseers' accounts 1735–43, 1745–46, 1747– 57, 1758–64 and 1765–71; b.26 and c.12 settlement papers

St Giles b.19 and b.20 overseers' accounts 1757–61 and 1761–76; c.26, b.34 and b.35 settlement papers; e.3 and e.4 accounts of parish charities 1724–1807

St Martin b.17–b.21 overseers' accounts 1725–72; b.26 and c.30 settlement-papers; a.2 churchwardens' accounts 1704–94; b.11 volume of churchwardens' notes 1693–1785; c.29 miscellaneous papers including overseers' receipted bills 1601–1768

St Mary Magdalen c.40–43, b.71 overseers' accounts 1736–48 and 1750–66; b.56 and c.51 settlement papers; b.43 and b.44 churchwardens' accounts 1719–40 and 1741–99; b.74 vestry minutes 1714–1849; c.55 accounts of Hody's charity 1737–1892; c.56 accounts of Morris's, Poole's and other charities 1741–1848; c.44 poor rate book 1751–53

St Mary the Virgin b.7–9 overseers' accounts 1723–71; c.22 and c.28 settlement papers

St Michael b.28–33 overseers' accounts 1738–70; c.29, c.30, b.40 and b.41 settlement papers; b.12 and b.13 churchwardens' accounts 1709–60 and 1760–95; c.26 Disbursements of Snowe's and Barker's charities 1720–86; b.28 volume of poor law notes 1741–70; b.38 volume concerning the workhouse to 1767; c.27 and c.28 overseers' vouchers 1663–1759 and 1761–72; c.31 miscellaneous papers including pauper inventories and correspondence

St Peter in East b.4, b.28 and b.29 overseers' accounts 1728–37, 1740–52 and 1758–69; c.3, c.7 and b.11 settlement papers; c.19 churchwardens' accounts 1738–85

St Peter le Bailey b.12 overseers' accounts to 1722; b.13–18 overseers' accounts 1722–66; c.7 settlement papers

NP lX/17 Inventory of goods at Northleigh workhouse 1800

Mss Oxf dioc. Papers d.556, d.559, d.562 and d.565 visitation returns 1759, 1768, 1771 and 1774

Mss Oxf Archd papers Oxon c.90–c.93 churchwardens' presentments

Mss dd Wills 118/4/14 John Brickland 1769

Handwritten transcript and index of Oxfordshire County Quarter Sessions Rolls 1687–1830 in eleven volumes

Handwritten and typed parish-register transcripts of baptisms, marriages and burials of all fourteen Oxford city parishes.

Oxford City Archives:

O.1.1. Gaol indentures 1720–1838

O.2.5–10 Oxford town quarter sessions minutes 1723–75

O.5.15 Oxford town quarter sessions recognizances 1739–70

Q.3.2. Receipts of Boyle's charity 1755–95

Q.3.3. Accounts of Harris's and Black Potts's charities 1764–1815, 1769–1870

Q.3.6. Alderman Nixon's charity 1752–1839

Q.4.9. Elections to charities 1715–1834

Q.5.1. Nixon's School deeds, rules and orders 1658–1825

AA.2.b List of officers in the city of Oxford 1683–1782

JJ.4.1. Bluecoat Boys' School subscribers and accounts 1748–81

Shropshire Archives

83/1/309 Shrewsbury House of Industry directors' order book 1784–1808

83/94/374 Shrewsbury House of Industry daily figures of poor in the house 1784–88

83/124/390 Shrewsbury House of Industry settlement certificates 1705–62

83/140/398 Shrewsbury House of Industry register of paupers admitted to the house 1784–1808

83/190/431 Shrewsbury House of Industry Holy Cross out relief 1784–92

681/56 *An Act for the better relief and employment of the poor belonging to several parishes within the town of Shrewsbury and the liberties thereof* (1783)

1831/2/1 Drapers' company accounts 1579–1745

1831/2/3 Drapers' company accounts 1756–61

1831/6 Drapers' company book of minutes 1607–1740

1831/10 Two bundles of petitions to drapers' company for relief

2133/11 Millington's trustees' minute book 1745–1805

2711/Ch/2 Shrewsbury St Julian churchwardens' accounts 1693–1724

2711/Ch/3 Shrewsbury St Julian churchwardens' accounts 1751–79

2711/Cy/82 Shrewsbury St Julian minute and account book of Richard Williams's charity 1766–1918

2711/P/1 Shrewsbury St Julian overseers' accounts 1753–65

2711/P/2 Shrewsbury St Julian overseers' accounts 1766–74

3909/1/1 Royal Salop Infirmary trustees' minute book 1747–56

3909/1/2 Royal Salop Infirmary trustees' minute book 1756–70

3909/1/24 Royal Salop Infirmary rough trustees' minute book 1778–84

3909/6/2 Royal Salop Infirmary Proposals and Annual Reports 1745–1847

3909/8/1 Royal Salop Infirmary pamphlets including Statutes (1752)

4791/1/1, 7, 9 Salop fire office policy books

DO4 1167.31 Shrewsbury charity school 1763 two reports and lists of subscribers

P257/B/3/3 Shrewsbury S Mary churchwardens' account book 1703–53

P257/B/3/4 Shrewsbury St Mary churchwardens' account book 1753–83

P257/L/3/2 Shrewsbury St Mary overseers' accounts 1695–1732

P257/L/3/3 Shrewsbury St Mary overseers' accounts 1732–47

P257/L/3/4 Shrewsbury St Mary overseers' accounts 1748–53

P257/L/3/5 Shrewsbury St Mary overseers' accounts 1754–64

P257/W/6/10/1–40 Shrewsbury St Mary churchwardens' presentments 1741–58

P250/C/1/2 Shrewsbury Holy Cross and St Giles churchwardens' accounts and parish meeting book 1729–1808

P250/L/1/3 Shrewsbury Holy Cross and St Giles articles of agreement for the maintenance of the poor 1741

P250/L/2/1 Shrewsbury Holy Cross and St Giles overseers' accounts 1721–54

P250/L/2/2 Shrewsbury Holy Cross and St Giles overseers' accounts 1755–88

P250/Q/1/1 Shrewsbury Holy Cross and St Giles Prynce's Charity 1733–90

Handwritten parish register transcripts of Shrewsbury St Julian and Shrewsbury Holy Cross

Shrewsbury Borough Records: 3365/

  77 Minutes of house meetings 1732–60

  274 Rate assessments for shop, carriage and horse taxes, 1778–86

  662 Mayor's accounts 1745

  664 Mayor's accounts 1759 (vouchers)

  665 Mayor's accounts 1761–62 (vouchers)

  683 Town public stock vouchers 1715–63

  723 St Chad's overseers Accounts 1702–55

  724 St Mary's overseers' Accounts 1604–1733

  725 St Alkmunds overseers' Accounts 1729–52

  726 St Julian overseers' Accounts 1648–1741

  727 Holy Cross overseers' Accounts 1638–1754

  2431 Town quarter sessions book of orders number 3 1746–70

  2446 Town quarter sessions miscellaneous papers 1755–67

  2642 Petitions to Mayors 1721–60

Shropshire County Quarter Sessions Records:

  QS/1/4 Order book 1757–72

  QF/1/1/1 Treasurer's account book 1666–1764

York City Archives

CC.33–CC.63 Chamberlain's account books 1722–82

Pawnbroker's pledge book 1777–78

Printed primary sources

Government Records

Calendar of State Papers, Domestic Series, Edward VI, Mary, Elizabeth 1547–1580 (London 1856)

Calendar of State Papers, Domestic Series, Anne, 1703–4 (London 1924)

Calendar of State Papers, Home Office Series, George III 1760–65 (London 1878)

Calendar of State Papers, Home Office Series, George III 1766–69 (London 1879)

Calendar of State Papers, Home Office Series, George III 1770–72 (London 1881)

Calendar of State Papers, Home Office Series, George III 1773–75 (London 1899)

Parliamentary Papers

House of Commons Sessional Papers of the Eighteenth Century ed. S. Lambert (Wilmington Delaware, 1975) 31, 'Abstracts of the returns made by the overseers of the poor' 1777; 60, 'Abstracts of the returns made by overseers of the poor' 1787

Abstract of the Answers and Returns made pursuant to 'An act for taking an account of the population of Great Britain 1801' (London, 1802)

Abstract of the answers and returns made pursuant to 'An act for procuring returns relative to the expense and maintenance of the poor in England' (London, 1804)

Abstract of the Returns of Charitable Donations for the benefit of poor persons, made by the ministers and churchwardens of the several parishes and townships of England and Wales. 1786–1788 (London, 1816)

Digest of Parochial Returns made to the Select Committee on the Education of the Poor (1819) volume 9 a, b and c, volume 10 a

Reports of the Charity Commissioners (1822) volume 9 (Oxford)

Reports of the Charity Commissioners (1831) volume 11 (Shrewsbury)

Reports of the Municipal Corporations Commissioners (1835) 23

Reports of the Municipal Corporations Commissioners (1835) 25

Reports of the Committee on Municipal Boundaries (1837) volume 28

Books and pamphlets

Account of the Charities of the late William Stratford LLD (Kendal, 1766)

An Account of Several Workhouses (London, 1732)

An Account of the Charity School at York (York, 1705)

An Account of the Hospitals, Alms-Houses, and Public Schools in Bristol (Bristol, 1775)

An Account of the Publick Hospital for the Diseased Poor in the County of York (York, 1746)

An Account of the Rise, Progress and Present State of the County Infirmary at Northampton (Northampton [1775])

Ackland, Rev. J., *A Plan for Rendering the Poor Independent on Public Contribution* (Exeter, 1786)

An Act for the better relief and employment of the poor belonging to several parishes within the town of Shrewsbury and the liberties thereof, and in the County of Salop (1783)

Alumni Oxoniensis 1715–1886 (Oxford, 1888)

Andrew, D. (ed.), *London Debating Societies 1776–1799* (London Record Society 30, 1994)

An Apology for the Business of Pawnbroking (London, 1744)

Appendices to the Assistant Charity Commissioner's Report on St Bartholomew's Hospital (1896)

Articles of Enquiry Addressed to the Clergy of the Diocese of Oxford at the primary Visitation of Dr Thomas Secker 1738 ed. Rev. H. A. Lloyd Jukes (Oxford Record Society 38, 1957)

Bailey's Northern Directory (Warrington, 1781)

Bailey, W., *A Treatise on the Better Employment and more comfortable Support of the Poor in Workhouses* (London, 1758)

Baker, J. B. (ed.), *Pleasure and Pain 1780–1818* (London, 1930)

Bearcroft, P. *The Wise and Useful Institution of Our Charity Schools* (London, 1748)

Bentham, J. *Defence of Usury* (London, 1787)

Bernard, Sir T. (ed.), *Reports of the Society for Bettering the Condition and Increasing the Comforts of the Poor* 5 volumes (1798–1808)

Bernard, Sir T. *Of the Education of the Poor* (London, [1809] 1970)

Bevan, H. *Records of the Salop Infirmary* (Shrewsbury, 1847)

Blakeway, J. B., and H. Owen, *A History of Shrewsbury* 2 volumes (London, 1825)

Bradley, J. *A Sermon ... the City of York Occasioned by the Erection of the Charity School* (York, 1706)

Bromehead, J. *An Oration on the Utility of Public Infirmaries* (London, 1772)

Broster, P. *The Chester Guide* (Chester [1780])

Burn, R. *History of the Poor Laws: With Observations* (London, 1764)

Butler, J. *A Sermon ... Yearly Meeting of the Children Educated in Charity Schools* (London, 1745)

Campbell, R. *The London Tradesman* (London, 1747)

Canning, R. *An Account of the Gifts and Legacies that have been given and bequeathed to Charitable Uses in the town of Ipswich* (Ipswich, 1747)

Chapman, J. *The Ends and Uses of Charity Schools for Poor Children* (London, 1752)

Colquhoun, P. *A Treatise on Indigence* (London, 1806)

Considerations on the Fatal Effects to a Trading Nation of the Present Excess of Public Charities (London, 1763)

Cox, J. C. (ed.), *The Records of the Borough of Northampton 1550–1835* (Northampton, 1898)

Crosby, A. G. (ed.), *The Family Records of Benjamin Shaw Mechanic of Dent, Dolphinholme and Preston 1772–1841* (Publications of the Record Society of Lancashire and Cheshire 130, 1991)

Darwin, E. *A Plan for the Conduct of Female Education in Boarding Schools* (Wakefield [1797] 1968)

Davies, D. *The Case of Labourers in Husbandry Stated and Considered* (London, 1795)

Deazley J. H. and Dodd, J. T. *Case Prepared on Behalf of the St Bartholomew's Committee of the Oxford City Council* (Oxford, 1896)

Defoe, D. *The Complete English Tradesman* (London, 1725)

Defoe, D. *A Tour Through England and Wales* 2 volumes (London [1727] 1959)

Department of Health, *Dietary Reference Values for Food Energy and Nutrients for the United Kingdom* (Report on Health and Social Subjects 41, HMSO, 1991)

A Dissertation on Credit [n.p., c. 1750]

Doble, C. E. (ed.), *Remarks and Collections of Thomas Hearne* volumes 1–3 (Oxford Historical Society volumes 2, 7, 13, old series 1884–88)

Eden, F. M. *The State of the Poor* (London [1797] 1928)

Fielding, H. *An Enquiry into the Causes of the Late Increase of Robbers* [London, 1751] edited by M. Zirker (Oxford, 1988)

Fielding, H. *Amelia* (London, 1751)

The Journeys of Celia Fiennes ed. C. Morris (London, 1947)

Gentleman's Magazine 1 (1731); 2 (1732); 4 (1734); 7 (1737); 9 (1739); 11 (1741); 14 (1744); 15 (1745); 21 (1751); 22 (1752); 28 (1758); 45 (1775); 51 (1781); 54 (1784); 67 (1797)

Godwin, W. *The Adventures of Caleb Williams* (Oxford [1794] 1982)

Gorsuch, W. 'An extract of the register of the parish of Holy Cross in Salop, from Michaelmas 1750 to Michaelmas 1760', *Philosophical Transactions of the Royal Society of London* 52 (1761–62)

Gorsuch, W. 'An extract from the register of the parish of Holy Cross in Salop, being a second decade of years from Michaelmas 1760 to Michaelmas 1770' *Philosophical Transactions of the Royal Society of London* 61 (1771)

Gorsuch, W. 'An extract of the register of the parish of Holy Cross Salop being a third decade of years from Michaelmas 1770 to Michaelmas 1780' *Philosophical Transactions of the Royal Society of London* 72 (1782)

Graham, M. (ed.), *Oxford City Apprentices 1697–1800* (Oxford Historical Society 31, 1987)

Grubb, S. *Some Account of the Life and Religious Labours of Sarah Grubb* (Dublin, 1792)

Hanway, J. *A Comprehensive View of Sunday Schools* (London, 1786)

Hart, C. 'Part of a Letter from Cheney Hart, M.D. to William Watson F.R.S. giving some account of the effects of electricity in the county hospital at Shrewsbury', *Philosophical Transactions of the Royal Society* 48 (1754), 786–8.

Heitzenrater, R. P. (ed.), *Diary of an Oxford Methodist Benjamin Ingham 1733–34* (Durham Carolina, 1985)

Hell upon Earth: or, the Town in an Uproar, &c (London, 1729)

Hendley, W. *A Defence of the Charity Schools* (London, 1725)

Hitchcock, T. (ed.), *Richard Hutton's Complaints Book: The Notebook of the Steward of the Quaker Workhouse at Clerkenwell, 1711–1737* (London Record Society, 1987)

Hobson, M. G. (ed.), *Oxford Council Acts 1702–1751* (Oxford Historical Society 10, 1954)

Hobson, M. G. (ed.), *Oxford Council Acts 1752–1801* (Oxford Historical Society 15, 1962)

The Honest London Spy: exhibiting the base and subtle intrigues of the town (Dublin, 1793)

Hughes, H. *Rise and Growth of Parochial Schools in Oxford* (Oxford, 1868)

Hughes, T. B. *The Advantages of Friendly Loan Societies contrasted with the ruinous effects of pawning* (London, 1841)

Jackson's Oxford Journal (Oxford, 1762, 1764, 1768, 1769, 1770, 1771, 1772, 1780)

Lackington, J. *Memoirs of the forty-five first years of the life of James Lackington* (London, 1795)

L'Estrange, R. *The Devil and Broker or a Character of a Pawnbroker in a Merry Dialogue* (London, 1677)

A Letter from a Discounter in Bishopsgate Street to a Pawnbroker in Long Acre (London, 1745)

A Letter to the Author of Considerations on Several Proposals for the Better Maintenance of the Poor (London, 1752)

Lewis, W. S. (ed.), *Correspondence of Horace Walpole* 48 volumes (New Haven, 1937–1983)

The Life and Real Adventures of Hamilton Murray (London, 1759)

A List of ... Subscribers to the Charity School for Girls in Sheffield ... with ... the Accounts of the ... Treasurer to the Charity ... August 28 1788 to August 28 1789 (Sheffield, 1789)

Lowth, R. *A Sermon Preached Before the Governors of the Radcliffe Infirmary* (Oxford, 1771)

McCance *et al.* (eds), *The Composition of Foods* (Royal Society of Chemists and Ministry of Agriculture Fisheries and Foods, 1991)

Mandeville, B. *The Fable of the Bees or Private Vices Publick Benefits* with commentary by F. B. Kaye (Oxford, 1988)

Map of the University and City of Oxford 1750 surveyed by I. Taylor 1750 (Oxford, 1751)

Medical Register (London, 1780)

Memoirs of the Noted Buckhorse (London, 1756)

Methods Used for Erecting Charity Schools (London, 1717)

The Mistery of Iniquity luckily Discover'd (London, 1708)

Mitchell, B. R., and P. Deane, *Abstract of British Historical Statistics* (Cambridge, 1962)

Mother Midnight's Comical Pocket-Book: or, a Bone for the Criticks (London [1753])

Nolan, M. *Treatise on the laws for the relief and settlement of the poor* (London, 1805)

Nolan, W. *An Essay on Humanity: or a View of Abuses in Hospitals* (London, 1786)

Orders Relating to the Almshouse &c at Dyvynog (London, 1731)

Owen, E. *A Sermon upon the Occasion of Opening a Charity School in Warrington* (Warrington, 1782)

Owen, H. *Some Account of the Ancient and Present State of Shrewsbury* (Shrewsbury, 1808)

Pawnbrokers Detected and Dissected: or the poor man's adviser (London, 1809)

Peet, H. *Liverpool Vestry Minutes 1681–1834* (Liverpool, 1912)

Phillips, T. *History and Antiquities of Shrewsbury* (Shrewsbury, 1779)

Pigott, I. *History of the City of Chester* (Chester, 1815)

A Plain Answer to a late pamphlet intitled The Business of Pawnbroking Stated and Defended (London, 1745)

A Plan for Recruiting the British Army (London [1780])

The Present Situation of the Town of Birmingham Respecting its Poor (Birmingham, 1782)

A Proposal for Erecting an Infirmary for the Poor-Sick and Lame of this County and Neighbourhood (Shrewsbury, 1737)

Proposals for a Regulation or an Entire Suppression of Pawnbrokers (London, 1732)

Rannie, D. W. (ed.), *Remarks and Collections of Thomas Hearne* volumes 4–11 (Oxford Historical Society 34, 42, 43, 48, 50, 65, 67, 72 old series, 1897–1918)

Reasons Against Licensing Pawnbrokers (London, 1745)

Report of a Committee of the Manchester Statistical Society on the State of Education in the Borough of Manchester in 1834 (London, 1835)

Report of a Committee of the Manchester Statistical Society on the State of Education in the City of York in 1836-7 (London, 1837)

Rouse, R. *A Collection of the Charities and Donations Given ... to the Town of Market Harborough* (Market Harborough, 1768)

Rowntree, B. S. *Poverty: A Study of Town Life* (London, 1901)

Rules and Orders for Relieving and Employing the Poor of the Township of Leeds (Leeds, 1771)

Rules and Orders for the Government of the Radcliffe Infirmary (Oxford, 1770)

Savary des Brulons, J., and M. Postlethwayt, *Universal Directory of Trade and Commerce* (London, 1757)

A Short Account of the Two Charitable Foundations at Kings-Cliffe in the County of Northampton (Stamford, 1755)

Short, T. *New Observations on City, Town and Country Bills of Mortality* (London, 1750)

Shrewsbury Burgess Roll ed. H. E. Forrest (Shrewsbury, 1924)

Shropshire Parish Registers Lichfield Diocese 12, Shrewsbury St Mary; 15, 16 and 17 Shrewsbury St Chad (Shropshire Parish Register Society, 1911–18)

Skelton, J. *Oxonia Antiqua Restaurata* 2 (Oxford, 1823)

Smith, D. M. (ed.), *The Company of Merchant Adventurers in the City of York: Register of Admissions 1581–1835* (Borthwick List and Index 18, 1996)

Smith, D. M. (ed.), *The Company of Merchant Taylors in the City of York: Register of Admissions 1560–1835* (Borthwick List and Index 16, 1996)

The Statutes of the General Infirmary at Chester (Chester, 1763)

Statutes of the Salop Infirmary (Shrewsbury, 1752)

Stebbing, H. *Of Charity to the Poor and the Religious Education of Poor Children* (London, 1732)

Stedman, Rev. T. *An Address to the Poor Belonging to the Several Parishes within the town of Shrewsbury* (Shrewsbury [c.1787])

Telford, J. (ed), *The Letters of the Rev. John Wesley* 7 (London, 1960)

The Tradesman's Lawyer and Countrey-man's Friend (London, 1703)

Universal British Directory (London, 1798)

White, W. 'Observations on the Bills of Mortality in York', *Philosophical Transactions of the Royal Society of London* 72 (1782)

Wilson, B. *A Discourse ... Against the misapplication of Public Charities* (London, 1768)

Wood, A. *The Antient and Present State of the City of Oxford* with additions by Rev. Sir John Peshall (London, 1773)

Wood's History of the City of Oxford 1 and 2 (Oxford Historical Society 15 and 17, old series, 1889–90)

The Life and Times of Anthony Wood 2 ed. Rev. A. Clarke (Oxford Historical Society 21, old series, 1892)

Wood, I. *Account of the Shrewsbury House of Industry* (Shrewsbury, 1791)

Woodman, J. *The Rat-Catcher at Chelsea College* (London, 1740)

Secondary sources

Books and Articles

Allison, K. J. (ed.), *Victoria County History of the East Riding of Yorkshire* 1 (Oxford, 1969)

Anderson, P. 'The Leeds workhouse under the old poor law: 1726–1834', *Publications of the Thoresby Society* 56: 2 (1980)

Andrew, D. *Philanthropy and Police: London Charity in the Eighteenth Century* (Princeton, 1989)

Andrew, D. 'Two medical charities in eighteenth-century London', in J. Barry and C. Jones (eds), *Medicine and Charity Before the Welfare State* (London, 1991)

Andrew, D. 'On reading charity sermons: eighteenth-century Anglican solicitation and exhortation', *Journal of Ecclesiastical History* 43: 4 (1992)

Andrew, D. '*Noblesse oblige*: female charity in an age of sentiment', in J. Brewer and S. Staves (eds), *Early Modern Conceptions of Property* (London, 1995)

Andrew, D. '"To the Charitable and Humane": appeals for assistance in the eighteenth-century London press', in H. Cunningham and J. Innes (eds), *Charity, Philanthropy and Reform* (Basingstoke, 1998)

Andrews, J. '"Hardly a hospital, but a charity for pauper lunatics"? Therapeutics at Bethlem in the seventeenth and eighteenth centuries', in J. Barry and C. Jones (eds), *Medicine and Charity Before the Welfare State* (London, 1991)

Anning, S. T. *The General Infirmary at Leeds volume 1: The First Hundred Years, 1767–1869* (Edinburgh, 1963)

Anning, S. T. 'The General Infirmary at Leeds 1767–1967', *University of Leeds Review* 10 (1966)

Arkell, T. 'The incidence of poverty in England in the later seventeenth century', *Social History* 12 (1987)

Armstrong, A. *Stability and Change in an English County Town: A Social Study of York 1801–1851* (Cambridge, 1974)

Ashton, T. S. *Economic Fluctuations in England 1700–1800* (Oxford, 1959)

Backhouse, A. *The Worm-Eaten Waistcoat* (York, 2003)

Barratt, S. 'Kinship, poor relief and the welfare process in early modern England', in S. King and A. Tomkins (eds), *The Poor in England 1700–1850: An Economy of Makeshifts* (Manchester, 2003)

Baugh, G. (ed.), *Victoria County History of Shropshire* 3 (Oxford, 1979)

Beattie, J. M. *Crime and the Courts in England 1660–1800* (Oxford, 1986)

Beier, A. L. 'The social problems of an Elizabethan country town, Warwick 1580–90', in P. Clark (ed.), *Country Towns in Pre-Industrial England* (Leicester, 1981)

Ben-Amos, I. K. *Adolescence and Youth in Early Modern England* (London, 1994)

Berry, A. 'Community sponsorship and the hospital patient in late eighteenth-century England', in P. Hordern and R. M. Smith (eds), *The Locus of Care: Families, Communities, Institutions and the Provision of Welfare Since Antiquity* (London, 1998)

Bittle, W. G., and R. T. Lane, 'Inflation and philanthropy in England: a re-assessment of W.K. Jordan's data', *Economic History Review* 29 (1976)

Black, J. *The English Press in the Eighteenth Century* (London, 1987)

Blaug, M. 'The myth of the old poor law and the making of the new', *Journal of Economic History* 23: 2 (1963)

Borsay, A. *Medicine and Charity in Georgian Bath: A Social History of the General Infirmary c.1739–1830* (Aldershot, 1999)

Boulton, H. E. 'The Chester Infirmary', *Chester and North Wales Architectural, Archaeological and Historical Society Journal* 47 (1960)

Boulton, J. *Neighbourhood and Society: A London Suburb in the Seventeenth Century* (Cambridge, 1987)

Boulton, J. 'Neighbourhood and migration in early modern London', in P. Clark and D. Souden (eds), *Migration and Society in Early Modern England* (London, 1987)

Boulton, J. 'Going on the parish: the parish pension and its meaning in the London suburbs, 1640–1724', in T. Hitchcock, P. King and P. Sharpe (eds), *Chronicling Poverty: The Voices and Strategies of the English Poor 1640–1840* (Basingstoke, 1997)

Boulton, J. '"It is extreme necessity that makes me do this": some "survival strategies" of pauper households in London's West End during the early 18th century', *International Review of Social History* 45 (2000)

Bowlby, J. *Charles Darwin: A Biography* (London, 1990)

Boyer, G. *An Economic History of the English Poor Law 1750–1850* (Cambridge, 1990)

Brears, P. 'Bastille soup and skilly: workhouse food in Yorkshire', in C. A. Wilson (ed.), *Food for the Community: Special Diets for Special Groups* (Edinburgh, 1993)

Briggs, W. G. 'Records of an apprenticeship charity 1685–1753', *Derbyshire Archaeological Journal* 74 (1954)

Broad, J. 'Parish economies of welfare, 1650–1834', *Historical Journal* 42: 4 (1999)

Broadbridge, S. R. 'The old poor law in the parish of Stone', *North Staffordshire Journal of Field Studies* 13 (1973)

Burne, R. V. H. 'The treatment of the poor in the eighteenth century in Chester', *Journal of the Chester and North Wales Architectural, Archaeological and Historic Society* 52 (1965)

Burnett, J. *Plenty and Want* (London, 1979)

Burnett, J. *Destiny Obscure: Autobiographies of Childhood, Education and Family from the 1820s to the 1920s* (London, 1984)

Burnett, J. *Idle Hands: The Experience of Unemployment, 1790–1990* (London, 1994)

Caffrey, H. 'The almshouse experience in the nineteenth-century West Riding', *Yorkshire Archaeological Journal* 76 (2004)

Cameron, H. C. *Mr. Guy's Hospital 1726–1948* (London, 1954)

Cardwell, J. H. *The Story of a Charity School* (London, 1899)

Caring: A Short History of Salisbury City Almshouse and Other Charities (Salisbury, 1987)

Carrié, J.-M. 'The contribution of papyri to the prosopography of the ancient world: evaluation and prospects', in A. Cameron (ed.), *Fifty Years of Prosopography* (Oxford, 2003)

Cavallo, S. 'Conceptions of poverty and poor relief in Turin in the second half of the eighteenth century', in S. J. Woolf (ed.), *Domestic Strategies: Work and Family in France and Italy 1600–1800* (Cambridge, 1991)

Cavallo, S. 'The motivations of benefactors: an overview of approaches to the study of charity', in J. Barry and C. Jones (eds), *Medicine and Charity Before the Welfare State* (London, 1991)

Chalklin, C. W. *The Provincial Towns of Georgian England: A Study of the Building Process 1740–1820* (London, 1974)

Chamberlain, A. 'Teaching surgery and breaking the law', *British Archaeology* 48 (1999)

Chambers, J. D. *Nottinghamshire in the Eighteenth Century* (London, 1966)

Cherry, S. 'The role of a provincial hospital: the Norfolk and Norwich hospital, 1771–1880', *Population Studies* 26 (1972)

Clark, P. (ed.), *The Cambridge Urban History of Britain. Vol. 2, 1540–1840* (Cambridge, 2001)

Cordery, S. *British Friendly Societies, 1750–1914* (Basingstoke, 2003)

Corfield, P. J. *The Impact of English Towns 1700–1800* (Oxford, 1982)

Corfield, P. J. 'Class by name and number in eighteenth-century Britain', *History* 72 (1987)

Corfield, P. J. *Power and the Professions in Britain, 1700–1850* (London, 1995)

Cornford, B. 'Inventories of the poor', *Norfolk Archaeology* 35 (1970)

Cox, J. S. *The Almshouse and St Margaret's Leper Hospital Ilchester* (Ilchester Historical Monographs 5, 1949)

Creighton, C. *A History of Epidemics in Britain* (London [1884] 1965)

Crittall, E. (ed.), *Victoria County History of Wiltshire* 6 (Oxford, 1962)

Crittall, E., and R. B. Pugh (eds), *Victoria County History of Wiltshire* 3 (Oxford, 1956)

Crosby, A. G. 'A poor diet for poor people?: workhouse food in Lancashire, 1750–1834', *Lancashire Local History* 9 (1995)

Crossley, A. (ed.), *Victoria County History of Oxfordshire* 4 (Oxford, 1979)

Croxson, B. 'The public and private faces of 18th century London dispensary charity', *Medical History* 41 (1997)

Cunningham, H. 'The employment and unemployment of children in England 1680–1851', *Past and Present* 126 (February 1990)

Cunningham, H. 'Introduction', in H. Cunningham and J. Innes (eds), *Charity, Philanthropy and Reform* (Basingstoke 1998)

Cunningham, H., and J. Innes (eds), *Charity, Philanthropy and Reform* (Basingstoke, 1998)

Cunnington, P., and C. Lucas, *Charity Costumes* (London, 1978)

Curthoys, J. '"To Perfect the College ...": the Christ Church almsmen 1546–1888', *Oxoniensia* 60 (1995)

Daunton, M. (ed.), *Charity, Self-interest and Welfare in the English Past* (London, 1996)

Davison, L. *et al.* (eds), *Stilling the Grumbling Hive: The Response to Social and Economic Problems in England, 1689–1750* (Stroud, 1992)

De Vries, J. *European Urbanisation 1500–1800* (London, 1984)

Dobson, M. J. *A Chronology of Epidemic Disease and Mortality in South-east England 1601–1800* (Historical Geography Research Series 19, 1987)

Dobson, M. J. *Contours of Death and Disease in Early Modern England* (Cambridge, 1997)

Doubleday, H. A., and W. Page (eds), *Victoria County History of Hampshire* 2 (London, 1903)

Drummond, Sir J., and A. Wilbraham, *The Englishman's Food: A History of Five Centuries of English Diet* revised with additions by D. Hollingsworth (London, 1958)

Dyer, A. D. *The City of Worcester in the Sixteenth Century* (Leicester, 1973)

Fasnacht, R. *A History of the City of Oxford* (Oxford, 1954)

Feingold, M. 'Jordan revisited: patterns of charitable giving in sixteenth and seventeenth century England', *History of Education* 8 (1979)

Fenwick, G. L. *A History of the Ancient City of Chester* (Chester, 1896)

Finnegan, F. *Poverty and Prostitution: A Study of Victorian Prostitutes in York* (Cambridge, 1979)

Fissell, M. *Patients, Power and the Poor in Eighteenth-Century Bristol* (Cambridge, 1991)

Fogel, R. W. *The Escape from Hunger and Premature Death, 1700–2100* (Cambridge, 2004)

Fontaine, L. 'Women's economic spheres and credit in pre-industrial Europe', in B. Lemire, R. Pearson and G. Campbell (eds), *Women and Credit: Researching the Past, Refiguring the Future* (Oxford, 2001)

Fuhrer, K. C. 'Pawning in German working-class life before the First World War', *International Review of Social History* 46 (2001)

Gaydon, A. T. (ed.), *Victoria County History of Shropshire* 2 (Oxford, 1973)

Geremek, B. *Poverty: A History* (Oxford, 1994)

Gittings, C. *Death, Burial and the Individual in Early Modern England* (London, 1984)

Glennie, P. *Distinguishing Men's Trades: Occupational Sources and Debates for Pre-Census England* (Historical Geography Research Series 25, 1990)

Godfrey, W. H. *The English Alms-House* (London, 1955)

Gorsky, M. *Patterns of Philanthropy: Charity and Society in Nineteenth-Century Bristol* (Woodbridge, 1999)

Gosden, P. H. J. H. *Self-Help: Voluntary Associations in the Nineteenth Century* (London, 1973)

Gove, P. B. 'An Oxford convict in Maryland', *Maryland Historical Magazine* 37 (1942)

Grady, K. 'The Georgian public buildings of Leeds and the West Riding', *Publication of the Thoresby Society* 62: 133 (1989)

Granshaw, L., and R. Porter, *The Hospital in History* (London, 1989)

Gutman, M. P. 'The future of record linkage in history', *Journal of Family History* 12 (1997)

Haagen, P. H. 'Eighteenth-century English society and the debt law', in S. Cohen and A. Scull (eds), *Social Control and the State* (Oxford, 1983)

Hadwin, J. F. 'Deflating philanthropy', *Economic History Review* 31 (1978)

Hampson, E. M. *The Treatment of Poverty in Cambridgeshire, 1597–1834* (Cambridge, 1934)

Hanly, M. 'The economy of makeshifts and the role of the poor law: a game of chance?', in S. King and A. Tomkins (eds), *The Poor in England 1700–1850: An Economy of Makeshifts* (Manchester, 2003)

Hans, N. *New Trends in Education in the Eighteenth Century* (London, 1966)

Harley, D. N. 'Ignorant midwives: a persistent stereotype', *Society for the Social History of Medicine Bulletin* 28 (1981)

Harley, D. N. 'Provincial midwives in England: Lancashire and Cheshire, 1660–1760', in H. Marland (ed.), *The Art of Midwifery: Early Modern Midwives in Europe* (London, 1993).

Harris, B. E. (ed.), *Victoria County History of Chester* 3 (Oxford, 1980)

Harris, M. 'Inky blots and rotten parchment bonds: London, charity briefs and the Guildhall Library', *Historical Research* 66 (1993)

Harvey, B. *Living and Dying in England 1100–1540* (Oxford, 1993)

Haverfield, F. J. 'Extracts from the *Gentleman's Magazine* relating to Oxford 1731–1800', in M. Burrows (ed.), *Collectanea II* (Oxford Historical Society 16, 1890)

Heal, F. *Hospitality in Early Modern England* (Oxford, 1990)

Henderson, J., and R. Wall (eds), *Poor Women and Children in the European Past* (London, 1994)

Herbert, N. M. (ed.), *Victoria County History of Gloucestershire* 4 (Oxford, 1988)

Hill, B. *Servants: English Domestics in the Eighteenth Century* (Oxford, 1996)

Hill, J. W. F. *Georgian Lincoln* (Cambridge, 1966)

Himmelfarb, G. *The Idea of Poverty* (London, 1984)

Hindle, G. B. *Provision for the Relief of the Poor in Manchester, 1754–1826* (Chetham Society Manchester 22, 1975)

Hindle, S. *On the Parish? The Micro-politics of Poor Relief in Rural England c. 1550–1750* (Oxford, 2004)

Hindson, J. 'The Marriage Duty Acts and the social topography of the early modern town: Shrewsbury 1695–8', *Local Population Studies* 31 (1983)

Hird, E. *The Lady Margaret Hungerford Almshouse and Free School, Corsham, Wiltshire 1668–1968* (Corsham, 1997)

Hitchcock, T. 'Paupers and preachers: the S.P.C.K. and the parochial workhouse movement', in L. Davison *et al.* (eds), *Stilling the Grumbling Hive: The Response to Social and Economic Problems in England, 1689–1750* (Stroud, 1992)

Hitchcock, T. '"Unlawfully begotten on her body": illegitimacy and the parish poor in St Luke's, Chelsea', in T. Hitchcock, P. King and P. Sharpe (eds), *Chronicling Poverty: The Voices and Strategies of the English Poor 1640–1840* (Basingstoke, 1997)

Hitchcock, T. *Down and Out in Eighteenth-Century London* (London, 2004)

Hitchcock, T. 'Begging on the streets of eighteenth-century London', *Journal of British Studies* 44 (2005)

Holt, P. 'Scottish pawnshops 1792–1820: a note on a neglected index of the condition of the working class', *Journal of the Scottish Labour History Society* 8 (1974)

Hoppit, J. 'Attitudes to credit in Britain 1680–1790', *Historical Journal* 33: 2 (1990)

Houlbrooke, R. 'Introduction', in R. Houlbrooke (ed.), *Death, Ritual and Bereavement* (London, 1989)

Howie, W. B. 'The administration of an eighteenth-century provincial hospital: the Royal Salop Infirmary 1747–1830', *Medical History* 5 (1961)

Howie, W. B. 'Finance and supply in an eighteenth century hospital 1747–1830', *Medical History* 7 (1963)

Howson, B. *Houses of Noble Poverty* (Sunbury, 1993)

Hudson, G. 'Negotiating for blood money: war widows and the courts in seventeenth-century England', in J. Kermode and G. Walker (eds), *Women, Crime and the Courts* (London, 1994)

Hudson, K. *Pawnbroking: An Aspect of British Social History* (London, 1982)

Hudson, P. *The Industrial Revolution* (London, 1992)

Hudson, P. 'A new history from below: computers and the maturing of local and regional history', *Local Historian* 25 (1995)

Hume, R. 'Educational provision for the Kentish poor 1660–1811: fluctuations and trends', *Southern History* 4 (1982)

Innes, J. 'Prisons for the poor: English bridewells 1555–1800', in F. Snyder and D. Hay (eds), *Labour, Law and Crime: An Historical Perspective* (London, 1987)

Innes, J. 'The "mixed economy of welfare" in early modern England: assessments of the options from Hale to Malthus (c. 1683–1803)', in M. Daunton (ed.),

Charity, Self-interest and Welfare in the English Past (London, 1996)

Innes, J. 'The state and the poor: eighteenth-century England in European perspective', in J. Brewer and E. Hellmuth (eds), *Rethinking Leviathan: The Eighteenth Century State in Britain and Germany* (Oxford, 1999)

Jacob, W. M. 'The eye of his master: children and charity schools', in D. Wood (ed.), *The Church and Childhood: Studies in Church History* 31 (Oxford, 1994)

Jackson, G. *Hull in the Eighteenth Century* (London, 1972)

James, R. R. 'Medical men in practice in Shropshire, 1779–1783', *Transactions of the Shropshire Archaeological and Natural History Society* 40 (1920)

Johnston, C. P. 'The charity school, the Church and the Corporation: aspects of educational provision for the poor in eighteenth-century Leeds', *Publications of the Thoresby Society* 3 (1993)

Johnston, V. J. *Diets in Workhouses and Prisons 1835-1895* (New York, 1985)

Jones, C. *Charity and Bienfaisance: The Treatment of the Poor in the Montpelier Region, 1740–1815* (Cambridge, 1982)

Jones, M. G. *The Charity School Movement: A Study of Eighteenth Century Puritanism in Action* (Cambridge, 1964)

Jordan, W. K. *Philanthropy in England 1480–1660* (London, 1959)

Jütte, R. 'Diets in welfare institutions and in outdoor poor relief in early modern Western Europe', *Ethnologia Europaea* 16: 2 (1988)

Jütte, R. *Poverty and Deviance in Early Modern Europe* (Cambridge, 1994)

Kaestle, C. F. '"Between the Scylla of Brutal Ignorance and the Charybdis of a Literary Education": elite attitudes toward mass schooling in early industrial England and America', in L. Stone (ed.), *Schooling and Society: Studies in the History of Education* (Baltimore, 1976)

Kidd, A. 'Historians or polemicists? how the Webbs wrote their history of the English poor laws', *Economic History Review* 40: 3 (1987)

King, P. 'Pauper inventories and the material lives of the poor in the eighteenth and early nineteenth centuries', in T. Hitchcock, P. King and P. Sharpe (eds), *Chronicling Poverty: The Voices and Strategies of the English Poor 1640–1840* (Basingstoke, 1997)

King, P. 'The rise of juvenile delinquency in England 1780–1840: changing patterns of perception and prosecution', *Past and Present* 160 (1998)

King, S. 'Poor relief and English economic development reappraised', *Economic History Review* 50: 2 (1997)

King, S. 'Reconstructing lives: the poor, the poor law and welfare in Calverley, 1650–1820', *Social History* 22: 3 (1997)

King, S. *Poverty and Welfare in England 1700–1850: A Regional Perspective* (Manchester, 2000)

King, S. *A Fylde Country Practice: Medicine and Society in Lancashire, circa 1760–1840* (Lancaster, 2001)

King, S. 'Reclothing the English poor, 1750–1840', *Textile History* 33 (2002)

King, S., and A. Tomkins (eds), *The Poor in England 1700–1850: An Economy of Makeshifts* (Manchester, 2003)

King, S. and A. Weaver, 'Lives in many hands: the medical landscape in Lancashire, 1700–1820', *Medical History* 45 (2000)

Landers, J. *Death and the Metropolis* (Cambridge, 1993)

Lane, J. *The administration of an Eighteenth-century Warwickshire Parish: Butler's Marston* (Dugdale Society Occasional Paper 21, 1973)

Lane, J. 'The provincial practitioner and his services to the poor 1750–1800', *Society for the Social History of Medicine Bulletin* 28 (1981)

Lane, J. *Worcester Infirmary in the Eighteenth Century* (Worcester Historical Society, 1992)

Lane, J. *Apprenticeship in England 1600–1914* (London, 1996)

Lane, P. 'Work on the margins: poor women and the informal economy of eighteenth and early nineteenth century Leicestershire', *Midland History* 22 (1997)

Langford, J. A. *A Century of Birmingham Life* (Birmingham, 1868)

Langford, P. *A Polite and Commercial People* (Oxford, 1992)

Laqueur, T. W. 'Working-class demand and the growth of English elementary school education, 1750–1850', in L. Stone (ed.), *Schooling and Society: Studies in the History of Education* (Baltimore, 1976)

Laqueur, T. W. *Religion and Respectability: Sunday Schools and Working Class Culture 1780–1850* (New Haven, 1976)

Laqueur, T. W. 'Bodies, death and pauper funerals', *Representations* 1 (1983)

Larson, E. S. 'A measure of power: the personal charity of Elizabeth Montagu', *Studies in Eighteenth Century Culture* 16 (1986)

Laslett, P. (ed.), *Household and Family in Past Time: Comparative Studies in the Size and Structure of the Domestic Group over the Last Three Centuries in England, France, Serbia, Japan, and Colonial North America, With Further Materials from Western Europe* (Cambridge, 1972)

Lees, L. H. *The Solidarities of Strangers: The English Poor Laws and the People, 1700–1948* (Cambridge, 1998)

Lemire, B. 'Consumerism in preindustrial and early industrial England: the trade in secondhand clothes', *Journal of British Studies* 27 (1988)

Lemire, B. 'The theft of clothes and popular consumerism in early modern England', *Journal of Social History* 24: 2 (1990)

Lemire, B. 'Peddling fashion: salesmen, pawnbrokers, taylors, thieves and the second-hand clothes trade in England c.1700–1800', *Textile History* 22: 1 (1991)

Lemire, B. *Dress, Culture and Commerce* (London, 1997)

Lemire, B. 'Introduction. Women, credit and the creation of opportunity: a historical overview', in B. Lemire, R. Pearson and G. Campbell (eds), *Women and Credit: Researching the Past, Refiguring the Future* (Oxford, 2001)

Lewis, C. P., and A. T. Thacker (eds), *Victoria County History of Chester* 5: 2 (Woodbridge, 2005)

Lis, C., and H. Soly, *Poverty and Capitalism in Pre-Industrial Europe* (Hassocks, 1979)

Litten, J. *The English Way of Death* (London, 1991)

Lloyd, S. '"Agents in their own concerns"? charity and the economy of makeshifts in eighteenth-century Britain', in S. King and A. Tomkins (eds), *The Poor in England 1700–1850: An Economy of Makeshifts* (Manchester, 2003)

Lloyd, S. 'Cottage conversations: poverty, and manly independence in eighteenth-century England', *Past and Present* 184 (2004)

Lobel, M. D. (ed.), *Victoria County History of Oxfordshire 5* (London, 1957)

Long, J. *Conversations in Cold Rooms: Women Work and Poverty in 19th-Century Northumberland* (Woodbridge, 1999)

MacCaffrey, W. T. *Exeter 1540–1640* (Cambridge Mass., 1958)

Mackay, L. 'A culture of poverty? the St Martin in the Fields workhouse in 1817', *Journal of Interdisciplinary History* 26 (1995)

MacKay, L. 'Why they stole: women in the Old Bailey, 1779–1789', *Journal of Social History* 32: 3 (1999)

Macleane, D. *A History of Pembroke College* (Oxford Historical Society 33, old series, 1897)

McCants, A. 'Petty debts and family networks: the credit markets of widows and wives in eighteenth-century Amsterdam', in B. Lemire, R. Pearson and G. Campbell (eds), *Women and Credit: Researching the Past, Refiguring the Future* (Oxford, 2001)

McClure, R. K. *Coram's Children: The London Foundling Hospital in the Eighteenth Century* (New Haven, 1981)

McInnes, A. *The English Town, 1660–1760* (London, 1980)

McInnes, A. 'The emergence of a leisure town: Shrewsbury 1660–1760', *Past and Present* 120 (1988)

McInnes, A. '1638–1780', in *Victoria County History of Shropshire* [Shrewsbury volume, forthcoming]

McIntosh, M. 'Networks of care in Elizabethan English towns: the example of Hadleigh, Suffolk', in P. Horden and R. M. Smith (eds), *The Locus of Care: Families, Communities, Institutions and the Provision of Welfare Since Antiquity* (London, 1998)

McLoughlin, G. *A Short History of the First Liverpool Infirmary 1749–1824* (London, 1978)

Magdalino, P. 'Prosopography and the Byzantine identity', in A. Cameron (ed.), *Fifty Years of Prosopography* (Oxford, 2003)

Marshall, D. *The English Poor in the Eighteenth Century* (London, 1926)

Midelfort, H. C. E. 'Madness and civilisation in early modern Europe: a reappraisal of Michel Foucault', in B. C. Malament (ed.), *After the Reformation: Essays in Honor of J. H. Hexter* (Manchester, 1980)

Miller, D. S., and D. J. Oddy, *The Making of the Modern British Diet* (London, 1976)

Mitchell, L. G., and L. S. Sutherland, *The History of the University of Oxford Volume Five: The Eighteenth Century* (Oxford, 1986)

Morrison, K. *The Workhouse: A Study of Poor Law Buildings in England* (Swindon, 1999)

Muldrew, C. 'Credit and the courts: debt litigation in a seventeenth-century urban community', *Economic History Review* 46: 1 (1993)

Muskett, P. 'A picturesque little rebellion? the Suffolk workhouses in 1765', *Bulletin of the Society for the Study of Labour History* 41 (1980)

Neuburg, V. E. *Popular Education in Eighteenth Century England* (London, 1971)

Ottaway, S. *The Decline of Life: Old Age in Eighteenth-Century England* (Cambridge, 2004)

Ottaway, S., and S. Williams, 'Reconstructing the life-cycle-experience of poverty in the time of the old poor law', *Archives*, 23 (1998)

Owen, D. *English Philanthropy 1660–1960* (Oxford, 1965)

Oxley, G. A. *Poor Relief in England and Wales 1601–1834* (Newton Abbot, 1974)

Page, W. (ed.), *Victoria County History of Hampshire 5* (London, 1912)

Page, W. (ed.), *Victoria County History of Northamptonshire 3* (London, 1930)

Page, W., and J. W. Willis-Bund (eds), *Victoria County History of Worcestershire 4* (London, 1924)

Palliser, D. M. *Tudor York* (Oxford, 1980)

Pennell, S. ' "Great quantities of gooseberry pye and baked clod of beef": victualling and eating out in early modern London', in P. Griffiths and M. Jenner (eds), *Londinopolis: Essays in the Cultural and Social History of Early Modern London* (Manchester, 2000)

Pickstone, J. V. *Medicine and Industrial Society* (Manchester, 1985)

Picton, J. A. *Memorials of Liverpool* (Liverpool, 1907)

Pinches, S. 'Women as objects and agents of charity in eighteenth-century Birmingham', in R. Sweet and P. Lane (eds), *Women and Urban Life in Eighteenth-Century England* (Aldershot, 2003)

Pollock, L. A. *Forgotten Children* (Cambridge, 1983)

Pooley, C. G., and J. Turnbull, *Migration and Mobility in Britain since the Eighteenth Century* (London, 1998)

Porter, D. and R. Porter, *Patients' Progress: Doctors and Doctoring in Eighteenth Century England* (Oxford, 1989)

Porter, R. 'Death and the doctors in Georgian England', in R. Houlbrooke (ed.), *Death, Ritual and Bereavement* (London, 1989)

Porter, R. 'The gift relation: philanthropy and provincial hospitals in eighteenth-century England', in L. Granshaw and R. Porter (eds), *The Hospital in History* (London, 1989)

Prescott, E. *The English Medieval Hospital 1050–1640* (London, 1992)

Prior, M. *Fisher Row: Fishermen, Bargemen and Canal Boatmen in Oxford 1500–1900* (Oxford, 1982)

Prochaska, F. K. 'Philanthropy', in F. M. L. Thompson (ed.), *The Cambridge Social History of Britain 1750–1950* (Cambridge, 1990)

Raymond, R. J. 'Pawnbrokers and pawnbroking in Dublin: 1830–1870', *Dublin Historical Record* 32: 1 (1978)

Razzell, P. *The Conquest of Smallpox* (Sussex, 1977)

Reay, B. *Microhistories: Demography, Society and Culture in Rural England, 1800–1930* (Cambridge, 1996)

Reinarz, J. *The Birth of a Provincial Hospital: The Early Years of the General Hospital, Birmingham, 1765–1790* (Dugdale Society Occasional Paper, 2003)

Richardson, R. *Death, Dissection and the Destitute* (London, 1987)

Risse, G. B. *Hospital Life in Enlightenment Scotland* (Cambridge, 1986)

Roach, J. P. C. (ed.), *Victoria County History of Cambridge and Ely* 3 (Oxford, 1959)

Roach, J. *The Shrewsbury Hospital, Sheffield 1616–1975* (Borthwick Paper York 104, 2003)

Robb-Smith, A. H. T. *A Short History of the Radcliffe Infirmary* (Oxford, 1970)

Roberts, M. J. D. 'Head versus heart? voluntary associations and charity organisation in England, c. 1700–1850', in H. Cunningham and J. Innes (eds), *Charity, Philanthropy and Reform* (London, 1998)

Robin, J. 'The relief of poverty in mid nineteenth-century Colyton', *Rural History* 1: 2 (1990)

Robson, D. *Some Aspects of Education in Cheshire in the Eighteenth Century* (Chettam Society Manchester 13, 1966)

Rogers, N. 'Confronting the crime wave: the debate over social reform and regulation 1749–1753', in L. Davison *et al.* (eds), *Stilling the Grumbling Hive: The Response to Social and Economic Problems in England, 1689–1750* (Stroud, 1992)

Rubin, M. *Charity and Community in Medieval Cambridge* (Cambridge, 1987)

Salzman, L. F. (ed.), *Victoria County History of Oxfordshire* 1 (Oxford, 1939)

Salzman, L. F. (ed.), *Victoria County History of Cambridge and Ely* 2 (Oxford, 1948)

Scola, R. *Feeding the Victorian City: The Food Supply of Manchester, 1770–1870* (Manchester, 1992)

Scott, B. 'Ackworth Hospital 1757–1773', *Yorkshire Archaeological Journal* 61 (1989)

Shammas, C. *The Pre-Industrial Consumer in England and America* (Oxford, 1990)

Shammas, C. 'Changes in English and Anglo-American consumption from 1550 to 1800', in J. Brewer and R. Porter (eds), *Consumption and the World of Goods* (London, 1993)

Sharpe, P. 'Poor children as apprentices in Colyton, 1598–1830', *Continuity and Change* 6: 2 (1991)

Sharpe, P. 'De-industrialisation and re-industrialisation: women's employment and the changing character of Colchester 1700–1850', *Urban History* 21: 1 (1994)

Sharpe, P. ' "The bowels of compation": a labouring family and the law, c.1790–1834', in T. Hitchcock, P. King, and P. Sharpe (eds*)*, *Chronicling Poverty : The Voices and Strategies of the English Poor, 1640–1840* (Basingstoke, 1997)

Sharpe, P. 'Survival strategies and stories: poor widows and widowers in early industrial England', in S. Cavallo and L. Warner (eds), *Widowhood in Medieval and Early Modern Europe* (Harlow, 1999)

Sherman, S. *Imagining Poverty: Quantification and the Decline of Paternalism* (Columbus Ohio, 2001)

Shore, H. *Artful Dodgers: Youth and Crime in Early 19th-Century London* (Woodbridge, 1999)

Siena, K. *Venereal Disease, Hospitals and the Urban Poor: London's 'Foul Wards', 1600–1800* (Rochester, 2004)

Sigsworth, E. M. 'Gateways to death? medicine, hospitals and mortality, 1700–1850', in P. Mathias (ed.), *Science and Society* (Cambridge, 1972)

Simon, B. (ed.), *Education in Leicestershire 1540–1940* (Leicester, 1968)

Simon, J. 'Was there a charity school movement? The Leicestershire evidence', in B. Simon (ed.), *Education in Leicestershire 1540-1940* (Leicester, 1968)

Simon, J. 'From charity school to workhouse in the 1720s: the SPCK and Mr Marriot's solution', *History of Education* 17: 2 (1988)

Simonton, D. 'Schooling the poor: gender and class in eighteenth-century England', *British Journal for Eighteenth-Century Studies* 23 (2000)

Slack, P. *Poverty and Policy in Tudor and Stuart England* (London, 1988)

Slack, P. *The English Poor Law 1531–1782* (London, 1990)

Slack, P. *From Reformation to Improvement: Public Welfare in Early Modern England* (Oxford, 1999)

Smith, B. G. *The 'Lower Sort': Philadelphia's Laboring People, 1750–1800* (Ithaca, 1990)

Smith, F. *A History of English Elementary Education 1760–1902* (London, 1931)

Smith, R. 'Relief of urban poverty outside the poor law, 1800–1850: a study of Nottingham', *Midland History* 2: 4 (1974)

Smith, R. M. 'Reflections from demographic and family history', in M. Daunton (ed.), *Charity, Self-interest and Welfare in the English Past* (London, 1996)

Snell, K. D. M. *Annals of the Labouring Poor: Social Change and Agrarian England 1660–1900* (Cambridge, 1985)

Sokoll, T. 'The pauper household small and simple?', *Ethnologia Europaea* 17: 1 (1987)

Sokoll, T. 'Negotiating a living: Essex pauper letters from London, 1800–34', *International Review of Social History* 45 (2000)

Sokoll, T. *Essex Pauper Letters 1731–1837* (Oxford, 2001)

Solar, P. 'Poor relief and English economic development before the Industrial Revolution', *Economic History Review* 48 (1995)

Souden, D. ' "East, west – home's best"? Regional patterns in migration in early modern England', in P. Clark and D. Souden (eds), *Migration and Society in Early Modern England* (London, 1987)

Spufford, M. *Contrasting Communities* (Cambridge, 1974)

Stapleton, B. 'Inherited poverty and life-cycle poverty: Odiham, Hampshire, 1650–1850', *Social History* 18 (1993)

Stephens, W. B. (ed.), *Victoria County History of Warwickshire* 7 (Oxford, 1964)

Stobart, J. 'Regional structure and the urban system: North-West England, 1700–1760', *Transactions of the Historic Society of Lancashire and Cheshire* (Liverpool, 1996)

Stone, H. 'The Ipswich charity schools of Greycoat Boys and Bluecoat Girls 1709–1809', *Proceedings of the Suffolk Institute of Archaeology* 25 (1952)

Stone, L. (ed.), *University in Society* 1 (Princeton, 1975)

Styles, J. 'Clothing the North: the supply of non-elite clothing in the eighteenth-century north of England', *Textile History* 25: 2 (1994)

Sweet, R. *The English Town 1680–1840: Government, Society and Culture* (Harlow, 1999)

Sweet, R. 'Introduction', in R. Sweet and P. Lane (eds), *Women and Urban Life in Eighteenth-Century England* (Aldershot, 2003)

Tate, W. E. *The Parish Chest: A Study of the Records of Parochial Administration in England* (Cambridge, 1946)

Tate, W. E. 'The charity sermons 1704–1732 as a source for the history of education', *Journal of Ecclesiastical History* 9 (1958)

Taylor, J. S. 'The unreformed workhouse 1776–1834', in E. W. Martin (ed.), *Comparative Development in Social Welfare* (London, 1972)

Taylor, J. S. *Jonas Hanway, Founder of the Marine Society* (London, 1985)

Taylor, J. S. *Poverty, Migration and Settlement in the Industrial Revolution: Sojourners' Narratives* (Palo Alto, 1989)

Tebbutt, M. *Making Ends Meet: Pawnbroking and Working-class Credit* (Leicester, 1983)

Thane, P. 'Histories of the welfare state', in W. Lamont (ed.), *Historical Controversies and Historians* (London, 1998)

Thane, P. *Old Age in English History: Past Experiences, Present Issues* (Oxford, 2000)

Thomas, E. G. 'The old poor law and medicine', *Medical History* 24 (1980)

Thompson, E. P. *The Making of the English Working Class* (London, 1980)

Thompson, E. P. *Customs in Common* (London, 1993)

Thomson, D. 'Welfare and the historians', in L. Bonfield, R. M. Smith and K. Wrightson (eds), *The World We Have Gained* (Oxford, 1986)

Thomson, D. 'The welfare of the elderly in the past', in M. Pelling and R. M. Smith (eds), *Life, Death and the Elderly: Historical Perspectives* (London, 1991)

Tillott, P. M. (ed.), *The Victoria History of Yorkshire: The City of York* (Oxford, 1961)

Tomkins, A. 'Charity schools and the parish poor in Oxford, 1740–1770', *Midland History* 22 (1997)

Tomkins, A. 'Paupers and the infirmary in mid-eighteenth-century Shrewsbury', *Medical History* 43: 2 (1999)

Tomkins, A. 'Cathedral almsmen: a new prosopographical project', *History and Computing* 12:1 (2000)

Tomkins, A. 'Almshouse *versus* workhouse: residential welfare in eighteenth-century Oxford', *Family and Community History* 7: 1 (2004)

Tomkins, A. 'Poverty, kinship support and the case of Ellen Parker, 1818–1827', in S. King (ed.), *The British Experience of Welfare* [forthcoming]

Tompson, R. *The Charity Commission and the Age of Reform* (London, 1979)

Treble, J. H. *Urban Poverty in Britain 1830–1914* (London, 1979)

Trinder, B. S. *The Industrial Revolution in Shropshire* (London, 1981)

Turner, B. C. *A History of the Royal Hampshire County Hospital* (Chichester, 1986)

Valenze, D. 'Charity, custom and humanity: changing attitudes towards the poor in eighteenth-century England', in J. Garnett and C. Matthew (eds), *Revival and Religion Since 1700* (London, 1993)

Valenze, D. *The First Industrial Woman* (Oxford, 1995)

Van Leeuwen, M. 'Histories of risk and welfare in Europe during the 18th and 19th centuries', in O. P. Grell, A. Cunningham and R. Jütte (eds), *Health Care and Poor Relief in 18th and 19th Century Northern Europe* (Aldershot, 2002)

Wales, T. 'Poverty, poor relief and life-cycle: some evidence from seventeenth century Norfolk', in R. M. Smith (ed.), *Land, Kinship and Life-Cycle* (Cambridge, 1984)

Wallis, P. 'Charity, politics and the establishment of York county hospital: a "party job"?', *Northern History* 38 (2001)

Wallis, P. J., and R. V. Wallis (eds), *Eighteenth-Century Medics* (Newcastle upon Tyne, 1988)

Wardle, D. 'Education in Nottingham in the age of apprenticeship 1500–1800', *Thoroton Society Transactions* 71 (1967)

Webb, S., and B. Webb, *English Poor Law History part one: The Old Poor Law* (London [1927] 1963)

Williams, K. *From Pauperism to Poverty* (London, 1981)

Williams, R. 'Stolen goods and the economy of makeshifts in eighteenth-century Exeter', *Archives* 31: 112 (2005)

Williams, S. 'Poor relief, labourers' households and living standards in rural England c. 1770–1834: a Bedfordshire case study', *Economic History Review* 58: 3 (2005)

Wilson, A. *The Making of Man-Midwifery: Childbirth in England 1660–1760* (Cambridge Mass., 1995)

Wilson, A. 'Conflict, consensus and charity: politics and the provincial voluntary hospitals in the eighteenth century', *English Historical Review* 111: 442 (1996)

Wilson, A., 'The Birmingham General Hospital and its public, 1765–79', in S. Sturdy (ed.), *Medicine, Health and the Public Sphere in Britain, 1600–2000* (London, 2002)

Wilson, C. 'Poverty and philanthropy in early modern England', in T. Riis (ed.), *Aspects of Poverty in Early Modern Europe* (Florence, 1981)

Wilson, C. A. *Food and Drink in Britain* (London, 1976)

Woodward, J. *To Do The Sick No Harm: A Study of the British Voluntary Hospital System to 1875* (London, 1974)

Woolf, S. J. *The Poor in Western Europe in the Eighteenth and Nineteenth Centuries* (London, 1986)

Woolf, S. J. *A History of Italy 1700–1860* (London, 1991)

Wrightson, K. 'The politics of the parish in early modern England', in P. Griffiths, A. Fox and S. Hindle (eds), *The Experience of Authority in Early Modern England* (Basingstoke, 1996)

Wrightson, K., and D. Levine, *Poverty and Piety in an English Village: Terling, 1525–1700* (New York, 1979)

Wrigley, E. A. *People, Cities and Wealth* (Oxford, 1987)

Wrigley, E. A. *Poverty, Progress and Population* (Cambridge, 2004)

Wrigley, E. A., and R. S. Schofield, *The Population History of England 1541–1871* (London, 1981)

Yudkin, J. 'Some basic principles of nutrition', in D. Oddy and D. Miller (eds), *The Making of the Modern British Diet* (London, 1976)

Unpublished material

Theses and dissertations

Barker-Read, M. 'The Treatment of the Aged Poor in Five Selected West Kent Parishes from Settlement to Speenhamland 1662–1797' (PhD thesis, Open University, 1988)

Barry, J. 'The Cultural Life of Bristol 1640–1775' (DPhil thesis, Oxford University, 1985)

Berry, A. 'Patronage, Funding and the Hospital Patient, c.1750–1815: Three English Regional Case Studies' (DPhil thesis, Oxford University, 1995)

Boss, B. 'The Bristol Infirmary 1761–2 and the "Laborious Industrious Poor"' (PhD thesis, Bristol University, 1995)

Hill, J., 'A Study of Poverty and Poor Relief in Shropshire 1550–1685' (MA dissertation, Liverpool University, 1973)

Hitchcock, T. 'The English Workhouse.: A Study in Institutional Poor Relief in Selected Counties 1696–1750' (DPhil thesis, Oxford University, 1985)

Lane, J. 'Apprenticeship in Warwickshire 1700–1834' (PhD thesis, Birmingham University, 1977)

Lloyd, S. 'Perceptions of Poverty in England 1660–1770' (DPhil thesis, Oxford University, 1991)

McNaulty, M. 'Some Aspects of the History of the Administration of the Poor Laws in Birmingham between 1730 and 1834' (MA dissertation, Birmingham University, 1942)

Sokoll, T. 'Household and Family among the Poor: The Case of Two Essex Communities in the Late Eighteenth and Early Nineteenth Centuries' (PhD thesis, Cambridge University, 1988)

Tomkins, A. 'The Operation of the Exeter Corporation of the Poor 1698–1710' (BA dissertation, Keele University, 1991)

Tomkins, A. 'The Experience of Urban Poverty: A Comparison of Oxford and Shrewsbury 1740–1770' (DPhil thesis, Oxford University, 1995)

Williams, S. 'Poor Relief Welfare and Medical Provision in Bedfordshire: The Social, Economic and Demographic Context 1770–1834' (PhD thesis, Cambridge University, 1998)

Papers

Adair, R. 'Pensioners under the Poor Law in Early Modern England', paper given at the Wellcome Unit for the History of Medicine, Oxford seminar (1991)

Adair, R. 'Age Composition of Pensioners in Early Modern England', paper given at the Wellcome Unit for the History of Medicine, Oxford seminar (1993)

Broadbridge, S. R. 'The Old Poor Law in the Parish of Stone (Staffs) 1691–1834', unpublished typescript in the William Salt Library, Stafford

Hudson, G. 'Negotiating for Relief: Strategies used by Victims of War in

Seventeenth-century England', paper delivered at Oxford University Social History of Early Modern Britain Seminar (1991)

Innes, J. 'Social Problems: Poverty and Marginality in Eighteenth Century England', unpublished paper (1985)

Trinder, B. S. 'The Textile Industry in Shrewsbury in the Late Eighteenth Century', paper given at the ESRC Colloquium on urban industry in the long eighteenth century (1993)

Internet sources

A. Brundage, 'Private Charity and the 1834 Poor Law', www.class.csupomona.edu/his/Tonyart, accessed 4 October 2000

ESRC-funded project on the Westminster poor headed by Jeremy Boulton and Leonard Schwarz, www.staff.ncl.ac.uk/j.p.boulton/esrcframeset.htm, accessed 10 October 2003.

Familysearch genealogy resource hosted by the Church of Jesus Christ of Latter-Day Saints, www.familysearch.org, accessed 6 September 2005

Old Bailey Proceedings Online, www.oldbaileyonline.org, accessed 24 August 2005

Index